A Jewish Ceremony for Newborn Girls

Sharon R. Siegel, *A Jewish Ceremony for Newborn Girls: The Torah's Covenant Affirmed*

Laura S. Schor, *The Best School in Jerusalem: Annie Landau's School for Girls, 1900–1960*

Federica K. Clementi, *Holocaust Mothers and Daughters: Family, History, and Trauma*

Elana Maryles Sztokman and Chaya Rosenfeld Gorsetman, *Educating in the Divine Image: Gender Issues in Orthodox Jewish Day Schools*

Ilana Szobel, *A Poetics of Trauma: The Work of Dahlia Ravikovitch*

Susan M. Weiss and Netty C. Gross-Horowitz, *Marriage and Divorce in the Jewish State: Israel's Civil War*

Ronit Irshai, *Fertility and Jewish Law: Feminist Perspectives on Orthodox Responsa Literature*

Elana Maryles Sztokman, *The Men's Section: Orthodox Jewish Men in an Egalitarian World*

Sharon Faye Koren, *Forsaken: The Menstruant in Medieval Jewish Mysticism*

Sonja M. Hedgepeth and Rochelle G. Saidel, editors, *Sexual Violence against Jewish Women during the Holocaust*

Julia R. Lieberman, editor, *Sephardi Family Life in the Early Modern Diaspora*

Derek Rubin, editor, *Promised Lands: New Jewish American Fiction on Longing and Belonging*

Carol K. Ingall, editor, *The Women Who Reconstructed American Jewish Education: 1910–1965*

Gaby Brimmer and Elena Poniatowska, *Gaby Brimmer: An Autobiography in Three Voices*

Harriet Hartman and Moshe Hartman, *Gender and American Jews: Patterns in Work, Education, and Family in Contemporary Life*

Dvora E. Weisberg, *Levirate Marriage and the Family in Ancient Judaism*

Ellen M. Umansky and Dianne Ashton, editors, *Four Centuries of Jewish Women's Spirituality: A Sourcebook*

Carole S. Kessner, *Marie Syrkin: Values Beyond the Self*

Ruth Kark, Margalit Shilo, and Galit Hasan-Rokem, editors, *Jewish Women in Pre-State Israel: Life History, Politics, and Culture*

Tova Hartman, *Feminism Encounters Traditional Judaism: Resistance and Accommodation*

Anne Lapidus Lerner, *Eternally Eve: Images of Eve in the Hebrew Bible, Midrash, and Modern Jewish Poetry*

A Jewish Ceremony for Newborn Girls

THE TORAH'S COVENANT AFFIRMED

Sharon R. Siegel

BRANDEIS UNIVERSITY PRESS | WALTHAM, MASSACHUSETTS

Brandeis University Press
An imprint of University Press of New England
www.upne.com
© 2014 Brandeis University
All rights reserved
Manufactured in the United States of America
Designed by April Leidig
Typeset in Garamond Premier Pro
by Copperline Book Services, Inc.

University Press of New England is a member of the
Green Press Initiative. The paper used in this book
meets their minimum requirement for recycled paper.

Yeshivat Chovevei Torah Rabbinical School grants permission
to reprint "Covenant, Women, and Circumcision: Formulating
a Covenantal Simhat Bat Ceremony," or parts thereof, which
originally appeared in *Meorot: A Forum of Modern Orthodox
Discourse* in Tishrei 5772 (September 2011).

Oxford University Press grants permission to reprint "Jewish
Welcoming Ceremonies for Newborn Girls: The Modern
Development of a Feminist Ritual," or parts thereof, which
originally appeared in *Modern Judaism: A Journal of Jewish
Ideas and Experience* in October 2012.

The editorial board of the *New York Jewish Week* grants
permission to reprint "A Covenant of Love," or parts thereof,
which originally appeared in the *New York Jewish Week* on
December 9, 2011.

Library of Congress Cataloging-in-Publication Data
Siegel, Sharon R.
A Jewish ceremony for newborn girls : the Torah's
covenant affirmed / Sharon R. Siegel.
    pages   cm. — (HBI series on Jewish women)
Includes bibliographical references and index.
ISBN 978–1–61168–473–5 (cloth : alk. paper)
ISBN 978–1–61168–417–9 (pbk. : alk. paper)
ISBN 978–1–61168–405–6 (ebook)
1. Brit bat — History. I. Title.
BM706.S54 2013
296.4'43—dc23   2013017429

5 4 3 2 1

To Dan, Dafna, Nurit, Yakir, Tamar,
and my parents

In loving memory of my grandparents,
Samuel and Senta Okolica

Contents

Preface

Nine years ago, I was pregnant for the first time, and my husband, Dan, and I chose not to find out the baby's sex. I knew that Judaism provided a circumcision ceremony for newborn boys, but was uncertain what ceremony, if any, was available for newborn girls. Always fascinated with the development of Jewish rituals, I was determined to have a meaningful, yet traditional, ceremony for our newborn child, whether boy or girl.

One Friday evening, after Shabbat (Sabbath) dinner, Dan and I were relaxing and talking in our living room. I had been reading some basic introductions on how to celebrate a daughter's birth and reviewing the Biblical chapters relating to God's communications to Abraham. I shared with Dan my observation that the episode where God mandates the circumcision of Jewish men is the fourth recorded interaction between God and Abraham. I therefore suggested viewing this episode in the context of the preceding interactions between God and Abraham, which make no mention of gender distinctions. I also noted that, elsewhere in the Torah, women are included in the covenant between God and Israel. Like me, Dan was intrigued, and he encouraged me to continue studying this subject.

I am an attorney, and, at that time, was working long hours at my law firm, as is customary for junior associates. Nonetheless, I continued in my off-hours to research, think, and consult about the ceremonies Dan and I would conduct for our soon-to-be-born child. I typed out two parallel ceremonies, one for a boy (which included circumcision) and one for a girl. Dan and I performed the latter ceremony with our daughter, Dafna Eliana, on the eighth day following her birth, in the presence of our family and friends. We did so notwithstanding the amazement of a number of our friends that we had "made up something ourselves."

I continued to develop a profound interest in this new type of ritual for newborn Jewish girls. As my curiosity grew, I read more on the topic and decided to write a short article about it. I began to think more critically and broadly about the evolution of Jewish rituals and the interplay between *halacha* (Jewish law) and popular customs. Drawing on my professional legal training and my Jewish education, I began traveling in my meager spare time to the world-class library at the Jewish Theological Seminary in New York City to conduct more extensive research. The librarians began to recognize me as my trips became more frequent. Soon, I was taking sporadic vacation days from my law firm to sit in my basement reviewing my library research and writing. I also slowly began calling and e-mailing professors with questions about their publications, as well as rabbis with questions about their communities' practices.

As my research progressed slowly over the years, Dan and I celebrated, in turn, the births of our daughter Nurit Avital and our son Yakir Eliezer. Our celebrations for Nurit and Yakir, as for Dafna, used the ceremonies I had formulated while I was pregnant for the first time. Toward the end of my third maternity leave, I even took ten-week-old Yakir on the train to midtown Manhattan to conduct research at the library of the Jewish Women's Resource Center.

Gradually, I produced a lengthy article. At that point, I consulted with my friend Chaim Saiman, currently a professor of law at Villanova University, and sent him a draft of my article. After reviewing the article, Chaim told me that he had good news and bad news for me. He said the good news was that he found the material interesting. He said the bad news was that I was, in fact, writing a book. This idea caught me off-guard. As a full-time practicing attorney and a parent of small children, I was doubtful that I would ever have enough time to devote to such a massive project.

Nonetheless, I continued to research and write and realized that I had a true passion for the topic of ceremonies for newborn Jewish girls. I also began to delve into a wide variety of related areas. Some of these include:

The theological role of the covenant in Judaism
The history of the circumcision ceremony
Traditional naming customs for Jewish girls
The history of modern welcoming ceremonies for girls
Jewish feminist rituals
The role of customs in the halachic system
The halachic ramifications of a covenantal ceremony for newborn girls
The history and current status of women's Torah learning and the Bat
    Mitzvah (a coming-of-age ritual for adolescent girls)
The histories of a variety of life-cycle and related Jewish customs and
The imagery of the tallit (prayer shawl)

The breadth of these areas of interest continues to astonish me.

As my research became more involved, I began to explore, as never before, the richness and beauty of the Jewish tradition. Each new discovery deepened my profound pride in the vibrancy of my heritage.

Ultimately, with my parents' unbelievably strong support and Dan's vigorous encouragement, I received the chance of a lifetime to write this book full time. By a quirk of fate or a measure of *hashgacha p'ratit* (the belief that God has a personal relationship with each individual), I confirmed with joy on the first day that I sat down to write on my "sabbatical" that I was pregnant with our fourth child. Dan jokes that the impetus for our new baby was to enable us to perform one of my ceremonies again. In truth, however, I found it very gratifying to write about newborn ceremonies while feeling a fetus kick inside me. Tamar Sarit was born a few days after I completed the first draft of this book.

I NOW HAVE the privilege of sharing my thoughts with you. My hope is that Jewish parents and expectant parents—who are in the same position that I was nine years ago—will benefit from the ideas and suggestions in this book. In addition, I hope that this book will be helpful to rabbis and Jewish organizations who advise parents about performing rituals for their newborn daughters. My intent in writing this book is to reach the entire Jewish community, without regard to denomination or personal outlook.

I also hope that this book will benefit anyone interested in the evolution of rituals or the interpretation of traditional practices. While there is a particular need for creative thinking about girls' welcoming ceremonies in the Jewish community, religious communities of all types are today considering the role of women in reshaping and performing rituals within the rubric of traditional belief systems. I hope that people of all faiths may find a Jewish approach fascinating and useful as they navigate their own paths.

My observations and experiences have led me to believe that we have arrived at a pivotal time in the development of modern ceremonies for newborn Jewish girls. Today, practices are coalescing in some Jewish communities, while, in others, parents continue to grapple with how to commemorate the birth of their daughters. Now is the time to assess these practices and look ahead to the next phase of their development. I hope that this book can play a role in working toward these goals.

Acknowledgments

My first thanks go to Phyllis Deutsch, editor-in-chief of the University Press of New England. She saw the potential in the sample chapter that I sent to her and in my vision for this book. She has given me astute advice at key moments and has skillfully guided the development of this book from beginning to end. I likewise appreciate the efforts of Ann Brash, Diana Drew, and Kate Mertes, whose collective expertise has made this book a reality.

Many thanks to Chaim Saiman, who critiqued early drafts of this book and gave me valuable suggestions for formulating my ideas. My thanks to Jeremy Meyerowitz and Ina Cohen, talented and tireless librarians at the Jewish Theological Seminary, who gave of their time to help me locate countless sources. I also thank Amy Bolton, who spent many months meticulously editing the first draft of this book.

A very special thank-you to my great-uncle and great-aunt, Rabbi Henry and Lisbeth Okolica, whose clear memories and wise observations are recounted in these pages. The insights of my beloved Uncle Henry and Aunt Lisbeth personalize and enrich this book in a way that is very special to me.

There are many others whom I would like to thank for their contributions to this book. They include Gila Ahdoot, Elisheva Baumgarten, Jennifer Bernstein, Yoram Bitton, Alisa Braun, Bill and Louise Braun, Michael Broyde, Eliezer Diamond, Paul Doherty, Yisrael Dubitsky, Aliza Dzik, Yechiel Eckstein, Jonathan Fox, Micky Goldschmidt, Myriam Goldschmidt, Elizabeth Goldstein, Blu Greenberg, Binyomin Hamburger, Abraham Kinstlinger, Annette Landau, Morty Landowne, Rose Landowne, Dov Linzer, Anna Mass London, Jonathan Malino, Tamar Malino, Michael Meyer, Shari Ness, Ethan Rotenberg, Sandy Eisenberg Sasso, Steven Sirbu, Daniel Sperber, Shira Vickar-Fox, Sid Vidaver, Daniel Wolf, Vitaly Zurkovsky, and Amy Zwas. Thank you also to the many congregational rabbis (in addition to those mentioned above) who took the time to describe to me the practices in their synagogues and communities. However, the opinions and positions taken in this book are mine alone, and should not be attributed or ascribed to any contributors mentioned here.

My profound thanks to my husband, Daniel Schlosberg, who has taken this long and exhilarating journey with me, side by side. It continues to surprise me how, even from the very beginning, Dan and I had the same ideas when it came to celebrating our newborn children. In our life together, Dan has always supported me wholeheartedly and has even encouraged me to take some unconventional paths. My gratitude for his love, companionship, and infinite patience.

My greatest appreciation goes to my parents, Judith Okolica and Marshall Siegel. This book never could have happened without their vision, enthusiasm, and extraordinary support. My parents edited every word I wrote, gave me new ideas, discussed with me every facet of this book, babysat endlessly, and always pushed me to do my very best. This is your book as much as it is mine.

Finally, I am indebted to those who, with ingenuity and devotion, created and perpetuated the modern ritual of welcoming newborn girls into the Jewish community. I also acknowledge the sincere devotion of the thousands of parents and rabbis who have performed these welcoming ceremonies and continue to do so. This book is my contribution to this ongoing process.

Introduction

I introduce this book—and each of its three parts—with a legal motion recently filed in federal court and the responsive judicial order. I was quite surprised that one set of documents could combine my knowledge of American legal procedure and my interest in Jewish ceremonies for newborns. I open with these documents not for their legal significance, but because they vividly capture many of the practices and beliefs that constitute the basis and motivation for this book.

On November 17, 2010, a criminal defense attorney, with a trial set to begin shortly, filed a motion called a "Writ of Possible Simcha [Celebration]" in a Manhattan federal court. He requested that the court grant a possible recess in the middle of the trial. Why did the attorney file this unconventional motion, and what is its purpose here? The relevance of this motion is evident from its colorful text:

> The facts are as follows: My beautiful daughter, Eva, married and with a doctorate no less, and her husband, Ira Greenberg (we like him, too) live in Philadelphia and are expecting their first child on December 3rd, *tfu tfu tfu* [the sound of spitting to ward off the evil eye]. They do not know whether it will be a boy or a girl, although from the oval shape of Eva's tummy, many of the friends and family are betting male (which I think is a mere *bubba meiseh* [old wife's tale] but secretly hope is true).
>
> Should the child be a girl, not much will happen in the way of public celebration. Some may even be disappointed, but will do their best to conceal this by saying, "as long as it's a healthy baby." My wife will run to Philly immediately, but I will probably be able to wait until the next weekend. There will be happiness, though muted, and this application will be mooted as well.
>
> However, should the baby be a boy, then hoo-hah! Hordes of friends and family will arrive from around the globe and descend on Philadelphia for the joyous celebration mandated by the *halacha* [Jewish law] to take place during daylight hours on the eighth day, known as the bris. The eighth day after December 3rd could be right in the middle of the

trial. My presence at the bris is not strictly commanded, although my absence will never be forgotten by those that matter.

So please consider this an application for maybe, *tfu tfu tfu,* a day off during the trial, if the foregoing occurs on a weekday. I will let the Court (and the rest of the world) know as soon as I do, and promise to bring pictures.[1]

While the sentiments expressed in this motion are startling in the context of an impending federal trial, some of them are extremely common in the traditional Ashkenazic community. (*Ashkenazic* refers to Jews with roots in Germanic and eastern European lands.) When a boy is born, grandparents and other relatives and friends, from near and far, make every effort to attend the festive circumcision ceremony performed eight days after the baby's birth. When a girl is born, relatives and friends, and sometimes even grandparents, may take their time in meeting the newborn and do so only at a convenient time. The public expression of happiness is subdued or even absent.

On the other hand, I believe that the sentiment that the birth of a girl is a disappointment, as expressed in this motion, is not typical today in the traditional Ashkenazic community, except perhaps for some Jews on the extreme right wing. To the contrary, many traditional *Ashkenazim* (Jews with roots in Ashkenazic regions) have demonstrated a burgeoning effort to celebrate newborn Jewish girls, whether with a *kiddush* (a public reception following synagogue services), a party, or a religious-themed ceremony, sometimes called a *Simchat Bat,* meaning "Celebration of a Daughter." To the extent that there is an overt celebration, however, it is often held weeks or months after a girl's birth. In addition, in the traditional Ashkenazic community today, this celebration is considered secondary and optional. By contrast, it is deemed primary and practically mandatory to perform a brief synagogue naming, at which the father of a newborn girl says blessings when the Torah is read, followed by the recitation of a simple prayer that names the baby. The baby's father is often the only close family member to attend the synagogue naming.

In contrast to standard practices in many traditional Ashkenazic communities today, some Sephardic (Spanish-Portuguese) and Mizrachic (North African, Middle Eastern, and Central and South Asian) traditions include rich ceremonies and customs for newborn girls. These rituals, often occurring within the first week or month of a child's life, demonstrate that practices for newborn girls in traditional Jewish communities are not as monolithic as the attorney's motion might lead us to believe. Furthermore, ceremonially welcoming a baby girl, in the synagogue or at home, has become commonplace in the wide range of liberal Jewish communities. Despite these differing practices, naming remains integral to marking the birth of a girl across Jewish communities at large, and Part I of this book examines how and why this emphasis on naming has developed.

The story of the attorney awaiting his grandchild continues. The day after the motion was filed, the presiding federal judge responded with the following handwritten order.

> [Defendant's counsel] will be permitted to attend the bris, in the joyous event that a son is born. But the Court would like to balance the scales. If a daughter is born, there will be a public celebration in Court, with readings from poetry celebrating girls and women.[2]

The news of this motion and order spread like wildfire within the legal community and beyond, appearing in the *Wall Street Journal*'s Law Blog[3] and the *American Bar Association Journal*.[4] The blogosphere buzzed with a variety of responses to this exchange. Some bloggers expressed disdain for the attorney's outlook and praised the judge's wisdom, while others maintained that this conversation belonged outside the federal courthouse. Other opinions abounded. This lively discussion is a testament to the combustive combination of traditional beliefs and modern egalitarianism, the motion's incongruously flippant tone, and the instantaneous communicative power of the Internet.

The judge admirably sought both to respect Jewish tradition (as the attorney presented it to her) and to highlight the value of a newborn, whether male or female. What the esteemed judge could not have known, however, is that there is no need to "balance the scales" by crafting a commemoration for girls from sources outside the Jewish tradition. To the contrary, the foundation for a meaningful religious ceremony for newborn girls lies squarely within the ancient Jewish tradition.

This foundation is the Jewish conception of the covenant between God and the Jewish people, the focus of Part II of this book. This cornerstone of the traditional Jewish belief system encompasses the Jewish people's fidelity to God and God's promise to bless and protect the Jewish nation. The covenant, embodied in the Torah, provides the basis for observing the Torah's commandments (*mitzvot*) and for building a relationship with the Land of Israel. From a theological perspective, the covenant is the raison d'etre for the Jewish people.

The attorney is correct that Jewish tradition dictates the circumcision rite for boys. It does so for reasons that we, as humans, do not understand, despite attempts that have been made to rationalize this practice. However, contrary to the attorney's outlook, the Jewish tradition does not also mandate the non-celebration of the birth of girls. Rather, this tradition views all Jews, male and female, as members of the fundamental covenant. A girl's initiation into the covenant as a newborn is a prerequisite for entering into the age of mitzvot as an adolescent at her Bat Mitzvah and embarking on a life of Jewish observance and values. It is highly appropriate to commemorate publicly the covenantal membership of girls, due to the centrality of the covenantal relationship in Judaism.

Furthermore, such a commemoration is no different than any of the other countless Jewish customs that have originated in the grassroots in response to changing societal, cultural, and economic norms over the millennia. Part III of this book contextualizes modern ceremonies for newborn girls in this vast universe of Jewish customs. Thus, notwithstanding the judge's thoughtful order, Jewish girls can and should be welcomed by specifically Jewish means.

FOR ME, JEWISH TRADITION is paramount. It is not, however, stagnant. It is impossible to think that the Judaism of today looks the same as that of two thousand years ago, or even five hundred years ago,[5] nor will Judaism look the same in the future as it does today. Jewish practices and ideologies evolve at a "legal" pace: overall slow and sometimes languorous, but occasionally punctuated with uncharacteristically rapid change in one specific area. Changes may occur in the grassroots or among the leadership, and often as a function of a dialectic between the two. The balance between tradition and change is very delicate, and the all-important question is where to place the fulcrum at any given moment.

Traditional rabbinic texts provide a firsthand account of Jewish rituals performed throughout the centuries and, in so doing, reflect the times and regions in which these texts were written. Studying traditional texts is, therefore, an effective means of understanding Jewish beliefs and practices and for unlocking how they have evolved over time.

The backbone of this book consists of a selection of these traditional texts, including those drawn from the analysis and explication of *halacha*, the intricate system that traditionally defines Jewish law and practice. Halachically observant Jews hold this system, from its broad principles to its technical minutiae, to be legally binding. As Professor Rachel Adler emphasizes, however, the challenges of halacha are not confined to the Orthodox, but rather [touch] "all Jews who believe the tradition possesses some relevance to modern Jewish life."[6] Furthermore, those who do not view halacha as binding or applicable today nonetheless generally recognize halacha as an underlying basis for the historical development of Jewish culture and societal structure, as well as a partial and subjective record of this development. Thus, halacha provides a sweeping historical perspective from which to consider and contextualize ceremonies for newborn girls. As Rachel Biale posited in her groundbreaking book *Women and Jewish Law,* "Comprehending the Halakhah is necessary for a Jewish life, whether one seeks to follow Jewish law or depart from it."[7]

In particular, halachic texts are indispensable in contemplating a framework for ceremonies for newborn girls. Only by studying the motivations and nuances of traditional rituals can Jewish customs expand organically. Indeed, this is precisely the tack taken by the earliest modern innovators of ceremonies for newborn girls in the 1970s. In an explicit fashion, they carefully based their ceremonies on traditional sources, themes, and practices. This approach was effective; today's ceremonies for newborn girls are here to stay.

Along the same lines, I suggest in this book that ceremonies for newborn girls should continue to ritualize essential Jewish principles and to incorporate traditional practices and imagery by reframing them. Underpinning this approach is my belief that the cautious, yet responsive, evolution of Jewish ritual practices is a positive value, not merely a survival tactic.

Halachic texts are not only sources of rituals and their history, but also the lifeblood of a system governing a specific way of life. These texts may be technical and extremely detailed-oriented. They also, however, demonstrate an abundance of creative thinking, an unbelievably vast expanse of ideas, and varying points of view. Furthermore, halachic texts can convey the humanity of the rabbis who wrote them. For example, we sometimes hear these rabbis' uncertainty about how to resolve conflicting rulings, their perplexity about popular practices of their day, or their accounts of personal experiences.

Nonetheless, classic halachic works were written in pre-modern times and reflect an ethos and set of expectations than many of us do not have today. In addition, these works are often sharply analytical and utilize hypotheses and strict categorizations, sometimes taking lines of reasoning to extreme conclusions. Significantly, it is also inescapable that only men wrote halachic texts.

In engaging with these texts, I take them at face value and try not to impose my modern sensibilities on them. In this way, I seek answers to my questions without getting mired in language or assumptions to which modern readers may have a difficult time relating. (At the same time, however, I am certainly not blind to these challenges.) This outlook also enables me to appreciate the intricate analytical process of halachic thinking as a distinctive hallmark of the Jewish tradition and as a source of pride. While I believe that more demonstrative responses to these texts are valuable, this is not the method that I employ in this book.

The vibrancy of studying halachic texts is palpable today across the spectrum of Jewish beliefs and practices. These texts are studied extensively and fervently at traditional religious seminaries (*yeshivot*). At the same time, the independent, international Limmud organizations, for example, confirm that Torah learning knows no boundaries in the Jewish community at large. Massive Limmud conferences draw men and women of diverse perspectives from the grassroots to learn Torah in a welcoming and energized environment.

Some people studying halachic texts today do so in order to fulfill the commandment to learn Torah. Traditionally minded Jews do not, however, hold a monopoly on pondering these classic writings. Rather, Torah study occurs throughout the Jewish community. Some learn halachic texts to understand Jewish history, literature, philosophy, or social structures, or simply because Torah study is a central feature of Jewish life.

It follows that disagreeing with the beliefs or values underlying these texts, or inherent in their method of discourse, is no reason to ignore them. To the contrary, those who are troubled by these texts should study them; those who are knowledgeable about them possess an understanding of where we have been and how our collective experiences can guide us into the future.

One important outcome of studying traditional texts is that one slowly gains an ability to distinguish between rules and customs, even as they sometimes blur. R. Haym Soloveitchik, a Torah scholar and historian of Jewish law, has brilliantly identified how, in recent years, the Orthodox community has embraced prescriptive written rules at the expense of well-accepted and unquestioned practices. As R. Soloveitchik explains, "traditional conduct, no matter how venerable, how elementary, or how closely remembered, yields [today] to the demands of theoretical knowledge."[8] I would add that, by contrast, liberal communities may extol customs, particularly new customs, and may downplay long-standing ritualistic rules. Many of these liberal communities have formulated new practices outside or alongside the rubric of the old rules.

Despite these opposing trends, both customs and halachic rules play crucial, intertwining roles in the evolution of Jewish beliefs and practices. Both customs and rules should, therefore, be studied rigorously with an eye toward differentiating between the two. I characterize ceremonies for newborn girls as customs that are developing within the halachic system, as we will see in Part III of this book.

THE EMERGENCE OF modern practices for newborn girls in Ashkenazic communities, beginning in the 1970s, is a prime example of this new genre of customs. These practices, while suffused with traditional notions, were sparked by feminism. The modern feminist movement, and, specifically, the so-called "second wave" of feminism, which began in the 1960s, demanded that women be construed and treated as "complete people"—shorn of confining gender roles, liberated from sexual stereotypes, and afforded the full range of social and economic opportunities. Concomitantly, there was a growing belief that women's experiences, which had often been pushed to the sidelines, should be recognized and embraced. The influence of this line of thinking spawned new and innovative ceremonies for newborn girls, with the aim of filling a void in Ashkenazic practices at that time.

Today, feminism has been adopted in modern societies to an extent that would have been unimaginable to pioneering feminist activists in the late 1960s and 1970s. For example, it is staggering to realize that women in the United States, as recently as the early 1960s, were barred from even the most basic economic functions, such as purchasing real estate or opening their own credit card accounts.[9] Today, economic opportunities are just the tip of the iceberg. While still a work in progress, the feminist revolution has changed the world—for both men and women.

The key point of feminism, in its ideal form, is that it affords men and women the opportunity to select from the complete spectrum of life choices (subject to biological and physical constraints) and to work together to maximize the full potential of every individual. Both men and women have the opportunities to actively raise their children and to enter the workforce. Feminism teaches that both men and women have the ability to cook dinner and do laundry, and that they are also both capable of being police officers or corporate raiders—or assuming any other role or vocation they see fit. In the feminist worldview, gender-based stereotypes and expectations are stifling, as well as inefficient in actualizing an individual's innate abilities.

Jewish women of all stripes have embraced the new opportunities that the feminist revolution has unleashed—even if some of these women do not acknowledge such changes as "feminist." The most striking change is the rapidity with which Jewish women, from secular to ultra-Orthodox, have seized the opportunity to work outside the home and to earn salaries in a fair-minded employment market. Thus, even those Jews who say they reject feminism benefit directly from it.

A brief encounter drove home this point for me. A friend of mine, who adheres devoutly to Orthodox Judaism, asked me during the course of a lighthearted conversation if I considered him a feminist. I asked him affably, with a twinkle in my eye, whether he thought that women should be able to work outside the home and whether he would enjoy a corresponding increase in his family's income. He responded in the affirmative to both questions, and, with a smile, mused to himself that maybe he is, in fact, a feminist.

The changes that have occurred in modern society since the advent of "second wave" feminism pervade every aspect of our lives, yet we still grapple with these changes and their repercussions. A prime example is the role of children: If both fathers and mothers are pursuing their dreams of self-fulfillment (or working jobs simply to make ends meet), who is raising their children? How does a feminist society take into account the needs of children? Indeed, to my mind, one failing of feminism is that, in expanding opportunities for adults, it has the effect of leaving children by the wayside, struggling to reclaim their parents' undivided attention. Fathers and mothers have an equal responsibility to acknowledge and remedy this situation. Raising our children should be our highest priority.

Such social and economic challenges affect the Jewish community, just as they impact other modern societies. Jews who are cognizant of traditional beliefs and rituals, like practitioners of other traditional religions or cultures, face the additional challenge of how to synthesize, if at all, longstanding belief structures with new feminist notions. The results of this interplay are complex, intensely personal, and sometimes unexpected. Some cursory examples can be drawn from the Jewish community. There are women who practice medicine, law, or finance while wearing wigs as an expression of their Jewish modesty. There are liberal-minded women who disavow certain traditional beliefs, yet immerse themselves in a *mikvah* (ritual bath) after the cessation of a menstrual period, in the manner of traditional Jewish practice. There are Hasidic women in the Chabad-Lubavitch sect who sponsor and lead rituals for women on Rosh Chodesh (the first day of a Jewish month), an innovation of early Jewish feminists. There is no end to these combinations and possibilities, and the underlying ideology of each individual is even more varied and complicated than the choices themselves.

The ability to even contemplate such possibilities is owed to the visions and scholarship of pioneering Jewish feminists such as Rachel Adler, Judith Plaskow, Arlene Agus, Blu Greenberg, and Alice Shalvi. These women, along with many other early Jewish feminist activists and thinkers, courageously grappled with the complexities inherent in an encounter between an ancient tradition and a new ideology. Their contributions (including the constructive controversies that arose) have enriched Judaism, and their insights have inspired others and continue to reverberate today.

CONTEMPLATING and performing rituals for newborn girls presents a particular challenge regarding the practice of Jewish traditions in a feminist age. How should this genre of newly created rituals, a product of feminist sensibilities, develop so that it continues to bring to light values and religious expressions that are wholly Jewish?

In considering my thoughts about ceremonies for newborn Jewish girls, I have drawn from one of my core feminist beliefs: that men and women are fundamentally more similar than they are different. They are not the same, but they are similar. I recognized how important this belief is for me on my first day of a first-year writing seminar in college. My professor asked that all the female students (including myself) stay after class for a few minutes, while all the male students were free to go. He told the female students that women are typically unassertive and quiet and have a tendency to be drowned out by their male counterparts. My professor explained that, as a result of this alleged disparity, he wanted to boost our morale and instill confidence in us so that we would succeed in his class. Despite recognizing his good intentions, I raised my hand—assertively—and pointed out the sexist stereotypes implicit in his remarks. My professor graciously conceded the point. This episode taught me how easy it is to disparage women by (needlessly) trying to strengthen their resolve.

I have held fast to this idea in my professional life as well. For example, I have consistently (and courteously) declined the invitation to participate in the "support groups" that each of my law firms established for their female attorneys. The idea for these groups is to enable women to discuss issues supposedly specific to them, establish mentoring relationships, and hold networking events. Law firms tout these support groups, and female colleagues have personally sought me out to encourage my attendance. I believe, however, that these groups hold female professionals back by lending credence to the misconception that women require extra support and a nurturing cocoon. In the law firm setting, I prefer to cultivate substantive relationships with both men and women based on similar practice areas and other shared professional interests, rather than superficial relationships with women based solely on the fact that we share the same physical form.

In the context of Jewish rituals for newborns, this notion of "gender similarity" has translated into my interest in examining whether ceremonies for girls could or should utilize a thematic and ceremonial structure similar to that traditionally used for boys. It is not uncommon in Judaism that practices resonate equally with men and women, despite originating with only one or the other. For example, there are men and women who find comfort in reciting the Kaddish prayer after the passing of a loved one, although this prayer was long recited only by men. Similarly, there are men and women who derive spiritual uplift from immersing themselves in a ritual bath (mikvah), although such immersions are traditionally reserved for women. The coming-of-age Bar Mitzvah ritual for boys, which coalesced slowly over centuries, has more recently spawned the Bat Mitzvah celebration for girls over the course of a few decades. There are countless other examples, since rituals that become deep-seated over time have a tendency to expand correspondingly in scope or intensity.

As a result, my instinct, like that of other parents, is to incorporate into a Jewish ceremony for newborn girls the covenantal theme and basic structure of the traditional circumcision ceremony (that is, a welcome, a covenantal ritual with prayers, and the naming), along with some covenantal liturgy and the eighth-day timing. I emphasize that this modeling does not include the circumcision act itself; I have never for a moment contemplated the possibility of a physically invasive ritual for newborn girls, nor would I ever advocate this type of ritual. Furthermore, the elements of a ceremony for newborn girls could be performed consistently, just as other Jewish life-cycle rituals have integral liturgical and structural components.

While this idea of modeling a welcoming ceremony for girls on the circumcision ceremony is not novel, it is apparently controversial. There are a number of reasons for this decades-long controversy, but I concentrate here on some broad, gender-based arguments. Some traditionalists maintain that women have different natures and proclivities than men and, thus, should only have a ceremony that in no way conjures up the circumcision practice or, alternatively, no ceremony at all. Some feminists might focus not only on the extreme "maleness" of circumcision, but also on the manner in which a highly structured ceremony for girls would run counter to the "feminist ritual" model, which is characterized by fluidity, flexibility, and openness. Some construe structure as a "male" trait and fluidity and changeability as "female" traits. Interestingly, in this context, there are both traditionalists and feminists who emphasize gender differences and agree that ceremonies for newborn girls should not be highly structured, like a circumcision ceremony, with standard rituals and prayers. Instead, they believe that each ceremony (if permitted at all) should be distinct and should reflect the personal tastes and interests of parents and/or rabbis.

I maintain that we should not push the pendulum too little (as in the traditional model) or too far (as in the feminist model), such that we are relegating newborn girls to something outside the Jewish mainstream, into the realm of "other." Working within the framework of a traditional model reinforces the aspiration of welcoming girls into the Jewish community on a consistent basis in a manner that fits comfortably into current life-cycle practices. Said otherwise, utilizing a traditional model as a starting point manifests an interest in moving rituals for newborn girls away from the narrow, and sometimes stigmatizing, category of "women and Judaism" and closer to the realm of "Jewish life-cycle rituals"—something that has already happened to varying extents in some communities. Clearly, practices for newborn boys and those for newborn girls are not congruent. Circumcision has been performed on Jewish boys for millennia in conformance with a Biblical commandment, whereas ceremonies for girls are much newer customs. Yet, as a practical matter, ceremonies for newborn girls need not, and should not, stand out as different from other Jewish rituals.

The key to this "mainstreaming" is to recognize a fundamental similarity —although, I emphasize, not a sameness—between boys and girls. In particular, both are members of the covenant and, as such, a ceremony for girls can and should incorporate traditional liturgies and structures that convey this truism simply and most effectively.

At the same time, boys and girls are not the same, and girls obviously cannot undergo penile circumcision. The act of circumcision in the Jewish tradition is an unquestionably male rite, and physical invasiveness has no place in a covenantal ritual for girls. Yet, the maleness of circumcision does not, and should not, impede the development of covenantal rituals for girls. Many beautiful rituals have already been created and performed to date. My preference is to perpetuate the ritual of swaddling baby girls in a prayer shawl (tallit), which first emerged in the 1970s. As we will see, this ritual lovingly embraces a newborn girl and ushers her into the covenant and the Jewish community in a manner that fits seamlessly with traditional Jewish practices and imagery, yet bears no resemblance to male circumcision. In this way, both boys and girls symbolically enter the covenant, but with wholly divergent rituals—a similarity with a difference.

I DO NOT BELIEVE this book could have been written prior to the emergence of the feminist movement of the 1960s, as modern ceremonies for newborn girls are a feminist innovation. At the same time, this book is steeped in halachic texts and longstanding Jewish practices and considers new ideas from a traditional perspective. In short, my approach is firmly rooted in the past while simultaneously looking to the future.

Part I

Naming and Welcoming

1

Traditional Ashkenazic Naming Practices for Girls

Naming is today a colloquial term for welcoming newborn Jewish girls. This terminology has become so pervasive that Hallmark, the leading American greeting card company, sells cards to be given to parents on the occasion of a daughter's naming. I was surprised the first time I saw such a card. Since Hallmark's aim is to create cards popular enough to be marketable, the company must have determined that Americans most commonly refer to rituals for newborn Jewish girls as *namings*. This is a remarkable conclusion.

Practically speaking, a girl today is deemed "officially welcomed" into the Jewish community when she is named. R. Yitzchak Yaakov Weiss (1905–1989; United Kingdom), for example, states that a new soul arrives when a naming occurs.[1] Naming a newborn girl has taken on a quasi-religious significance, based on the belief that there is nothing else to which she is ceremonially entitled. As a result, a certain parallelism has developed where the formative event for girls is their naming, and the formative event for boys is their circumcision. Boys are publicly named as well; however, the drama of a boy's circumcision sometimes overshadows the announcement of his name, which occurs at the conclusion of the circumcision ceremony.

One ritual that appears regularly, across the denominations (various streams of Judaism), as part of synagogue practices for newborn girls, is a naming coupled with an aliyah to the Torah for the father (in Orthodox communities) or the parents (in more liberal communities). An *aliyah* (plural, *aliyot*) consists of an honoree being called up to make blessings in front of an open Torah scroll before and after the Torah portion is chanted by either the honoree or a designated reader. After the aliyah, a rabbi, sexton (*gabbai*), or prayer leader announces the baby's name, thereby officially bestowing this name on her. One prayer used for this purpose is the *Mi Shebairach*, so called because it begins with *Mi Shebairach avoteinu* ("He

4 NAMING AND WELCOMING

who blessed our forefathers"). More generally, the Mi Shebairach is a genre of prayers recited for a range of different purposes, such as blessing an individual for communal contributions or praying for one's health and safety. The specific Mi Shebairach for naming girls has multiple formulations, one of which is as follows:

> He who blessed our ancestors Abraham, Isaac, and Jacob, Sarah, Rebecca, Rachel, and Leah, may He bless [mother's name] and the daughter born to her. Her name shall be called in Israel (*v'yikara sh'ma b'yisrael*) [baby's name]. May the parents raise their daughter to Torah, the wedding canopy, and good deeds; and let us say, Amen.

We will use the term *synagogue naming* to refer to this ritual of a parent's aliyah followed by a Mi Shebairach prayer in which a baby girl is named. While the synagogue naming is not utilized in many communities today, there are many other communities (particularly traditional ones) in which the synagogue naming is believed to be the singularly "traditional" means of recognizing newborn girls. Indeed, there are Ashkenazic prayer books (*siddurim*; singular, *siddur*) across the denominational spectrum in which the central ritual for newborn girls is a Mi Shebairach during the Torah service.[2]

Nonetheless, when the synagogue naming is used, it is sometimes modified or embellished. Typically occurring on Shabbat, a synagogue ritual may include, in addition to the aliyah and/or Mi Shebairach, readings, prayers, blessings, and an explanation of the baby's name, either by the rabbi or the parents. Parents may also be presented with a gift from the community. However, one purpose of these synagogue ceremonies—and often the primary one—is to publicly announce the baby's Hebrew name.

On the other hand, in many traditional Ashkenazic communities, the synagogue naming may constitute the entire ritual performed shortly after a baby girl's birth. At the first public Torah reading following a girl's birth (Shabbat, Monday, or Thursday) or on the first Shabbat after the birth, a Mi Shebairach prayer is recited after the newborn's father receives an aliyah. Some communities utilize the Mi Shebairach prayer, described above, while the following is another popular version of this prayer:

> He who blessed our ancestors Abraham, Isaac and Jacob, Moses and Aaron, David and Solomon, and Sarah, Rebecca, Rachel, and Leah, may He bless the woman who gave birth [mother's name] and her daughter

who was born to her in "mazal tov," and her name shall be called in Israel [baby's name], since their husband/father will give charity on behalf of [the mother and daughter]. As a reward for this, may [the daughter's] father and mother merit raising her to Torah, the wedding canopy, and good deeds; and let us say, Amen.[3]

A related form of this Mi Shebairach includes prayers for the mother's recovery from childbirth and then briefly blesses and names the daughter.[4] Other details differ among various Mi Shebairach texts. For example, there are traditional prayer books that mention only the father as raising his daughter or that do not include the hope that a girl be raised to Torah.[5]

In these communities, besides the Mi Shebairach, little or nothing else is typically said at this juncture by the rabbi, the father, or anyone else. Generally, neither the baby nor her mother is present for this aliyah. Grandparents and other close relatives similarly may not be present, choosing to wait for a more convenient time, sometimes much later, to meet the baby for the first time. As expressed by Blu Greenberg, "All who were paying attention [when the father had his aliyah] would wish the new father a mazel-tov and that, for the most part, was that!"[6] In short, the momentous occasion of a girl's naming may pass virtually unnoticed.

There is another custom that may, or may not, occur in conjunction with a synagogue naming. A mother, on her first post-partum visit to the synagogue, or someone on her behalf, recites *Birkat HaGomel* (meaning a "blessing of one who is grateful"). This is a thanksgiving prayer said by those enduring specified dangerous experiences, including one who is sick and recovers.[7] A mother who subscribes to this custom says: "Blessed are You God, King of the universe, who provides good things to those who are obligated to Him[8] and who has provided me with such good," and the congregation responds, "Amen, may He who has provided you with such good always provide you with good, selah." By reciting this responsive prayer, a mother thanks God for her "return" to good health (even if she did not encounter complications during or after childbirth). In some traditional communities, the Birkat HaGomel is utilized to give a mother a voice and a public role that she would not otherwise have.

The naming practices of certain Sephardic and Mizrachic communities provide a basis of comparison. In some of these communities, girls are named at ceremonies conducted in the parents' home, and these ceremonies are as diverse as the communities where they are found. In others, such as the Syrian, Egyptian, and some Spanish and Portuguese communities, baby girls are more commonly named in the synagogue on Shabbat with a Mi Shebairach prayer recited after a father's aliyah. (Alternatively, some recite this prayer when a mother attends the synagogue on Shabbat for the first time post-partum.)[9] The Sephardic Mi Shebairach is as follows:

> He who blessed our foremothers Sarah and Rebecca, Rachel and Leah, Miriam the prophet and Abigail, and Queen Esther the daughter of Avichayil, may He bless this lovely girl, and her name shall be called [girl's name] the daughter of [father's name] in "mazal tov" and at a blessed time. May He cause her to grow up in health, peace, and tranquility. May her father and mother merit to see her joy and her wedding canopy, with male children, riches and honor, and may they be thriving and fresh, fruitful into old age; and may this be the will [of God], and let us say, Amen.[10]

This Mi Shebairach focuses on the daughter, while the Ashkenazic Mi Shebairach blesses both mother and daughter and, in some versions, also prays for the mother's speedy recovery. In addition, the Sephardic Mi Shebairach invokes foremothers only, whereas the Ashkenazic Mi Shebairach frequently invokes both foremothers and forefathers. As noted by others,[11] it is ironic that a baby girl's welcome in the Sephardic Mi Shebairach includes the hope that she should produce male offspring.

The Sephardic Mi Shebairach is part of a broader traditional liturgy called Zeved HaBat ("Gift of a Daughter"). This liturgy is recited, in some communities, in the synagogue with an aliyah or, in other communities, as a ceremony that takes place at home, without an aliyah. The Zeved HaBat liturgy begins with Song of Songs 2:14:

> My dove in the clefts of the rock,
> In the hiding places on the mountainside,
> Show me your face,
> Let me hear your voice;
> For your voice is sweet,
> And your face is lovely.

In some traditions, Song of Songs 6:9 is then recited if the baby girl is a firstborn:

But my dove, my perfect one, is unique,
The only daughter of her mother,
The favorite of the one who bore her.
Maidens saw her and called her blessed;
Queens and concubines praised her.

The Italian Zeved HaBat includes the recitation of Genesis 24:60: "And they blessed Rebecca, and said to her 'You are our sister, may you be the mother of thousands or ten thousands, and may your descendents inherit the gate of those who despise them.'"[12] The Zeved HaBat liturgy may also incorporate Psalm 128, additional passages from Song of Songs, and other songs and lyrical poems (*piyutim*).[13]

In some Sephardic communities that utilize the Zeved HaBat liturgy with a father's aliyah, this ritual occurs in a spirited atmosphere. For example, the Zeved HaBat ritual in the synagogue begins when the "arranger" (*mesader*) announces *avi habat* (the father of the daughter), and the congregation chants choruses (*pizmonim*).[14] In some Bucharian (central Asian) and Persian communities, when the father of a baby girl is called up to the Torah, the congregation sings *"Dror Yikra L'Ven Im Bat"* (a song traditionally sung on Shabbat, meaning "He will call freedom to a son with a daughter"), and repeats and emphasizes the word *bat* ("daughter"), the last word of each line of the song. In the Bucharian tradition, a father recites poetic texts and passages from Song of Songs, and he is showered with candy before his aliyah.[15]

There are a number of questions that arise with respect to the broad range of synagogue naming practices today: Why are newborn girls commonly named using a Mi Shebairach recited after a parent receives an aliyah to the Torah? In Ashkenazic communities, and particularly more traditional ones, how did an aliyah and Mi Shebairach become so integral to the point that some today conceive of these naming practices as virtually required? Why is this Ashkenazic practice so sparse that it is barely acknowledged in traditional communities and affirmatively supplemented in more liberal ones? We address these questions below by tracing the historical development of the Mi Shebairach and the Ashkenazic customs associated with new mothers.

HISTORY OF THE MI SHEBAIRACH NAMING TEXT

The practice of naming newborn girls with a Mi Shebairach developed relatively late, as Avraham Yaari (twentieth century, Mandate Palestine and Israel) demonstrates in his comprehensive study of the development of the Mi Shebairach prayer.[16] Yaari explains that it was customary in the early medieval period (circa seventh–eleventh centuries CE) to recite two prayers before the Torah was returned to the ark on Shabbat, both beginning with the Aramaic formula, *Y'kum Purkan Min Shemaya*—"May deliverance arise from heaven." The first such prayer was a blessing for the *Rosh HaGolah* (the Head of the Diaspora), Torah academy leaders, and all other Torah scholars and students. The second one blessed the congregation as a whole. However, neither prayer appears in the siddurim of R. Amram Gaon or R. Saadia Gaon in ninth- and tenth-century Babylonia. By this time, Aramaic was no longer widely understood in Europe, and congregations had stopped reciting *Y'kum Purkan Min Shemaya* prayers in Spain, North Africa, Italy, and the Middle East.

As the use of *Y'kum Purkan Min Shemaya* prayers declined, the Mi Shebairach prayer developed as a means of blessing the congregation in Hebrew. The first Mi Shebairach appears in the ninth-century siddur of R. Amram Gaon in the prayer service for Monday and Thursday mornings when the Torah is read:

> May He who blessed [Mi Shebairach] Abraham, Isaac, and Jacob, our forefathers, bless all of our brothers and sisters the Children of Israel who come to synagogues for prayer and charity. May the Holy One Blessed Be He listen to the voice of their prayers and satisfy their needs and fulfill their requests with good, and let us say amen.[17]

Since people wanted to say this new prayer, its recitation on Monday and Thursday encouraged people to attend synagogue on those days. People might otherwise have attended communal services and heard the Torah reading only on Shabbat.

The second appearance of the Mi Shebairach is in the Shabbat liturgy of the *Machzor Vitry*, a compendium of Jewish practices and rules compiled by Simcha ben Samuel of Vitry and published in France in 1107. This Mi Shebairach is a blessing for those who "busy themselves with the needs of the community and the heads of the academies that are everywhere and from which Torah emerges. . . ."[18] The Machzor Vitry comments that this prayer was established to imbue the Jewish masses with a fear of God and to increase their participation in communal affairs. Other Mi Shebairach prayers blessing the community subsequently appeared in Germany and France, as well as in Italy, Spain, Yemen, and Holland. Special formulations of this prayer also developed for various Jewish holidays.

The third phase is the development of Mi Shebairach prayers for individuals. In Germany and elsewhere, these prayers were said for those performing good deeds for the community, such as taking care of the needs of the synagogue, giving charity, attending to the dead, and the like. Mi Shebairach prayers were also recited to warn against restricted activities and to publicize rabbinic edicts. One such edict, for example, outlawed non-designated wines, while another prohibited talking in the synagogue during services.

In the fourth phase, Mi Shebairach prayers developed for individuals in distress, such as those who were sick or in captivity, as well as women laboring in childbirth. By the twelfth century, these Mi Shebairach prayers spread throughout Germany and northern France and to many communities in Spain. R. Judah ben Barzillai (twelfth-century Spain), however, disapproved of reciting these prayers, due to his concern that one should not seek divine mercy on Shabbat.[19]

The fifth stage of development—and the most significant one for our purposes—featured Mi Shebairach prayers for individuals for reasons not related to distress. Recipients included those who received aliyot or led prayer services, grooms, women who recently gave birth, fathers of newborn boys, and baby boys placed in their cradles. R. Ismar Elbogen (1874–1943, Germany)[20] notes that the first mention of a Mi Shebairach for those receiving aliyot appears in *Ohr Zaruah* by R. Isaac ben Moses of Vienna, written circa 1260.[21] Based on Yaari's observation that the Mi Shebairach prayer for birthing mothers developed in the same era as the Mi Shebairach for those receiving aliyot, the Mi Shebairach for birthing mothers likewise probably originated in approximately the mid-thirteenth century. This estimate conforms with Yaari's determination that the previous stage in the Mi Shebairach's development (for individuals in distress) was ongoing in the twelfth century.

Yaari notes that a liturgy for naming girls became incorporated into the Mi Shebairach for birthing mothers. "In Ashkenazic communities, they would bless the woman who recently gave birth at the time that her husband went up to the Torah [to receive an aliyah], and if a daughter was born, they added to the [Mi Shebairach] blessing the announcement of the name for the newborn daughter."[22] Professor Elisheva Baumgarten concludes, however, that in the High Middle Ages (circa eleventh–fourteenth centuries) in Germany and northern France, naming a girl in the synagogue using a Mi Shebairach does not appear in the sources.[23] It seems, therefore, that the formula for naming a newborn girl in the Mi Shebairach for birthing mothers (*V'yikara sh'ma b'yisrael*—May her name be called in Israel) may have developed later than this Mi Shebairach itself.

At least one modern source may support the hypothesis that the text for naming a baby girl was added to an already extant Mi Shebairach for birthing mothers. *Tikkun Hasofer V'Hakoreh*, a standard German guide for Torah scribes and readers, compiled by R. Yitzchak Baer in 1886, records a Mi Shebairach for birthing mothers that does not include a clause for naming a newborn girl. This Mi Shebairach contains parallel language for boys and girls:

> He who blessed our forefathers Abraham, Isaac, and Jacob may He bless the birthing mother [____] the daughter of [____] with her son who was born [her daughter who was born] in mazal tov, since her husband made a vow on their behalfs. . . . In merit of this, the Holy One Blessed Be He will help them and protect them, and the mother will merit to raise her son [her daughter] with goodness and with pleasantries, and to guide him [her] on a straight path for mitzvot and good deeds, and let us say amen.[24]

The omission of a naming formula in this Mi Shebairach demonstrates that not all Ashkenazic newborn girls were historically named in the synagogue in conjunction with a father's aliyah, even as recently as the late nineteenth century. Thus, one custom in Germany at this time was to bless a birthing mother and her child, whether boy or girl, but without announcing a name.

Another observation about the development of the Mi Shebairach for birthing mothers is that none of the Mi Shebairach texts recited for the occasion of a birth, as cited in Yaari's study, make any mention of a mother's recovery. This prayer is included, however, in some Ashkenazic Mi Shebairach texts today.

Finally, Yaari notes differences between Ashkenazic and Sephardic practices. "In the communities in Spain and the Middle East, they would announce the name of a daughter in the home (and not in the community [i.e., synagogue]), and at the time of announcing the name, they blessed the daughter (and not the birthing mother) with a special blessing."[25] By contrast, in Ashkenazic communities, a Mi Shebairach was recited in the synagogue, and this prayer focused on the mother, not the baby. Yaari states that the home ceremony performed in Spain and the Middle East is called the Zeved HaBat.[26]

Despite these significant differences, it seems that both the Ashkenazic and Sephardic Mi Shebairach prayers for naming girls have their roots in the Mi Shebairach form that originated in the early medieval period. This parallel development of purpose may have been the result of ongoing social or business interactions between Ashkenazim and Sephardim.[27]

EARLY NAMING PRACTICES

We now expand our scope from the Mi Shebairach naming text to customary naming practices, more generally. Examining these customs will enable us to begin to piece together how the contemporary synagogue naming evolved.

In Biblical times, both boys and girls received their names at birth.[28] For example, Abraham named Isaac upon birth. Thus, when Isaac was circumcised on his eighth day of life, he had already been named (Genesis 21:3–4). The twelve sons and one daughter of Jacob were all likewise named upon birth by either Leah or Rachel (Genesis 29:32–30:24). Similarly, Hannah immediately named her son Samuel when he was born (I Samuel 1:20).

Although there is no explicit Talmudic source that describes at what point girls or boys were named,[29] newborn boys in late antiquity began to receive their Hebrew name at the time of their circumcision. Boys may have been named at their circumcisions even as early as the time of the Second Temple.[30] This Jewish practice is explicitly noted in the first century CE in the book of Luke (1:59–60, 2:21) that describes how John the Baptist and Jesus were circumcised and named. Pirkei d'Rabbi Eliezer (Chapters of R. Eliezer; ch. 48), a ninth-century *midrash* (rabbinic homiletic story; plural, *midrashim*), notes that Moses was circumcised and named Yekutiel when he was eight days old. Similarly, the circumcision liturgies recorded by R. Amram Gaon (ninth century) and R. Saadia Gaon (tenth century) include a naming.[31] Today Jewish boys who undergo ritual circumcision are universally named at this ceremony.

The early history of naming baby girls is much murkier than that of boys. The Biblical custom of naming babies at birth apparently persisted for girls for some length of time.[32] In addition, there is an allusion to an obscure festival known as the *Shavuah HaBat* ("Week of the Daughter") that some believe may have been held in the Mishnaic/Talmudic era (second–fifth centuries CE) or later. (The Mishnaic legal code serves as the basis for subsequent Talmudic discourses, and a *mishna* is a paragraph containing succinct legal rules, disputes, and discussions.) The only original reference to the Shavuah HaBat festival is a *baraita* (an uncodified *mishna*) from the "minor tractate" *Semachot* that states, "[In the case of both] *Shavuah HaBen* ["Week of the Son"] and Shavuah HaBat, Shavuah HaBen precedes; [in the case of both] a burial and a circumcision, the circumcision precedes."[33] In the High Middle Ages, R. Isaac ibn Giat (eleventh-century Spain)[34] and R. Moses ben Nachman (Nachmonides; thirteenth-century Spain and Israel)[35] both quote this baraita excerpt, but neither one explains it. In the nineteenth century, R. Seligman Baer Bamberger (Germany, 1807–1878) hypothesizes that Shavuah HaBat may refer to a baby girl's naming.[36] The term Shavuah HaBen, by contrast, is mentioned a handful of times in the Babylonian Talmud (e.g., Bava Kama 80a, Bava Batra 60b, Sanhedrin 32b), at least once in the Jerusalem Talmud (Ketuvot 1:5), and once in the Tosefta, a compilation of Mishnaic-era texts (Megillah 3:15).

Even today, the meaning of Shavuah HaBen and Shavuah HaBat remains unresolved and vigorously disputed. One group of modern scholars suggests the possibility that Shavuah HaBen and Shavuah HaBat were parallel birth celebrations that lasted for the entire week following the birth of a boy or a girl, respectively,[37] with at least one commentator maintaining that girls may have been named at the Shavuah HaBat.[38] R. Reuven Margoliot (twentieth century, Israel) posits that the Talmud's use of the double language "Shavuah HaBen, Shavuah HaBen" (BT Sanhedrin 32b) is unnecessary and that this passage should actually read "Shavuah HaBen, Shavuah HaBat."[39]

Another group of modern scholars strongly rejects the hypothesis of a week-long celebration for a girl, maintaining that this idea is unsubstantiated. Some in this group maintain, in conformance with the interpretation of R. Shlomo Yitzchaki (Rashi; eleventh-century France),[40] that Shavuah HaBen is a circumcision ceremony and thus unrelated to a Shavuah HaBat for girls.[41] Others conclude that there was no ancient Jewish birth celebration for boys or girls on the seventh day or for a full week following birth.[42]

In any event, to the extent there was a Shavuah HaBat birth celebration—and this is unknown and unconfirmed—there would apparently be no connection between this type of early practice and the later Mi Shebairach synagogue naming practice for girls, which is the focus of our examination.

MEDIEVAL ASHKENAZIC CUSTOMS FOR BIRTHING MOTHERS

The story of naming practices for baby girls continues in the Middle Ages in Ashkenaz (Germany, northern France, and adjacent provinces). The customs for birthing mothers (also known as *parturients*), as practiced in this era and region, provide the context necessary to unravel how the Ashkenazic synagogue naming developed over time. Three of these customs include: a mother's ceremonious first post-partum appearance in the synagogue, the creation of *wimpels,* and the *Hollekreisch* ritual. We discuss each in turn.

First Post-Partum Synagogue Visit

Birthing mothers, whether they had a boy or girl, remained in their homes for four weeks, or approximately thirty days, following childbirth. Friends and neighbors accompanied birthing mothers constantly (*sh'mira*) and provided them with food and the like. These practices resulted from the belief that mothers are sick after childbirth and also susceptible to spirits and the evil eye.[43] For the first two-and-a-half to three weeks after birth, a mother lay in bed, and her friends attended to her. On the Shabbat approximately three weeks after giving birth, a mother "got out of bed, changed her sheets and clothing and hosted her friends who came to visit. This stage was called the *Pfühl* [literally, "pillow"]. She then spent an additional week in bed."[44]

On the Friday at the end of this additional week, when approximately four weeks had elapsed since childbirth, the new mother

> changed her clothes and put white sheets on her bed. She cleaned and dressed the baby. This was called *die weisse Pfühle* ["the white pillow"]. That Sabbath morning, she proceeded to the synagogue, accompanied by her female friends and neighbors. She wore her Sabbath clothes covered with shrouds and on her head she wore a hat covered with a veil or scarf. . . . The woman's arrival in the synagogue was timed to coincide

with the beginning of the morning blessings that preceded the recital of the Shema, and special tunes were sung in her honor. If the baby was a boy, the woman gave the synagogue the embroidered wimpel. . . . The father of the baby was called to the Torah [for an aliyah] and said a blessing for his wife. The parturient herself did not play any active role in the synagogue ritual. After services, she took off the scarf she had covered her head with and the shrouds she had worn and returned to her home accompanied by her friends. She prepared a meal for them and gave them small gifts of baked goods and fruit. That same afternoon, the Hollekreisch ritual took place.[45]

These practices on the fourth Shabbat after giving birth signal the end of the period of "maternal seclusion" and a mother's return to her communal roles and household responsibilities.[46] Ashkenazic women typically did not bring their newborn babies to synagogue with them on their first appearance after childbirth.

Medieval and modern rabbis emphasize the importance of a new father's aliyah.[47] This aliyah took place thirty days (or four weeks) after the birth of a child, on the Shabbat morning that the mother returned to the synagogue post-partum, regardless of whether she gave birth to a boy or a girl.[48] The aliyah was the means by which a new mother fulfilled her obligations to give thanks to God for the recent birth of her child and to request atonement. These obligations stem from a new mother's Biblical requirement to bring, in Temple times, a burnt offering (*olah*) and a sin offering (*chatat*). A new mother brought these sacrifices at the end of her post-partum ritual impurity—forty days following birth for a boy and eighty days following birth for a girl (Leviticus 12:1–8). The burnt offering became conceptualized as a *karban todah,* a thanksgiving sacrifice by which a mother expressed her gratitude to God for the safe delivery of her newborn child. The sin offering was interpreted as a *karban yoledet,* a birthing sacrifice. While one Talmudic source holds that a birthing mother brings an atonement sacrifice not to atone for sins, but rather to enable her to partake of consecrated food (BT Keritot 26a), R. Simon bar Yochai states that a mother seeks atonement for swearing on her birthing bed never again to have intercourse with her husband (BT Niddah 31b). The shroud that a new mother wore to the synagogue in medieval Ashkenaz may represent her request for atonement, just as one today wears the *kittel,* a shroud-like garment, on Yom Kippur as a symbol of atonement.

A father's aliyah thus functions as a remembrance for the mother's sacrificial offerings.[49] When the father said, *"Barchu et Hashem hamivorach—* Blessed is God the Blessed"* as part of the aliyah ritual, he kept in mind that he was giving thanks on behalf of his wife. When the father completed the blessings of his aliyah, the mother would say "Amen" to acknowledge this thanksgiving rite and to fulfill her obligations. In addition, some women recited prayers recognizing these Temple sacrifices and offering supplications in their place.[50] Along the same lines, a father typically donated wax or candles to the synagogue, as mentioned in some versions of the Mi Shebairach, in commemoration of the animals that a birthing mother would have brought to the Temple to sacrifice. Interestingly, with the advent of gas and electric lighting in the nineteenth century, it became customary in the Frankfurt synagogue of R. Samson Raphael Hirsch (1808–1888) for fathers of newborn babies to donate money to the synagogue's general maintenance (*bedek habayit*) fund, since there was no longer a need for wax or candles.[51]

According to traditional Jewish law (halacha), a new father's aliyah is considered to be an obligation (*chiyuv*) because it satisfies a mother's responsibilities to give thanks and seek atonement. As a chiyuv, this aliyah has priority over almost all other aliyot, with the possible exception of that of a groom on the Shabbat preceding his wedding. It is noteworthy that a new father's aliyah occurs prior to the expiration of eighty days, the juncture at which the mother of a daughter would have offered sacrifices in Temple times. The aliyah is nonetheless obligatory because it is conducted in remembrance of Temple rituals (*zecher l'mikdash*), rather than as an independent practice.[52]

It was considered crucial for a birthing mother to be present for her husband's aliyah because this ritual was conducted solely for the mother's benefit. It follows that this aliyah took place thirty days following childbirth, at which point a mother's recovery was considered complete and she was, therefore, able to attend synagogue services and respond "Amen" to the aliyah's blessings.[53] Furthermore, there was no obligation for this aliyah if a mother died. If a mother was sick, the aliyah became obligatory only when she was well enough to make her way to the synagogue.[54] There is evidence that, in twentieth-century Berlin, if a birthing mother died before appearing in the synagogue, a gabbai recited a Mi Shebairach to name a baby girl on the Shabbat that the mother would have come to the synagogue, thirty days after the birth, but the father did not receive an aliyah.[55]

Moreover, R. Jacob Emden (the Yabetz; northern Germany, 1697–1776) remarks that, in the absence of her husband, a woman can apparently even receive her own aliyah to the Torah if the prayer service takes place in her home.[56] This appears to be an extraordinary leniency, since women were barred from participating in the Torah service in the synagogue. This exception is a creative solution, since it permits the aliyah while upholding the traditional notion that women's primary "ritual space" is in the home. The possibility of a woman receiving an aliyah at home demonstrates a strict adherence to the rule that the post-partum aliyah requires the mother's presence.

In Ashkenaz, this first synagogue appearance of a new mother after giving birth was a day of great joy and celebration, a personal holiday (*yom tov*) for the woman. She wore her finery and jewelry, along with the shroud and veil. The prayer leader sang special tunes for selected prayers in honor of the birthing mother, and the father was accordingly obligated to offer a monetary gift to the prayer leader. These practices, as well as the festive atmosphere, may have been similar to those occurring today at a traditional *Shabbat chatan* (*aufruf* in Yiddish) on the Shabbat prior to a wedding day, when a groom is called up for an aliyah, receives a Mi Shebairach, and is acknowledged and celebrated during the service.

A birthing mother also hosted at least one meal at her home for women in the community. Alternatively, she gave small plates of food to the rabbi, sexton, prayer leader, relatives, and neighbors, and particularly those who provided her with food during her home stay.[57] Like the aliyah, these elaborate and festive rituals commemorate the Temple sacrifices, express a mother's gratitude for surviving childbirth, and constitute a request for atonement.[58]

New mothers in medieval Ashkenaz did not recite Birkat HaGomel (the prayer for surviving harrowing experiences) in connection with childbirth.[59] This prayer would have been superfluous in light of the aliyah and other customs by which a mother expressed her thanksgiving. There were, however, prayers recited for mothers who were in danger or serious distress after giving birth. For example, R. Israel Isserlin (fifteenth-century Austria) describes a special Mi Shebairach that was recited specifically under these difficult circumstances. This prayer, which is separate from the Mi Shebairach recited for all birthing mothers, invokes Sarah, Rebecca, Leah, and Hannah, and deliberately omits Rachel who died in childbirth (Genesis 35:16–20).[60]

Creation and Presentation of Wimpels

A second related ritual pertains only to mothers of baby boys. A *wimpel* (in Yiddish, or *mappah* in Hebrew) is a diaper or cloth used at a baby's circumcision, which was subsequently embroidered and donated to the synagogue as a binder for Torah scrolls. In chapter 7, we will learn how the wimpel custom can serve as a basis for enhancing modern life-cycle rituals.

The wimpel is either the baby's diaper, a cloth wrapped on top of his actual diaper, or a cloth placed under the baby during his circumcision. After the circumcision, the baby's mother and her friends artistically decorated and embroidered this diaper. A mother undertook this project during the three weeks that she was ensconced at home after her son's circumcision. Some mothers, however, retained artists, scribes, or other craftsmen to decorate their sons' wimpels.[61]

A wimpel's embroidery typically included the boy's Hebrew name, his birthday, his father's Hebrew name, and the expected date that the boy would eventually be called to the Torah for the first time. In modern times, the family name and the boy's mother's name were sometimes included. Some wimpels recorded unfortunate circumstances, such as a newborn boy's death, or, in fewer instances, the death of a baby's mother. Italian wimpels occasionally depicted the family symbol and the donor's name. Due to its wealth of demographic information, the wimpel "became a record of a new male member of the community." Stored in the synagogue, a collection of wimpels thus "formed a birth registry for boys only."[62]

The embroidery also sometimes contained an inscription that just as the boy entered the covenant, so may he enter a life of Torah, the marriage canopy, and good deeds. Other inscriptions were prayers that God should guard and protect the boy, or confirmations that he was born under a good constellation.[63]

By the seventeenth century in western and southern Germany, Switzerland, Denmark, and Bohemia, wimpel embroidery or painting had become a prevalent religious art form, exhibiting a torrent of creativity. Biblical passages were embroidered on wimpels, despite some rabbinic prohibitions against doing so, and the words artistically incorporated colorful, decorative touches. Some wimpels depicted Biblical scenes, or pictures relating to circumcision, Jewish holidays, or the boy's name or time of birth. Other embroidered or painted motifs included the signs of the zodiac, birds, fish, snakes, lions, other animals, leaves, flowers, branches, crowns, the marriage canopy, stars of David, and Torah scrolls. By the late nineteenth and early twentieth centuries, patriotic themes, such as national flags, began to emerge. Notwithstanding these embellishments, some communities were careful to leave on the wimpel the blood of circumcision, due to its believed mystical qualities.[64]

Different customs developed regarding the public donation of the wimpel to the synagogue. One custom was that a birthing mother presented a wimpel when she came to the synagogue for the first time since her baby boy's birth, typically on the fourth Shabbat following birth (as mentioned at the beginning of this section).[65] An alternate custom developed that a boy between the ages of six months and five years, depending on local practices, delivered his wimpel on the first day that he came to the synagogue. The rabbi blessed the boy and a special Mi Shebairach prayer was recited in the boy's honor.[66]

The synagogue then used the adorned wimpel as a binder with which to tie a Torah scroll. At least one source points out how the wimpel connects the covenant of circumcision with the covenant of Torah and, as a result, fulfills the precept that an object used for one good deed (circumcision) should also be used for another (binding a Torah scroll).[67] In some communities, a bar mitzvah (a thirteen-year-old boy who assumes his religious obligations) used his wimpel to tie up the Torah from which he received his aliyah; a groom likewise did so on the Shabbat preceding his wedding.[68]

Some attribute the genesis of the wimpel custom to the impromptu use of a Torah binder as a diaper at a circumcision by R. Yaakov ben Moses Levi Molin (the Maharil; fourteenth–fifteenth centuries, Germany) when he was serving as *sandek* (the person who holds the baby as the circumcision is performed). Others, however, reject this hypothesis. Regardless, once circumcision diapers began to be used as Torah binders in Ashkenaz, they completely supplanted the use of other items for this purpose.[69]

The wimpel custom may have begun as early as the fourteenth century, and persisted until the eve of the Holocaust particularly in southern and western Germany.[70] For example, my family retains the wimpel of the father of my great-aunt Lisbeth Okolica. My great-uncle Henry Okolica—a rabbi ordained at the Breuer's Yeshiva in Frankfurt, Germany at age nineteen—

presciently retrieved his father-in-law's wimpel from a synagogue in Tann (Röhn), Hesse, in central Germany. He did so a few short months before *Kristallnacht* ("the night of the broken glass," November 9–10, 1938), when the Nazis ransacked countless synagogues and Jewish businesses in Germany and Austria and deported thousands of Jewish men to concentration camps. My great-uncle took the one wimpel he recognized; he believes that many others in that synagogue were destroyed on Kristallnacht. Uncle Henry ultimately brought the wimpel to the United States, and it now hangs proudly in his son's living room.

The Hollekreisch Ceremony

A third related ritual brings us back to the naming of newborns. From the eleventh century until the Holocaust,[71] it was customary among Jews in Germany and neighboring lands to announce a newborn's name at a Hollekreisch ceremony.[72] As we will see, this practice waxed and waned at different times in different regions. The predominant purpose of the Hollekreisch was to announce the name or nickname that a boy or girl would use on an everyday basis, such as a German, French, or Yiddish name. This "unholy" or "secular" name stands in contrast to the "holy" or "Jewish" name, derived from the Torah or Talmud, which boys received at their circumcision and then used for aliyot, marriage contracts, and the like. Ashkenazic girls traditionally received only an "unholy" name.

Much less commonly, the Hollekreisch could instead incorporate a baby's "holy" name. For example, the reiteration of a boy's Jewish name at the Hollekreisch indicated the intent to use this name regularly.[73] In the twentieth century, some girls received a Jewish name at the Hollekreisch,[74] although the extent of this practice is unclear. My great-uncle Henry recounted to me that, in his experience in pre-Holocaust Germany, a baby girl's Jewish name was announced at her Hollekreisch, just as a baby boy's Jewish name was announced at his circumcision. Uncle Henry explained that both boys and girls received their German names when their births were registered with the civil authorities.

The Hollekreisch traditionally occurred on the afternoon of the Shabbat when a new mother attended the synagogue for the first time post-partum, approximately four weeks or thirty days after giving birth. The first evidence of this timing is from the fifteenth century.[75] In "emancipated" regions where Jews no longer lived in ghettos, the Hollekreisch was sometimes performed on weekdays.[76] My great-uncle is adamant that, in his experience in Germany, the Hollekreisch never occurred on Shabbat, in order to ensure that no attendees would use motorized vehicles or otherwise violate Shabbat prohibitions.

The ceremony proceeded as follows: children from the family and/or neighborhood—traditionally boys for a baby boy and girls for a baby girl[77]—came to the home of the new parents and gathered around the baby's crib. The baby was dressed up for the ceremony. The children lifted the crib, or, in other variations (particularly in modern times), an adult such as the father or a rabbi did so while surrounded by the children. The children shouted three times, "Hollekreisch! Hollekreisch!" (or, alternatively, "Holle! Holle!"), followed by *Wie soll das kindschen heissen?—*How shall the baby be called?" This question was shouted either once or three times and, in some versions, may have been asked by the baby's father rather than the children. Then, either the children (informed by the baby's parents) or one of the parents responded with the baby's name. At the ceremony's conclusion, the children received sweets, cakes, and fruits. In at least one modern account, the children received a small toy as a surprise.[78]

At a boy's Hollekreisch, the children recited a number of Biblical passages, which varied according to era and region. For example, a prayer book published in Rodelheim, Germany in 1901 contains nine verses in its Hollekreisch text, including the first verse of each book of the Pentateuch.[79] According to one source, school-age boys in attendance chanted these passages from their printed Pentateuch volumes (*chumashim;* singular, *chumash*) while sitting around a table.[80] Writing in northern Germany in the eighteenth century, R. Jacob Emden mentions *p'sukei bracha* (Biblical verses functioning as blessings) read at Hollekreisch ceremonies for girls,[81] but it appears that Biblical passages were more commonly not recited at all for baby girls.[82] To the extent that they were recited, however, the verses for a girl were not fixed, as they were for a boy.

In Avignon, France, the Hollekreisch ceremony for baby boys included a special prayer about learning and following the Torah, as well as a Mi Shebairach that concluded with the hope that the boy would merit "Torah, the marriage canopy, and good deeds." Some versions of the ceremony included the placement of a chumash (Leviticus, according to one source) under a baby boy's head as part of the ceremony.[83]

An additional aspect of the Hollekreisch is that baby boys may have been covered in a special tallit. The extent to which this custom was practiced is unclear, but it is recorded in one source from seventeenth-century Worms, Germany.[84] It is also not clear whether baby girls were likewise covered with a tallit,[85] but there is at least one adamant opinion that this never occurred.[86]

Different theories surround the origin of the name *Hollekreisch.* Fifteenth- and sixteenth-century rabbis explained that *Hollekreisch* is derived from *hol,* meaning "not holy," and *kreisch,* meaning "cry out," and thus refers to crying out an everyday name, which is what occurred at the ceremony.[87] Another hypothesis is that *Hollekreisch* signifies "holy *gorash,*" meaning that "the sickness, connected with childbirth, has been driven out."[88] Others have interpreted *Hollekreisch* as deriving from the French *haut la crèche* ("up with the cradle"),[89] although modern scholars reject this interpretation as not credible or forced.[90] These scholars posit that *Holle* refers to Frau Holle, a "Germanic goddess-like figure" believed to attack or kidnap unbaptized infants. To ward off Frau Holle by tricking her into thinking children were baptized, medieval Christian women took unbaptized children to church, picked them up three times, called out "Holle, Holle, Holle," and gave them a name. These scholars maintain that the Hollekreisch may have been one of a variety of means by which Jews handled their fear of evil spirits.[91] Interestingly, my uncle Henry, an Orthodox rabbi, matter-of-factly told me that *Hollekreisch* means to cry to the demon Holle. He was unoffended by what he considered to be a well-understood explanation.

R. Binyomin Shlomo Hamburger of the Institute for German Jewish Heritage (Machon Moreshes Ashkenaz) in Bnei Brak, Israel, has a different perspective. He views the Hollekreisch as a custom that is neither well-known nor well-understood. He stresses that one should never mock customs, since they are a source of Jewish life and strength and a reflection of a Torah outlook.[92] Another opinion is that of R. Leo Trepp (Germany and United States, 1913–2010), who emphasizes the importance of Jewish folk-ways and maintains that the Hollekreish "instilled values of which I have become more aware with the passage of time." According to R. Trepp, the Hollekreish also manifests a belief, even among "deeply traditional Jews" that "girls should also have something," since circumcision and other rituals were not available to them. He points out that, in this way, "[p]ractice over-rode instruction" and that since the Hollekreisch "was done in the home, this became easier."[93]

In some regions, the Hollekreisch practice disappeared for boys—who continued to receive Hebrew names at their circumcision—and remained for girls only.[94] R. Yoel Sirkis (the Bach, 1561–1640) observed that the Hollekreisch was no longer practiced, at least for boys, where he lived in Poland and ·Ukraine, calling this custom *minhag kadmonim* ("a custom of those living in earlier times"). The prevailing custom in Poland and the Ukraine by the early seventeenth century was that a boy received two names at his circumcision: his Hebrew name and his vernacular name; the latter functioned as a nickname.[95] R. Samuel HaLevi Segal of Mezeritch, Ukraine, noted that, in the sixteenth and seventeenth centuries, the Hollekreisch was performed for boys and girls in Germany, but was performed only for girls in Poland, Moravia, and Austria.[96] In late sixteenth to early seventeenth-century Poland and seventeenth-century Worms, Germany, the Hollekreisch was performed only for girls.[97]

While it was a dominant Ashkenazic practice for many centuries, the Hollekreisch persisted into modern times in only a few places, for example, in Alsace, Switzerland, and Holland for girls only.[98] In addition, up until the Holocaust, the Hollekreisch was retained in parts of Germany; depending on the region, this ceremony was performed either for both boys and girls or for only one or the other.[99] My great-uncle and great-aunt, Rabbi Henry and Lisbeth Okolica, clearly recall the Hollekreisch ceremony as a standard practice in Tann, in central Germany, but for girls only.

When my parents and I broached the topic of the Hollekreisch with my great-aunt Lisbeth, her face lit up with excitement; this is a well-remembered practice from her childhood, one that she may not have spoken about for decades. It is amazing that my own family can provide the "living history" for a practice that is all but extinct. At the same time, I have been pleasantly surprised to discover that at least a handful of families are attempting to keep the Hollekreisch's memory alive. For example, I have identified two texts for modern welcoming ceremonies for girls—one from 2002, the other from 2005, and both performed in New York City—which incorporate the Hollekreisch practice.[100]

NAMING GIRLS WITH A "JEWISH" NAME

In the High Middle Ages (circa eleventh–fourteenth centuries), a father's aliyah to the Torah, the blessing for his wife, and the Hollekreisch were all functioning Ashkenazic customs, and were practiced upon the birth of a boy or girl. The wimpel was also a functioning custom, but for boys only. All these practices occurred on the Shabbat of the fourth week (or approximately thirty days) following a baby's birth. For girls, an "everyday" or "unholy" name was announced at the Hollekreisch and no "holy" or "Jewish" name was given. As noted above, historian Elisheva Baumgarten observes that, in the High Middle Ages, aside from the Hollekreisch, "no other naming ritual [for girls] is mentioned in the sources."[101] A "holy" name was deemed unnecessary for girls since they did not have aliyot or perform other public rituals. Even as late as the twentieth century, some German-Jewish women did not receive a "holy" name. For example, my own maternal grandmother, Senta Okolica, was not given a Jewish name at birth; she was born in Aschaffenburg, in central-west Germany, in 1919. Many years later, in the United States, she adopted Sarah as her Hebrew name.

At some point after new fathers began to receive aliyot, however, a new practice appeared; newborn girls in certain Ashkenazic regions began to receive a "holy" or Jewish name in the synagogue. This naming occurred on the fourth Shabbat following a girl's birth when her mother made her first post-partum appearance at the synagogue. Also that Shabbat, the father received an aliyah at the synagogue in the morning, and the Hollekreisch was performed at home in the afternoon. A baby girl, therefore, received her "holy" or Jewish name in the morning in conjunction with her father's aliyah, and received her "unholy" or "everyday" name that afternoon at the Hollekreisch.[102] As discussed above, the Mi Shebairach text for birthing mothers apparently developed in approximately the mid-thirteenth century. Thus, the blessing that a husband recited for his wife after receiving his aliyah transitioned into the Mi Shebairach around this time. Regardless of exactly when this Mi Shebairach for birthing mothers emerged, a baby girl's naming as part of this Mi Shebairach was apparently added later, since there was a point in time when the aliyah and the husband's blessing occurred but the girl's "holy" naming did not.

This custom of synagogue naming for girls spread to different regions at different times, and interacted with the pre-existing Hollekreisch custom in different ways. For example, while the synagogue naming custom never took hold in some communities, it ultimately became the sole means of naming baby girls in others. In seventeenth-century Worms, Germany, girls were named only at home at the Hollekreisch ceremony.[103] In the same era, however, R. Samuel HaLevi Segal of Mezeritch, Ukraine, observes that the Hollekreisch was no longer performed for girls in many larger communities; instead, a Mi Shebairach was recited in the synagogue.[104]

By the eighteenth century, R. Joseph ben Menahem Mendel Steinhardt (1720–1776) recounts that in Germany and Poland, baby girls were named twice on the same day. They received a "holy" name in the synagogue Mi Shebairach following a father's aliyah and, later that day, received their "unholy" name at the Hollekreish ceremony. However, he also emphasizes the importance of the synagogue naming: "[I]t is a mitzvah for the father leading services to make a Mi Shebairach for his wife and the child, in order to publicize the name of the child in the community, both for a boy or a girl."[105] This statement may signal a shift toward the emergence of the synagogue naming as a primary mode of naming newborn girls, at least in certain regions and perhaps in certain larger cities. This statement also demonstrates that, in the eighteenth century, fathers continued to be honored in the synagogue on the fourth Shabbat whether the child was a boy or a girl. Finally, it is interesting that the Mi Shebairach was used to "publicize" a boy's name, although it had apparently already been announced at his circumcision.

The description by R. Jacob Emden of the synagogue naming and Hollekreish in northern Germany in the eighteenth century[106] may likewise indicate a shift in this region, or in certain cities, toward the primacy of the synagogue naming. R. Emden describes that a girl is named in the synagogue via a Mi Shebairach in conjunction with her father's aliyah in the morning and that the Hollekreisch is performed that afternoon. R. Emden does not explicitly mention a naming as part of the Hollekreisch, although he does state that p'sukei bracha (Biblical verses functioning as blessings) are recited for the baby. If this omission of a Hollekreisch naming is significant, it might suggest that, in R. Emden's experience, the synagogue naming was becoming primary and that the Hollekreisch, while still performed, was losing significance.

Furthermore, R. Emden explains that the synagogue naming occurs on the fourth Shabbat following childbirth when a birthing mother goes to synagogue for the first time. On this day, her husband has an obligation to receive an aliyah in remembrance of a mother's required Temple sacrifices. R. Emden adds, however, that the father or someone else gives a baby girl her name at the end of her first four weeks of life, even if the mother is not present in the synagogue. This is a significant change from the earlier accepted practice that a Mi Shebairach is recited only in the mother's presence, since the father has no obligation to be called to the Torah in the mother's absence. This notion of naming a girl even in her mother's absence may demonstrate that, in some regions, the synagogue naming was gaining prominence, since the naming demanded performance even when the aliyah's primary purpose—thanksgiving and atonement for the mother—went unfulfilled.

Also noteworthy is R. Emden's comment that the Hollekreisch ceremony "is not a simple and established custom among the Ashkenazim, and it is not written in a book." (My great-uncle likewise emphasizes that the Hollekreisch is not recorded in any book.) By contrast, R. Emden declares that "[c]ertainly among the customs of the Sephardim, I have seen the Zeved HaBat [a practice described earlier in this chapter]," and proceeds to record the passages and Mi Shebairach recited at the Zeved HaBat. Thus, in northern Germany in the eighteenth century, R. Emden viewed the Hollekreisch custom as in flux, particularly as compared to what he considered a well-established Zeved HaBat custom among Sephardim.

R. Salomon Carlebach (Germany and United States, twentieth century) reports both a synagogue naming and a Hollekreisch ceremony for baby girls in Berlin, Germany, in 1918. R. Carlebach describes how a baby girl was given her name "in front of the Sefer Torah" (the Torah scroll) in the synagogue on the first Shabbat when a mother appeared in the synagogue after giving birth. Then, that afternoon, the children of the community gathered for the Hollekreisch ceremony.[107]

In many areas of Europe, the Hollekreisch disappeared over an extended period of time. For example, R. Menachem Gottlieb describes that in 1897 in Hanover, north-central Germany, a new father received an obligatory aliyah on the first Shabbat that his wife came to the synagogue postpartum. After this aliyah, the prayer leader (*shaliach tzibur*) recited a Mi Shebairach for the mother and daughter and announced the daughter's name.[108] R. Gottleib does not, however, mention the Hollekreisch. Similarly, there were Hungarian communities using the Ashkenazic *nusach* (liturgical style) where, up until the eve of the Holocaust, a baby girl was named only when her father had an aliyah on the first Shabbat that her mother returned to the synagogue.[109]

On the flip side, some German communities did not adopt the custom of naming baby girls in the synagogue even as late as the nineteenth and twentieth centuries. For example, R. Markus Horovitz notes in a book of responsa, published in 1891, that in his Frankfurt-am-Main community in

Germany, it was not customary to give a *yad v'shem* to girls (that is, to name them) in the synagogue.[110] This observation corresponds with the absence of a naming formula for either girls or boys in the Mi Shebairach text in *Tikkun HaSofer V'HaKoreh*, a guide for Torah readers published in Germany in 1886, as mentioned above.

Likewise, in the experiences of my great-uncle and great-aunt in southeastern Germany on the eve of the Holocaust, newborn girls were named for the first or only time at the Hollekreisch ceremony. While the father of a baby girl had the option of receiving an aliyah, he could do so only after the baby was already named at the Hollekreisch, and the Mi Shebairach in the synagogue merely reiterated this name. Uncle Henry commented that, in his experience in Germany, fathers typically would not receive an aliyah, as many of them were not religiously observant. Naming a baby girl for the first time in the synagogue was a practice with which my great-uncle and great-aunt became familiar only upon their arrival in the United States.

THE WANING OF MEDIEVAL ASHKENAZIC CUSTOMS FOR NEW MOTHERS

Despite the longevity of the Hollekreisch and wimpel customs, the only Ashkenazic practices for birthing mothers that have survived to the present day are the father's aliyah and the Mi Shebairach with a "holy" naming for girls. Prior to the Holocaust, this "synagogue naming" was inconsistently, yet increasingly, performed in Germanic and eastern European regions, as we have seen. More recently, this practice has become widely accepted in traditional Ashkenazic communities because it emerged as the surviving traditional means of naming a girl.

It is not clear why the bulk of Ashkenazic customs for birthing mothers have disappeared. Some "emancipated" communities may have developed an interest in emphasizing formal, synagogue-centered rituals and scaling back informal or folk-based customs. It follows that a mother's participation on the fourth Shabbat following birth was downplayed and that the father's role on this day—most prominently, his aliyah—was magnified.

In some Ashkenazic communities, a rabbi's involvement in the Hollekreisch ceremony may represent a turning point, where the synagogue's influence, as represented by the rabbi, was incorporated into the home ritual. For example, R. Joshua Falk (1555–1614, Poland) mentions in his Derisha commentary on the *Arba'ah Turim,* an early halachic code, that community rabbis in late sixteenth- to early seventeenth-century Poland would customarily go to the home of a birthing mother to name a baby girl at the Hollekreisch.[111] As anthropologist Harvey Goldberg has observed in the context of men asserting dominance in the home to conduct a circumcision, "[p]erhaps the historical thrust of rabbinical culture was less about excluding women than about asserting control over domestic affairs, wherein 'women' represent the home and 'men' are emblematic of communal authority."[112]

In communities where the Hollekreisch persisted, a rabbi's officiation at this ceremony may have been a cultural accommodation that promoted the custom's longevity. I was intrigued when my great-uncle Henry, a practicing rabbi in pre-Holocaust Germany, told me that he officiated at Hollekreisch ceremonies for newborn girls as a matter of course. After the children shouted to ask for the baby's name and the mother responded, Uncle Henry recited two Mi Shebairach prayers, one blessing the baby girl and the other praying for the mother's health. If a father chose to have an aliyah subsequently, these Mi Shebairach prayers were repeated. Uncle Henry recounts that parents would arrange their daughter's Hollekreisch ceremony, hold it privately in their home, and invite the community rabbi to attend and preside. Fathers, however, were typically absent. Thus, the Hollekreisch, as practiced in my great-uncle's personal experience, welcomed one male presence (that of the rabbi) but discouraged another (that of the father).[113]

Another hypothesis for the decline of customs for new mothers is that some communities became more interested in identifying girls with a Hebrew or "holy" name when civil authorities began to assume a role in registering the "unholy" names of newborns. Since the synagogue naming had become associated with a girl's "holy" name and the Hollekreisch with her "unholy" name, there was less need for the Hollekreisch and more interest in the synagogue naming. In a break with earlier customs, however, my great-uncle's community in Tann, in central Germany, announced a girl's "holy" name at her Hollekreisch ceremony. This particular community apparently held so tightly to the Hollekreisch custom that it shifted its emphasis from the "unholy" to the "holy" name, yet resisted a corresponding shift from the Hollekreisch to the synagogue naming.

RECENT CHANGES AFFECTING ASHKENAZIC NAMING PRACTICES

This story of Ashkenazic naming practices for girls does not end, however, with the disappearance of most medieval Ashkenazic customs for new mothers and the persistence of the aliyah and Mi Shebairach, which comprise the synagogue naming. Rather, this story continues with the substantial changes that the surviving synagogue naming has undergone in recent years. Prominently, this custom's timing has shifted from four weeks (or thirty days) to no more than a few days following birth. On this new timetable, a baby girl is named at the first public Torah reading after her birth (Shabbat, Monday, or Thursday) or, alternatively, on her first Shabbat. This timing is no longer tied to the mother's post-partum return to the synagogue.

R. Binyomin Hamburger of the Institute for German Jewish Heritage observes that the evolution of the Ashkenazic Mi Shebairach text tells the tale of this timing shift. He observes that the primary purpose of the contemporary Mi Shebairach is to pray for the mother's recovery. In addition, the Mi Shebairach, when recited for the mother of a newborn boy, today includes a prayer requesting the merit to enter him into the covenant of circumcision. Both features reflect that the Mi Shebairach is recited three to four weeks earlier now than in the past. Since a mother's condition is thought to be most acute immediately after birth, it follows that a prayer for her recovery would be recited at this early juncture. Likewise, a prayer referencing an upcoming circumcision is recited within the first week of a boy's life, since circumcision occurs on the eighth day. As R. Hamburger emphasizes, however, the substantive cause of this timing shift and the liturgical changes that followed is the loss of the "special connection" between the Mi Shebairach and a mother's first appearance in the synagogue after giving birth.[114] In other words, when the special customs for new mothers fell away, the Mi Shebairach text changed accordingly to reflect this reality.

Another important observation is that the baby's father is central to the few customs that remain from the array of traditional Ashkenazic practices for new mothers. In traditional communities, a father receives an aliyah, and the Mi Shebairach prayer that follows is recited while the father stands prominently next to the Torah and in front of the congregation. It appears that when the many customs overtly involving mothers disappeared, the aliyah's purpose of enabling mothers to commemorate their Temple sacrifices was accordingly neglected. Thus, the aliyah and the Mi Shebairach, which outwardly involve only fathers, gradually lost their significance for new mothers and evolved into rituals solely for new fathers.

Furthermore, the synagogue naming originally occurred on the fourth Shabbat following birth to correspond to a mother's emergence from her post-partum seclusion. Reframed as rituals for new fathers, however, the aliyah and Mi Shebairach were severed from the four-week timing that is specific to mothers. Since fathers had no particular reason to wait for four weeks to perform these rituals, they began to do so as early as possible—on the first Shabbat or the first Torah reading following a baby girl's birth.

Mothers apparently stopped attending the synagogue naming when fathers assumed the central role in this practice and the four-week timing broke down. As a cultural norm, mothers were not expected to emerge in public earlier than four weeks following childbirth. In addition, there was no reason for mothers to attend the synagogue naming since all the rituals significant to them had faded away. As a result, when the aliyah began to occur within mere days of childbirth, not only did mothers no longer attend, but the expectation of their attendance likewise dissipated. This continues to hold true today in traditional Ashkenazic communities, where mothers often do not attend a daughter's synagogue naming. The historical reasons for this peculiar situation are now clear in light of the evolution of the father's aliyah.

We also appreciate the resulting legal (halachic) anomaly in which a mother remains obligated to respond "Amen" to a Mi Shebairach in remembrance of her compulsory Temple sacrifices, yet she may not be present in the synagogue in traditional Ashkenazic communities today. Moreover, in the birthing mother's absence, her husband does not even have an obligation (chiyuv) to be called to the Torah. Yet, he continues today to receive the benefit of this chiyuv, in that his aliyah is granted a high priority. A halachic difficulty occurs, however, when the father receives his aliyah before or instead of someone with an actual chiyuv (for example, one reciting the Kaddish prayer to mark the death of a family member). Today, these halachic difficulties are not well known, yet they should be regarded as troublesome.

We now also understand why some birthing mothers today give thanks for a safe childbirth by reciting Birkat HaGomel, although this was not the historical practice. In medieval Ashkenaz, mothers had no need for Birkat HaGomel. They satisfied their post-partum thanksgiving obligation by attending a husband's aliyah, responding "Amen" to the Mi Shebairach, and preparing meals for those who were helpful to them. Mothers, however, sought a new mode to give thanks when they were no longer present for the aliyah because it occurred too soon after childbirth. It appears, therefore, that some mothers more recently began to make use of the Birkat HaGomel. They could recite this prayer (or have it recited on their behalf) when convenient, anytime after the synagogue naming.

Today, mothers sometimes recite Birkat HaGomel on their first post-partum appearance in the synagogue, which could be a number of weeks after the synagogue naming. The short Birkat HaGomel blessing, however, is no substitute for the special treatment and recognition that a mother enjoyed as part of the customs she performed and experienced in medieval Ashkenaz. Furthermore, it seems that Birkat HaGomel was adopted as an accommodation associated with the waning of a mother's central role in the synagogue on the fourth Shabbat after birth. Therefore, despite common perceptions to the contrary, the recitation of Birkat HaGomel today is not a "traditional" practice; rather, it may have resulted from the decline of long-standing customs.

The waning of Ashkenazic customs for mothers of newborns also explains why a newborn girl is typically absent at her own synagogue naming. The original purpose of the Mi Shebairach was to bless the mother, not to bless or name the baby. In medieval Ashkenazic communities, the Shabbat four weeks post-partum was a special day for a mother. Even with the subsequent introduction of a girl's "holy" naming on this Shabbat, a newborn remained at home and did not accompany her mother to the synagogue. This was the prevailing norm perhaps because the synagogue naming was a minor feature on a day still dominated by practices for the new mother or simply because, as a general rule, babies did not attend synagogue in medieval Ashkenaz. When these practices for the mother receded, the custom persisted that a baby girl did not attend the synagogue, even though the "holy" naming is conducted for her. This is still the case in some traditional Ashkenazic communities today. The practice that occurred in a newborn girl's presence was the semi-private Hollekreisch ceremony. Where this ceremony disappeared, there was no other extant Ashkenazic ritual that welcomed a baby girl in person.

By contrast, Spanish and Portuguese Jews were more likely to bring new-borns to the synagogue on Shabbat than were Ashkenazim, although some Ashkenazim in England, for example, adopted this Sephardic practice. In nineteenth-century England, on Shabbat, an Ashkenazic birthing mother would stand holding her baby in the hallway of the synagogue. There, she recited Psalms, the Birkat HaGomel, and a "Prayer for the Birthing Mother," composed and instituted by R. Nathan Marcus Adler (1803–1890), Orthodox Chief Rabbi of the British Empire. The baby was then brought into the sanctuary (seemingly without her mother), and the rabbi bestowed on the baby the priestly blessing (*Birkat Kohanim; Numbers* 6:24–26).[115]

The original purpose of the Mi Shebairach also explains some oddities of the Ashkenazic Mi Shebairach text with respect to a girl's naming. This naming consists of the three words "*V'yekara sh'ma b'yisrael*—May her name be called in Israel," followed by the girl's name. This naming, while commonly considered today to be the main point of the Ashkenazic Mi Shebairach, reads as a mere parenthetical in the overall prayer, which blesses the mother and daughter and, in some versions, asks for the mother's full recovery. The prayer's title in the popular contemporary ArtScroll siddur, "Prayer for Mother and Newborn Child (and Naming a Baby Girl)," starkly reflects the naming's secondary role in the overall text. By contrast, the Mi Shebairach associated with the Sephardic Zeved HaBat ceremony focuses on the daughter.

It is no surprise that the Ashkenazic Mi Shebairach concentrates more on the mother than the baby, since the original purpose of this prayer was to bless the mother and to enable her to fulfill her thanksgiving and atonement obligations. It is likewise not surprising that the naming reads like a misplaced afterthought since it was apparently added to the pre-existing Mi Shebairach for the mother. A prayer intended for a birthing mother does not easily translate into a prayer for a baby. (This history does not explain, however, why some traditional prayer books mention only the father as raising his daughter, or include a blessing for a girl to be raised to marriage and good deeds but not to Torah.)

THE CONTEMPORARY SYNAGOGUE NAMING

We now turn to the bigger picture. The common element of the various medieval customs associated with birthing mothers is that they all signify entrance or re-entrance into the Jewish community. The mother's presence in the synagogue indicated her re-emergence into society and her assumption of household responsibilities after her four-week post-partum seclusion.

Donating a wimpel to the synagogue likewise signified a baby boy's entrance into the Jewish community, since a collection of wimpels, each embroidered with demographic information, functioned as a communal birth registry for boys. The announcement of a baby's Hebrew name in the synagogue and/or a vernacular name at the Hollekreisch also marked an entrance into the Jewish community, since a name is a means of recognizing an individual's communal membership. By the end of the fourth Shabbat following a baby's birth, a mother and baby were fully re-integrated or integrated, respectively, into the fabric of the Jewish community.

When a father's aliyah and his daughter's "holy" naming were displaced from their original context, they gradually lost much of their significance. In the absence of the full complement of Ashkenazic customs for new mothers, the synagogue naming for girls no longer made a strong statement of integrating a newborn girl and her mother into the community. In short, the aliyah and Mi Shebairach became vestiges of the rich collection of customs geared toward incorporating a birthing mother, as well as her newborn, into the community.

In progressive communities, the vestigial aliyah and Mi Shebairach customs have been recast and reinterpreted. Both parents may receive aliyot or a "joint aliyah," often while holding their newborn. In some communities, the baby is named with a Mi Shebairach, which may incorporate new or modified language. Moreover, these practices are typically part of broader synagogue ceremonies that celebrate the newborn and welcome her into the community of Israel. These ceremonies, which are led by a rabbi during regular synagogue services, include the naming, along with blessings and prayers, a speech by the rabbi, and sometimes other rituals. Some of these synagogue ceremonies, however, use naming liturgies other than the Mi Shebairach, while others omit an aliyah altogether or de-emphasize it by making other prayers or rituals central to the ceremony.

In traditional Ashkenazic communities, however, the synagogue naming (aliyah and Mi Shebairach) has become increasingly entrenched as other practices for newborns and mothers have gradually disappeared. This may be the result of an interest in preserving the only remaining Ashkenazic means of naming a newborn girl.

Today, there are traditional Ashkenazic communities that have supplemented the synagogue naming, while still maintaining its primacy. In this type of practice, which generally occurs on Shabbat, the rabbi draws the attention of the congregation to the father's aliyah and to the Mi Shebairach. The mother might publicly recite Birkat HaGomel, and the rabbi then offers words of Torah to sanctify the moment.

More commonly, however, the synagogue naming has been further eroded in many traditional Ashkenazic communities. As we saw at the beginning of this chapter, even those attending services might miss a girl's synagogue naming because it occurs quickly and inconspicuously. As a result, this ritual may not even serve its core purpose as a simple announcement. Often, neither the baby being named nor her mother attends the brief proceedings, and close family and friends likewise make no effort to attend. Under these circumstances, there is an absence of anything resembling a significant life-cycle ritual.

Along the same lines, parents in these communities sometimes heave a sigh of relief that their baby is a girl so that they need not go to the trouble of preparing a *simcha* (celebration)—or certainly not right away. In fact, some expectant parents in this modern age decide to find out via ultrasound or amniocentesis if the baby is a boy or a girl for the purpose, at least in part, of determining whether they will need to organize a party and whether their parents and other relatives will need to make travel plans. The preparations occur and the plans are made only if the baby is a boy.

It follows that family and friends may not even meet a baby girl in her first few weeks of life. Sometime prior to 1984, sociologist Rela Geffen Monson observed that one event that is "likely to startle a Jewish woman into an awareness of her inequality in the tradition" is "the birth of a daughter, when all the people who'd planned to come for the bris [i.e., circumcision] cancel their reservations."[116] More recently, Professor Rochelle Millen similarly recounted that her father would have closed his store and traveled to meet a newborn grandson and attend a circumcision, but that he waited "for a more convenient time" to meet his newborn granddaughter.[117] I am likewise personally aware of grandparents who have affirmatively chosen not to meet their new granddaughters for many months, although they would have certainly made immediate travel arrangements to attend a circumcision for a grandson. This is consistent with the practice espoused by the attorney awaiting his first grandchild whom we met in this book's Introduction.

A friend of mine summed up these practices by observing that, in many traditional Ashkenazic communities, "it is simply too easy to miss the opportunity to meet a newborn girl." Indeed, the fact that the *Rabbinical*

Council of America Madrikh, a manual for Orthodox rabbis, finds the need to remind rabbis that "[t]he birth of a girl is as great a joy as the birth of a boy"[118] speaks volumes about the norms in these communities.

PRACTICES BEYOND THE SYNAGOGUE NAMING

While the synagogue naming remains primary in traditional Ashkenazic communities, other noteworthy practices have developed as well. For example, parents often mark the birth of a daughter with a Shabbat *kiddush* (plural, *kiddushim*), a community-wide buffet served following the blessing over wine at the end of synagogue services. This is a significant expression of recognizing and celebrating the birth of a daughter with the entire community.

When my husband and I sponsored a kiddush in our synagogue in memory of his beloved grandfather on the first anniversary of his passing (*yartzeit* in Yiddish), an acquaintance of mine at the kiddush asked me the age of our youngest daughter. Puzzled, I responded that she was three months old. Only later did it occur to me that this acquaintance—quite mistakenly—assumed that this kiddush was our means of recognizing our daughter's birth. This personal experience reflects the widespread expectation that parents in traditional communities sponsor a kiddush to publicly celebrate the birth of a daughter. It also demonstrates that, if parents choose to sponsor a kiddush, they may wait some period of time after a daughter's birth to do so. It is less common that parents sponsor a kiddush on the Shabbat of a naming, within a few days of the baby's birth, despite some twentieth-century halachic opinions encouraging a festive meal at this juncture.[119]

In many traditional communities, a kiddush is deemed appropriate in that it is commemorative but without adding "specific or detailed rituals."[120] According to R. Moshe Sternbuch, chief rabbi of the Eidah HaChareidit (a prominent ultra-Orthodox organization in Jerusalem), the dual purposes of the kiddush are to publicize a girl's name and to give thanks. R. Sternbuch also mentions that a kiddush provides an opportunity for people to bestow on the father the blessing that he should derive joy from his daughter.[121]

Possibly a more mystical motivation for holding a kiddush for a baby daughter is provided in a story, although it is disputed whether this story ever happened and, if so, which rabbi was involved. The father of an unmarried adult daughter asks his rabbi why this daughter has not yet married. The rabbi responds that the reason is that the father never held a proper kiddush for his daughter when she was born. The rabbi explains that a kiddush results in many blessings being recited on behalf of the girl, including the blessing that she will get married, and that it is never too late to have this kiddush. The father holds a kiddush for his adult daughter, and she becomes engaged soon afterwards.[122]

I slowly began to realize that this motivation for holding a kiddush for a daughter is apparently well-known in some communities. A friend, who would identify himself as modern Orthodox, mentioned to me that his father sponsored a kiddush for my friend's adult sister in the hopes that she would marry. I was surprised to hear this, particularly when my friend reported that his sister did not attend the kiddush. I was even more surprised when my husband told me that a character on the first season of the Israeli soap opera *S'rugim* hosted a kiddush for herself to increase her chances for marriage and, furthermore, that she married during the show's second season. To the extent that traditional Jews are aware of the notion that holding a kiddush may result in eventual marriage, this may be a reason that a kiddush is a relatively popular means of recognizing newborn girls in traditional communities. The idea is to hold a kiddush for a newborn so that she need not require one as an adult.

A much newer practice, which today has a firm foothold in some traditional communities, is to hold, often at home, religious-themed ceremonies to welcome newborn girls in the presence of family and friends. Sometimes held weeks or months after a synagogue naming, these ceremonies incorporate prayers, songs, Scriptural readings, an explanation of the baby's name, and other speeches. There are liberal practitioners who likewise conduct religious welcoming ceremonies outside the rubric of synagogue services. A different type of event held across the spectrum of Jewish practice is a nonsectarian "birthday party" which incorporates no religious or quasi-religious overtones and may feature a birthday cake.

Another custom found in traditional communities is for parents, upon the birth of a daughter, to privately recite, "Blessed are You God, our God, King of the Universe, who has kept us alive and preserved us and brought us to this season—*Shehechiyanu v'kiyamanu v'higiyanu la'z'man hazeh*" (referred to as *Shehechiyanu*). This blessing is traditionally recited for specified new experiences (BT Brachot 58b, 59b–60a). The idea of reciting Shehechiyanu to recognize a daughter's birth appears briefly in the works of at least four nineteenth and twentieth century halachic authorities. R. Naftali

Tzvi Yehuda Berlin (Netziv; 1816–1893, Lithuania) innovated this idea from the rule that Shehechiyanu is said upon the purchase of new clothing, bed linens, dishes, and the like. He also mentions that a daughter is a gift for her father.[123] R. Yisrael Meir Kagan (Chofetz Chaim; 1838–1933, Lithuania) derives the recitation of Shehechiyanu for a daughter from the requirement to say this blessing upon seeing someone for the first time in thirty days. He asks rhetorically: "Can [seeing one's daughter for the first time] be worse than one who sees his friend for the first time in thirty days, is happy to see him, and says 'Shehechiyanu'?"[124] Both R. Chaim Elazar Spira (Munkacser Rebbe; 1868–1937, Ukraine), whose only child was a beloved daughter, and R. Eliezer Waldenberg (1915–2006, Jerusalem) mention parental joy as a reason for reciting Shehechiyanu on the birth of a girl.[125]

A related custom is to recite the *Hatov v'Hameitiv* blessing ("Blessed are You God, our God, King of the Universe, who is Good and who causes good"). I first became aware of this custom when a centrist Orthodox rabbi mentioned to me that he recited Hatov v'Hameitiv immediately upon the birth of his daughters. I was surprised to hear this because Hatov v'Hameitiv is traditionally recited in connection with the birth of a son (BT Brachot 59b).[126] I have become increasingly interested in the Hatov v'Hameitiv blessing, and suggest the possibility of parents reciting this blessing as part of a communal ceremony for a daughter, if they have not already done so privately upon the baby's birth. One ultimate manifestation of divine Good is the birth of a child, and Hatov v'Hameitiv gives thanks for this beneficence. Furthermore, Hatov v'Hameitiv has long been specifically associated with newborns (albeit sons), while Shehechiyanu, for example, is a broad-based blessing that has been reconfigured in modern times for the wholly new purpose of welcoming newborns. Hatov v'Hameitiv is arguably better suited for a communal ceremony than Shehechiyanu, since the Talmud cites the former as appropriate for that which is "for oneself and others," while the latter is meant only for that which is "for oneself" (BT Brachot 59b). I have examined elsewhere, from a technical halachic perspective, the recitation of Hatov v'Hameitiv for a newborn daughter.[127]

THIS IS WHERE we conclude our journey through the history of the Ashkenazic synagogue naming for girls. In the next chapter, we turn our attention to how this history can inspire our practices for newborn girls today.

A First and Only Naming

By exploring the history of how newborn girls received their names in Ashkenazic regions over the centuries, we now understand that the contemporary synagogue naming for girls, which consists of an aliyah and a Mi Shebairach prayer, is the only surviving component of a larger complement of medieval Ashkenazic practices. We have also learned that the vestigial synagogue naming plays different roles in different communities today. While the aliyah and Mi Shebairach are frequently reinterpreted, supplemented, or downplayed in progressive communities today, the status of the synagogue naming has been elevated in many traditional Ashkenazic communities to the point that this ritual is deemed virtually obligatory.

Detached from its original historical context, however, the synagogue naming conducted today for newborn girls has devolved into a perfunctory and inconspicuous practice in many traditional Ashkenazic communities. Parents are relieved that they need not organize a festive event, and family and friends know that they are not expected to make any immediate plans. This situation persists overall in these communities, despite the existence of countervailing customs, such as kiddushim and religious-themed ceremonies, which are considered decidedly secondary and optional. Even traditional synagogues that embellish the synagogue naming do so with the clear understanding that the aliyah and Mi Shebairach are the primary rituals.

In traditional Ashkenazic communities today, the dominance of the synagogue naming perpetuates a minimization of the religious significance of newborn girls. This approach does not warmly welcome a baby who has been created in the image of God (*tzelem Elohim*), nor does it optimally satisfy the Jewish concept of respecting others—the baby and her parents—with the respect due to oneself (Leviticus 19:18; BT Shabbat 31a). Furthermore, by not publicly honoring a newborn, an opportunity is missed for glorifying

God and the baby with a beautified ritual ("This is my God and I will praise Him"; Exodus 15:2). As a result, the synagogue naming today is broken.

These observations lead us to inquire: How can we revitalize and reshape the contemporary Ashkenazic naming ceremony for newborn girls in light of the rich traditional naming customs of the past?

In this chapter, we address this question by considering, first, the notion of consistently incorporating a girl's naming into a larger ceremony that welcomes her into the Jewish community. We then consider the possibility of decoupling this ceremony from the parental aliyah in a way that highlights the special roles of both newborns and parents, respectively. As we will see, these ideas draw inspiration from the medieval Ashkenazic customs for new mothers. We also contextualize these ideas by approaching them from the perspective of halacha, the classic system of Jewish law, and by noting a comparable structure in certain traditional Sephardic and Mizrachic customs for newborn girls. Although our inquiry derives from prevalent practices in traditional Ashkenazic communities, the hope is that the ideas that we develop here are broadly applicable to all Jewish communities.

NAMING AT A WELCOMING CEREMONY

We begin by recalling from the previous chapter that girls have not been consistently named with an aliyah and Mi Shebairach in Ashkenazic lands over the centuries, and that the interaction between this synagogue naming and the Hollekreisch naming has varied according to time and place. More recently, the time for reciting the Mi Shebairach has changed dramatically, from four weeks to a few days after a girl's birth. Since synagogue practices for newborn girls have been continuously evolving over time, it follows that these practices may be susceptible to further change in the future. Said otherwise, the synagogue naming, as practiced today by traditional Ashkenazim, has become accepted as a result of historical happenstance, not from a deliberate rabbinic requirement—and certainly not a divinely ordained one.

Second, we suggest that when customs lose their purpose and context, it is appropriate to examine the possibility of revitalizing and reframing them, according to the traditional dictum of the prophet Jeremiah to "renew our days like that of old" (*chadesh yameinu k'kedem*) (Lamentations 5:21). We have a responsibility to connect past with future and to ensure the vitality of tradition.[1] This is a particularly important exercise if it enables us to revisit practices that may be currently inconsistent with traditional Jewish values.

Applying these two principles, we see that a first step toward remedying the current situation in traditional Ashkenazic communities would be to name a girl for the first and only time at a well-attended ceremony that focuses on her importance to the Jewish people. The idea is to have a "unified" ritual, one that discloses a girl's name for the first and only time, while also honoring her, in person, as a new member of the Jewish people.

One initial outcome of this approach is to restore a girl's naming so that it truly becomes an announcement for a community of family and friends. According to R. Joseph ben Menahem Mendel Steinhardt (eighteenth-century Germany), one reason that the naming Mi Shebairach following a father's aliyah has been assigned the status of a "mitzvah" is because this prayer "publicize[s] the name of the child in the community."[2] Two centuries later in Israel, R. Moshe Sternbuch likewise emphasizes the importance of publicizing a girl's name.[3] This goal is attained simply by announcing a name when family and friends are gathered and listening closely.

More importantly, receiving a name is a milestone in that it assigns an identity to a newborn. It follows that a girl's name should be revealed for the first time at a ceremony in her honor because this naming constitutes part of her welcome into the Jewish nation. Futhermore, a girl is welcomed with respect when there is a communal expectation for a full-fledged ritual, which her parents plan as a labor of love, and when family and friends make travel plans to attend this special life-cycle event. A girl then receives her name in person, while she is held tenderly in her parents' arms.

Today, if a baby girl is ceremonially welcomed in the traditional Ashkenazic community, this welcome often occurs weeks or months after a perfunctory synagogue naming. The baby's name is revealed in the synagogue ritual within days of her birth and, at a subsequent event, the naming Mi Shebairach is repeated and the name's significance is explained. In this configuration, the synagogue naming is deemed mandatory, while the separate ceremony or celebration is considered a secondary addition.[4] This model retains the standard synagogue naming and, therefore, also its inherent difficulties—despite supplementing it with a meaningful ceremony at a later time. It is also noteworthy that explaining a name immediately after it is announced compounds the interest and excitement of the naming itself. By contrast, reiterating and explaining a name that has already been known for a period of time feels to me somewhat anti-climactic.

Combining a girl's welcome and naming into one ceremony is one way to resolve these concerns. There would no longer be a lingering contrast between the invisibility of the synagogue naming and the warm embrace of the welcoming ceremony that follows. A new dynamic is at play when a baby's name is announced for the first time at a welcoming ceremony where she is front and center; the girl is welcomed as she is named, and she is named as she is welcomed. Both indicate her inclusion in the Jewish community, and both take place in her presence. There is a palpable sense of anticipation not only because a name is about to be revealed, but also because a new person is joining the Jewish people.

EMPHASIZING THE ROLES OF PARENTS AND NEWBORNS

A first and only naming as part of a welcoming ceremony could occur either in the synagogue during services or at a "freestanding" ceremony (that is, outside the framework of synagogue prayers). Many progressive Ashkenazic synagogues today bestow a girl's Hebrew name in the synagogue, as part of a broader ritual that is integrated into regular Shabbat services and that initiates girls into the Jewish community. The entire congregation listens as the rabbi blesses the baby and speaks publicly about her name and her family. Sephardic and Mizrachic communities that utilize an aliyah and Mi Shebairach to name baby girls in the synagogue often do so with a spirited tone that communicates the significance of the naming event. We see, therefore, that the synagogue can be an effective setting for welcoming and naming newborn girls. Indeed, there are some traditional Ashkenazic communities where the synagogue naming has expanded to publicly welcome a baby girl with speeches, songs, and the like.

Nonetheless, Jewish communities—including the vast majority of traditional Ashkenazic communities—might consider adopting the practice of announcing a girl's name and formally welcoming her in a single freestanding ceremony that is held in the baby's honor and in her presence. At the same time, the father or the parents of a newborn girl (in traditional or egalitarian communities, respectively) could continue to be called up to the Torah and, as before, a Mi Shebairach would be recited to bless the mother.

The primary change is that a baby would no longer be named in the synagogue, since she would be named for the first and only time at a separate ceremony. As a result, "*V'yekara sh'ma b'yisrael*—May her name be called in Israel" would no longer be said in the synagogue Mi Shebairach.

This approach highlights the importance of both parents and newborns to the community. Neither overshadows the other, and parents and newborns are each central to their own ritual—the aliyah and Mi Shebairach (for parents) and the welcoming ceremony (for the baby). As we will see, this structure also affords other benefits (some of which may likewise apply if a baby's welcome occurs in the synagogue).

As independent events, the parents' ritual and the baby's ceremony could occur in different venues and at different times. With respect to venue, the aliyah for parents would continue to take place in the synagogue, whereas the baby's ceremony would, preferably, be conducted at home. It is fitting to acknowledge parents in the synagogue, their primary forum of communal engagement, and to initiate a newborn in the home, the locus of her existence and a source of warmth and comfort. In this way, the home functions for a baby as a "second womb." The home is an intimate setting for initiating one who is so small and fragile.[5]

With respect to timing, the aliyah would no longer be tied to a concern about naming the baby by a certain time. It follows that the aliyah could occur when a mother attends the synagogue on Shabbat for the first time after giving birth—regardless of how much time has passed since the birth, and regardless of when the baby is named. In this way, both parents are certain to be present for the aliyah, and the baby can be named and welcomed at a time that is appropriate and significant.

These adjustments regarding location and timing would also provide an opportunity to recapture the medieval Ashkenazic paradigm where newborns and parents were honored separately. On the one hand, the baby's name could be announced at an intimate home ceremony, as it was at the Hollekreisch. Indeed, the practice of naming girls at the Hollekreisch ceremony apparently preceded that of the synagogue naming. Therefore, naming girls today at a freestanding welcoming ceremony might be construed as a reversion to an older practice.

On the other hand, performing the aliyah on the Shabbat that a mother returns to the synagogue for the first time post-partum restores this ritual into a distinctive public occasion for both parents. As in medieval

Ashkenaz, fathers would receive this special aliyah (as would mothers, in egalitarian communities today), and parents would be honored with songs and enjoy a festive ambience. Furthermore, parents could formally reconnect with the community after a period of post-partum privacy. Today, there is evidence that birthing mothers are seeking ways to ritualize their reintegration into the community.[6] In sum, Jews today have the opportunity to enhance the present by evoking the past and to make parents and newborns feel special and appreciated at a turning point in their lives.

Holding this aliyah on a mother's return to the synagogue also restores the ritual's original, important purpose: to fulfill a mother's obligation to give thanks and seek atonement, as she would have done in the Temple by bringing sacrifices. Today the impulse to give thanks for a safe childbirth remains as strong as ever. A mother may wish to thank her Creator for the opportunity to participate in the miracle of birth and for giving her strength throughout this primal physical experience.

Seeking atonement also resonates today, since we strive for atonement at other major life-cycle milestones. The Ashkenazic customs of fasting and wearing a kittel, a white shroud-like garment, transform one's wedding day into a *Yom Kippur katan,* a diminutive Day of Atonement. In addition, a person lying on a deathbed recites the *viduy* confession prayers in order to seek atonement. The idea that a post-partum aliyah functions as a means of seeking atonement thus fits easily into existing life-cycle practices. It also dovetails with a custom that, when a woman goes on to the birthing stool as labor begins, she promises to perform zealously a specific mitzvah of her choosing,[7] in the hope that the merit of this mitzvah will sustain her and give her strength. More broadly, a modern commentator has conceptualized a birthing mother's atonement sacrifice as commemorating the "start of a new page" for the family, in the manner that atonement sacrifices were brought after the dedication of the Tabernacle, among other examples.[8] According to this interpretation, the atonement sacrifice symbolizes the momentous change that a newborn brings, a sentiment experienced just as much today as in Temple times.

A mother's presence at the aliyah today is not only personally meaningful, but also has the critical effect of reinstating the aliyah's status as an obligation (chiyuv) and rectifying the halachic anomalies that result when a father receives an aliyah without a chiyuv. Every time that a father has this aliyah without the birthing mother in attendance, she is not fulfilling her halachic obligations to give thanks and to atone. Furthermore, halachic complications arise if a father's aliyah, which does not constitute a chiyuv in his wife's absence, is afforded higher priority than the aliyah of someone who has an actual chiyuv. It follows that halachically observant Jews should make a particular effort to perform this aliyah when a birthing mother comes to the synagogue for the first time after giving birth, and no sooner.

This brings us to the role of Birkat HaGomel, the responsive prayer recited for having recovered from an illness.[9] While some birthing mothers customarily recite Birkat HaGomel today, this was not the case in medieval Ashkenaz. In the Ashkenazic tradition, birthing mothers did not recite Birkat HaGomel; rather, they were present for their husband's aliyah and responded "Amen" to the blessings. If birthing mothers did not recite Birkat HaGomel in the Middle Ages when childbirth was quite dangerous, it is arguable that today, when childbirth has become so much safer, birthing mothers should likewise, as a general rule, not recite Birkat HaGomel.

More importantly, since childbirth is a natural process experienced by healthy women, birthing mothers arguably should not say a prayer that is recited on account of recovering from an illness. Today, a mother might recite Birkat HaGomel only if she has endured a dangerous pregnancy or birth. In addition, one could pray for a mother experiencing post-partum complications using a Mi Shebairach specific to these circumstances, such as that reported by R. Israel Isserlin in fifteenth-century Austria, which invokes all the foremothers except for Rachel who died in childbirth.[10] Today, healthy birthing mothers returning to the synagogue the first time post-partum, and attending the special aliyah and other festivities, could develop different ways of expressing their thanks to God for the miracle of childbirth.

HALACHIC CONSIDERATIONS FOR NAMING NEWBORN GIRLS

Although we have now learned about various means of reorienting the synagogue naming, we return to the observation that many traditional Ashkenazic Jews today have become attached to the synagogue naming to the point that some believe it is practically mandatory. A new father once complained to me that he went to the synagogue to receive an aliyah and name his newborn daughter with a Mi Shebairach, although he would have preferred a ritual that is more personally meaningful to him. I asked him why he did so, given his perspective about the synagogue naming ritual. He responded,

"Because I had to." Similarly, I am aware of a couple who named their daughter with a Mi Shebairach following the father's aliyah. The mother expressed her distaste for this ritual, but nonetheless attended services and invited a few close relatives to attend in an effort to make the occasion more expansive. In response to my cautious questioning about why she and her husband chose this mode of naming, she said, "I didn't know there was any other way to name a daughter." Thus, for traditional Ashkenazim, it is critical to examine what the Jewish legal system of halacha prescribes with respect to naming newborn girls. Moreover, this is a significant exercise for all those who are interested in the interplay between law and customs and how the distinction between the two can sometimes become obscured.

We begin with the key observation that the synagogue naming at the first Torah reading or the first Shabbat following birth is customary, and not legally mandated.[11] Viewed from a broader sociological perspective, naming girls is an interesting example where certain customs have become entrenched although the legalistic halachic system allows for a fairly extensive amount of flexibility.

Our first question involves the halachic expectations about when to name a girl. R. Yitzchak Yaakov Weiss (1905–1989; United Kingdom) states that there is no obligatory, proper, or defined time to name a daughter.[12] R. Eliezer Waldenberg (1915–2006; Israel) similarly explains that the question of when to name a daughter is not legally determinable (*ein mizeh b'halacha*).[13] Even contemporary sources mention a number of halachically acceptable times for naming a girl, such as the day of her birth, the first Torah reading following her birth, her first Shabbat, at the end of her first month of life, or within eighty days of birth (corresponding to the time at which her mother brings a birthing/atonement sacrifice).[14] Thus, we see that the frantic rush to name girls in traditional Ashkenazic communities is a recent phenomenon and not a longstanding requirement.

Moreover, for centuries, girls in some Ashkenazic regions received their "holy" names in the synagogue four weeks (or thirty days) following birth. In eighteenth-century Germany, R. Jacob Emden commented that a baby girl is named after four weeks of life, when she is about to emerge from the status of a *nefel* (an infant susceptible to death).[15] My great-uncle Henry Okolica, an Orthodox rabbi for eighty years, emphasized to me that, in his experience in early twentieth-century Germany, a girl's name was never revealed prior to the Hollekreisch ceremony conducted four weeks following birth. Indeed, as late as the eve of the Holocaust, the synagogue naming was not a universal practice among traditional Ashkenazim, nor did every Jewish girl even have a "holy" name. Today, however, newborn girls are named in the synagogue as soon as possible, when they are no more than a few days old. This contrast demonstrates that, even as a practical matter, there is no mandated time for naming girls.

Our second question is the extent to which halacha associates a girl's naming with an aliyah in the synagogue. R. Yitzchak Yaakov Weiss plainly states that "it is possible to name a daughter even without having an aliyah."[16] It is also noteworthy that the *Koren Siddur,* published in 2009 as a joint venture of Chief Rabbi Lord Jonathan Sacks of the United Kingdom and the Orthodox Union of the United States, provides for the option of naming a girl for the first and only time at a freestanding ceremony.[17] It is therefore not an overstatement to say that naming a girl without an aliyah has the imprimatur of the Orthodox rabbinate of Great Britain and the premier Orthodox organization in the United States.

This rabbinic standpoint is consistent with historical realities. We saw that the father of a girl could receive an aliyah without reciting a naming Mi Shebairach (for example, Yitzchak Baer's 1886 *Tikkun*), and that this Mi Shebairach could be recited without a father receiving an aliyah (for instance, if a mother dies prior to her first synagogue visit). A girl's naming, therefore, is not a priori linked to either the aliyah or the Mi Shebairach. The reason for this disconnect is that the original purpose of the Mi Shebairach was to bless a mother, not to name her daughter.

SEPHARDIC AND MIZRACHIC HOME NAMING CEREMONIES

Additional support for naming girls for the first and only time at ceremonies unrelated to a Torah service derives from the fact that some Sephardic and Mizrachic communities have been doing this for centuries. Home ceremonies and other customs for naming and welcoming newborn girls, which are part of certain Sephardic and Mizrachic traditions, constitute precedents for Ashkenazim seeking to develop a similar model. However, the modern practice of naming a daughter at a freestanding ceremony (beginning in the 1970s) is not, as a historical matter, a product of these much older Sephardic and Mizrachic customs.

Not every Sephardic and Mizrachic community recognizes newborn girls with a home ceremony or other practice; indeed, many do not. Furthermore, some of these communities traditionally prize sons and deem daughters to be undesirable (as evidenced, for example, by the Zeved HaBat's prayer that a girl be blessed with "male children"). However, some Jewish cultures that traditionally deride daughters also paradoxically value them, particularly for their help in performing housework and caring for their siblings, or even for their beauty and grace. Thus, outlooks regarding the value of sons and daughters have varied substantially according to regions and even towns, and attitudes toward daughters have sometimes been conflicted.[18] That said, it is significant that, in some Sephardic and Mizrachic traditions, ceremonies for newborn girls have developed outside the framework of synagogue services and often occur in parents' homes.

One such ceremony is the Zeved HaBat ("Gift of a Daughter"). The Zeved HaBat liturgy recited in conjunction with a father's aliyah in some Sephardic communities, as we have seen, is incorporated into a home ceremony in other traditions.[19] This liturgy consists of selected passages from the Song of Songs, other Biblical verses, a special naming Mi Shebairach, and sometimes songs and lyrical poetry. In the Spanish and Portuguese communities that hold a Zeved HaBat at home, a mother recites Birkat HaGomel, and a prayer leader (*chazzan*) recites the Zeved HaBat liturgy, concluding with the naming. Some Moroccan families likewise hold this ceremony at home with members of the community in attendance. In the Judeo-Spanish tradition, all the guests sing the Zeved HaBat liturgy, in conjunction with the Las Fadas ceremony described below.[20] Jews in India, Yemen, and Bucharia have also welcomed and named newborn girls using the Zeved HaBat ceremony.[21] The timing of a Zeved HaBat home ceremony is at the parents' discretion.[22]

The role of an officiant, such as a rabbi, chazzan, or mesader, is prominent in Zeved HaBat rituals, particularly in the home setting. A presiding rabbi may hold the baby in his hands or on his knees when reciting the liturgy. It is customary in some communities that a *kohen* (priest) takes the baby in his hands and blesses her and all the gathered guests with the priestly blessing (Numbers 6:24–26).[23]

During the Zeved HaBat ceremony, women in attendance may sing songs of praise to both the mother and daughter and provide them with gifts, such as incense and candles. Women may also bring to the ceremony fertility symbols, such as live chickens and "star water," which is water exposed to the sky for seven nights. In the Moroccan tradition, "women raise their voices in undulations while the naming of the child is taking place in order to express their great joy at the birth of the lass."[24] Whether the Zeved HaBat occurs in the synagogue or at home, the family typically sponsors a festive meal (*seudat mitzvah*) and/or a kiddush (*sabt*) for all those in attendance. Often, fruits of the seven special species of Israel are served at the celebration.[25]

Las Fadas is another type of welcoming ceremony held at home for baby girls. It is conducted in the Judeo-Spanish and Turkish traditions, among others. At a ceremonial feast approximately two weeks or sometimes thirty days after a girl's birth, the newborn is dressed up in a miniature white bridal gown. A young relative carries her into the room on a pillow, and the guests pass the baby from one to the other, each giving her a blessing. The rabbi then holds the baby on his lap, recites a blessing for her health and happiness, and announces her name. Verses from the Song of Songs are also recited.[26] In Turkey, an embroidered silk veil is placed over the heads of a mother and her daughter. The mother wears this veil throughout her life, and the daughter wears it at her wedding. In another version of this custom, the newborn is wrapped in a veil while she is named.[27] The word *fadas* derives from the Spanish *hadas,* meaning "fairies." Jews apparently adapted the Spanish custom of having fairies bless a newborn by infusing this custom with Jewish symbolism.[28]

Jews from Iraq and, less frequently, Kurdistan hold a *Shisha* (or *Shasha*) festival at home on the sixth night of a baby's life. In the Iraqi tradition, a Shisha is identical for boys and girls, except that only girls are named at this festival, since boys are named at a circumcision later that week. A Shisha features singing and feasting and may include the recitation of blessings, verses from the Song of Songs, and other Biblical verses, as well as songs praising the baby's beauty.[29]

Indian Jews of Iraqi extraction hold a similar festive gathering at home called a *Sitti* or *Leylat-el-sitti*. This celebration is held on the sixth night following a birth, but for newborn girls only.[30] A baby girl is brought to her family's living room in her cradle, the assembled guests greet her, and the midwife or community chazzan announces her name. The baby wears "a silk and lace dress and underdress and a bonnet decorated with gold-thread embroidery."[31] The Sitti has been described as "reminiscent of that preceding a boy's circumcision, attended by a quorum of men and friends who read the Zohar or Song of Songs and then bless the baby. The guests feast, accompanied by much singing and music."[32] The Sitti is practiced today; for example, I know a couple in the United States who have held this ceremony, along with an elaborate party, for each of their young daughters.

Neighborhood children were invited to the home of a newborn on the day preceding a Sitti ceremony. "On the way they made as much noise as possible—shouting 'shasha, shasha' [a nonsense word], stamping their feet and banging tin cans... in order to ward off evil spirits." Then, "[w]hen the children reached the baby's home, the adults there encouraged them to make even more noise; as a reward they were given... treats, such as watermelon and pumpkin seeds, roasted chick peas, and sugar cubes, which were proffered on a table or large tray that sometimes also held coins and amulets."[33]

Indian Jews known as the Bene Israel (distinct from Iraqi Indian Jews), traditionally perform the *Barsa* ceremony at home on the twelfth day following a birth to introduce a newborn to his or her cradle. Despite its Hindu origins, the Barsa is a social custom that enables friends and neighbors—primarily women and children—to meet a newborn and to bring gifts. A girl receives her name at this time, while a boy has already been named at his circumcision. The baby's aunt or another woman "holds the baby in her arms, blesses her, whispers her new name into her ear, then places her in the cradle." Boiled chickpeas, sweets, and other foods are arranged around the baby in the cradle and are later distributed to the children. In addition, "[l]adies sing lullabies to the child. The mother sits on the bed rocking the cradle. She also wears new clothes and her hair is decorated with flowers."[34] The baby likewise receives a special new garment, and the cradle is decorated with flowers and colored paper. After the baby is rocked to sleep, the women sing, dance, and play with the children. The women hide five species of fruit in the hem of the mother's sari and give treats to children who act as if they are robbing sweets from the baby's cradle. Each woman also gives the mother a coconut to ensure her continued fertility and other foods to guarantee sufficient breast milk for the baby.[35]

In sum, certain Sephardic and Mizrachic communities have developed rich customs for naming and recognizing newborn girls at home. These customs are important precedents because they demonstrate the longstanding acceptability of naming a daughter for the first and only time at home or elsewhere, rather than in the synagogue after an aliyah. At the same time, these practices provide only a glimpse into the complex and diverse attitudes regarding newborn daughters in traditional Sephardic and Mizrachic societies.

A CONSISTENT PRACTICE of naming girls for the first and only time at a home ceremony is one means of reshaping the contemporary synagogue naming to show respect to newborn girls and to give them a prominent role in their own rituals. Parents could be separately honored with the aliyah and other synagogue-based practices. While there are today a variety of approaches for naming newborn girls, my hope is that the observations and ideas in this chapter are pertinent across the range of Jewish communities.

But what else should a welcoming ceremony for newborn girls contain, aside from a naming? We begin to address this question by exploring the modern rituals for newborn Jewish girls which emerged in the 1970s and have expanded since then into a robust life-cycle genre. These rituals, which contain namings and much more, are the focus of the next chapter.

3

New Modern Practices for Baby Girls

My four-year-old son Yakir was once speaking proudly about his baby sister and remarked, "People have parties for their babies because the babies are new." He also explained to me that God, parents, and a nurse all work together to make a new baby, and this is why God "comes to the party and says 'hi' to the new baby." Intrigued, I asked Yakir if God welcomes the baby at the party, and he responded in the affirmative. Thus, even a young child instinctively recognizes a religious imperative to welcome every newborn.

The story that unfolds in this chapter is about how modern innovators have applied this idea of initiating every newborn into the Jewish people by building Jewish rituals for baby girls practically from scratch. In these modern rituals, which first appeared in the 1970s, a baby girl is named and/or recognized in a religious framework, and she participates in the event. While many different names are used to refer to this ritual form, one is Simchat Bat which means "Celebration of a Daughter." *Simchat Bat* is the generic term used here to refer to the full range of rituals that have been created since the 1970s in primarily Ashkenazic communities, and which consist of something more than an aliyah, Mi Shebairach, celebratory meal, or kiddush. These new practices have developed in a predominantly Ashkenazic framework since each Sephardic and Mizrachic community has its own set of relevant customs.

The Simchat Bat is predicated on a belief that daughters should be formally welcomed into the Jewish community. The original motivation for creating these practices was a perception that no satisfactory traditional means of commemorating and celebrating the birth of a girl had developed in Ashkenazic communities, and that the Simchat Bat filled this void. This motivation remains palpable among parents holding welcoming ceremonies for their daughters in traditional communities where the standard practice is an aliyah and a Mi Shebairach and nothing more. By contrast, some lay-people in progressive communities today may be so accustomed to their syn-agogue's particular Simchat Bat practice that they may not feel that a ritual for girls had been previously lacking.[1]

While the Simchat Bat is widely practiced in liberal communities and increasingly popular in some traditional communities, it is not performed among the ultra-Orthodox. It is noteworthy that the *Artscroll Siddur* in the Ashkenazic nusach (style), which is commonly used across the Ortho-dox spectrum, does not include any ritual for newborn girls, aside from a Mi Shebairach in the Shabbat Torah service. (The *Artscroll Siddur* in the Sephardic nusach does not even include the traditional Zeved HaBat cere-mony.) Furthermore, the lesser-known *Artscroll Simchah Handbook,* a com-pendium of liturgies for Jewish celebrations,[2] does not make any mention of rituals for newborn girls, although it devotes many pages to an array of other life-cycle events. It also includes liturgies for a *siyyum* (completion of a course of Torah study), the entry of a Torah scroll to a synagogue, and the dedication of a new home—occasions that, while significant, are arguably less momentous than a birth of a daughter.

One dominant feature of the Simchat Bat genre is its overall variability. The appearance of Simchat Bat ceremonies in the 1970s led to an explosion of creative energy that has spawned to date "thousands upon thousands" of unique welcoming ceremonies.[3] This diversity means that there are no stan-dard Simchat Bat prototypes. It also means that a small selection of "sample ceremonies" does not effectively communicate the full extent and impact of the Simchat Bat practice.

Nonetheless, a Simchat Bat frequently follows a loose outline that con-sists of welcoming or acknowledging the baby girl; reciting prayers, bless-ings, readings and/or performing a ritual; naming the baby; explaining the baby's name and/or speaking on a Torah-related topic; and a festive meal or kiddush. More significantly, common themes, readings, prayers, and rituals have emerged as Simchat Bat ceremonies have proliferated. In short, the creative surge that characterized the Simchat Bat in its early years has been tempered as this practice continues to mature.

In this chapter, we trace the development of the modern Simchat Bat practice from its inception until the present day. Only by understanding this story can we proceed to consider the future development of practices for newborn Jewish girls.

HISTORICAL SETTING

While the Simchat Bat has used traditional themes, symbolism, and texts as a foundation from the outset, it is not the continuation or result of any previous Jewish ritual form for newborn girls. For example, it is not an outgrowth of any traditional Sephardic or Mizrachic practices. The Simchat Bat also has no historical connection to a little-known (and possibly never performed) Reform ceremony, crafted in Germany in the 1840s, that welcomes both boys and girls into the covenant. While this ceremony looks and feels like a Simchat Bat, its purpose was to replace the circumcision ceremony, which had come under attack by the Reform movement at that time.[4] Instead, the distinctive Simchat Bat arose in the 1970s in the grassroots, as a product of the feminist and countercultural social movements and of related movements particular to the Jewish community.

Jews have long been prominent in the feminist movement, having joined its ranks since its inception in the 1960s and 1970s. Some emerged as leaders, such as Betty Friedan, whose book *The Feminine Mystique* sparked this movement. Others began taking a hard look at the feminist ideals of women's humanity and worth and evaluating how they intersect with Jewish values and principles. As a result, "Jewish feminism" emerged.

Some early milestones of Jewish feminism occurred in the political and intellectual realms. For example, in 1971, the Jewish feminist organization Ezrat Nashim was formed in the United States. In 1972, Ezrat Nashim issued a "Call for Change" at the annual convention for Conservative rabbis. R. Saul Berman published his seminal article, "The Status of Women in Halakhic Judaism" in the Orthodox journal *Tradition* in 1973.[5] Also that year, over five hundred Jewish women met for four days at the first National Conference of Jewish Women in New York City, sponsored by the North American Students' Network, an event that one participant described as "exploding with energy."[6] This was followed in short order, in 1974, by the National Conference on Jewish Women and Men, which in turn initiated the Jewish Feminist Organization. The journal *Response* approached some participants to contribute to a special issue devoted to Jewish feminist topics. This issue was published in 1973, and editor Elizabeth Koltun expanded upon it to develop the groundbreaking book *The Jewish Woman: New Perspectives,* published in 1976.[7] Another publication that year was *The Jewish Catalog* (discussed further below), which suggests a number of ways to begin changing women's status in Judaism. Also in 1976, the Jewish feminist magazine *Lilith* began and another landmark book, *The Jewish Woman in America,* by Charlotte Baum, Paula Hyman, and Sonya Michel, was published.

Modern Jewish feminism made inroads somewhat more slowly in Israel, where there was a "small but active political feminist force at work" in the late 1970s.[8] By 1984, the American Jewish Congress's annual U.S.-Israel Dialogue about Jewish women, attended by hundreds of participants, resulted in a march of one hundred women to the King David Hotel in Jerusalem. There, they submitted a list of demands to the leading candidates for prime minister. That afternoon, the Israel Women's Network, an organization to further women's status in Israel, was founded. Some of its early activism involved challenging the Israeli rabbinical establishment. The first International Jewish Feminist Conference was held in Jerusalem in December 1988. "Women of the Wall," a group devoted to ensuring that women have the opportunity to carry Torah scrolls and wear religious garments safely at the Western Wall, was founded in the aftermath of this conference.[9]

While political and intellectual changes were beginning to swirl in the 1970s, the impact of Jewish feminist thinking was perhaps nowhere "more revisionary and revolutionary than in the areas of religious knowledge, spiritual experience, and ritual practice."[10] For example, the Reform movement ordained its first female rabbi in 1972, and the Reconstructionist and Conservative movements followed suit in 1974 and 1985, respectively. In 1979, R. David Silber founded the Drisha Institute for Jewish Education, which expanded opportunities for women to study Jewish texts, including Talmud, on the most advanced levels. The Women's Tefillah Network, devoted to creating prayer services led by women yet within the rubric of halacha, was founded in 1982, and the Task Force on Jewish Woman drew hundreds of women and men in 1983 to a national conference in New York City called "Women, Prayer, and Tradition."[11]

More broadly, women began to express their self-determination and impact by creating innovative religious rituals that commemorate women's connection to Judaism and highlight their personal experiences. Simchat Bat ceremonies emerged in the 1970s as one manifestation of this trend. By formally welcoming newborn girls into the Jewish people, these ceremonies ritualized the religious significance of newborn girls and affirmed their value. Another example is the appearance of free-form women's gatherings to mark Rosh Chodesh, the first day of the month on the Jewish lunar calendar and traditionally a women's holiday (due in part to an association between the lunar cycle and the menstrual cycle). Using innovative rituals and readings and engaging in wide-ranging discussions, participants create a "women's space" to give voice to their Jewish spirituality.[12] Finally, feminists sought to sanctify female biological milestones (such as menarche, miscarriage, childbirth,[13] lactation, weaning, and menopause) by framing them as significant religious events with newly crafted or reinterpreted rituals and blessings.[14]

The Simchat Bat and these other Jewish feminist expressions are paradigmatic of the "feminist ritual" model that was developing in the wider feminist community at this time. In this model, rituals are fluid, open, and non-hierarchical. Indeed, "sometimes it appears to be largely structural openness that defines a ritual as feminist." Along the same lines, flexibility and creativity mark feminist rituals, and some have considered highly structured rituals to be inherently "unfeminist."[15] The influence of relationalism is also prominent in this model, in that participants form relationships and make connections in a "ritual space." These relationships typically extend "horizontally" among all participants evenly, rather than "vertically" between a leader and the rest of the group. In a feminist ritual, therefore, interactions are informal and sometimes unscripted. R. Debra Orenstein articulates why "many women, and especially feminists, feel a deep harmony with the whole ritual enterprise." She explains: "The women's movement has worked to achieve some of the same ends that ritual serves: Namely, to rely on and build community, while providing support and opportunities for self-expression to individuals in transition."[16]

The 1960s and 1970s witnessed the explosion of not only feminism but also other types of "identity politics," in which people connected with their heritage or other aspects of their persona. One example is that some previously unaffiliated or disenchanted American Jews experienced a renaissance of Jewish identification and expression. This engagement with Judaism often occurred within the framework of the broader counterculture, which prized free expression and individualism and incorporated a measure of anti-establishmentarianism. In the Jewish community, this trend manifested in the *chavurah* (literally, "group"; plural, *chavurot*) movement and so-called "Catalog Judaism."[17] The influence of these movements dovetails with that of feminism in promoting the rise of the Simchat Bat and its hallmarks of personalized expression, openness, and creativity.

The Chavurah movement developed from the dissatisfaction of young, well-educated American Jews with Jewish institutions, which they viewed as "sterile, impersonal, and divorced from Jewish tradition." As a result, these Jews "sought deepened religious experience and warm personal ties in close-knit communities and less formal styles of prayer." Chavurot typically met in private homes for prayer services. While Chavurah participants regarded Jewish tradition as their guide and its revitalization as an aim, they also introduced the new principle of egalitarianism.[18]

"Catalog Judaism" refers to the innovative Jewish trends and practices inspired by *The Jewish Catalog,* published in 1973, as well as the second and third volumes, published in 1976 and 1980, respectively. Edited by Michael and Sharon Strassfeld (Richard Siegel also edited the first Catalog), these revolutionary volumes "documented emerging Jewish rituals and promoted the creative spirit that would lead to more." The Catalogs are characterized by "[d]emocracy and open access" and "seeker-oriented spirituality."[19] With their hand-drawn illustrations and accessible layout, the Catalogs speak directly to readers about wide-ranging areas of Jewish expression and encourage readers to craft new rituals using flexibility and creativity. The Catalogs also provide lists of resources, publications, and organizations to facilitate this output. The introduction to *The Jewish Catalog* explains:

> The orientation is to move away from the prefabricated, spoon-fed, nearsighted Judaism into the stream of possibility for personal responsibility and physical participation. This entails a returning of the control of the Jewish environment to the hands of the individual—through accessible knowledge of the what, where, who, and how of contemporary Judaism. ... The hope, in fact, is that the catalog will facilitate the development of a "repertoire of responses" so that a person can accommodate himself to the rapid pace of societal and environmental change—as well as to his own personal, emotional, and spiritual flux.[20]

EARLY SIMCHAT BAT CEREMONIES

Simchat Bat ceremonies for newborn girls in the 1970s and early 1980s were created by motivated parents and rabbis who were inspired by the feminist movement and drew on the teachings of the Chavurah movement and Catalog Judaism (although sometimes without explicitly recognizing these influ-

ences). Thus, from the outset, Simchat Bat ceremonies were highly innovative and personally meaningful. These parents and rabbis were not afraid to
engage in experimentation; as a result, this early period was an exceptionally
creative time.

Many of the Simchat Bat ceremonies crafted at this time focused on the
covenant (brit) between God and Israel. The architects of these ceremonies
understood the covenant, into which a boy enters upon his circumcision,
as the generalized covenant between God and Israel. This covenant constitutes God's eternal promise to regard the Jewish people as His people, and
the people's reciprocal promise to keep God's commandments. Those who
conceptualized the covenant in this way viewed circumcision as a means of
entering into the covenant, and fashioned the Simchat Bat genre as a means
of commemorating girls' covenantal entry.

To this end, many early Simchat Bat ceremonies incorporated novel covenantal rituals or themes and, particularly in the United States, included new
or adapted English readings relating to these rituals. However, early ceremonies performed by Orthodox families—like those performed today—
welcomed girls typically with Scriptural readings, classic prayers, and
speeches, rather than with new covenantal rituals or references to the covenant. Unlike their more liberal counterparts, Orthodox adherents sought
to distance their daughters from the covenant, which they viewed as tied
to circumcision. It is important to remember that, regardless of content, all
these early ceremonies were ground-breaking, as they together constituted
a brand-new ritual form.

The timing of early ceremonies is not consistently recorded, but they
seem to have been held at a variety of different times after a baby girl's birth.
Likewise, these early ceremonies have many different names. Some names
are general, such as Simchat Bat. Others reflect the ceremony's substantive
content, such as *Brit ha-Nerot* ("Covenant of Candles") or *Brit Rechitza*
("Covenant of Washing"). We will discuss these rituals below.

R. Sandy Eisenberg Sasso (who in 1974 became the first female Reconstructionist rabbi) describes that, in 1970, a "small group of rabbinical students were sitting around our friends' living room welcoming our friends'
new daughter into the covenant of the Jewish people."[21] R. Sasso and her
husband, R. Dennis Sasso, created this welcoming ceremony, which they
called *Brit B'not Yisrael* ("Covenant of the Daughters of Israel"). The center-

piece of the ceremony is a blessing recited by the baby's parents: "Praised are You, Eternal God, Ruler of the Universe, who sanctified us with Your commandments and commanded us to bring our daughter into the covenant of the people of Israel." In addition, the newborn girl is named on Shabbat, such that Shabbat functions as a broad covenantal symbol. This ceremony is meant to occur at home on the first Shabbat on which both parents can attend and participate.[22]

Published in 1973, this is one of the earliest recorded modern welcoming ceremonies for girls. R. Sandy Eisenberg Sasso recently emphasized to me the centrality of the covenant in her Brit B'not Yisrael. She explained that this ceremony is, therefore, not a *Simchat Bat*, which connotes for her a ceremony bereft of covenantal significance.

Two other ceremonies were also published in 1973. Michael and Sharon Strassfeld described a ceremony in which they immersed their newborn daughter Kayla in a miniature ritual bath (mikvah). This representative mikvah, a small tub filled with water, constituted the ceremony's central covenantal symbol. (Traditionally, menstruating women do not engage in sexual relations, and resume relations only upon immersion in a mikvah one week after menstruation has ended.) Citing traditional sources that link circumcision and mikvah immersion (for example, BT Yevamot 46a–46b), the Strassfelds explain that the symbolism of circumcision, with its connection to procreation and the covenantal chain of generations, finds a parallel in mikvah immersion with its prominent role in female sexuality and procreation.[23]

That same year, R. Daniel I. and Myra Leifer created a ritual incorporating a modified version of the *sheva brachot,* seven blessings traditionally recited at a Jewish wedding. The Leifers recited these blessings two hours after their daughter's birth and again at a kiddush following an aliyah for the family.[24]

In 1974, Ellen and Dana Charry published a ceremony called *Brit Kedusha* ("Covenant of Holiness"), at which they presented their daughter with a kiddush cup, traditionally used on Shabbat and holidays to sanctify wine. They filled the cup with wine and recited the blessing over wine, thereby expressing the hope that their daughter will ritually use the cup in years to come.[25] Along similar lines, Marty and Melissa Federman in 1976 describe a covenantal ceremony in which they presented to their daughter a prayer shawl (*tallit*), doorpost marker (*mezuzah*), and phylacteries (*tefillin*). These sacred ritual objects represent Torah, marriage/home, and good deeds, respectively.[26]

Other early ceremonies include: the *Brit Ceremony* in which Shoshana and Mel Silberman recited Biblical passages, prayers, and blessings to convey the theme of Shabbat as a covenant;[27] the Brit Rechitza, composed by a group of nine rabbis and rabbinical students, in which a baby's feet were washed to symbolize covenantal entry;[28] and a ceremony weaving the timely themes of Chanukah and Rosh Chodesh, by Elaine Shizgal Cohen and Stephen Cohen.[29] The *Brit ha-Nerot* by Paul Swerdlow, incorporates lit candles and wine, along with the recitation of Deuteronomy 29:9–14, which explicitly includes the entire Jewish people in the Sinaitic covenant.[30] In another covenantal ceremony performed in the mid-1970s, parents wrapped their one-month-old baby in the tallit that had been their wedding canopy, washed her feet, and then passed her among family members who bestowed blessings on the girl.[31]

Two proposals for ceremonies with physically invasive covenantal symbolism were suggested in the mid-1970s. In 1975, Mary Gendler suggested hymenectomy as a covenantal ritual paralleling circumcision, based on the notion that both procedures facilitate reproduction, a prime element of the Abrahamic covenant. Gendler explains that she proposed "an equivalent 'opening' of the girl's generative area so that her seed, also, can be directly and symbolically dedicated to God."[32] The *Second Jewish Catalog,* published in 1976, mentions Margarita Freeman and Leonard Levin's proposal for an ear-piercing ceremony. This ceremony evokes the idea that all of Israel heard the covenantal word of God at Sinai.[33] It is not clear whether either of these proposed ceremonies has ever been performed.

Some early ceremonies consist of prayers, readings, and songs and do not incorporate specific covenantal rituals. For example, in 1977, Professor Judith Plaskow published a ceremony that focuses on the achievements of women in a covenantal context. The ceremony's core is a set of Biblical excerpts describing the contributions of Sarah, Miriam, Deborah, and Chulda (all female Biblical figures) and a reference to the contributions of Jewish women throughout history whose names are unknown today. The ceremony also includes the blessing of "command[ing] us to bring our daughters into the covenant of the people of Israel." Plaskow comments that, "after much thought and with some misgivings, I gave up on finding a physical symbol and decided to focus my ceremony on women's experiences within the Jewish tradition."[34] Aviva Cantor composed a prayer in 1982 that similarly invokes the wish that her daughter embody the positive characteristics of the foremothers.[35] In 1984, Susan Weidner Schneider observed that "[w]hether the ceremonial welcoming of a daughter into the Jewish people (and into the people's covenant with God) should include some physical component . . . is an issue much debated."[36]

Self-identified Orthodox adherents likewise produced welcoming ceremonies in this early period. The content of these ceremonies is not explicitly covenantal, focusing instead on a girl's name and on welcoming her into the Jewish people. In 1974, Joseph C. Kaplan and Sharon Kaplan designed and conducted a Simchat Bat ceremony, which may have been the first such ceremony held by Orthodox parents. After the baby ceremonially entered the room greeted by songs and passed from one family member to another, Joseph announced that both sets of grandparents planted trees in the baby's honor, a custom described in the Talmud (BT Gittin 57a). Blessings were recited, including Birkat HaGomel. In addition, the baby's name was inscribed in a family tree prepared for the occasion. This ceremony was held on the first Sunday two weeks after the baby's birth.[37] Joseph recounts: "Although we consulted with our rabbi, Steven Riskin, as to the appropriateness of the ceremony and received his approval, it was our ceremony, saying what we wanted to say, and bringing our daughter into the covenant between God and the Jewish people."[38]

Gary Rosenblatt (now publisher and editor of the *New York Jewish Week* newspaper) recently recounted that he and his wife, Judy Rosenblatt, held a Simchat Bat for their newborn daughter in Baltimore in 1976. He explains: "We included prayers, songs, and readings to go with talks by my father and grandfather, both Orthodox rabbis, and explanations of how we chose the name Talia Sarah for our daughter to honor the memory of special women in our family." Rosenblatt comments that, at this early date, the practice did not catch on in his Orthodox Baltimore community.[39]

In 1977, R. Yechiel Eckstein (who today heads the International Fellowship of Christians and Jews) and his then-wife Bonnie held a Simchat Bat for their nine-day-old daughter in West Hempstead, New York. After women carried in the baby, R. Eckstein recited the Shehechiyanu blessing, and Bonnie read from the Song of Hannah (I Samuel 2). Others recited selections from Psalms, and the baby was named with a Mi Shebairach. Songs and a festive meal followed. The *New York Times* reported R. Eckstein's comment at that time:

> All rabbis, including the Orthodox, agree that women share equally with men in the covenant with God . . . . So, as I see it, if women share equally, it is not only permissible to devise an appropriate symbol for girls entering the covenant, it is a religious obligation. The technical problem is how to put together a ceremony.

R. Eckstein emphasized, both then and now, that this ceremony is halachically acceptable.[40] He recently recalled that "the 'waves' we created were simply from having [an] event and sending invitations out to [a] 'simchat habat.'" R. Eckstein also noted that the ceremony took place at his in-laws' home since the local synagogue deemed such an event too radical.[41]

Gary and Sheila Rubin published a ceremony in 1982 that included the recitation of Biblical readings, blessings, and acrostics. (An acrostic is a unique poem in which the first letter of each line, read vertically, is a word or words—in this case, the baby's name—and each line consists of a Biblical verse beginning with that letter.) In addition, the guests in attendance recited, "Just as she has been inducted into the community of Israel [*kehilat am yisrael*], so shall she be introduced to the Torah, to the marriage canopy, and to a life of good deeds."[42] This blessing, which conveys the baby girl's entry into the "community of Israel," is a variation on the traditional blessing recited at a boy's circumcision, which marks his entry into the covenant.

At this time, other segments of the Orthodox population had a vastly different viewpoint, denouncing the burgeoning Simchat Bat movement in no uncertain terms. This swift reaction demonstrates that the Simchat Bat phenomenon was closely observed even in its earliest days. For example, in his book *Jewish Woman in Jewish Law,* published in 1978, R. Moshe Meiselman (head of Yeshiva Toras Moshe in Jerusalem) refers to an eighth day covenantal ceremony for girls as a "ridiculous" practice "that mocks the very concept of *brit.*" R. Meiselman also critiques this type of ceremony with pointedly—and gratuitous—negative sexual imagery. He states that an attempt to create for girls "a unilateral executed covenant with God is, at best, a meaningless form of spiritual autoeroticism." Also, "to insist that a woman needs a form of spiritual self-stimulation to enter into the covenant is to place her on a lower level than classical Judaism has viewed her."[43]

In the December 1983 issue of the journal *Sh'ma,* which was dedicated to discussing creative new rituals, a heated debate plays out between advocates for innovation and those for halachic conservatism. Professor Judith Bleich strongly criticizes the mikvah immersion ritual that Sharon and Michael Strassfeld, editors of the *Jewish Catalogs,* held for their newborn daughter in the early 1970s. Bleich argues that this ritual is unacceptable because it is akin to a Christian baptism. She also criticizes a foot-washing ceremony for girls because it is framed in terms of the Noachide covenant, which is not specifically Jewish, and because washed-off dust has been interpreted as relating to idolatry. While commending the innovators' sincerity, Bleich describes the new rituals as "embarrassingly inappropriate" because they incorporate "alien concepts and foreign traditions."[44]

Sharon and Michael Strassfeld aggressively retort:

> In the last few years, we have noted the same pattern of response by the Orthodox; a pat on the head for those of us involved in creating new ritual and a word about our "sincere, at times passionate desire to give expression to deeply-rooted religious feelings" followed by an impassioned attack on why the ritual itself is inappropriate and the entire enterprise halachically unacceptable.[45]

The Strassfelds characterize this type of critical response as "patronizing" and observe that Bleich's criticism may result from her "complacent belief that none of us involved in this Jewish approach are familiar with Jewish sources, or even, perhaps, know Hebrew." They continue: "Wrong again, Dr. Bleich. We know sources and approach them differently than you do, and are, frankly, surprised by the intellectual dishonesty of your comments." The Strassfelds also strenuously argue that to "claim, as you seem to, that Judaism does not contain elements of tradition integrated from other religions is simply wrong." They maintain that they "are living, growing, [and] *breathing* tradition," while Bleich believes that "what was done until the modern time must be regarded as holy; what might be added as innovation in the modern time is profane." The Strassfelds conclude that it is "pointless to carry on dialogues with . . . [those in] the Orthodox world who oppose change." Furthermore, in one hundred years, "no one will remember, except as a footnote in history, the time when such ceremonies were not normative practice. The people who *live* Judaism, rather than those who intellectualize and distort it, will, in the end, be the ones who decide what will be encoded as a part of the holy Jewish tradition."[46]

While other contributors to this *Sh'ma* issue took a more even-tempered approach, the tenor of the discourse between Bleich and the Strassfelds is highly charged, with fierce language and strongly held worldviews.

Reflecting on this extraordinary dialogue, I agree with the Strassfelds that Judaism is shaped by continuous evolution and reinterpretion and that this process is ongoing and valuable. I also agree that neighboring cultures are perpetually interacting and reacting, and that Judaism is no exception to this dynamic. Yet, Bleich's comments illustrate that, as a practical matter, new rituals are most likely to endure if they connect easily with common sensibilities. The shift in symbolism demanded by the Strassfelds' ritual—from menstrual purity to covenantal entry—may have been too drastic for many practitioners (not just Bleich).[47] As a result, this particular ritual did not catch on.

EARLY COMPILATIONS AND GUIDES

We have seen that the early development of the Simchat Bat ceremony was a grassroots surge of boundless creativity, despite the vehement criticism of some in the Orthodox community. By the late 1970s and early 1980s, this cross-denominational process had attained a critical mass. For example, in 1977, the Reform movement published an initiation ceremony for girls in its prayer compilation for the home,[48] and R. Steven Riskin of Lincoln Square Synagogue, an Orthodox synagogue in New York, was actively seeking at this time to advance his interpretation of the Simchat Bat.[49] Despite this trickle of institutional direction, parents and expectant parents were clamoring for more extensive information and tools to create ceremonies for their daughters.

The collections of ceremonies and other guidance materials that emerged provided the models that these parents were seeking. *The Second Jewish Catalog,* published in 1976, contained the first such collection, in which the Strassfelds provide eight model ceremonies, one of which is their own. The Strassfelds explain: "With the new interest in Jewish feminism, many people have reassessed their needs and values and have written their own *brit* ceremonies. We include some of the many sent to us with the hope that they inspire other parents to explore the tradition and their own Jewish needs."[50]

Also in 1976, R. Daniel I. Leifer summarized and critiqued three covenantal ceremonies in an article in the journal *Sh'ma*. R. Leifer observed, "All of these ritual innovations seek to celebrate the birth of a daughter with the same or comparable equality and dignity with which the birth of a son is traditionally celebrated." Furthermore, all are "rooted in traditional forms," yet are innovative or even radical. Interestingly, R. Leifer proposed for both boys and girls the combination of a covenantal ceremony on the eighth day and a synagogue naming on Shabbat.[51] Less than a month after R. Leifer's article was published, Sharon and Joseph Kaplan, whose ceremony was one of those analyzed, responded to R. Leifer's analysis in yet another *Sh'ma* article.[52] The Kaplans respectfully explain their reasons for formulating their particular ceremony, commenting that they "feel somewhat schizophrenic" in arguing for both "freedom and innovation" and "adherence to tradition."

Another significant resource from this early period is R. Sandy Eisenberg Sasso's *Call Them Builders: A Resource Booklet about Jewish Attitudes and Practices on Birth and Family Life,* published in 1977.[53] As R. Sasso explains in her Introduction, this booklet identifies traditional customs for naming and welcoming newborns, examines modern issues relating to procreation, and offers suggestions for contemporary practices and ceremonies. R. Sasso includes in *Call Them Builders* the Brit B'Not Yisrael ceremony that she and her husband, R. Dennis Sasso, formulated in 1970. This wide-ranging guide also contains supplemental readings for ceremonies, the music for lullabies, and a Sephardic song for a girl's naming.

In 1978, Toby Fishbein Reifman, with the Jewish feminist organization Ezrat Nashim, published a historic pamphlet titled, *Blessing the Birth of a Daughter: Jewish Naming Ceremonies for Girls.* In her pamphlet, Reifman compiles six articles, each of which describes an early welcoming ceremony for newborn girls. (These rituals are all presented in the previous section.) Reifman explains that the authors of these ceremonies "are all grappling with the same problem—when and how to celebrate the birth of their daughter and mark her entrance into the Jewish community." Reifman, therefore, frames *Blessing the Birth of a Daughter* as a start toward filling in the missing pieces in Jewish life-cycle events for women. She concludes with the hope that her pamphlet "will assist parents in celebrating the entrance of their daughters into the covenant."[54]

Also in this early time period, the Reconstructionist Rabbinical College maintained a "Creative Liturgy Library," which collected and distributed welcoming ceremonies for newborn girls, as well as rituals for other women's life events. One rabbi notes that, prior to the establishment of this library, innovative ceremonies "were passed down from one rabbi's files to the next."[55]

Another collection of ceremonies was housed at the Jewish Women's Resource Center (JWRC), an arm of the New York Division of the National Council of Jewish Women. By the mid-1980s, the JWRC had "a large loose-leaf notebook filed with copies of ceremonies sent in by parents who know that whatever models people can find for such events will be welcome, since there are few formal guidelines."[56]

In 1984, Susan Weidman Schneider, the founding editor of the Jewish feminist magazine *Lilith,* published her groundbreaking book, *Jewish and Female.* This user-friendly book provides a comprehensive, erudite examination of virtually every aspect of life encountered by Jewish women at that time. In discussing life-cycle practices, Schneider describes how and why Jews have begun "honoring the birth of a daughter" and provides the texts of three ceremonies for newborn girls. Like the *Jewish Catalogs, Jewish and Female* closes each section with a list of resources to enable further study, and the section on ceremonies for girls is no exception. Schneider lists a handful of booklets, organizations, and individuals for parents to consult for additional information.[57]

As parents continued to craft more unique Simchat Bat rituals using ceremony collections or relying on the help of enterprising friends, observers began to systematically identify and document popular prayers, readings, rituals, and themes, as well as when, where, and how to hold ceremonies. These efforts at categorization resulted in the development of guides that offer "how-to" instructions to parents creating their own personalized ceremonies.

The earliest of these "how-to" resources is *A Guide toward Celebrating the Birth of a Daughter,* attributed to the JWRC.[58] This watershed document, which is believed to date from 1980,[59] presents a step-by-step outline of a ceremony for girls, including the following: a welcome and introduction; prayers of thanksgiving; reading rabbinic lore relating to children; the blessing over wine (kiddush); naming the baby; a Torah exposition (d'var Torah), including an acrostic of the baby's name; parental blessings, both personal and communal; the priestly blessing; and a festive meal. The guide explains each of these elements, which are drawn from performed ceremonies, and emphasizes that these elements are "merely suggestions" and "not binding." The guide also provides a wide range of options for when to hold the ceremony, and suggests the use of "embellishments and objects" to represent "an eternal sign" for the child. These include printed programs, Shabbat candles, a kiddush cup, a tallit, and a siddur or Bible.

The guide characterizes its detailed advice as "an opportunity for parents to celebrate the life of their new creation in a fitting manner" and "within a Jewish framework." It also stresses the individuality of each ceremony:

> These suggestions represent ideas which have been found successful by different couples. Everyone has different views and themes to put forward. You may pick and choose as you feel most comfortable. But remember that you are putting together a whole. It should have some cohesion, some basic theme to hold it together. It could be a word, a thought, an item, whatever. It should also be fun.

Appended to the guide is a handwritten boilerplate letter, dated 1976, which Carol Glass and Nina Beth Cardin, then students at the Jewish Theological Seminary in New York, sent in response to those seeking advice on how to create welcoming ceremonies for girls. The introduction to this letter evidences, only a few years after the first Simchat Bat appeared, the remarkably pervasive interest in holding these ceremonies:

> I was very glad to receive your excited inquiry concerning our collection of naming ceremonies. There is such an abundance of them, however, that to send them all to you would not be possible. What I have tried to do instead is to summarize the background for doing the ceremonies, and the elements that comprise them, with a few examples to help illustrate how best to carry them out.

This documentary "piece of history" is consistent with a *New York Times* article, published in 1977, which reports that these students have "received so many inquiries that they have started a consultation service."[60]

This guide continued to circulate until at least 1987 when Debra Cantor included it in her booklet *Jewish Naming Ceremonies for Girls: A Sourcebook for Rabbinical Students*.[61] At this time, R. Cantor was a rabbinical student at the Jewish Theological Seminary. This booklet also incorporates the December 1983 issue of *Sh'ma* (including the debate between Bleich and the Strassfelds) and two sample ceremonies, one of which is that of Joseph and Sharon Kaplan.

These ceremony collections and guides demonstrate how, even in the

1970s and early 1980s, the creators of Simchat Bat rituals had already begun to draw from a set of well-used texts and readings while still maintaining the model that every ceremony should be different from its predecessors. Ironically, therefore, these ceremonies slowly began to exhibit some patterned or even expected elements, reflecting a somewhat different conception of the open and flexible "feminist ritual" model.

SIMCHAT BAT RITUALS TODAY

While retaining many of the characteristics of their predecessors, Simchat Bat practices have noticeably started to mature. Today, two types of Simchat Bat practices have emerged, as we learned in chapter 1. One is a freestanding ceremony that is generally held at home, a synagogue's social hall, or another venue and, significantly, not during regularly scheduled synagogue services. Either the parents or a rabbi lead the proceedings. Much is written about these types of Simchat Bat ceremonies and their unique texts. This genre is most similar to its predecessors from the 1970s and 1980s although, on the whole, the experimental cauldron has cooled somewhat. The second type of Simchat Bat practice is no less interesting and likely more prevalent overall, yet sometimes overlooked. This is the Simchat Bat that is led or officiated by a congregational rabbi, conducted in a synagogue's sanctuary, and integrated directly into regularly held prayer services. We will refer to the first type as a "freestanding Simchat Bat" and the second type as a "synagogue Simchat Bat." (One Reform rabbi with whom I spoke differentiated between "off-bimah" and "on-bimah," respectively.) Both varieties of Simchat Bat practices include a naming, but its centrality varies, and sometimes the naming is actually a reiteration of a previously disclosed name.

I began to recognize these two distinct, yet related, types of Simchat Bat practices when, years ago, I visited the office of a suburban Conservative synagogue to investigate what liturgy for newborn girls is recorded in the Conservative movement's *Siddur Sim Shalom*. I took the siddur (prayer book) off the shelf and asked an administrative assistant if I could please use the photocopy machine. She looked at me somewhat suspiciously and asked what I was looking for. I explained that I was interested in rituals for newborn girls. She smiled and exclaimed, "Why didn't you just say so?" Quicker than I could respond, she clicked her computer's mouse, pulled two pages off the printer, and handed them to me. She said, "This is the ceremony that we use in this synagogue for a girl's naming." When I inquired who created this ceremony, she replied "the rabbi" in a tone that indicated she considered this answer to be obvious.

Until that point, I had been primarily aware of freestanding rituals, such as those held by my husband and me, as well as some of our friends. I began to understand, however, that the various practices that rabbis conduct in the synagogue during scheduled services are part of the same genre of modern, creative expressions of welcome for baby girls. I also realized that the synagogue Simchat Bat is a normative practice today in liberal communities.

Currently, there are a number of permutations of practices for welcoming newborn girls. Some communities, particularly Orthodox ones, offer an aliyah and Mi Shebairach, with nothing more. In other communities, parents commemorate their daughter's birth with either a synagogue or freestanding Simchat Bat. The baby is named in all these rituals (although sometimes the baby's vernacular name may already be known). Another variation is to name the baby in the synagogue, typically with an aliyah and Mi Shebairach, and then to reiterate and explain this name later at a freestanding Simchat Bat. Finally, it is feasible to hold a freestanding Simchat Bat with a naming, followed by a name reiteration in the synagogue, but I am not aware of anyone today welcoming a daughter in this particular sequence.

The differences between synagogue and freestanding Simchat Bat rituals are significant. A congregational rabbi leads a synagogue Simchat Bat since it is conducted during services. The rabbi also may meet with parents in advance of a ceremony to prepare them for the occasion. The rabbi's role at a freestanding Simchat Bat is more variable. A rabbi might lead or participate in the ceremony, or the parents might lead it themselves. This decision is frequently made by the parents.

It appears that, in Orthodox settings, parents often take charge of a freestanding Simchat Bat. While there are Orthodox rabbis who involve themselves in planning and conducting a Simchat Bat, there are many others who do not. Some of these rabbis believe that parents prefer to be left in charge, while others may have limited knowledge about the Simchat Bat or may feel it is unnecessary, inappropriate, or disallowed. In my personal experience, I have attended one freestanding Simchat Bat where the parents' Orthodox rabbi presided. I have also been to a handful of ceremonies where an Orthodox rabbi was in attendance or contributed a speech or a song, although the parents clearly remained the lead participants. To the extent that Orthodox parents encounter a lack of rabbinic interest or participation, they turn to the freestanding Simchat Bat structure to create unique ceremonies held on their own terms and often in their own homes.

There are, however, some Orthodox synagogues today that offer a synagogue Simchat Bat. One such example occurs at the Hebrew Institute of Riverdale in New York. R. Avraham Weiss asks the congregation to rise when the father receives an aliyah, and, afterwards, he invites the mother and baby to ascend to the central podium (bimah). When the family gathers on the bimah, a standard Ashkenazic Mi Shebairach is recited and the baby girl is named. The congregation sings a congratulatory song ("*Siman Tov U'mazal Tov*"), and R. Weiss provides a few words of Torah to conclude the ritual.

Timing is another basis of comparison between freestanding and synagogue Simchat Bat practices. Unconstrained by a schedule of synagogue services, the freestanding Simchat Bat is conducted at a time of the parents' choosing, frequently on a day that is convenient for them and the invited guests. By contrast, the synagogue Simchat Bat typically occurs on Shabbat (either on Friday night or Saturday morning), when the synagogue is most widely attended. If held during Shabbat morning services, a Simchat Bat ritual is often inserted during the Torah service, although this placement may vary. For example, there is at least one Reform synagogue where the rabbi conducts a Simchat Bat ceremony immediately following the recitation of the thanksgiving segment of the Shabbat Amidah (literally, "standing") prayer.

Another point is that, broadly speaking, the synagogue practice tends to be more streamlined than the freestanding ceremony. It seems that some rabbis do not want to elongate already expansive prayer services in the synagogue. A rabbi also may carefully use familiar prayer elements in order to remain within a community's zone of comfort. By contrast, since freestanding ceremonies occur independent of scheduled synagogue services, these ceremonies are not time-constrained and need not conform to the sensibilities of fellow community members. Another, more subtle difference is that a greater number and wider range of relatives and friends are likely to participate in a freestanding Simchat Bat (for example, by reading a passage or holding the baby), than in a synagogue Simchat Bat. All told, a freestanding ceremony has the potential to be more elaborate and creative than the synagogue Simchat Bat—although many today are not, as we will see.

To illustrate these general characteristics of synagogue and freestanding Simchat Bat rituals, we will proceed to examine the content of these two varieties of Simchat Bat in greater detail. We will also consider the themes that these ceremonies sometimes convey, as well as the times when they are held.

Synagogue Simchat Bat

Although neither the synagogue Simchat Bat nor its freestanding counterpart has a standard liturgy or a fixed structure, each type of Simchat Bat includes certain common elements, some of which overlap. The synagogue Simchat Bat often includes an aliyah for one or both of the baby girl's parents, although it may or may not be a focal point of the ceremony. In some traditional Conservative communities, for example, an aliyah and Mi Shebairach serve as the centerpiece of a synagogue Simchat Bat. I have heard more than one Conservative rabbi comment that the aliyah is indispensible and that new parents are strongly encouraged to come to the synagogue for this ritual. This emphasis highlights a perception by some today that the aliyah and Mi Shebairach are the traditional means of recognizing newborn girls. One Conservative rabbi with whom I spoke characterized having only a home ceremony as "selfish." In a similar vein, Orthodox synagogues performing a Simchat Bat during services likewise retain an aliyah for the father as a central ritual.

In some Reform synagogues, both parents are invited to have an aliyah, although one Reform rabbi mentioned to me that, in his experience, parents have declined this honor based on their belief that an aliyah is not integral to a baby naming. More than once, someone has described to me a ceremony held for a baby girl in a Reform synagogue, but neglected to mention the aliyah until I specifically inquired about it. In other Reform communities, synagogue Simchat Bat practices do not include the option of an aliyah; rather, parents are invited to light the Friday night candles or to perform some other synagogue ritual.

Announcing the baby's name is a central feature of a synagogue Simchat Bat, and this occurs after the aliyah, if there is one. The rabbi or prayer leader inserts the baby's name when reciting a Mi Shebairach or an alternative liturgy. One such liturgy is a modified version of the more elaborate naming prayer recited at a circumcision ceremony, which begins, "Our God and the God of our forefathers—*Eloheinu veilo-hei avoteinu.*" Some Reform synagogues, in particular, appear to utilize liturgies other than the Mi

Shebairach. After the naming, the rabbi offers a few words of Torah and speaks about the family, including grandparents and siblings, and the parents or the rabbi discuss the baby's new name. The mother may also recite Birkat HaGomel. Finally, "*Siman Tov U'mazal Tov*" is sung, and a kiddush sponsored by the parents follows services. These elements, including the aliyah, may constitute the totality of a synagogue Simchat Bat.

However, a synagogue Simchat Bat may include additional elements. One commonly recited blessing is Shehechiyanu ("Blessed are You God, our God, King of the Universe, who has kept us alive and preserved us and brought us to this season"). Another prevalent ritual is that the parents or rabbi recite Birkat Banim (the Blessing of Children), which parents more typically bestow upon their children weekly as part of the rituals for welcoming Shabbat. For girls, this blessing begins, "May God make you like Sarah, Rebecca, Rachel, and Leah" and continues with the priestly benediction: "May God bless you and keep you / May God shine His light upon you and be gracious to you / May God lift His Face to you and grant you peace" (Numbers 6:24–26). A rabbi often presents parents with a gift on behalf of the synagogue, and the baby's siblings may ascend to the podium to receive or recite a blessing. Less frequently, the ceremony may include the blessing over a cup of wine ("Blessed are You God . . . Creator of the fruit of the vine"), as well as modern readings or poems about thanksgiving, new Jewish life, or related topics.

One final element that appears in some synagogue Simchat Bat rituals is a reference to the covenant between God and Israel. Introductory and/or concluding remarks by the rabbi or parents may frame the ceremony as covenantal. In addition, the rabbi and/or congregation may signify the baby's covenantal entry by reciting the following prayer, adapted from the traditional circumcision liturgy: "Just as she has entered into the covenant, so shall she be entered into Torah, the marriage canopy, and good deeds." Some liberal communities have adapted a blessing from the circumcision ceremony. For example: "Blessed are You God, King of the Universe, who sanctified us with Your commandments and commanded us to enter her into the covenant of Abraham our forefather and Sarah our foremother" or ". . . who has entered our daughter into the covenant of Abraham our forefather and Sarah our foremother." In different variations, the blessing ends by referencing only Abraham, only Sarah, or "the Jewish nation," "the community of Israel," or the like.

Some synagogues use a variety of "active" rituals (that is, doing something rather than saying something) to represent covenantal entry. For example, a rabbi may touch the baby's hand to the Torah, or parade the baby around the sanctuary in the manner of carrying a Torah scroll. However, some synagogue Simchat Bat ceremonies do not use such rituals or do not mention the covenant at all.

Freestanding Simchat Bat

Despite its greater potential for originality, the freestanding Simchat Bat nonetheless often incorporates many of the same familiar blessings and other traditional liturgies used in synagogue Simchat Bat ceremonies. These elements include the Mi Shebairach, Shehechiyanu blessing, Birkat HaGomel (or other prayers for birthing mothers), Birkat Banim, and the blessing for wine, along with some words of Torah and an explanation of the girl's name. Another blessing sometimes recited is Hatov v'Hameitiv ("Blessed are You God, our God, King of the Universe, who is good and who causes good"). Freestanding ceremonies also commonly include passages from Psalms or Proverbs. For example, one popular selection is Psalm 128; another is the text of *Eshet Chayil* (the "Woman of Valor" passage, Proverbs 31:10–31), a song extolling the virtues of the ideal woman, which some Jewish husbands sing to their wives on Friday evening.

In addition, freestanding Simchat Bat ceremonies often integrate a broad repertoire of other readings drawn from classic Jewish texts, such as the Bible, Talmud, or Midrash (body of rabbinic homiletic stories), formulated according to the personal preferences of parents or rabbis. For example, some popular Biblical readings include part of the blessing that Rebecca's mother and brother Laban bestowed upon her ("May you be the mother of thousands and tens of thousands," Genesis 24:60); the blessing that Jacob bestowed on his grandsons, Menashe and Ephraim ("The angel who redeemed me from from all evil will bless the youngsters," Genesis 48:16); and Moses's description of the Israelites' entrance into a covenantal relationship with God ("You stand today, all of you, before the Lord your God," Deuteronomy 29:9–14). Other recited texts include a midrash about children as guarantors in receiving the Torah (Song of Songs Rabba 1, 24) and a Talmudic story about a man planting a carob tree for the benefit of the next generation (BT Taanit 23a).

Another increasingly popular "traditional" element of freestanding ceremonies is the Sephardic Zeved HaBat liturgy, especially the standard Song of Songs verses (2:14 and 6:9) and the special Mi Shebairach. In this way, Ashkenazim performing Simchat Bat ceremonies borrow openly from Sephardic practices. For example, in the *Koren Siddur,* the first Ashkenazic siddur published under Orthodox auspices to include a Simchat Bat ritual, the ceremony for newborn girls is titled "Zeved HaBat" and includes the traditional Song of Songs verses. The *Koren Siddur's* Zeved HaBat, however, features an Ashkenazic Mi Shebairach, thus creating a hybrid of Ashkenazic and Sephardic customs.[62] Many traditional Ashkenazim likewise cherry-pick the Zeved HaBat liturgy for their freestanding Simchat Bat ceremonies in combination with other blessings and prayers.[63]

This appropriation is fairly surprising, since traditional Ashkenazim today generally would not knowingly adopt Sephardic customs in most other contexts. Believing that there is no acceptable Ashkenazic precedent, however, some Ashkenazim resort to the practice of using long-standing Sephardic liturgy as a means of imbuing tradition into a brand-new practice. Relying on an accepted Sephardic tradition makes the novel Simchat Bat practice more palatable for traditionally minded Jews. As a result, some may erroneously infer that the Zeved HaBat practice is the basis and impetus for the modern Simchat Bat. To the contrary, the Simchat Bat incorporates blessings, prayers, and themes drawn from traditional sources, but the use of these elements in the context of the Simchat Bat is, in fact, only decades old.

Ashkenazic parents consistently make one specific change to the traditional Zeved HaBat liturgy. These parents are careful to modify the Sephardic Mi Shebairach's prayer that a girl be blessed with "male children" to include both male and female children. This is an interesting example of making a traditional liturgy conform to feminist values in order to uphold the purpose of the Simchat Bat.

It is also noteworthy that the first verse recited at a Zeved HaBat characterizes a girl as coy ("My dove in the clefts of the rock / In the hiding places on the mountainside / Show me your face / Let me hear your voice") and focuses on her physicality ("For your voice is sweet / And your face is lovely"). It is ironic that parents making an effort to celebrate their daughter in a modern way would bless her to be coy and beautiful, rather than kind and intelligent or other more substantive traits. Many Ashkenazic parents nonetheless recite these verses at a Simchat Bat as a means of infusing a traditional element into their daughter's ceremony.

In some traditional communities, a selection from the liturgies and read-ings described above may constitute the totality of a freestanding Simchat Bat ceremony. That said, some ceremonies in traditional communities inte-grate other practices, which are just as likely to appear in more progressive ceremonies as well. Some of these practices revive and reformulate traditional customs. For example, at a Simchat Bat, parents may acknowledge that a tree has been (or will be) planted in honor of a newborn, in conformance with Talmudic advice (BT Gittin 57a). Another example is the formulation and recitation of acrostics for the baby's name. Hebrew acrostics may have existed as early as the seventh century BCE, and acrostics for both names and other words and phrases have been popular (among Jews and gentiles) since at least the early Middle Ages.[64] In addition, new prayers in the manner of *techines,* a genre of personal Yiddish prayers written by and for women, have been com-posed and incorporated into modern ceremonies.[65] There are liturgies that evoke the foremothers, other Biblical women, and Jewish women through-out the generations.[66] Combining a baby's Simchat Bat with a celebration marking her parents' completion of a course of Torah study (*siyyum*)[67] is a less familiar practice. A siyyum recasts Torah study, which has been tradi-tionally male-dominated, as a joint endeavor for a husband and wife.

Some Simchat Bat practices—such as those described below—are more likely to be found in progressive communities than in more traditional communities. One example is the inclusion of texts (in Hebrew or English) by eminent, modern Jewish philosophers and poets such as Martin Buber, Abraham Joshua Heschel, and Chaim Nachman Bialik, as well as lesser-known writers. On the whole, traditional families are more comfortable re-citing classic prayers, blessings, and Biblical or midrashic excerpts, although, by doing so in the context of a Simchat Bat, they are reinterpreting these texts in a distinctly modern way.

More prominently, the recitation of brand-new blessings is prevalent in Simchat Bat ceremonies in progressive communities. Some new blessings maintain the traditional template, but modify the substantive content. For example: "Blessed are You God, King of the Universe, who sanctified us with Your commandments and commanded us to enter her into the covenant of Abraham our forefather and Sarah our foremother." This blessing and its variants are also sometimes recited in synagogue rituals, as we have seen. Other new blessings include, "Blessed are You God . . . who commanded us to sanctify life" and "Blessed are You God . . . who causes parents to rejoice with their children." Moreover, some progressive Simchat Bat ceremonies incorporate blessings with feminine God language. In particular, feminine grammatical forms and imagery replace those that are masculine (*b'rucha at Ya* instead of *baruch ata Adonai,* and so on) and "King of the Universe" becomes "Spirit [*Ruach*] of the Universe," an allusion to the *Shechina*—the feminine divine presence. As a result, the traditional blessing template is changed. In stark contrast, however, traditional practitioners steadfastly believe that it is halachically forbidden to recite newly created blessings or use modified blessing templates, and carefully avoid these new and modified forms in formulating ceremonies for their daughters.

Some Simchat Bat practices are derived from the traditional circumcision ceremony. For example, some recite liturgy adapted from the circumcision ceremony to express the parallel theme of covenantal entry. My husband and I used this type of liturgy at our daughters' ceremonies. Another example is the designation of a symbolic Miriam's Chair at a Simchat Bat to represent the presence of the Biblical prophetess Miriam, in place of the Elijah's Chair used at a circumcision ceremony. There are Simchat Bat ceremonies that have directly addressed circumcision by referencing Biblical passages about "circumcision of the heart" (e.g., Deuteronomy 30:6). There is at least one ceremony where participants recited verses that highlight three types of non-physical "circumcision," that of the heart, ears, and lips (Jeremiah 9:30, 6:10; Exodus 6:30).[68]

Simchat Bat practices are drawn from other Jewish life-cycle customs as well. For example, some recite the seven traditional wedding blessings (sheva brachot) or use a wedding canopy (*chuppah*) at a Simchat Bat. These may convey the idea of childbearing as a desired result of marriage. A less common practice is to read from a Torah scroll at home, with aliyot for both parents. This puts a new gloss on the synagogue naming practice for girls.

Various rituals are used at a Simchat Bat specifically because of their traditional relationship to women. Candlelighting is a popular choice. Some have reinterpreted this practice, however, by lighting seven candles to symbolize the seven days of creation, an allusion to beginnings and birth. Alternatively, parents may give the baby a candlestick to grasp, or they present candlesticks to the baby as a gift for her use in adulthood.

On the other hand, a handful of Simchat Bat practices reflect the evolution of gender roles in Judaism. For example, guiding a baby girl's hand to touch a Torah scroll handle connects her with Torah reading and study.

Until at least the early twentieth century, however, women and girls had been effectively barred, or at least discouraged, from studying Torah. Another example is reciting at a Simchat Bat the Shabbat kiddush prayer or presenting a kiddush cup to the baby. Many women recite kiddush today, although it has been traditionally recited only by men.

Other Simchat Bat rituals originate in disparate Jewish contexts. One example is performing the Havdalah service that separates Shabbat from weekdays; this service includes drinking wine, smelling spices, and lighting a candle. While Havdalah marks the transition from Shabbat to weekdays, a Simchat Bat transitions a baby into the covenant. In addition, smelling spices at a Simchat Bat evokes the Sephardic custom of smelling myrtle and reciting a blessing for spices at a circumcision. Another example is reciting an adaptation of the traditional blessing for a good and productive life, which appears in the liturgy for a Shabbat preceding Rosh Chodesh. Reciting the blessings for seeing lightning ("Blessed are You God . . . who makes the works of creation") or rainbows ("Blessed are You God . . . who remembers the covenant, is faithful in His covenant, and upholds His statements") is another interesting example of re-contextualizing traditional liturgies for a Simchat Bat. The former characterizes a newborn as a "work of creation," while the latter uses the symbolism of the Noachide covenant.

Some Simchat Bat practices are particularly inventive. For example, there have been suggestions to use salt water to stimulate each of the five senses,[69] to perfume a baby's ears with myrtle, or to rub olive oil on her forehead. One ceremony includes readings that focus on the labor of childbirth to highlight a woman's role in perpetuating the chain of generations and to compare childbirth to the redemption from Egypt.[70] Finally, there are ceremony texts that incorporate everything from culturally diverse poetry to excerpts from a children's Dr. Seuss book. While some parents continue to devise distinctive features for freestanding Simchat Bat ceremonies, this exceptional creativity is, on the whole, far less common today than previously.

Themes

Following in the footsteps of Simchat Bat practices from the 1970s and 1980s, some ceremonies focus on a theme, although many others do not. Both freestanding and synagogue practices may have themes, although a well-developed theme is more likely to be found in freestanding ceremonies.

The most prevalent Simchat Bat theme is the covenant between God and Israel. That said, this theme is not universal. For example, in my limited personal experience, I have yet to attend a ceremony held by self-identified Orthodox parents that explicitly centers on a covenantal theme. A friend of mine, who would characterize himself as modern Orthodox, said that my eldest daughter's covenantal ceremony was the first and last one that he ever attended. In addition, an Orthodox-affiliated acquaintance commented to me that, in the ceremony she and her husband recently performed, they intentionally omitted any reference to the covenant. At the same time, I have been told about ceremonies held by modern Orthodox parents that employ a covenantal theme.

Liberal parents and rabbis use the covenantal theme to a considerable extent. Yet, there are some liberal synagogues where the ceremonies held for newborn girls do not specifically reference the covenant or mention it in passing. For example, the covenant might be cited prominently in the ceremony's introduction, but then not reappear again in the body of the ceremony.

Other relatively popular themes are Torah, water, and light. Some more creative themes include the foremothers, Shabbat, Rosh Chodesh, other Jewish holidays, charity, sanctity, femininity, religious objects, and witnessing Revelation. One particularly innovative theme is that of tents, such as those in which Abraham and Sarah lived.[71] Again, it seems to me that the use of these more creative themes has, generally speaking, declined today overall. Nonetheless, ceremonies may incorporate any one of these themes, a completely different theme, or a combination of two or more. The most likely combination is an overarching covenantal theme that is expressed using a different subsidiary theme.

Verbal expression is a primary means of conveying a theme, for example, by reciting relevant readings and prayers, explaining the reasons for using a particular theme, or introducing the overall ceremony. One illustration is a freestanding, covenantal Simchat Bat ceremony that appeared in the 1980s. In it, R. Saul Berman, the rabbi of Lincoln Square Synagogue in New York, used various readings and sophisticated explanations to affirm the creation of three distinct covenantal relationships into which the newborn girl was embarking: those with the Jewish people, her extended family, and her parents.[72]

Today, a freestanding ceremony might include covenantal prayers and blessings such as those recited at a synagogue Simchat Bat. For example:

"Just as she has entered into the covenant, so shall she be entered into Torah, the marriage canopy, and good deeds," or the more progressive "Blessed are You God . . . who sanctified us with Your commandments and commanded us to enter her into the covenant of Abraham our forefather and/or Sarah our foremother." Other covenantal blessings might include, "Blessed are You God, who makes the covenant" (adopted from the circumcision ceremony) or ". . . who remembers the covenant" (adopted from Rosh HaShana prayers). Introductory and closing remarks by parents or a rabbi might also frame the ceremony as one of covenantal entry.

Among freestanding ceremonies with a central theme, some convey this theme with one or more "active" rituals, where something is done rather than said. These rituals are rooted in traditional imagery, yet formulated specifically for Simchat Bat ceremonies. Many were devised in the 1970s and 1980s to welcome girls into the covenant, as described above. One example of a covenantal ritual is washing the baby's hands or feet, evoking how Abraham welcomed visiting angels by washing their feet (Genesis 18:4). One Conservative rabbi commented to me that this is an increasingly popular choice for those performing an active ritual. A related, but seldom performed, covenantal ritual is immersing a baby in an actual mikvah or, alternatively, a miniature bath, set on a table. This mikvah ritual is construed as parallel to circumcision, based on the *aggada* (rabbinic lore; plural, *aggadot*) that the women and men redeemed from Egypt utilized these rituals, respectively, to "convert" to Judaism (BT Yevamot 46a–46b, Keritot 9a). In other ceremonies, the baby is carried between two lines of guests to symbolize communal acceptance and to evoke the Abrahamic "covenant between the parts" in which God lights a fire between halves of animals (Genesis 15). It also echoes a similar custom performed for mourners at a burial. Another covenantal ritual performed today is swaddling the baby in a tallit to symbolize the loving embrace of her family and the Jewish people. This is a practice that my husband and I adopted for our newborn daughters' ceremonies.

Various other active rituals mentioned above have been used to convey covenantal entry, such as touching a Torah, anointing the newborn with oil, lighting candles, or smelling spices. There have also been some distinctive rituals, such as touching breast milk or lochia (afterbirth blood) to the baby's body,[73] which bring an intimate physicality to a Simchat Bat. As such, these rituals are formulated in the same vein as Mary Gendler's hymenectomy proposal, but without the physical invasiveness that Gendler suggested (although the lochia ritual includes drawing blood with a pinprick from the baby's finger). In another ceremony, the word *Sha-dai,* the name of God, is marked on the baby's body with a semi-permanent dye and olive oil, as a "sign of the covenant" to parallel that of circumcision.[74] Since the dye lasts for two weeks, this ceremony seeks a measure of physical permanence akin to that of Gendler's more extreme proposal. A different proposed ritual is to tap a newborn girl's cheek "to evoke the folk tradition of a 'menstrual slap' which a mother gives her daughter [on the face] when she reaches menarche."[75] This references female blood, paralleling the male blood of circumcision. While all of these are evocative and creative, they are far from the mainstream today.

Active rituals were some of the earliest expressions of girls' covenantal entry (and were correspondingly viewed in some circles as a threat), but it appears that active covenantal rituals, such as those described here, might be less popular today than previously. This may be due, in part, to the ascent of the synagogue Simchat Bat and its emphasis on familiar practices. While many contemporary Simchat Bat practices do have themes, many others do not, and, of those with themes, some do not incorporate active rituals.

Timing

Thus far, we have seen the emergence of some common features in Simchat Bat practices today, despite the wide-ranging choices that persist. But one feature that stands out for its relative consistency is timing. Simchat Bat rituals are frequently held on a day that is convenient for the parents and for those traveling or working. Synagogue Simchat Bat rituals, therefore, are held on a convenient Shabbat. Since freestanding Simchat Bat ceremonies are unconstrained by synagogue schedules, the timing is selected based primarily, if not solely, on convenience. This consideration typically translates to Sundays or civil holidays in the Diaspora and, in Israel, weekday evenings, holidays, or sometimes Fridays. Shabbat is avoided by those who do not want guests traveling on Shabbat or who are inviting faraway guests who do not travel on Shabbat. Minor holidays like Rosh Chodesh (traditionally celebrated by women) or Chanukah are sometimes favored—but only to the extent that they are convenient.

Another aspect of this convenient timing is that ceremonies are often held weeks, months, or even a year following a baby's birth, when new parents feel they have regained some "normality" in their lives. Said otherwise, a ceremony is often held when a mother feels that she has "recovered" sufficiently from the birth and when parents feel they have garnered the strength to prepare a celebration in the midst of caring for a newborn. Some parents may also believe that delaying the ceremony will enable their family and friends to make travel plans, as necessary.

It follows that many parents eschew the notion of conducting a Simchat Bat a specific, preordained number of days following a daughter's birth. For example, while my daughters ceremonially entered the covenant on their eighth day of life, many parents view this timing as highly inconvenient, as well as unnecessary. Others deem the eighth day to be inappropriate for girls, perceiving that it is reserved exclusively for circumcising boys. Some consider holding a ceremony approximately a month following a daughter's birth to be enough time to enable a family to acclimate to a new baby. This juncture also corresponds to when a baby is halachically deemed viable. For many families, however, this timing is likewise much too soon.

There is an uncommon practice of holding a ceremony on the fifteenth day following birth. This day marks the end of the two-week period during which a woman who has given birth to a girl is considered ritually impure (*niddah*).[76] (The mother of a boy is considered ritually impure for only one week.) There is also at least one example of holding a ceremony on the first Sunday two weeks after a baby's birth. This hybrid timing combines this niddah rationale with the convenience of a Sunday.[77] Some have suggested holding a Simchat Bat on the twenty-first day following birth, at which point the mother of a girl traditionally immersed herself in the mikvah, or on the eightieth day following birth, when a birthing mother brought her sacrifices in the Temple.[78] I do not know whether any family has ever used these timetables for these specific reasons.

One family held a freestanding ceremony on the seventh day following birth, one day earlier than the eighth day on which a boy's circumcision occurs. This one-day difference reflects the traditional one-year difference between the Bat Mitzvah for twelve-year-old girls and the Bar Mitzvah for thirteen-year-old boys.[79] Another proposed time for holding a Simchat Bat is the twentieth day, when the she-devil Lilith can no longer attack and kill infant girls, according to rabbinic lore.[80] I am not aware of any ceremony actually held on this day for this reason. While interesting to note, these times are seldom encountered today.

MODERN SIMCHAT BAT RESOURCES

Another component of current Simchat Bat practices is the set of resources, compiled by laypeople and Jewish professionals in the last twenty years, which provide models and detailed advice for parents who want to create freestanding Simchat Bat ceremonies for their daughters. These ceremony collections, anthologies, and websites are, like similar materials from the 1970s and 1980s, inspired by the do-it-yourself approach of the Chavurah movement and Catalog Judaism. The current resources thus follow squarely in the footsteps of the earlier ceremony collections and guides but are more expansive than their predecessors.

Since the 1970s and 1980s, new collections of Simchat Bat texts from performed ceremonies have slowly accumulated. Parents and rabbis use these texts as models in creating new ceremonies. Today, at least a handful of synagogues keep informal files of ceremonies that congregants consult. Other institutions and organizations likewise house files, such as the Jewish Theological Seminary (JTS) Library of the Conservative movement in New York City, and Machon Itim, a non-profit organization in Jerusalem with the goal of making Judaism accessible to all. A JTS reference librarian recently remarked to me that the welcoming ceremony collection had been one of the library's most popular items, but that this was much less the case today. The library of the Jewish Women's Resource Center (JWRC) in New York City, which began collecting Simchat Bat texts as early as the 1980s, made its extensive file of ceremonies for girls available to the public, until the JWRC closed its library in 2010 and donated its materials to JTS. The JWRC's librarian told me in 2007 that she encouraged individuals to send her copies of their newly created ceremonies so she could include them in the file to inspire the next person's creativity.

Some individuals also keep files of texts that they received upon attending ceremonies or that they otherwise acquired. These private collections appear to be some of the most vibrant ones in use today. Like that of the JWRC, at least one such private collection functions as a highly effective "chain letter." Parents and expectant parents are invited to review the file and strongly encouraged to add their own ceremony text for the benefit of future users.[81]

More recent anthologies and guides, like their predecessors from the 1970s and 1980s, speak directly to parents who are searching for ways to celebrate their newborn daughters. These resources provide parents with tools to craft rituals and give parents step-by-step advice for how to use these tools to formulate and hold ceremonies. Unlike earlier guides, however, the newer resources are detailed, providing parents with every bit of information they could possibly need.

I have identified a number of current hard-copy "how-to" resources, and likely there are others. Two of these are books written by American laypeople, Deborah Nussbaum Cohen and Anita Diamant, respectively.[82] Another is a folder with information sheets compiled by the Women's League for Conservative Judaism, an arm of the Conservative movement, with an introduction by R. Nina Beth Cardin.[83] Two others are pamphlets published in Israel, one by Machon Itim with a traditional bent,[84] and the other by Kehilat Kol Haneshama, a Progressive congregation in Jerusalem.[85] Also noteworthy is a pamphlet with a collection of relevant articles that the Jewish Orthodox Feminist Alliance makes available on its website.[86]

The essence of these resources is an outline of the elements of a ceremony for girls (for example, welcome, prayers, rituals, readings, songs), coupled with a wide range of options for each element. In this way, each anthology presents a "mix-and-match" menu, thus adopting the same format as the JWRC's *Guide toward Celebrating the Birth of a Daughter*. The contemporary anthologies encourage readers to select one or more options for each element, add or eliminate elements, and then combine the various selections into a new, personalized "do-it-yourself" ceremony. Most anthologies also present full-length sample ceremonies. Some of these resources emphasize the theme of covenant, while others do not. A pattern emerges in which the American anthologies present the option of covenantal rituals, whereas the Israeli ones do not.

These contemporary guides also provide comprehensive practical information, such as when to have the ceremony, what to call it, and where to have it. All the guides recommend handing out a program, and some include advice on handling logistics, contingencies, food preparation, photography, and helpful supplies. Deborah Nussbaum Cohen summarizes the purpose of her book: "Enough has been developed so that it's no longer necessary for each Jewish parent of a new daughter to reinvent the wheel." Furthermore: "It's a wonderful opening to do something personal, creative, and individual to welcome your daughter. It can also seem overwhelming . . . to try to create something from scratch. This book is here to help."[87]

As technology has evolved since the 1990s, parents seeking guidance on how to celebrate their newborn daughters began to do what they usually do when seeking information or advice—they search the Internet. There are at least two popular websites that include this type of guidance, while also covering a wide range of other Jewish rituals: those of Ritualwell (www.ritualwell.org) and Machon Itim (www.itim.org.il). Ritualwell is a project of Kolot, The Center for Jewish Women's and Gender Studies at the Reconstructionist Rabbinical College in Philadelphia. Its website "is a source for innovative, contemporary Jewish rituals . . . and empowers Jews to shape and renew Jewish tradition." Operating in an Israeli environment, dominated by an Orthodox religious culture and governmental establishment, Itim's website presents more conservative options. For example, the Ritualwell website provides for explicitly covenantal rituals for girls, while Itim's website does not.

The websites share with their hard-copy predecessors an ethos of personalization and a "how-to" approach to appeal to a wide audience. Both formats also present model ceremonies, an array of options, and an abundance of information. However, the websites have the added benefit of powerful Internet capabilities, which the websites use effectively and innovatively to make ceremonies more easily accessible and to streamline their production.

For example, the Ritualwell webpages devoted to welcoming and raising children function as a ceremony collection,[88] just like any of the hard-copy collections in synagogues or personal files. These webpages also include articles and other relevant information for those creating new ceremonies. However, rather than going to the library or asking friends to borrow their personal collections, users can quickly and easily browse Ritualwell's online collection to find the information they seek. The Ritualwell website also has videos and blogs that disseminate ideas directly from ritual builders. Users can also post their own personal rituals, prayers, or articles by creating an account and clicking on "Add Your Own Ritual." Posting new ceremonies to the Ritualwell website evokes how librarians and private collectors encourage individuals to add their ceremonies to hard-copy collections. However, the Ritualwell website can accomplish this instantaneously and can reach the countless individuals browsing the web at any given moment.

In a similar way, the Simchat Bat pages on the Itim website function like their predecessor hard-copy anthologies and guides by providing detailed information about every aspect of performing welcoming ceremonies and then facilitating the creation of new ceremonies. In particular, the Itim website explains when and where to hold a ceremony, what to call it, how to prepare for it, and how to select a name. It also describes a range of contemporary practices and provides historical background. Unlike the hard-copies, however, the Itim website presents all this information in an easily accessible point-and-click format. Significantly, Itim capitalizes on the power of the Internet with an online "mix-and-match" menu with which a user can create a ceremony online in a matter of minutes. To select a particular option on the menu (such as a reading, prayer, poem, or blessing), a user clicks and places a checkmark in the box associated with that option. When satisfied with the selections comprising a new ceremony, the user clicks on the option for "Create the Ceremony" and enters an e-mail address. The complete, formatted ceremony appears in the user's inbox moments later.[89]

In sum, all these collections, anthologies, and websites encourage parents to create new and distinctive freestanding Simchat Bat ceremonies and, in the process, to revel in the opportunity for flexibility and creativity that these ceremonies ostensibly present. To this end, these resources provide models for creating new ceremonies and/or systematically identify and categorize prevalent patterns within the universe of existing ceremonies. While each resource presents an abundance of different options, the mere identification and presentation of these options may, paradoxically, slow down the creative process and contribute to a homogenizing trend. Despite exhortations to devise new ceremonies, parents faced with so many choices may perceive no need to innovate further.

Laura Janner-Klausner, editor of Kehillat Kol Haneshama's anthology, has recognized this risk. As a result, she pleads with her readers to resist the ossification that her anthology might invite: "The evolutionary nature of writing your celebration based on your own ideas, as well as those of others, might be inhibited by this anthology. PLEASE read, enjoy, adapt, accept or reject different ideas and DON'T STOP CREATING."[90] Despite their intent to promote fresh ideas, these Simchat Bat resources may be working in the opposite direction.

That said, who is actually using these resources and to what extent are they using them? First of all, rabbis in progressive communities may consult with anthologies and websites in crafting the Simchat Bat ceremonies they use. Some parents read these resources to educate themselves before or after meeting with their rabbi. Other audiences for these resources include those who participate in chavurot, independent minyanim, or other communities without formal rabbinic leadership. Likewise, those who are not affiliated with a synagogue or other community, yet interested in holding a ceremony, would consult these guides.

Another significant audience is Orthodox-affiliated parents formulating ceremonies for their daughters in the absence of rabbinic guidance. Perhaps in no other aspect of their religious lives do Orthodox adherents reach so far outside their usual modus operandi of following communally accepted liturgies. These highly motivated parents utilize unlikely sources, sometimes a bit uncomfortably, to cobble together a personally meaningful ceremony. Orthodox parents consult anthologies and websites (many of which have a progressive outlook), seek advice from enterprising friends or relatives who have formulated their own ceremonies, and peruse ceremony collections to get ideas and identify models. Indeed, when these parents request help from friends or acquaintances, the initial response is most often an enthusiastic willingness to provide them with a collection of performed ceremonies. It follows that the Simchat Bat is one of the few ritualistic areas that Orthodox adherents deem susceptible to creativity, and parents seize upon this opportunity for the relative amount of innovation and personalization that they believe it permits. This leeway is granted, at least in part, because parents have already conducted the "required" synagogue naming by the time they have an "optional" Simchat Bat ceremony. Interestingly, Orthodox involvement in the Simchat Bat enterprise presents a counterpoint to this community's simultaneous veer toward stringencies and its growing emphasis on the rigorous demands of rules and technicalities.[91]

The process of creating new ceremonies using available resources remains robust overall. For example, Machon Itim's director reported in 2007 that this organization distributed its pamphlet each month to 4,000 new mothers in maternity wards in Israel, and that Machon Itim receives two to three new ceremonies each week from people who have used the organization's resources.[92] Nonetheless, it appears that affiliated American Jews outside the Orthodox community are guided more by their rabbis than by popular resources in preparing Simchat Bat rituals.

MODERN TRENDS

In her seminal analysis of the emerging Simchat Bat phenomenon in the late 1970s, Professor Chava Weissler observed that "our first impression is of chaos."[93] Today, a diversity of practices recognizing newborn Jewish girls is still evident. These include not only a wide variety of Simchat Bat ceremonies and rituals, but also celebrations without explicit religious significance, such as kiddushim and birthday parties.

Even Weissler, however, noticed tinges of a "symbolic focus" in the ceremonies she examined, and a trend toward some measure of commonality among Simchat Bat practices has become more pronounced in the years that have followed. While the Simchat Bat genre remains innovative and fluid in the sense that parents and rabbis perceive a great amount of freedom to craft and modify rituals, the Simchat Bat is grounded today less in experimentation and more in the utilization of model ceremonies that have already been performed. Many today are not interested in creating something new. As parents have continued to look to precedents rather than create rituals out of whole cloth, common elements have emerged and, with each subsequent use, they have become increasingly accepted. Rachel Adler describes this process as the product of "antithetical poles" whereby ritual "both preserves traditions and transforms them; it is highly patterned and predictable, yet changeful and surprising."[94] Professor Vanessa Ochs likewise observes this irony, calling Jewish rituals "naturalized" when they are new, yet well-practiced and almost fixed.[95]

These glimpses of homogenization have resulted in changing the tone and texture of Simchat Bat rituals. Even in progressive communities, the Simchat Bat practice has evolved since the days when the Strassfelds immersed their baby daughter in a miniature mikvah. In many communities across the denominational spectrum, a ceremony or ritual for newborn girls is no longer exotic or extraordinary. It has even become expected in some communities (although among the ultra-Orthodox, the Simchat Bat remains alien). Whether in the synagogue or at home, the Simchat Bat has been toned down since its early days when it was highly creative and literally brand-new. This modulated tone has resulted in greater acceptance, and greater acceptance has resulted in this modulated tone.

Why have certain common elements among Simchat Bat practices begun to emerge and, to some extent, become normative? First, the advent of the synagogue Simchat Bat has gently moved the center of gravity of the overall Simchat Bat practice, especially in North America, toward greater cohesion. The synagogue Simchat Bat is geared toward a wider audience than its freestanding counterpart, since it is a "public event" led by a rabbi and held in the synagogue during regularly scheduled services, rather than privately in a home or social hall. The synagogue Simchat Bat, therefore, is designed to be streamlined, and it tends to incorporate a group of familiar or easy-to-understand liturgies. It follows that as the synagogue Simchat Bat has become more prevalent, a collection of commonly used liturgies has gradually emerged.

Furthermore, many rabbis are inclined to use and reuse Simchat Bat templates that they have created. Some rabbis keep these templates as computer files that can be easily e-mailed to parents (or researchers like me), and others even post these ceremonies on their synagogue's website. This use of templates—although there are many of them—may have a homogenizing effect.

The synagogue Simchat Bat demonstrates single-handedly just how much the Simchat Bat has evolved since it began with experimental and diverse rituals. One is hard-pressed to conceive of the synagogue Simchat Bat as a classic "feminist ritual" that is open, fluid, and non-hierarchical. Instead, the synagogue Simchat Bat, particularly within a given community, is a structured and expected synagogue ritual with a clear "vertical" demarcation between the rabbi leading the ritual and the congregation observing it. While synagogue Simchat Bat practices vary among communities, the emergence of this type of ritual represents a significant shift in the span of a few short decades.

The influence of the collections, anthologies, and websites that enable the formulation of new ceremonies likewise results in a pool of commonly used prayers, rituals, and readings—although this pool is fairly large. To the extent that parents and rabbis consult these resources, they encounter a library of model ceremonies and/or a menu of pre-selected elements. The elements that are used, passed on, and reused gradually become popularized, while outlying or unconventional ideas are largely ignored or forgotten. The idea that the Simchat Bat practice can be encapsulated in a single book or webpage may demonstrate that the vast universe of Simchat Bat options is slowly contracting.

Finally, in general, traditional parents tend to use a narrower range of Simchat Bat elements than their more progressive counterparts. Many traditional parents who have Simchat Bat ceremonies for their daughters are careful not to violate halachic rules or sensibilities and, for example, do not create or recite new blessings. These limitations may affect Simchat Bat practices as a whole.

As common elements emerge, it becomes increasingly feasible to identify some generalized characteristics of the Simchat Bat practice. Even so, the Simchat Bat today remains an evolving and diverse practice, and we therefore draw conclusions gingerly.

Our initial observations relate to the content of Simchat Bat ceremonies. First, a girl's naming is frequently a component, and sometimes a central component, of Simchat Bat practices across the denominations. A girl is named with a Mi Shebairach or some other type of liturgy. An aliyah is often performed at a synagogue Simchat Bat and, if so, it may or may not be a focus of the ceremony. A baby girl's Hebrew name is announced for the first and only time at a synagogue Simchat Bat or a freestanding Simchat Bat if no other ritual is performed. However, in traditional communities, a freestanding Simchat Bat is often preceded by a synagogue naming, in which case, the girl's name is reiterated at the Simchat Bat ceremony.

Second, while the covenant is a common theme, it is not universally utilized. For example, a synagogue Simchat Bat, with its streamlined format, may be overall less likely to have a well-developed covenantal theme than a freestanding Simchat Bat. It follows that, while the covenant is mentioned in many Simchat Bat practices, it is not consistently central to the ceremony. For example, parents might recite, "Just as she has been entered into the covenant, so shall she enter Torah, the marriage canopy, and good deeds" or a blessing about the covenant (such as "Blessed are You God . . . who enters her into the covenant of Abraham"). However, this may be the only reference to the covenant, among a number of other disparate elements. In other ceremonies, a rabbi or parent introduces the occasion as entering the baby girl into the covenant, but the covenant is not mentioned as part of the ceremony itself. In sum, not every Simchat Bat practice incorporates the covenant as a unifying theme.

As a result, active covenantal rituals (such as candlelighting, tallit swaddling, and touching a Torah handle) are not widespread today, although some ceremonies with a covenantal focus do incorporate these rituals. These sorts of rituals—as opposed to the verbal expressions that dominate many Simchat Bat ceremonies—have captured the imagination of some innovators. However, active covenantal rituals are perceived as too avant-garde for many others. In some communities, these rituals are ill-suited to the synagogue Simchat Bat with its emphasis on inclusivity and familiarity.

Another observation is the cross-denominational prevalence of holding a Simchat Bat at a time that is convenient for the parents and guests and when the mother has sufficiently "recovered" from the childbirth. A convenient time also often means delaying a Simchat Bat until weeks or months after the birth. Ceremonies held a specific number of days following birth for an articulated reason are unusual today. The anthologies and websites are unanimous in recommending that parents enjoy the flexibility and convenience of holding a ceremony at a time of their choosing, and parents frequently follow this advice.

Finally, there is little, if any, effort today toward consciously developing a more unified Simchat Bat liturgy and practice, and this is the case across the spectrum of Jewish practice and belief. Instead, parents and rabbis generally welcome the opportunity to innovate (or at least to rearrange and personalize preselected elements). The anthologies and websites reinforce this practice by encouraging parents to produce unique ceremonies. While some Simchat Bat components have become popular as a function of the practice's natural maturation process, standardization would require a collective reorientation of purpose.

FROM THESE OBSERVATIONS, it follows that contemporary Simchat Bat practices do not fully embrace certain components that, to my mind, are critical for welcoming newborn girls, namely:

- A first and only naming;
- An "active" symbolic covenantal ritual;
- A cohesive covenantal theme that is reflected in what is said, when it is performed, and what it is called; and
- A uniform core practice.

I suggest that these should be key elements of a welcoming ceremony for newborn girls, whether this ceremony occurs at home (my preference) or in the synagogue. Taken together, these elements constitute my approach for the future development of practices for newborn Jewish girls.

Naming a newborn girl for the first and only time at a ceremony in her honor is an important means of welcoming a girl (as it is for a boy), for reasons described in the previous chapter. At the same time, the naming should not be the focal point of an initiation ceremony for girls. Rather, the covenant should be a ceremony's central theme, as in some—but not all—Simchat Bat practices today. Part II, which follows, explores why and how the covenant is crucial to the identity of Jewish women and men, and explores ways of incorporating the covenantal theme into a ceremony for newborn Jewish girls. In Part III of this book, we consider how a gradual move toward standardization would enhance the long-term sustainability of practices for newborn girls.

While many of these ideas for further developing the Simchat Bat are not new, our aim here is to bring these ideas to the fore and to think about them with a fresh perspective. By studying current practices and making suggestions for their continuing evolution, I hope to advance the conversation about where girls' welcoming practices are heading and where we, as a community, want them to go.

Part II

Covenant

Women and Covenant

I went for a checkup a few weeks after the birth of my fourth child, Tamar. In the course of making conversation, a medical technician asked me about my occupation. I responded that I am writing a book about rituals for newborn Jewish girls. He looked at me incredulously and said, "I didn't think such a thing existed; I thought only Jewish boys had a ritual."

Around the same time, I took Tamar for an appointment with her pediatrician. My eldest child, Dafna, was having a pageant at her elementary school, and my husband and I were planning to take Tamar. I inquired about how best to shield my newborn from the swarms of germs she would likely encounter on this outing. The doctor offered little advice, noting that "had Tamar been a boy, she would have already been exposed to many people at a circumcision ceremony." The doctor's assumption was that no one had gathered to celebrate Tamar's birth.

In fact, both were wrong. On her eighth day of life, Tamar was joyously welcomed at a ceremony at home, in the presence of family and friends, at which she was symbolically entered into the eternal covenant (brit) between God and the nation of Israel.

The importance of ceremoniously initiating every newborn Jewish girl into the covenant is a key message of this book. In the previous chapter, we learned about the dominance of the covenant as a theme in some early Simchat Bat ceremonies, and how the role of the covenant appears to have diminished somewhat since then. Before more closely considering the content of covenantal ceremonies, however, we must first delve into the Jewish conception of *covenant*.

The covenant is the central pillar of Jewish faith and nationhood in that it embodies (1) the Jewish people's fidelity to God as the one and only God, and their agreement to keep God's commandments, and (2) God's promise to keep the Jewish people as His people, make them multitudinous, and give them the land of Israel as an inheritance.

After Moses's first encounter with Pharaoh, God declares the essence of His covenant with the Jewish people: "I have taken you to Me for a nation, and I will be God for you" (Exodus 6:7). Toward the end of his life, Moses articulates the terms of the covenant: "God establishes you [the Israelites] today as a nation for Him, and He will be a God for you, as He has said to you and as He swore to your forefathers, to Abraham, Isaac, and Jacob" (Deuteronomy 29:12). The Torah functions as the written embodiment of this everlasting covenant, which God made with the Jewish people at the Sinaitic Revelation (Exodus 34:27, Deuteronomy 5:2–3). In addition, the Land of Israel is a significant feature of the covenant. God first promises this homeland to Abraham and his descendants by dramatically commanding Abraham to journey to this faraway land (Genesis 12:1).

Encapsulating the essence of Jewish existence and the eternal relationship between God and the Jewish people, the covenant is the centerpiece of traditional Jewish faith. The covenant inextricably links God, Torah, the Jewish people, and the Land of Israel by defining the Jewish national character and traditional religious belief system. The covenant is thus both a national charter and a raison d'être for the Jewish people. The foundational role of the covenant in Judaism, manifested in the Torah and the Land of Israel, cannot be overstated.

While modern thinkers have articulated the concept of covenant in different ways, the centrality of the covenant remains unquestioned. For example, R. Joseph B. Soloveitchik (1903–1993), head of the Yeshiva University rabbinical school for forty-five years, conceptualizes the covenant as consisting of a "covenant of fate" and a "covenant of destiny," which together comprise all of Jewish existence. The covenant of fate was made in Egypt when God imposed His sovereignty and compelled the Israelites to become His people. While the covenant of fate has produced loneliness, alienation, and suffering, it has also resulted in shared experiences, mutual responsibilities, and the obligation to perform acts of loving-kindness for other Jews. By contrast, the covenant of destiny results from free will, when the Jewish people affirmatively consented to receive the Torah at Sinai. This existence is active, directed, substantive, and holy. "Destiny is the font out of which flow the unique self-elevation of the nation and the unending stream of Divine inspiration that will not run dry so long as the path of the People is demarcated by the laws of God." The covenant of Destiny elevates and completes the covenant of Fate and transforms the Jewish people into a nation. These two covenants join together into an "integrated whole ... [and] a distinct covenantal unit."[1]

R. Lord Jonathan Sacks, Chief Rabbi of the United Hebrew Congregations of the Commonwealth (United Kingdom), places the covenantal relationship "[a]t the core of Jewish faith," with Torah as "the constitution of the covenant." He explains that "there is theology, but beyond that there is covenant, the bond between God and a singular people." For R. Sacks, "one of [Judaism's] primary expressions is narrative: telling the story of the covenantal people through time."[2] He understands "covenantal societies" as existing "to honor a pledge, a moral bond, an undertaking, and that is why you have to tell the story to successive generations ... because it reminds everyone who is there and why they are there." This covenantal storytelling is how "Jews sustained a sense of belonging to a nation."[3] R. Sacks characterizes the covenant as "immune to history" yet paradoxically "realised in history," and thus conceives of Judaism as "peculiarly posed between timelessness and time."[4] R. Sacks also understands the covenant as radically ahead of its time. In particular, the covenant "set moral limits to the exercise of power[,]" "inspired the birth of freedom" that exists today in Western society, and established that "there is no legitimate government without the consent of the governed."[5]

R. Eugene Borowitz, a distinguished professor at Hebrew Union College, uses the covenant as the central metaphor in his groundbreaking theology of post-modern Judaism. R. Borowitz uses this metaphor to explain the relationship among God, the Jewish people, and the Jewish individual. The newfound need to factor in the self-determining individual is due to a modern "commitment to the religious significance of the autonomous self." In this new configuration, God remains primary, and the Jewish community continues to be essential. R. Borowitz's innovation is that "Jewish autonomy becomes the use of our freedom in terms of our personal participation in the people of Israel's covenant with God as the latest expression of its historic tradition." Said otherwise, "We employ our will rightfully when God serves as its limiting condition, better, as our partner in decision making."[6] In R. Borowitz's conceptualization, the covenant has broadened from bilateral (God and the Jewish people) to trilateral (God, the Jewish people, and the individual Jew), but it remains as central as ever.

For all three of these thinkers, the covenant is not only fundamental, but also all-encompassing. The covenant embraces the full sweep of Jewish history, including the Holocaust and the establishment of the State of Israel, as well as the relationships among Jews and between Jews and all of humanity. The covenant spans religion, society, and politics. Yet, for all its breadth, the covenant begins with a series of interactions and agreements between God and Abraham described in Genesis 12 to 17. These interactions progressively depict the full extent of the covenant, beginning with God's promises to multiply Abraham's descendants and give them the Land of Israel, followed by Abraham's acceptance of God as the one and only divine Ruler. As the covenant evolves, it becomes binding not only on Abraham but also on all the generations that follow for eternity.[7]

The essential role of covenant in Jewish identity is evident from its wide range of manifestations in the Torah. As we will see, the covenant plays a prominent role in the Biblical precept of reward and punishment and in pivotal episodes in the Biblical epic, most prominently, the Exodus from Egypt, the Sinaitic Revelation, and entry into the Land of Israel. The covenant is inextricably bound up with sacred objects, such as the tablets inscribed with the Ten Commandments and the ark that carried them. The covenant is also central to Shabbat, a quintessential cornerstone of Jewish life.

During the First Temple period, the later prophets focus on the covenant to frame their plea that the Jewish people should return to God. In this context, the covenant is mostly bereft of its legal implications; rather, these prophets emphasize God's love and the covenant's eternality despite the Jewish people's infidelity. While the covenant is not as prominent in the rabbinic legal texts of the Talmud, the rabbis nevertheless understood the importance of the covenant as the overarching reason for their legal discourses and religious belief system. Explicit references to the covenant also appear in a few prayers that we traditionally recite daily today in the morning service, such as a meditation following the morning blessings ("We are Your people, the children of Your covenant")[8] and the *U'vah L'Tzion* prayer at the service's conclusion ("'As for Me, this is My covenant with them,' says God").[9] More prominent is the *zichronot* ("memories") section of the Musaf service on Rosh HaShana, which is, in part, a plea to God to remember His covenant despite our straying ways.

The covenant defines Jewish life and is the most basic premise of Jewish existence. Without the covenant binding God and the Jewish people, there would be no a priori reason to observe the Torah's commandments (mitzvot), no concept of divine reward and punishment, and no particular significance to the Land of Israel. Membership in the covenant characterizes the totality of Jewish religious identity; it precedes the ability to distinguish between good and evil, to perform mitzvot, and to relate meaningfully to other human beings. The covenant constitutes the starting point for every Jewish life, just as it embodied the starting point for the Jewish nation. It seems to follow that one cannot be Jewish if one is not a member of the covenant.

This understanding of the covenant as a bedrock of Jewish theology and history brings us to our next line of inquiry: Are women members of the covenant? Is the covenant so fundamental that it transcends the biological, social, and ritualistic differences that characterize traditional Jewish gender-based roles and responsibilities? These are critical threshold questions in considering a covenantal ceremony for newborn girls.

On an anecdotal basis, I have received a range of responses when posing the question of whether women are included in the covenant. Some people immediately answer that women are certainly covenantal members. Others hesitate and ponder a question that they had never before considered. Upon reflection, some ultimately respond that women share in the covenant. Others express doubt about this proposition, but, in my limited personal experience, I have not encountered anyone who has outright disagreed with it.

Rochelle Millen has had a somewhat different experience. She vividly recounts how a young, Orthodox-affiliated man refused to accept her gift of a silk screen on the occasion of the birth of his daughter. This gift was inscribed with the phrase, "Just as she has been entered into the brit [covenant], so shall she be entered into Torah, the marriage canopy, and good deeds," and the young man's explanation for his refusal was that a "girl is not part of the brit." Millen comments, "It is hard to forget even now the certainty—even arrogance—with which this young man excluded all women from the covenant of Israel."[10]

The goal of this chapter is to step beyond contemporary perceptions about the relationship between women and the covenant and to explore the Biblical and rabbinic texts that speak to this crucial issue. In delving into this aspect of the Jewish theology of covenant, we recognize that classic Jewish religious texts are often addressed to men and overall impart to women a social and legal status based on their relationship with men or as "enablers."[11] However, the perspective we use here in exploring these texts is focused and dispassionate. Our aim is simply to ascertain whether classic Jewish texts consider women as covenantal members—regardless of the texts' tone, audience, result, or the like—and, thus, whether newborn girls should symbolically and ceremonially enter into the covenant. We start this journey at the beginning, with Abraham.

COVENANT OF ABRAHAM

As we will see, the covenant between God and Abraham gradually develops from a series of interactions that are recorded in the book of Genesis. The relationship between God and Abram (Abraham's original name) begins in Genesis 12 with God's promise to make Abram into a great nation, bless him, and make his name great. Abram, in turn, agrees to leave his home in Mesopotamia and move to the Land of Canaan, later called Israel, with his wife Sarai (Sarah's original name) and his nephew Lot. Once they move to Canaan, God appears to Abram and promises to give Canaan to his descendants. Abram and his family take the resolute step of leaving all that is familiar and traveling to an unseen land because God commands them to do so.

In a second episode in Genesis 13, God again promises to give Abram and his descendants the Land of Canaan forever and to make his descendants innumerable like the dust of the earth. In response to both promises, Abram builds an altar, an indication that he is ready to accept his responsibilities and that Abram and God will have an ongoing relationship.

Abram's third interaction with God is the "covenant between the parts" (*brit ben habitarim*) in Genesis 15. Here, God tells Abram in a vision not to be afraid, since God will protect him and reward him greatly. Despite Abram and Sarai's childlessness, God promises to make their descendants countless like the stars in the sky. Furthermore, God promises to grant Abram a long life, return Abram's descendants to Canaan after an exile, and give them Caanan as an inheritance. For his part, Abram accepts the responsibilities that God has given him; he believes in God and thinks of God favorably. Commenting on Genesis 15:6, R. Obadiah ben Jacob Seforno (sixteenth-century Italy) interprets Abram's belief as an unquestionable conviction that God will always do what He says, and Nachmanides explains that Abram realizes for the first time that God's promises are unconditional. Abram divides three animals down the middle and lays each half against the other. God then lights a fire between these halves. With these mutual symbols, God makes a covenant (brit) with Abram that day.

A fourth experience occurs in Genesis 17 when God appears to Abram and instructs him to walk before Him and to be perfect or complete (*tamim*). God promises to make a covenant with Abram, and changes Abram's name to Abraham (meaning "a father of many nations"). God reiterates His earlier promises that Abraham will spawn a numerous and great nation and that God will be the eternal God for this nation and give them Canaan "for an everlasting holding." God establishes an eternal covenant throughout the generations "to be a God to you and your descendants who follow." Accepting God's command to keep the covenant, Abraham circumcises himself, his son Ishmael, and all the men in his household. God says of circumcision, which must occur on a boy's eighth day of life, that "this is my covenant that you will guard between Me and you and between your descendants" and that it is a "sign of the covenant between Me and you." God then changes Sarai's name to Sarah. God blesses Sarah and proclaims that she will give birth to a son in a year and that kings will emanate from her. This son's name will be Isaac, and God will establish His covenant with Isaac and his descendents.

In a fifth scene, recorded chapters later, Abraham binds Isaac as a sacrifice (the *akeida*) in an astounding show of faith. It is significant that, after Isaac is released, the angel who speaks with Abraham promises him multitudinous descendants and an inheritance (Genesis 22:17–18).

By following the flow of these interactions between God and Abraham, we realize that all these episodes, along with their corresponding agreements, together comprise the covenant of Abraham. As each encounter unfolds, we see how God and Abraham, over time, nurture a relationship based on mutual trust and some amount of give-and-take. R. Menachem Leibtag of Yeshivat Har Etzion (Alon Shevut, Israel) identifies the unifying theme that, in the first four episodes recounted above, "God tells A[b]raham four times that his offspring [*zera*] will become a nation in a special land [*aretz*]." R. Leibtag therefore considers these episodes to be "revelatory." He also provides specific contextual reasons for each interaction,[12] thereby reinforcing the notion that these interactions are each distinct, yet collectively significant. In addition, due to the angel's covenantal promises to Abraham, the binding of Isaac could be construed as a culminating episode of the covenant of Abraham.

All told, the substantive content of the covenant of Abraham is that (1) God will make Abraham the father of a nation with innumerable descendants and will give this nation a land of its own, and (2) Abraham believes in God and accepts the responsibility of fathering a nation. It follows that Abraham's acceptance of circumcision is one episode in a long series of interactions in which God and Abraham cultivate their relationship and the terms of the covenant of Abraham coalesce. While circumcision is distinguishable as a physical mark and a commandment for all generations, it draws significance from the broader context of the covenant's development.

The result of this interpretation is that the covenant of Abraham, which ultimately becomes the covenant between God and Israel, is by no means exclusive to men—despite the fact that circumcision is. As Abraham's descendants, all Jews are, at birth, part of the Jewish nation and members of the covenant that has embraced every generation since Abraham. The primary elements of the covenant are the establishment of a Jewish nation in Israel, a steadfast belief in God, and God's eternal love for the Jewish people. These elements are so fundamental to the core of Jewish existence that they apply to both men and women, regardless of the secondary differences between the sexes and regardless of the fact that penile circumcision is feasible only for men.

The text of the Torah does not imply that Abraham somehow represents Jewish men and Sarah represents Jewish women.[13] Rather, Abraham and Sarah work together as a unit to found the Jewish nation on God's command. For example, R. Isaac Ben Judah Abrabanel (the Abrabanel; fifteenth to early sixteenth-century Portugal, Spain, and Italy) explains that God changed Sarai's name to Sarah to signify to Abraham that "it is appropriate that [Sarah] will be a partner with you [Abraham] in all the good that will accrue to you, since [Sarah] is from your self, and flesh of your flesh."[14] The Abrabanel thus views Abraham and Sarah as partners or even as practically a single entity.

According to this interpretation, the text assumes that the acts of Abraham and Sarah together deepen the covenantal relationship. For example, it is significant that Abraham and Sarah journey together to Canaan. Furthermore, Abraham's name change, articulated belief in God, and circumcision are all components of the covenant, as are Sarah's name change and her birthing of Isaac.[15] Another crucial constituent is Sarah's recognition that Ishmael, Isaac's half-brother, must be exiled in order to preserve the covenantal lineage through Isaac (Genesis 21:10).[16]

All these components work in concert and occur in a particular order; together, they comprise one covenant. For example, R. Nissim ben Reuven (the Ran; fourteenth-century Spain) emphasizes that God did not change Abram's name until he was circumcised and "complete," and that God did not change Sarai's name, in turn, until Abram's name was changed (Genesis 17:15–16). Along the same lines, the Tosafists (schools of primarily French Talmudists, circa twelfth–fourteenth centuries) explain that Sarah did not become pregnant with Isaac until Abraham was circumcised.[17]

Thus, the totality of all these covenantal actions and interactions—whether involving Abraham, Sarah, or both—comprise the covenant of Abraham. The fact that Abraham, who interacts directly with God, happens to be a man does not limit covenantal membership to men. Indeed, identifying one's covenantal status with either Abraham or Sarah based on one's sex misses the key point of the non-physicality, transcendence, and singularity of the covenant. The covenant of Abraham, which represents the genesis of the eternal covenant, encompasses all Jews—men and women alike.

OTHER PENTATEUCHAL TEXTS

Other Biblical passages support the premise that both women and men are members of the covenant. One dramatic example is the requirement to stone to death "a man *or a woman* who perpetuates wickedness in the eyes of God, transgressing His covenant" (Deuteronomy 17:2). If the person is found, after an investigation, to have worshipped other gods, then "you will take that man *or that woman* that did this wicked thing to your gates and stone them until they die" (Deuteronomy 17:5). Likewise, the "curses of the covenant" will befall "any man *or woman* or family or tribe whose heart turns today from the Lord your God to go to worship the gods of these nations" (Deuteronomy 29:17, 20). If both men and women are expected to adhere to the covenant on pain of death (and idol worship is anathema in the covenantal framework), it follows that both men and women must be members of the covenant in the first place.

In its description of the commandment for a national assembly and public Torah reading (*hakhel*), the Pentateuch explicitly mentions women alongside men, and defines the "nation" of Israel to encompass both:

Moses commanded them saying: "Every seven years . . . when all of Israel comes to appear before the Lord your God in the chosen place, you will read this Torah before all of Israel in their ears. Gather the nation: the men, the women, and the children, and the strangers that are in your gates, in order that they will listen, and in order that they will learn and fear the Lord your God, and be careful to observe all of the words of this Torah (Deuteronomy 31:10–12).

Hakhel embodies the covenant by dramatically reinforcing the Jewish people's inextricable connection to the Torah's commandments and their fear of God. Indeed, R. Jonathan Sacks characterizes hakhel as a "covenant renewal ceremony."[18] Women's explicit obligation for hakhel thus demonstrates their inclusion in the Jewish nation and the covenant.[19]

Deuteronomy 29:9–13 also explicitly includes women as members of the covenant:

You stand today, all of you, before the Lord your God, your heads of your tribes, your elders, and your officers, all the men of Israel, your children, your wives . . . to enter you into the covenant of the Lord your God and His oath that the Lord your God makes with you today. In order to establish with you today for a nation for Him, and He will be for you a God. . . .

These passages, unlike others, are spoken to the men who functioned in ancient times as the heads of their households. As a result, Jewish feminists have noted that the content of the covenant here, in both grammar and substance, is addressed to these male heads of household, rather than directly to both men and women.[20] Despite this indisputable point, it is nonetheless clear that all of those mentioned—men, women, and children—entered into the covenant that day and, therefore, that these passages confirm women's membership in the covenant. It is noteworthy that the last of the Ten Commandments (Exodus 19:14), for example, is likewise spoken to men ("Do not covet the wife of your fellow man"). Yet, one would be hard-pressed to argue that, on this basis, women need not adhere to the Ten Commandments.

The Revelation at Sinai, where the Israelites accept God's commandments, is a defining moment in the covenantal relationship, and the vast majority of Scriptural references to the covenant in the context of Revelation do not differentiate according to gender (notwithstanding the language of the final commandment). For example, in Exodus 24, Moses builds at the foot of Mount Sinai an altar upon which young people bring sacrifices. He reads from the "book of the covenant," whereupon the people dramatically answer, "*Na'aseh v'nishma*—We will do and we will listen." Moses then sprinkles the sacrificial blood on the Israelites and says, "Here is the blood of the covenant that God has made with you regarding all of these matters" (Exodus 24:8). It is significant that this sacrificial blood at Revelation constitutes "covenantal blood" in the Pentateuch. Although the association between covenantal blood and male circumcision has become magnified over time (as we will see later), the covenantal blood that appears at Revelation represents the covenant for all Israelites, without distinction between men and women.

Other examples involving Revelation are likewise not gender-specific. Immediately before the Revelation, God says that if the Israelites listen to God and keep His covenant, then they will be a treasure (*s'gulah*) for Him (Exodus 19:5). In addition, after the sin of the golden calf, when God gives Moses the second set of tablets, God says that He is making a covenant with the nation (Exodus 34:10). After Moses writes down a compilation of laws and precepts, God says that He has made a covenant with Moses and the people and calls these writings *divrei habrit,* the words of the covenant (Exodus 34:27–28). None of these stirring passages distinguish between men and women.

A verse that initially appears more difficult to understand is Moses's instruction to "the nation" immediately before the Sinaitic Revelation to "[b]e ready in three days; do not come near a woman" (Exodus 19:15). Professor Judith Plaskow has termed this verse a paradigm of "the profound injustice of the Torah itself." She asserts that this verse highlights the invisibility of women even at a time as crucial as the Revelation, thereby "provok[ing] a crisis for the Jewish feminist." She also mentions, however, that the rabbis re-interpret this verse to include women.[21] Along similar lines, Rachel Adler envisions the foremothers sitting under Mount Sinai, "eavesdropping between God and man, wondering if there is anything God wants you to do and, if so—why doesn't He tell you so Himself?"[22]

These are thoughtful reactions to the difficulty inherent in this verse. However, given our limited focus here, we respond with the observation that this pre-Revelation passage is a prooftext for women's inclusion in the covenant. Even a reference to separating from women evidences that women were present at Mount Sinai. Plaskow observes this point as well.[23] In addition, midrashim commenting on Exodus 19:15 affirmatively insert women into the Revelation scene, as we will see later in this chapter. This exegetical gloss speaks volumes about the rabbis' discomfort with Exodus 19:15 and their belief that women are indeed covenantal members.

This midrashic inclusion of women at Revelation comports with the distinction posited by R. Eliezer Berkovits (1908–1992, Europe, Australia, the United States, and Israel) between "Torah-tolerated" Judaism, an early phase in the evolving status of women when they are considered nonpersons, and "Torah-taught" Judaism, a later phase in this evolution when women are respected as people. R. Berkovits outlines the goal of eliminating the "Torah-tolerated" phase and cementing women's status today based on the "Torah-taught" phase.[24] R. Berkovits' cutting-edge interpretation dovetails with Blu Greenberg's observation that "[t]he stratification of men and women in Judaism simply reflects the male-female hierarchical status in all previous societies in human history."[25] This is not an apology, but rather a fact. The Torah both reflects the times in which it was given and innovates in substantial ways within these bounds.

Furthermore, focusing on Exodus 19:15 overlooks the vast majority of references to the covenant not only during Revelation, but also throughout the Pentateuch, which do not differentiate between men and women. The Torah exhorts the Israelites in dramatic language about the terms of the covenant: if the Israelites follow God's laws and commandments, then they will be blessed with plentiful food, offspring, rain, land, and military success, but if they forsake the covenant, then they will be cursed with suffering and destruction (Leviticus 26; Deuteronomy 4, 7, 8, and 28). The Torah emphasizes that although God will avenge violations of the covenant, He will remember the covenant with the patriarchs and will not destroy Israel or the covenant (Leviticus 26:25, 42–44; Deuteronomy 4:31). While the covenant demands that Israel keeps God's commandments, it also encompasses God's love (Deuteronomy 7:7–9) and His promise to keep Israel as His special nation and not to forsake them (Leviticus 26:44; Deuteronomy 4:31, 7:6). All these passages, and many others, articulate a fundamental reward and punishment dynamic, coupled with God's promise of perpetual nationhood, and none of these passages are gender-specific or speak only to men. Women, like men, are required to keep commandments (a point discussed below) and are subject to punishment for failing to do so.

PROPHETS AND WRITINGS

As in the Pentateuch, references to the covenant in the Prophets and Writings are largely gender-neutral. Many of these references relate to the covenant's continuity despite Israel's straying from the covenant through idol worship and other transgressions. These passages often use gentle, loving language[26] and speak of restoration, forgiveness, and praise to God for remembering His covenant.[27] Some of these passages refer to the everlasting covenant (*brit olam*)[28] and the ultimate salvation.[29] A few passages refer to breaking the covenant.[30] Jeremiah 34:18–19 even refers to the *brit ben habitarim*, Abraham's "covenant of the pieces" (Genesis 15). Taken together, these broadly worded, sometimes-lyrical passages provide a clear picture of the brit as a sacred and resilient covenant between God and the Jewish people, both men and women. By contrast, circumcision is referenced only a handful of times in the Prophets and Writings, typically as a descriptor or metaphor (for example, Jeremiah 6:10, 9:24–25). Even the account of the mass circumcision that occurred after the Israelites crossed the Jordan River (Joshua 5:2–8) makes no explicit mention of the covenant (although it does refer to the Exodus from Egypt). The covenant thus transcends the physical symbolism of circumcision.

Ezekiel 16 bolsters this conclusion. This is a well-studied chapter, in which the prophet uses a female character to allegorize Jerusalem and its covenantal relationship with God. The episode opens with a baby girl who is unwashed and uncared for, wallowing in her birth blood. God says to the baby, "in your bloods live; . . . in your bloods live" (Ezekiel 16:6). God causes this baby to mature into a woman, covers her nakedness, enters into a covenant with her, and proclaims, "You became Mine." God washes off the birth blood, anoints her with oil, and gives her food, jewelry, and beautiful clothes. Not remembering her youth, however, the woman prostitutes herself to the nations, even worshipping idols using the gifts that God gave her. As a result, God promises to uncover her nakedness and judge her, and to cause her lovers to stone her and attack her with swords. The moral of this story is that God will cause Jerusalem to own up to its abominations since it "desecrated the oath in destroying the covenant." Still, God will remember His covenant with Jerusalem from the "days of its youth," establish an everlasting covenant, and forgive Jerusalem. With its central female character, this poignant chapter conveys a connection, albeit allegorical, between women and the covenant.

Ezekiel 16:6–9 describes how the allegorical girl matures and enters into a covenant with God. However, as we will see in the following chapter, Ezekiel 16:6 ("in your bloods live") is today commonly deemed integral to the circumcision liturgy. I was intrigued, therefore, when I saw that Ezekiel 16:6 was recited as part of a girl's welcoming ceremony that was held in 1998.[31] The most interesting aspect of this ceremony is that it reclaims this dramatic Biblical verse by presenting it as an expression of women's inclusion in the covenant. The ceremony text even characterizes Ezekiel 16:6–9 as "God's words of covenant to a female Israel."

Like Ezekiel 16, passages in Zechariah referring to the Messiah (9:9–11) present an allegory that connects women, blood, and the covenant. God speaks directly to a "daughter of Zion" and a "daughter of Jerusalem," saying, "Also for you [aht], in the blood of your covenant [dam b'riteich], I have sent your prisoners from the pit that has no water." This is a particularly striking linkage between women and covenant, since the phrase *the blood of your covenant*—which would likely be associated today with male circumcision—refers to a woman, and the pronouns *you* and *your* are in the female grammatical form. Significantly, R. Shlomo Yitzchaki (Rashi; eleventh- to twelfth-century France) states that Zechariah's "blood of your covenant" refers to the blood sprinkled on the people during Revelation in Exodus 24. With this interpretation, we come full circle. Rashi expands upon the joining of women, blood, and covenant in Zechariah 9 to demonstrate that women share in the covenantal blood of Revelation.

Other episodes in the Prophets and Writings vividly illustrate a different pertinent point: the importance of voluntary reaffirmations of the covenant. In II Kings 22 and 23,[32] King Josiah of Judea reads a book of the Torah (thought to be Deuteronomy), which was found in the Temple. A believer in God at a time of rampant idol worship among his people, Josiah tears his clothes and seeks the counsel of the prophet Chulda. She prophesies that God will "bring evil" to the Judeans because of their idol worship, but only after Josiah's death. In an effort to lead his people back to God, Josiah reads the Book of the Covenant (*Sefer HaBrit*) in the Temple to the entire gathered nation. Josiah reaffirms the covenant "to walk after God, keep His commandments, testimonies, and laws with every heart and soul, and to establish the words of this covenant written in the book." At this point, "the entire nation stood with the covenant." Josiah proceeds to destroy idolatry and root out idolatrous priests, and commands the entire nation to observe Passover.

A second covenantal reaffirmation is found in Nehemiah 8. This chapter speaks of the faith of the Jews who returned to Israel following the First Temple's destruction and the Babylonian exile. After repairing the walls of Jerusalem, "the entire nation" requests that Ezra the Scribe bring "the Book of the Torah." Standing on a wooden platform, Ezra reads the Torah for many hours to the congregated men and women. When Ezra opens the Torah, the assembly stands, and when Ezra blesses God, the assembly answers "Amen, Amen" and bows down before God. Ezra and Nehemiah declare the day holy and instruct the people to feast and not to mourn or cry; the people nonetheless cry upon hearing the words of Torah. They then study Torah and celebrate the Sukkot festival (Feast of Tabernacles).

These episodes in II Kings and Nehemiah demonstrate that voluntary reaffirmations of the covenantal bond are valued and encouraged and that such activities do not require divine instruction or invitation. Furthermore, the explicit involvement of both men and women in the reaffirmation in Nehemiah substantiates the inclusion of women in the covenant.

EXEGETICAL SOURCES

The rabbis of the Talmudic and post-Talmudic periods did not address at any length the philosophical question of whether women are included in the covenant. It apparently was not a relevant issue in their exhaustive discussions of Jewish law and lore. This may be because the rabbis simply assumed that women were part of the fundamental covenant of God and Israel. Nonetheless, rabbinic sources, taken together, convey the viewpoint that women are covenantal members. Professor Shaye Cohen reports that he has not been able to locate a single rabbinic text that implicitly or explicitly excludes women from the covenant.[33]

The exegesis of midrashic texts demonstrates the belief that women are covenantal members. The Sifra (Bechukotai 8:9), for example, notes that the foremothers are not included in the verse, "I will remember My covenant with Jacob, and even my covenant with Isaac, and even My covenant with

Abraham I will remember, and I will remember the Land" (Leviticus 26:42). The midrash's solution is that the untranslatable article *et,* which precedes each of the verse's three mentions of *covenant,* actually refers to the foremothers.[34] Thus, God remembers His covenant with both the forefathers (stated explicitly) and the foremothers (understood implicitly). Here, the rabbis go out of their way to insert women affirmatively into the covenant.

Other examples specify both men and women as covenantal members. The Fourth Commandment states that Shabbat restrictions apply to "you, your sons and daughters, your male servants and female servants, your cattle, and the strangers within your gates" (Exodus 20:10). In its exegesis on this verse, the Mechilta characterizes both male and female servants as "children of the covenant" (*b'nei brit*).[35] Men and women, therefore, both have a place in the covenant.

The Damascus Document (circa 100 BCE or earlier),[36] one of the Dead Sea Scroll texts, demonstrates a similar point with different terminology. The Damascus Document's language is fiery and covenant-centric, exhorting sectarians to uphold the responsibilities and expectations of members of the covenant of God.[37] A statute in the document instructs that a man "shall not sell to [gentiles (*goyim*)] his manservant and maidservant, for [the servants] entered with him into the covenant of Abraham [Brit Avraham]."[38] Sectarian Jews living in the late Second Temple era thus believed that both men and women (that is, Jewish manservants and maidservants) are members of the covenant of Abraham, a term typically (yet erroneously) associated today with circumcision. The Damascus Document demonstrates a belief that the covenant of Abraham is not defined by circumcision, but rather, is synonymous with the broader covenant between God and the Jewish people. This statute also supports the notion that the covenant of Abraham is the amalgamation of several episodes in Genesis, and is not limited only to the episode in Genesis 17, which introduces the commandment of circumcision.

A different set of midrashim and aggadot go to great lengths to insert women into the defining experience of the Sinaitic Revelation. These texts recast Moses's pre-Revelation instruction to the "nation" to "[b]e ready in three days; do not approach a woman" (Exodus 19:15).[39] At first glance, this verse seems to exclude women from the covenant, since men are instructed to refrain from contact with women, apparently to ensure the men's purity so that they can receive the Torah. The Mechilta, however, flips this interpretation around. The midrash explains that this verse refers to the specific halachic precept that women with residual, post-coital seminal discharge, who are considered ritually impure (*tameh*), become ritually pure (*tahor*) after three days elapse.[40] Centuries later, R. Menachem Meiri (thirteenth- and early fourteenth-century Spain) confirms that women can avoid this type of ritual impurity as long as they refrain from intercourse for three days. It follows that Moses's instruction to "not approach a woman" is actually for the benefit of the Israelite women, since this abstinence ensures the women's ritual purity and their participation in Revelation.[41] In a similar vein, the Tanchuma notes that the Israelite women did not menstruate in the desert since the presence of God (Shechina) was with them.[42] As a result, these women remained ritually pure both during and after Revelation. Some today view with distaste, or even contempt, the Jewish tradition's character- ization of uterine discharges as "impure," while others justify, re-interpret, or embrace traditional attitudes toward female blood. Regardless, these mi- drashic glosses on Exodus 19:15, taken at face value, demonstrate the rabbis' staunch belief that women were integral participants in Revelation and that women received the Torah, the written embodiment of the covenant.

Relatedly, the Mechilta's exegesis has God, through Moses, address- ing both men and women as members of the covenant. When Moses is on Mount Sinai, God instructs him to say to "the House of Jacob" (*Beit Yaakov*) and "the Children of Israel" (*B'nai Yisrael*) that God has "put you on the wings of eagles and brought you to Me." Furthermore: "If you will listen to My voice and keep My covenant, and you will be for Me a trea- sure . . . and a holy nation" (Exodus 19:3–6). The Mechilta interprets "the House of Jacob" to mean the women and "the Children of Israel" to mean the men. This midrash also provides an alternate explanation that Moses should speak to the women (the House of Jacob) using soft language and provide them with basic information, whereas Moses should detail the in- formation for the men (the Children of Israel). In so doing, Moses relays divine statements "even to the women."[43] This second, alternate interpre- tation exhibits a bias against women's capabilities and accordingly limits their access to the full extent of God's communication to the people. This perspective reflects the gender-based societal expectations that prevailed at the time that the midrash was written.

However, the key point is that both midrashic glosses explicitly regard women as participants in Revelation. The Mechilta is addressing why the

Biblical text here refers to the Israelites in two different ways (House of Jacob and Children of Israel), and there is no particular impetus to answer this question by identifying women (or men) in the narrative. This interpretation is therefore significant and signals an intent to portray women at Revelation. Centuries later, Pirkei d'Rabbi Eliezer (chapter 41) echoes the Mechilta's exegesis and even has the men and women "answer[ing] altogether in one voice, 'All that God has spoken we will do and we will hear'" (Exodus 24:7).

Women's inclusion at Revelation is also evident in the Talmudic opinions (BT Yevamot 46a–46b, Keritot 9a) that the Israelites who left Egypt "converted to Judaism" upon receiving the Torah. In particular, the Israelite men "converted" via circumcision and the Israelite women did so via mikvah immersion. By immersing, the Israelite women "enter[ed] under the wings of the Shechina [God's presence]." These Talmudic sources indicate, therefore, that the generation of women who left Egypt entered into the covenant, since their ritual of mikvah immersion runs parallel to the covenantal ritual of circumcision. Furthermore, these texts depict women as participating in Revelation alongside men, perhaps to dampen the impact of Moses's instruction to the men not to "approach a woman."

Many centuries after these midrashim and aggadot were expounded, R. Yair Chaim Bachrach (seventeenth-century Germany) stated that women were "without a doubt present at the holy standing," that is, the Revelation, and were included as Israelites present there. R. Bachrach adds that women are "certainly included in the acceptance of the entire Torah."[44] Women's receipt of the Torah—the covenant's charter—indicates their inclusion in the covenant itself.

In some midrashim, the women take the lead at Sinai, based on the text's placement of the *House of Jacob* (the women) before the *Children of Israel* (the men) (Exodus 19:3). The Tanchuma, for example, states that women received the Torah before the men.[45] In a related formulation, Pirkei d'Rabbi Eliezer (chapter 41) recounts that God instructs Moses at Mount Sinai to first ask the women if they wish to receive the Torah, "since it is the way of men to go after the minds of the women." While modern readers may be uncomfortable with this phrasing and its underlying assumptions, the upshot is the rabbinic belief that women are Torah recipients and covenantal members (and that they may even have an elevated covenantal status).

The rabbinic sources that are most interesting to me innovatively reframe the commandment of circumcision to affirmatively place women in the covenant. These medieval interpretations not only validate women's covenantal membership, but also shine a positive, inclusive light on women's relationship with the distinctively male rite of circumcision. Joseph ben Isaac (the Bechor Shor; twelfth-century northern France), commenting on Genesis 17:11, asserts that menstruation rituals are the covenantal symbol for women, just as circumcision is the covenantal symbol for men. He explains that these practices—in which menstruating women refrain from sexual relations until immersing in a mikvah a week after uterine bleeding stops—are for women "blood of the covenant [dam brit]." Thus, not only are women covenantal members, but they even have their own blood-centric, covenantal rituals directly analogous to circumcision.

The Bechor Shor's interpretation appears to draw on the Talmud's parallel treatment of the forefathers' circumcision and the foremothers' mikvah immersion (BT Yevamot 46a–46b, Keritot 9a). The Bechor Shor, however, substantially broadens this parallel. He boldly pronounces menstruation rituals as analogous to circumcision for all generations (rather than only for the generation redeemed from Egypt), and explicitly characterizes these practices as a covenantal symbol. The Bechor Shor's thinking likely reflects the trend in the early and high Middle Ages of attributing spiritual power to the blood of circumcision.[46] But ultimately, the Bechor Shor's interpretation answers the question, "Why don't women have their own covenantal symbol?" The response is, "They do." It is noteworthy that the Bechor Shor's line of thinking has resurfaced today from a wholly different vantage point, in that menstruation itself and childbirth have been mentioned as potential female covenantal symbols, since they are centered on both blood and genitals, just like circumcision.[47]

Several centuries after the Bechor Shor, the Abrabanel provides a different innovative spin on circumcision. The Abrabanel states that circumcision imparts holiness not to a circumcised man, but rather to the children he sires, both boys and girls. Thus, "women will be saved with the same covenant as men, since they are born with the same holiness,"[48] that is, since boys and girls are both sired by circumcised men. In this way, circumcision applies for all generations, as God promised Abraham. Furthermore, the outcome of the Abrabanel's novel interpretation is that the covenant encompasses both men and women. Even more interesting is that women are beneficiaries of circumcision itself, which—for obvious reasons—is typically associated only with men.

A beautiful aspect of the Abrabanel's novel interpretation is its emphasis on future generations, since the children of a circumcised man are the primary beneficiaries of circumcision's holiness. The Abrabanel wrote his commentary on Genesis at the end of his life (between 1505 and 1507),[49] after enduring the Spanish Inquisition and the Jewish expulsion from Spain. He suffered, despite the advantage of being born into a wealthy and prominent family. By the end of his life, the Abrabanel may have been frustrated with the present and focused on the future, hoping that the Jewish condition would improve for subsequent generations.

Finally, one exceptional modern source from the commentary of R. Yehuda Brandes (head of Beit Morasha in Jerusalem) compares a woman's first intercourse (defloration) with circumcision,[50] thereby introducing a different perspective on the relationship among women, the covenant, and circumcision. R. Brandes comments on a statement by the French Tosafists (twelfth–fourteenth centuries), which defines the Talmudic term "sexual intercourse of mitzvah" (Ketuvot 4a) to mean the first intercourse of marriage, performed for purposes of procreation. The Tosafists elaborate that "a woman does not enter into a covenant [koretet brit] except with one who makes her into a vessel," that is, a sexual partner. While covenant apparently means marriage in this context, R. Brandes highlights the Tosafists' covenantal language by pointing out a striking parallelism between a boy's circumcision and a woman's first intercourse. Both events involve the genitals, the release of blood, and the removal of "something extra" (a foreskin or a hymen, respectively). R. Brandes elaborates that both circumcision and defloration constitute the fulfillment of commandments and a reason for rejoicing. Furthermore, both bodily changes "complete" the individual; midrashim emphasize that circumcision made Abraham "perfect" (Genesis 17:1), and a woman is deemed "complete" when she is able to procreate. The end result is that R. Brandes implies that a woman's defloration has covenantal overtones. It is interesting that Mary Gendler—who suggested hymenectomy as a covenantal ritual for newborn girls—also identifies parallels between the rupture of the hymen and circumcision, despite her vastly different worldview from that of R. Brandes.

HALACHIC SOURCES

Like the exegetical texts, there are relatively few classic halachic sources that explicitly address whether women are covenantal members. In general, these sources are concerned with the practical issue of structuring the interaction of men and women to maintain their respective religious and social roles. To this end, halachic obligations of women are traditionally fewer than those of men. Rabbinic texts exempt women from positive time-bound commandments, and consistently exclude women from the public religious roles that evolved in rabbinic and post-rabbinic times. As a result, some Jewish feminists conclude that halacha marginalizes women, while traditionalists accept or even praise halacha's sex-role differentiation as natural and socially stabilizing. Our aim, however, is not to consider the halachic system as a whole. Our goal is modest; we simply seek to examine whether the halachic obligations incumbent upon women allow for the conclusion that the rabbis recognized women as covenantal members.

One side of the covenantal relationship is the responsibility of the Jewish people to perform God's commandments. Prominently, R. Moses ben Maimon (Maimonides; 1135–1204, Spain and Egypt) states that forty-six of the sixty "unconditional commandments" are "binding on women and constitute their special covenant." Significantly, these forty-six commandments include the first nine entries on Maimonides's list of positive commandments.[51] These nine—which include believing in God, believing in the unity of God, loving God, fearing God, and worshipping God—are integral to the traditional Jewish belief system and the covenantal framework. Ultimately, therefore, women are obligated to perform these commandments because they are covenantal members.

In the seventeenth century, R. Yair Chaim Bachrach explicitly addresses women's relationship with mitzvot. He asserts that women are fundamentally obligated to perform all 613 Biblical commandments, but that women have been exempted from time-bound positive commandments as a practical matter because of their "particular nature" (a term he does not clarify). R. Bachrach explains that since women received the Torah at Mount Sinai, a woman who takes it upon herself to observe a specific time-bound positive commandment is deemed "obligated" to perform it, and may recite the blessing that God "sanctifies us with His mitzvot and commands us" to perform that mitzvah.[52] Said more broadly, women's essential connection to commandments evidences their inclusion in the covenant, the underlying reason for performing commandments in the first place.

We turn now to some specific, illustrative commandments. For example, Nachmanides is adamant that there is a "negative commandment" that one must not forget the experience of standing at Mount Sinai.[53] This idea is so intrinsic that some medieval and modern scholars do not count it as a commandment, explaining that it encompasses the entire Torah. However, to the extent that not forgetting Revelation is a Biblical commandment, it applies to men and women, both of whom are obligated in all negative commandments. This halachic obligation is consistent with the midrashic portrayal of women receiving the Torah at Mount Sinai and evidences women's inclusion in the covenant that was consecrated that day.

Another pertinent example is the commandment to study Torah. Women are exempt from this commandment,[54] and there is Talmudic rhetoric regarding women's exclusion from Torah study that is nothing short of extreme.[55] This vehemence, however, is juxtaposed with the praise heaped upon the pursuit of Torah study.[56] It follows that women's exemption from the mitzvah of learning Torah was apparently used as a practical means of separating men's public sphere from women's private sphere. This prevalent societal configuration, however, does not impact women's transcendent relationship with the covenant. As R. Eliezer Berkovits explains, "It is true that women are not commanded to study Torah, but are they not still part of the Jewish people to whom the Torah was given? They are Jews because of the Torah!"[57] It is also noteworthy that R. Moses of Coucy (circa thirteenth-century France) holds that women are obligated to learn the laws that pertain to them (although not to fulfill the commandment to learn Torah),[58] and late medieval and early modern authorities agree.[59]

The mitzvah of prayer also implicates women's connection to the covenant. Women are obligated to pray (M. Brachot 3:3), and this obligation applies although prayer could be construed as a time-bound mitzvah from which women are generally exempt. Fundamentally, women are required to pray since prayer is "considered [a request for divine] mercy" (BT Brachot 20b) and may be offered at any time. Late medieval and modern rabbinic authorities reiterate these points.[60] These rulings recognize women's relationship with the Divine and, by extension, with God's eternal covenant.

Two specific prayers bear mention. First is the central prayer of Shema (which begins, "Hear O Israel, the Lord is our God, the Lord is One"). The Talmud states that women are exempt from reciting this prayer despite the Shema's declaration of the "kingdom of heaven," the belief that God rules the world.[61] Many centuries later, the foremost halachic code, the *Shulchan Aruch* (by R. Joseph Caro, sixteenth century), echoes this conclusion, but adds that it is proper for women to accept "the yoke of the kingdom of heaven," the belief in God's omnipotence.[62] Some sixteenth- and seventeenth-century halachic authorities go one step further. R. Mordechai Yoffe (the Levush, circa 1530–1612, Bohemia and Poland) says that women should be taught to recite the first two verses of Shema,[63] and R. Yoel Sirkis (the Bach, 1561–1640)[64] and R. Joshua Falk (1555–1614, Poland)[65] hold that women are obligated to accept "the yoke of the kingdom of heaven" and to recite the first verse of Shema. In chipping away at the Talmud's exemption of women from saying the Shema, these rabbis recognize that women should accept the unity and majesty of God—precisely what the covenant demands. Women's recitation of the beginning of Shema rather than the entire prayer speaks to the limitations of women's traditional role in Judaism. For our specific purpose, however, this distinction is beside the point; the key is that these sixteenth- and seventeenth-century opinions confirm women's covenantal membership. These opinions also may draw on the plain assertion of a post-Talmudic "minor tractate" that women are required to recite Shema and to listen to public Torah readings (Sofrim 18:4).

Another significant prayer is the blessing on the Torah (Birkat Ha-Torah), which is recited every morning: "Blessed are You, the Lord our God, King of the Universe, who chose us from all nations and gave us His Torah. Blessed are you God, who gives us the Torah." In his Shulchan Aruch, R. Joseph Caro states that women recite this blessing[66]—despite his warning that one "must be very cautious" in saying Birkat Ha-Torah[67] and his earlier opinion that women are not obligated to recite this blessing.[68] R. Mordechai Yoffe nonetheless expands on R. Caro's statement in the Shulchan Aruch to hold explicitly that women are obligated to recite Birkat Ha-Torah.[69] This blessing is the most exalted of all Torah blessings (BT Brachot 11b) because, as Rashi explains, it gives thanks to God and praises Torah and Israel. Since these are prime components of the covenant, women's recitation of Birkat Ha-Torah, or their requirement to do so, demonstrates their covenantal membership.

We close this section by addressing the technical halachic principle that "All Israel are responsible for one another" (kol yisrael areivim ze l'ze).[70] This rule of "responsibility" (areivut) means that one who has fulfilled a halachic obligation can (or should) repeat it to effect another's fulfillment of the same obligation. R. Asher ben Yechiel (the Rosh; thirteenth–fourteenth centuries, Germany and Spain) states that areivut does not apply to women.[71] However, R. Akiva Eger (eighteenth–nineteenth-century

Poland) and R. Yechiel Michal Epstein (eighteenth-century Lithuania)[72] clarify that women are included in the concept of areivut with respect to those who, for any given mitzvah, have the same obligation as they do. This is the same principle that applies to men. R. Eger and R. Epstein also agree that the Rosh differentiates between men and women only to the extent that there is a difference in personal obligations between them. As R. Epstein explains, "In the mitzvot for which a woman is obligated, she is entirely equal to a man." He furthermore characterizes as "astonishing" the idea that women might not be included in the community of areivut.

This explication of the Rosh's perspective underscores the broader point that areivut is a halachic construct, not a philosophical precept. Said otherwise, although women's exemption from certain mitzvot may limit their opportunities to exercise areivut, women's status as covenantal members remains steadfast. Similarly, midrashim that appear to exclude women from "Israel"[73] are predicated on women's halachic exemption from positive, time-bound commandments and do not affect women's overarching inclusion in the covenant. Moreover, the narrow halachic application of areivut is distinguishable from the more generalized idea that Jews are responsible for each other. For example, the Talmud cites the phrase "all of Israel is responsible for one another" in homelitical contexts where gender differentiation is not relevant (BT Sh'vuot 39a, Sanhedrin 27b). Furthermore, there is at least one mishna that explicitly includes women in "Israel" (M. Terumot 8:12).

MODERN PERSPECTIVES

Contemporary scholars have recognized that classic Jewish sources do not expound upon the question of whether women are covenantal members and, therefore, have addressed this issue head-on. Some modern rabbis answer this question in the affirmative. R. Daniel Sperber states that women are "certainly included" in all the Biblical covenants, excluding that of circumcision.[74] R. Eliezer Berkovits likewise asserts that women are members of the community of Israel and the covenant. In his words: "There is no doubt today that women are part of the Jewish people no less than men. The covenant was concluded with [all of] the Jewish people, and the land [of Israel] and the Torah were given to all of the Jewish people."[75] R. Jonathan Sacks emphasizes that "the partners to the covenant were to be 'all the people'—men, women, and children" and that "citizenship is conceived as being universal." He goes as far as to contrast the universality of the ancient Jewish covenant with women's exclusion from voting in the United States and Britain until as late as the twentieth century.[76] Even R. Moshe Meiselman, who strongly opposes ceremonies marking the covenantal status of girls, agrees that "a woman becomes a member of the covenant automatically at birth."[77]

Some have taken a different tack, raising doubts about whether the Jewish tradition includes women in the covenant. For example, in 1983, Rachel Adler boldly asked, "Have [women] ever had a covenant in the first place? Are women Jews?" She also observed that the "normative contractor of the covenant is the Jewish male." While first theorizing that Jewish women are not "considered to have [been] covenanted," she determines "that the Jewish female cannot be other than a partial and diminished participant" in the covenant.[78] Other scholars agree that women are secondary, lesser, or "nonnormative" players in the covenantal relationship,[79] although at least one scholar maintains that women are "full" members of the covenant.[80]

OUR PERSPECTIVE is narrower and, arguably, more simplistic. We are interested in whether women are members of the covenant and, as a result, whether this status should be ceremonially commemorated. The traditional Jewish sources we have examined—spanning the Bible, Talmud, Midrash, and halachic texts—support the conclusion that women are members of the covenant.

A related result is that the gender-based socio-religious roles of men and women in rabbinic Judaism have no bearing on women's covenantal membership.[81] Traditionally, men have a public religious role and a duty to study Torah, while women have a private and facilitative role and a concomitant exemption from public life. I do not advocate for the perpetuation of these roles today, and many have called for their modification or elimination. The point, however, is that even within this traditional framework, both men and women are members of the covenant. The covenant is singular, transcendent, and integral to Jewish identity, regardless of how that identity is manifested. I therefore cannot conceive of drawing distinctions between "classes" or "levels" of covenantal membership.

Some classic texts go to great lengths to include women in the covenant. For example, the Bechor Shor and Abrabanel characterize women as covenantal members based on a relationship with circumcision, and some midrashim and aggadot insert women into the Revelation experience in response to Biblical texts that, at first glance, appear to marginalize women. Likewise, there are halachic opinions that obligate women to pray and recite Birkat Ha-Torah despite halachic precepts that seem to dictate otherwise. Even the sources that portray women in a negative light or speak only to men nonetheless include women in the covenant. We do not justify or rationalize these difficulties, nor do we deny that rabbinic texts record the opinions of men only. Rather, the point is that focusing on the texts' audience or tone distracts from the substantive conclusion that these texts conceive of women as covenantal members.

Since newborn girls are automatic members of the covenant from birth, it follows that they can and should begin their lives by ceremonially marking the formative symbolism of covenantal entry. Indeed, some Biblical sources (such as II Kings 22–23 and Nehemia 8) demonstrate that voluntary covenantal affirmations are valued and encouraged exercises. The next question is how women's inclusion in the covenant reconciles with their exclusion from the commandment of circumcision. We turn to this question in the next chapter.

The Conflation of Covenant
and Circumcision

We have learned that women are members of the covenant, according to Biblical and rabbinic sources. Why, then, particularly among traditional Jews, is there a pervasive discomfort in connecting women with the covenant? I have observed reactions such as nervous laughter and an obvious sense of uneasiness when, in the course of conversation, I have mentioned the covenantal entry of girls. An immediate, instinctual association of the covenant with boys has also become apparent to me. For example, one friend invited to my youngest daughter's Brit Bat (Covenant of a Daughter) ceremony saw the word *brit* ("covenant") on the invitation and automatically assumed that our newborn was a boy. What is it about the covenant that makes some people think that it is only for males?

To answer these questions, we begin with a story. R. Joseph B. Soloveitchik (the Rav), a leader of American modern Orthodoxy, recounts that his grandfather, R. Hayyim Soloveitchik (R. Hayyim; 1853–1918, Lithuania), head of the illustrious Volozhin Yeshiva, attended a conference of Torah scholars in St. Petersburg in the late nineteenth century. This conference addressed the issue of whether the names of uncircumcised infant boys should be written in the official registers of the Jewish community.[1] The parents of these boys were, in the Rav's words, "assimilationists" who affirmatively chose not to circumcise their sons. From the 1840s to the 1870s, a number of community councils in Germany excluded uncircumcised boys from their registers, thus denying these boys entry into the Jewish community. This controversy was vigorous, with a spectrum of voiced opinions and even the intervention of civil authorities. The rabbis at the conference supported the aggressive move of not registering uncircumcised boys, with the aim of compelling parents to circumcise their sons.[2]

R. Hayyim stood up at the conference and said:

My masters, please show me the halakhah [Jewish law] which states that one who is not circumcised is not a member of the Jewish people. I am aware that a person who is not circumcised may not partake of the sacrifices or the heave offering [*teruma*, food set aside for priests] but I am unaware that he is devoid of the holiness belonging to the Jewish people. To be sure, if he comes of age and does not circumcise himself he is liable to excision [*karet*, a severe divine penalty]. However, he who eats blood and he who violated the Sabbath are also liable to excision. Why then do you treat the uncircumcised infant so stringently and the Sabbath violator so leniently? On the contrary, this infant has not as yet sinned at all, except that his father has not fulfilled his obligation.

Even in the face of a furor over a rejection of circumcision, R. Hayyim asserts that circumcision is not required for membership in the Jewish people, and that refusing to circumcise is no more violative than desecrating Shabbat or transgressing in other ways. After relaying this story about his grandfather, the Rav comments that the rabbis who refused to enter the names of the boys into council registers were correct "[f]rom a political and practical perspective." The Rav thus approves of the rabbis' attempts to compel circumcision. For our purposes here, however, the crux of the Rav's statements is that "on the basis of the pure Halakhah, R. Hayyim was correct."[3]

This story starkly illustrates the pervasive conflation of covenant and circumcision. The rabbis at the conference automatically associated circumcision with joining the Jewish people and, thus, with Jewish identity and the covenant itself. These rabbis therefore suggested that uncircumcised boys are not members of the Jewish people and should not be recorded as such in the municipal registers. The rabbis made these assumptions despite the fact that, as R. Hayyim pointed out, many other Jewish practices and symbols are halachically as weighty as circumcision. Furthermore, the rabbis' assumptions overlook the absence of a halachic basis for singling out circumcision for special treatment or exceptionally stringent enforcement. The rabbis surely felt that the German Reform movement at that time was attacking circumcision in advocating that it has no place in modern society. However, the Reform movement was likewise espousing the belief that other "archaic" practices, such as traditional Shabbat prohibitions, were no longer necessary or required, yet these deviations did not meet with as vociferous a reaction.

The other key point of this story is that both R. Hayyim and the Rav agree that, according to Jewish law, whether a boy is circumcised or not has no impact on his membership in the Jewish people or, said otherwise, in the covenant. This membership is automatically conferred upon birth from a Jewish mother,[4] regardless of whether a circumcision ever occurs. It follows that circumcision and the covenant are distinct and separable concepts in the Jewish tradition, despite the widespread conflation of the two.

As we will learn in this chapter, circumcision and the covenant have been conflated for many centuries, and this prevalent belief remains entrenched today—despite clear evidence to the contrary in traditional Jewish legal texts. The unfortunate result of this misconception is that the commandment of circumcision, which is a covenantal symbol, has obscured and overshadowed the covenant as an independent tenet. Many people, therefore, mistakenly assume that the covenant applies only to the extent that one is or can be circumcised. Since women cannot be circumcised in the manner of men, many Jews today are viscerally uncomfortable with the notion of associating women and the covenant. A few may even outright believe that, on this basis, women are not members of the covenant. Confusing covenant and circumcision, therefore, has the actual or potential effect of wrongly excluding women from the covenant as a matter of common perception.

BLENDING COVENANT AND CIRCUMCISION

Today, the covenant and circumcision have become conflated to such an extent that the two have become practically synonymous. As a result, circumcision has come to represent the covenant to the exclusion of virtually all else. When asked for their first immediate, instinctive association to covenant, Jews of all types invariably respond "circumcision."

One foremost contemporary example of this phenomenon is that people commonly refer to the act of circumcising as *brit milah* ("covenant of circumcision"), rather than simply as *milah* ("circumcision"). This usage first appeared in the Mechilta (on Exodus 19:5),[5] a halachic midrash compiled in the third to fourth century. The term *brit milah* apparently became more widespread by the Middle Ages.[6] It is significant that the Mechilta passage that first used *brit milah* also uses the terminology *brit Shabbat*. This is not surprising since the Torah refers to both circumcision and Shabbat as *ote*, a sign or symbol, and as *brit olam*, an everlasting covenant for all generations

(Genesis 17:7–19; Exodus 31:16). Yet, no one today refers to Shabbat as *brit Shabbat*. This observation highlights the point that, today, circumcision has accrued much greater covenantal recognition than even Shabbat.

In English-speaking countries today, the semantic covenantalization of circumcision has gone one step further with the rampant use of the word *brit* or *bris* (the Ashkenazic pronunciation) to refer to circumcision and the circumcision ceremony. I cannot remember the last time I heard the circumcision ceremony referred to, among English speakers, as anything but *bris*. Thus, *brit* or *bris* is an ill-conceived shorthand for *brit milah*, and *brit milah* is itself a term created long after the word *milah* appeared in the Biblical text.[7] Using *brit* or *bris* ("covenant") to mean the rite of circumcision compounds the entrenched—yet erroneous—notion that the covenant and circumcision are one and the same.

An experience with my six-year-old daughter, Nurit, brings this point into stark relief. At a Shabbat dinner, Nurit showed us the journal that she had just completed in her Jewish day school. Our family had recently attended a circumcision ceremony, and Nurit recounted this experience in her journal by writing that she and her family went to a *bris*. I was incredulous, not believing that this terminology becomes ingrained as early as kindergarten. I was particularly astounded that my own daughter would use the term *bris*. Since my husband and I always carefully refer to a baby boy's ceremony as a *brit milah*, Nurit had not heard the term *bris* in our home. When I asked Nurit where she learned this term, she replied nonchalantly that her teachers said that the ceremony was called a *brit milah* in Hebrew and a *bris* in English. No story could better demonstrate how, in English-speaking societies, the term *bris* has become virtually universal and how the covenant (brit or bris), in turn, has effectively subsumed circumcision (milah).

Other examples abound. A number of halachic works on circumcision use only the term *brit* in the title.[8] The mention of *milah* in the subtitles is not necessary; *brit* clearly conveys to readers the topic of these works. Other illustrations of this practice are found in English-language newspaper articles. For example, a simple search on the *New York Times* website in the archives since 1981 reveals more than thirty articles referring to circumcision as *bris*. The point is not so much the newspaper's inaccurate use of the term *bris* to mean circumcision as the accurate belief that its readership (both Jewish and gentile) understands this intended meaning. This semantic practice has become so commonplace that it has even seeped into the popular culture, turning up on the television show *Seinfeld* in a well-known episode titled "The Bris" (aired in October 1993). In this episode, the show's main characters attend a circumcision ceremony.

In a final example, the terminology *bris* showed up in the legal motion discussed in the Introduction in which an attorney seeks a trial recess in the event that his daughter gives birth to a boy. This attorney defines *bris* as "Hebrew for 'covenant,' for the covenant of Abraham, i.e. ritual circumcision, joyous to everyone except, apparently, the baby."[9] This definition demonstrates how *bris* morphs almost imperceptibly from "covenant" to "circumcision."

The widespread, yet careless, usage of *bris* or *brit* to mean circumcision conveys that circumcision is the only expression of the covenant or, worse, implies that covenant and circumcision actually mean the same thing. While likely meant as a shorthand, this usage has unwittingly stripped the covenant of its independent, prominent status in Judaism.

A different illustration of this conflation is that there are Jews today who circumcise their sons even when most of their other ties to Judaism have frayed. This phenomenon prevails despite oscillating trends and studies about the health effects of circumcision. In the United States, many Jews employ a surgeon in the hospital to circumcise their sons without any ritual, whereas, in Israel, parents employ a ritual circumciser (*mohel*).[10] R. Lawrence Hoffman recounts a story about an American grandmother, unaffiliated with any synagogue and "alienated from contemporary Jewish life," who desperately sought the presence of a rabbi at her grandson's hospital circumcision. In this way, the grandmother attempted to infuse some "Jewishness" into a clinical procedure. R. Hoffman explains that, for this grandmother, "not to have her grandson circumcised in at least a marginally Jewish way seemed to her tantamount to apostasy."[11] Circumcision thus continues to evoke "Jewishness" even when all other observances fall by the wayside.

The most startling manifestation of this blending of circumcision and covenant is that there are parents who express their distaste or outright contempt for circumcision, calling it "genital mutilation" or "child abuse," but who nonetheless circumcise their sons.[12] For example, a friend of mine had mentioned to me, when he was single, that were he to have a son, he would never consider performing circumcision since it mutilates the body. Now that he is married, my friend told me that he would likely circumcise a son. This turnabout is due to the deep-seated misconception that a boy is not

Jewish if he is uncircumcised and that not circumcising a son would sever him completely from his Jewish heritage—something my friend, like many others, is not inclined to do.

Another example brings us back to nineteenth-century Germany. Reform Jews who refused to circumcise their sons were met by a traditional rabbinate that used every ounce of influence it had to compel the practice. "The result was that, unlike many medieval or even ancient ritual practices [that] the German Reform Jews jettisoned, circumcision was brought to North America and practiced. Thus, even among those Reform Jews whose revised form of Judaism hails from Germany, circumcision is generally the norm."[13] Even a movement promoting modernization could not quash the circumcision practice that many deem primitive or irrational and that some earlier Reform practitioners had steadfastly rejected.

Circumcision has been described as "an age-old ritual that has defied all attempts to end it."[14] It is surprising that there is today such strong fidelity to a peculiar practice that some Jews find offensive and that all find difficult to understand. The reason, however, is that there is an ingrained feeling that circumcision is the ultimate symbol of "Jewishness" and that the rite is required to establish a boy's Jewish identity. This feeling stems directly from the prevalent cultural equation of circumcision with covenant.

One modern context for this feeling is where "circumcision may function as the positive assertion of a Jewish refusal to surrender to anti-semitism."[15] Sociologists Eva Kovacs and Julia Vajda, observing the great efforts of post-Holocaust Hungarian Jewry to perform circumcision, conclude that these efforts may "constitute a complex testament to the endurance of Jewish identity under conditions of stress and adversity."[16] Psychologist Elizabeth Wyner Mark takes this idea one step further, commenting that "a discussion that might engender doubt or hesitation about circumcision may be viewed, from a Jewish survivalist point of view, as a morally questionable act."[17] The fact that communities facing anti-semitism would prioritize circumcision as an assertion of Jewish pride demonstrates the belief that circumcision is inextricably bound up with Jewish identity and its covenantal foundation.

SOME EXEGETICAL AND LITURGICAL examples illustrate that this conflation of covenant with circumcision has been long-standing.[18] The first use of the term *brit milah* in the Mechilta is itself a conflation of circumcision and covenant. The basis for the Mechilta's exegesis is God's message to Moses on the eve of the Revelation: "If you [the Israelites] listen to My Voice and keep My covenant, you will be for Me a treasure from among all the nations..." (Exodus 19:5). This verse captures the essence of the covenant between God and Israel at the critical covenantal juncture of Revelation. As the Mechilta continues to explain, however, *covenant* in this verse refers to either the covenant of Shabbat or the covenant of circumcision and against idol worship.[19] The Mechilta thus conflates the covenant with its manifestations of circumcision, Shabbat, and the obliteration of idolatry.

In the same vein, a mishna (Nedarim 3:11) states, "Circumcision [*milah*] is great since, without it, God would not have created the world," and cites God's invocation of "My covenant [*briti*] with day and night" (Jeremiah 33:25). This verse, however, has nothing to do with circumcision and everything to do with the overarching covenant between God and Israel. The passages that follow this verse describe the fall of the House of David (due to a breach of the covenant) and Israel's ultimate return from captivity (due to the perpetuity of the covenant). A related baraita from the Tosefta (Nedarim 2:6) likewise draws "evidence" for the importance of circumcision from a passage depicting the covenant between God and Israel. The baraita proclaims, "Circumcision is great since it equals in value all of the commandments in the Torah," and cites the verse that begins, "This is the blood of the covenant that God entered into" (Exodus 24:8). However, this is not circumcision blood, but rather the blood of sacrifices brought by the Israelites during the Sinaitic Revelation, the moment of communal covenantal entry. By injecting circumcision into Biblical passages describing the covenant, this mishna and baraita imply a one-to-one relationship between circumcision, which is commanded only for men, and the covenant. While linking halachic concepts with tenuously related Biblical verses (*asmachta*) is common in the Talmud, the use of this semantic technique in this particular context allows for the mistaken belief that women are excluded from the covenant.

Another rabbinic text that blends covenant and circumcision is the second blessing of Grace After Meals, "We thank You, the Lord our God, ... for Your covenant that You have sealed into our flesh." This phrase attributes physicality to the covenant, transforming the metaphysical covenant into the physical mark of circumcision. This liturgy also transforms circumcision into the primary—or perhaps the only—manifestation of the covenant. In short, this phrase encapsulates the conflation of circumcision and covenant.

This liturgy for the second blessing of Grace After Meals, which is well-established today, is the product of a relevant discussion in the Babylonian Talmud (Brachot 48b–49a). The Talmud explains that this covenant, which has been "sealed into our flesh" was given in thirteen covenants. This refers to the thirteen times the word *covenant* appears in Genesis 17, the chapter where circumcision is introduced. The Talmud thus equates circumcision with the covenant and continues to use the term *covenant* to mean circumcision in the discussion that follows. The Jerusalem Talmud (Brachot 1:5), however, states that one who does not mention brit (covenant) in the second paragraph of Grace After Meals must return and repeat the paragraph. As Shaye Cohen has pointed out, the Jerusalem Talmud—in stark contrast to the Babylonian Talmud—is referring to the covenant between God and Israel, without any mention of circumcision.[20] This contrast between the two Talmudic collections may demonstrate an evolving conception of identifying the covenant primarily or exclusively with circumcision during the Talmudic era in Babylonia. This connection between covenant and circumcision apparently was not evident a priori or else it would have been referenced in both the Babylonian and Jerusalem traditions.

The Jerusalem Talmud's conception of the covenant in Grace After Meals as the covenant between God and Israel apparently persisted for many centuries after the Talmudic era, and even in Babylonia. Grace After Meals in the siddur of R. Saadia Gaon, written in tenth-century Babylonia, refers to the covenant without mentioning circumcision: "We give thanks to you God our God because you caused us to inherit a pleasant, good, and broad land, covenant and Torah, life and food. . . ."[21] In addition, manuscripts from the Cairo Geniza (discovered in a storeroom of the Ben Ezra Synagogue in Cairo, Egypt, 1896–1897) demonstrate that, in the Mediterranean region in the tenth to thirteenth centuries, the dominant covenantal reference in Grace After Meals was to the covenant between God and Israel, although the interpretation of covenant as circumcision was also extant.[22] Thus, the Grace After Meals reference to the covenant between God and Israel persisted widely even as late as the High Middle Ages, although the association between covenant and circumcision was making inroads as well.

Finally, an excerpt from Pirkei d'Rabbi Eliezer (chapter 29), a ninth-century midrash, provides a particularly colorful example of blending covenant and circumcision. The first part of this excerpt provides that the Israelites were circumcised en masse on the day they left Egypt, based on the verse,

"For the entire nation that went out were circumcised" (Joshua 5:5). This verse, however, recounts a mass circumcision not at the time of the Exodus, but rather when the Israelites entered the Land of Canaan forty years later. By citing this verse out of context, the midrash alludes to the requirement that the Israelite men redeemed from Egypt had to be circumcised prior to partaking of the pascal lamb (Exodus 12:48). Although the Biblical text describing the pascal lamb simply states this requirement, the midrash paints the picture of a dramatic mass circumcision. This exegetical embellishment highlights the connection between circumcision and the Exodus, a pivotal episode in the covenantal epic.

Pirkei d'Rabbi Eliezer proceeds to describe how, on the night before the Exodus, the Israelites eluded the final plague that killed all firstborn Egyptians:

> And [the Children of Israel] would take the blood of circumcision and the blood of Passover [that is, the pascal lamb] and put it on the doorpost[s] of their houses. And when the Holy One, Blessed Be He, passed over to plague Egypt and saw the blood of the covenant [that is, circumcision] and the blood of Passover, He was filled with compassion on Israel, as it is said, "When I passed over you and I saw you wallowing in your bloods, I said to you: 'In your bloods live' (Ezekiel 16:6)."

Here, the midrash understands the plural *bloods* in Ezekiel 16:6 to mean two types of blood, and imagines that the Israelites put a mixture of two bloods on their doorposts to indicate their exclusion from the final plague. This mixture combines the blood of the pascal lamb (as Exodus 12:7 indicates) and the blood of the mass circumcision that the midrash appends to the Exodus narrative. The blood of the pascal lamb represents God's covenantal beneficence in redeeming the Israelites from Egypt. Therefore, by mixing pascal lamb blood with circumcision blood, the midrash is *literally* blending covenant and circumcision.

Not only is *bloods* in the plural in Ezekiel 16:6, but the entire phrase, "I said to you, 'In your bloods live'" is stated twice. The midrash interprets the repetition of this phrase to mean that, on account of these bloods, God first delivered the Israelites from Egypt and then will deliver them again in messianic times.[23] While contemplating the possible reasons for this exegesis (and volumes have been written about Ezekiel 16:6), we cannot overlook that this verse has nothing to do with circumcision and everything to do with the covenant. Ezekiel 16 provides an allegory of the Jewish people's infidelity to God and their desecration of the covenant. Moreover, the blood in Ezekiel is a mother's birth blood, a "female" blood that bears no relationship to circumcision. Thus, by using the covenantal allegory in Ezekiel 16 to represent the blood of circumcision, the midrash vividly conflates covenant and circumcision.

Based on this midrash, the practice has developed to recite Ezekiel 16:6 at a circumcision ceremony immediately after announcing the boy's name.[24] Reciting this verse is deemed integral to the circumcision ceremony across the spectrum of Jewish practices.[25] I found this out at my son's circumcision. Our wonderful mohel (who also became my friend) readily acknowledged that I would "run the show," as he good-naturedly put it, despite a mother's frequent exclusion today from the circumcision ceremony. In the program that I created and handed out to our guests, I intentionally omitted Ezekiel 16:6, reasoning that it has no connection to circumcision. Even our easygoing mohel, however, would not abide by this omission. When my husband and I recited the naming liturgy for our son Yakir, our mohel gently interjected Ezekiel 16:6 as the traditional liturgy prescribes. When he later mentioned to me the extreme importance of this verse, I responded with my rationale. However, our mohel would not agree that this verse had been taken out of context. Years later, I still maintain that this practice of reciting Ezekiel 16:6 at a circumcision perpetuates not only the conflation of circumcision and covenant, but also the mistaken assumption that this verse is referring to circumcision blood.

WHY HAVE CIRCUMCISION AND COVENANT BECOME CONFLATED?

One possible factor spurring this erroneous conflation is that circumcision is, simply, the first commandment predicated explicitly on the Jewish covenant. Indeed, the covenant and circumcision are textually linked, in that the word *brit* (covenant) appears thirteen times in Genesis 17, the chapter in which God commands Abraham to circumcise himself and his family.[26]

Another possible reason is that many covenantal symbols, such as the ark, the Sinaitic tablets, and the showbread (*challot*), disappeared with the destruction of the Second Temple. In turn, the symbols that remained—such as circumcision, Shabbat, phylacteries (tefillin), ritual fringes (tzitzit), and doorpost markers (mezuzot)—took on enhanced significance. In addition, circumcision is the only one of these surviving covenantal symbols that is physically permanent and, therefore, an ever-present reminder of the covenant.[27] This distinction may have contributed to circumcision's perceived conflation with the covenant itself.

Likely, the most potent cause of this conflation, however, is that circumcision is an exceptionally difficult commandment to understand, particularly since it is performed on newborn babies.[28] Furthermore, circumcision poses a potential for conflict with other commandments. For example, when a circumcision occurs on Shabbat (for a baby born the previous Shabbat, unless via Caesarian section), the demands of the circumcision supersede the Shabbat prohibitions against cutting, tearing, and using tools (BT Shabbat 131b–132b). Some may even argue that circumcision seemingly contradicts the Biblical injunction not to mutilate one's body (Leviticus 19:28, Deuteronomy 14:1). It follows that elevating circumcision by equating it with the covenant is an effective means of mitigating circumcision's incomprehensibility and conceptualizing this commandment's special treatment.

From a historical perspective, it appears that the conflation of covenant and circumcision is one aspect of the extreme praise of circumcision, a prevalent theme in rabbinic texts from the Mishnaic era until the early Middle Ages. Rabbis used this "meta-halachic" tactic to encourage the performance of circumcision in the face of antagonistic cultural and political influences that threatened this sacred ritual. One means of praising circumcision was to inflate its importance by characterizing this rite as the embodiment of Jewish identity and tantamount to the eternal covenant itself. This conflation, as well as the extreme lauding of circumcision more generally, both developed as impetuses to persuade and motivate Jews to circumcise their sons.

Male circumcision was vehemently derided in the Greco-Roman culture of late antiquity. In this society, "[p]ublic nudity both during work and at play was prevalent and . . . the perfection of the unaltered male physique was prized." Circumcision thus prevented Jewish men from using gymnasia and bathhouses—popular sites for conducting business—and from participating in the athletic events that were "often a prerequisite for social advancement." After the Jewish revolt against Rome in 66–70 CE, Roman authorities examined men's genitals as a means of enforcing the "punitive Jewish tax." Also, circumcision was a potential bar to citizenship in Greek cities such as Alexandria.[29]

As a result of these Greco-Roman influences, some Jews stopped circumcising their sons when a gymnasium was built in Jerusalem (I Maccabees 1:17). Some Jewish men even attempted to reverse their circumcisions via epispasm, a procedure that stretches foreskin remnants. Epispasm was practiced from at least the second century BCE until the second century CE or later, with its height in the first century CE. It is no surprise that early Christians rejected circumcision as a religious requirement, focusing instead on the importance of faith (Acts 15).

These pressures were coupled with outright bans on circumcision over the course of many centuries. In the second century BCE, Antiochus IV Epiphanes outlawed circumcision in the Seleucid Empire on pain of death, among other edicts aimed at aggressively assimilating Jews in the Empire (I Maccabees 1:47–48, 58–59). Upon discovering two women who had circumcised their sons, the Seleucid authorities tied the boys to their mothers' breasts, humiliatingly paraded the mothers and sons, and threw all of them off the city walls (II Maccabees 6:11). Furthermore, it is generally accepted that, in the second century CE, the Roman Emperor Hadrian (who reigned 117–138 CE) prohibited the Jews in the Empire from performing circumcision.[30] Even according to a divergent historical interpretation, Emperor Antoninus Pius (who reigned 138–161 CE) proscribed circumcision for gentiles.[31] Centuries later, the Visigothic Code of Christian kings ruling Spain from 586 to 711 CE outlawed Jewish circumcision, punishing "with the utmost severity of the law" anyone performing or undergoing the rite.[32]

Due to these extreme pressures imposed on Jews circumcising their sons, rabbis in late antiquity and the early Middle Ages fervently sought to impel Jews to perform circumcision. Beginning in the Mishnaic era, one means to this end was the codification of new legal requirements for ritual circumcision. One innovation was *periah,* the complete uncovering of the penis head, and another was the removal of residual foreskin shreds (*tzitzin*) (M. Shabbat 19:2). These procedures make it physically impossible to perform epispasm. The rabbis even legally equated periah with actual circumcision, mandating that periah was necessary to fulfill the circumcision commandment (M. Shabbat 19:6).[33] Today, although the threat of epispasm has disappeared, periah and tzitzin removal remain integral requirements of ritual circumcision.

Heightening the importance of circumcision was another means by which rabbis promoted and invigorated the circumcision practice in the face of Greco-Roman culture and early Christian influences. Most prominently, from Mishnaic times and for many centuries following, the rabbis lauded circumcision in an extreme fashion.[34] One prevalent theme of this over-the-top praise is that circumcision is "great," and a mishna even provides six reasons to this effect (Nedarim 3:11).[35] This mishna introduces the powerful ideas that the world would not have been created but for circumcision and that circumcision supersedes Shabbat. Yet another reason for circumcision's "greatness" is that it results in a man's perfection and completion. Some later midrashim elaborate on this notion (derived from Genesis 17:1), vividly explaining that circumcision made Abraham complete and perfect.[36] In the same vein, Pirkei d'Rabbi Eliezer (chapter 29) says that Abraham was circumcised on Yom Kippur (the Day of Atonement), the day when Jews become pure and blameless.

A related theme of praise compares performing circumcision to bringing a Temple sacrifice. Pirkei d'Rabbi Eliezer (chapter 29) says that an altar was built where Abraham was circumcised, while later midrashim explicitly compare those who circumcise their sons with priests bringing sacrifices and libations on an altar.[37] In the Tanchuma's lore, God remarks hyperbolically: "I would come to bless one who slaughters an ox or lamb and spilled a little blood, ... how much more so must I bless Abraham, from whose house a river of blood exits due to the circumcision."[38] Indeed, sacrificial motifs, including that of the binding of Isaac, became prevalent on circumcision bowls, plates, and knives, among other artifacts.[39]

According to the Tosefta (Nedarim 2:6), another powerful reason that circumcision is "great" is that it "equals in value all of the commandments in the Torah."[40] Many centuries later, the Shulchan Aruch opens its exposition on the commandment of circumcision by stating that "circumcision is greater than all other positive commandments."[41] One modern halachic treatise mentions that *brit* is equivalent to 612 in *gematria* (the system of assigning numeric values to Hebrew letters) and adding one, to represent the one word of "circumcision," brings this value to 613. Since there are 613 Biblical commandments, circumcision is equivalent to all the other commandments combined.[42]

It follows that such a great mitzvah would be single-handedly responsible for a range of epic rewards and punishments. According to various midrashim, performing circumcision resulted in the Exodus from Egypt,[43] the splitting of the Red Sea,[44] and entry to the Land of Israel,[45] and will result in the ultimate redemption.[46] Furthermore, Abraham is envisioned as sitting at the entrance of Gehinnom (hell) and permitting no circumcised Israelite to descend.[47] On the other hand, not performing circumcision is understood as the singular reason for the Egyptian enslavement.[48] Also, Abraham is believed to remove the foreskins from babies who die uncircumcised and to bring sinners to Gehinnom after putting these foreskins on them.[49] The uncircumcised will descend to Gehinnom,[50] and even those of the uncircumcised who perform good deeds have no share in the "world to come" (M. Avot 3:11). The stigma of non-circumcision is thus impossibly weighty.

From this review of how circumcision came to be praised in the extreme, we see that this praise and the conflation of covenant and circumcision follow similar historical trajectories. Both trends are rooted in the Mishna and Talmud and then developed and expanded over the centuries, particularly in midrashic sources. The conflation of covenant and circumcision is, therefore, one facet of this extreme praise for circumcision. Circumcision is praiseworthy not only for all the reasons mentioned above, but also because it is singularly tantamount to the eternal covenant, the basis for all fundamental Jewish beliefs. Like all other forms of this praise, conflating circumcision with the covenant responds directly to virulent anti-circumcision influences and provides a vital impetus for performing circumcision in the face of these pressures.

The tactics of conflating covenant and circumcision, and praising circumcision more generally, have worked exceptionally well. Not only have these tactics preserved circumcision, they have even elevated it. In modern times, the peculiar commandment of circumcision has been threatened by other forces, such as secularism, religious skepticism, and selected medical studies. Yet, the conflation of covenant and circumcision and the extreme praise of circumcision both continue to color our thinking today. Jews of all persuasions remain influenced by the long-standing beliefs that circumcision is singularly praiseworthy and constitutes the essence of Judaism. As a result of these subliminal beliefs (along with the prevalence of circumcision among gentiles in the United States and elsewhere), a high percentage of Jewish men today are circumcised. As noted above, even those who are disdainful of the ritual or who outright oppose it sometimes nonetheless circumcise their sons.

DISTINCTION BETWEEN COVENANT AND CIRCUMCISION

We have seen how the covenant and circumcision became conflated over the centuries and remain so today. This conflation, however, is erroneous from a traditional theological standpoint, as we will learn below. Furthermore, a result of this conflation is the mistaken belief that Jewish women are not members of the covenant, since they are not circumcised. It is therefore crucial that we clarify the distinction between covenant and circumcision.

Brit milah is the common terminology used to refer to circumcision or the circumcision ceremony. This phrase literally means "covenant of circumcision"—*brit* means covenant, and *milah* means circumcision. As its name indicates, the brit milah ceremony incorporates both the commandment of circumcision and the theme of covenantal entry. Chava Weissler identified in the 1970s this duality of purpose, observing that the circumcision ceremony incorporates the "twin themes" of circumcision blood and the covenant.[51] Biblical and rabbinic sources demonstrate that circumcision and covenant are, in fact, distinct, although circumcision is a Biblically mandated symbol of the covenant. Thus, circumcision is but one component—albeit an important one—of the larger conception of covenant, and the metaphysical notion of covenant transcends the physicality of circumcision. To assess this proposition, we examine below selected excerpts from the Bible and Talmud, as well as the viewpoint of Maimonides.

Biblical Sources

The Bible's use and placement of the terms *brit* and *milah* strongly support the point that these are distinguishable concepts. In particular, it is significant that the Pentateuch nowhere explicitly articulates a connection between the covenant and circumcision except in Genesis 17, where circumcision is introduced as an eternal commandment. However, it may be noteworthy that, in this chapter, God demands the circumcision not only of the men in one's family, but also of any man living in one's house or bought with one's money, even if they are "foreign-born" (*ben-neichar;* Genesis 17:12). In addition, immediately after God excludes Ishmael from the covenant (Genesis 17:20–21), Abraham circumcises Ishmael, along with all members of Abraham's household (Genesis 17:23–27). Thus, even in Genesis 17, being circumcised does not necessarily mean that one is included in the covenant; there is no one-to-one relationship between circumcision and the covenant.

More broadly, there are a handful of references to circumcision in the Torah narrative that may implicitly portray circumcision as a symbol of the covenant. Two examples are the commandment that a man must be circumcised in order to eat the pascal lamb (Exodus 12:44, 48), and the mass circumcision following the Israelites' entry into the Land of Canaan (Joshua 5:2–8). Both evoke the Exodus from Egypt; the pascal lamb was eaten on the eve of the Exodus, and the mass circumcision removed the "shame of Egypt" and preceded the first celebration of Passover in Canaan (Joshua 5:9–11). As a result of their connection to the Exodus, both examples allude to the covenant, since God's promise to redeem the Israelites from Egypt is an integral covenantal component (Genesis 15:13–16). Furthermore, one could argue that, in Genesis 34, when the sons of Jacob demand that Shechem the Hivvite circumcise himself in order to marry their sister Dena, they are presenting circumcision as necessary to perpetuate the covenantal line of Abraham. (On the other hand, the sons of Jacob are actually using circumcision as a ploy by which to slaughter Shechem and his people.) One could also argue that the circumcision that Moses's wife Tzipporah performs on their son (Exodus 4:24–26) depicts circumcision as a covenantal precondition to remain holy, as does the Torah's juxtaposition of a birthing mother's seven days of ritual impurity with her son's circumcision on the eighth day (Leviticus 12:3). Finally, Deuteronomy 30:6 uses the phrase *circumcision of the heart* in a covenantal context. Other verses likewise use the term *foreskinned* metaphorically (e.g., Exodus 6:30).

But these passages are the exception, not the rule. The Torah uses the independent term *covenant* (*brit*) in countless passages to mean the covenant between God and Israel, without any mention of circumcision. Contrary to R. Lawrence Hoffman's characterization of the Bible as a "logbook of circumcision,"[52] the covenant is mentioned in the Bible far more frequently than circumcision. Moreover, the covenant is the central theme of the Torah's narrative and the raison d'être of the Jewish people in this narrative. If anything, the Bible is a logbook of the covenant.

The Pentateuch spells out the terms of the covenant every time it articulates God's eternal love for the Jewish people and their obligations to worship God, observe the commandments, and remain holy. Likewise, every mention of God's punishing the people for their idol worship and other transgressions reflects a violation of the covenant. These frequent statements of covenantal responsibilities and repercussions suffuse the Torah, yet nowhere in these references does the Torah mention circumcision. For example, in Deuteronomy 27 and 28, six Israelite tribes are commanded to stand on Mount Gerizim to declare the plentiful blessings that the Israelites will enjoy if they keep the commandments, and six tribes are commanded to stand on Mount Evel to rail against the people with the harsh curses that will befall them if they do not. This ritual is performed after the Israelites cross the Jordan River (Joshua 8:33–35). God calls this litany of rewards and punishments "the words of the covenant" (Deuteronomy 28:69), but nowhere in these pivotal passages is circumcision mentioned. Leviticus 26 and Deuteronomy 8 likewise present the rewards and punishments that the Israelites will merit, depending on whether they follow or flout God's commandments, respectively. These two chapters specifically refer to this reward-and-punishment dynamic as the covenant,[53] without any reference to circumcision.

Furthermore, the Pentateuch prominently associates the covenant with fundamental components of Jewish existence—without a single reference to circumcision. For example, a covenant is made at Revelation when Moses reads "the book of the covenant" and sprinkles the sacrificial "blood of the covenant."[54] The Ten Commandments are called the "covenant" or "the words of the covenant."[55] They are inscribed on the "tablets of the covenant,"[56] which are, in turn, carried in the "ark of the covenant of God."[57] God promises not to forget the covenant that He swore to the forefathers.[58] In addition, the covenant is linked to Shabbat, a foundational aspect of Jewish life. Exodus 31:16 refers to Shabbat as an "everlasting covenant" (*brit olam*) and a "sign" *(ote)* of the covenant. Some passages likewise describe the Exodus from Egypt as an independent element of the covenant.[59]

It is also significant that, as Jewish sovereignty unravels, the prophets Ezekiel, Isaiah, and Jeremiah plead with the people to stop desecrating the covenant and tell them about God's forthcoming punishments and ultimate forgiveness. These prophets even go to great lengths to disassociate the covenant from ritualism, emphasizing the importance of fidelity to God and of good deeds toward fellow human beings.[60] Despite this overwhelming emphasis on the covenant, the physical act of circumcision is nowhere mentioned. In a few instances, circumcision is used as a metaphor for covenantal adherence.[61]

All these observations strongly support the conclusion that the covenant is a core concept that transcends the circumcision rite. This distinction also reinforces the conclusion that the covenant encompasses every Jew regardless of sex, even though circumcision—one important symbol of the covenant, among others—is, in the Jewish tradition, performed only on men.

THERE IS ONE Biblical passage, however, that some might argue equates circumcision with the covenant. Genesis 17:10 states: "This is My covenant that you will guard between Me and you [plural] and between the descendants after you [singular]; circumcise for you [plural] every male." The medieval commentators do not appear concerned with the question of how the metaphysical covenant can be equated with physical circumcision. R. Samson Raphael Hirsch (nineteenth-century Germany), however, directly addresses this question in his commentary on this verse:

> In a striking manner the Mila [circumcision] itself is first called Brit [that is, covenant, in Genesis 17:10], so that the performance of it itself seems to be fulfilling the covenant, and then, in the following verse [verse 11, "You shall circumcise the flesh of your foreskin, and it will be a sign of the covenant between Me and you"], it is declared to be "ote brit," the sign of the covenant, as a symbol to represent the brit, so that the fulfillment of the covenant itself must be something transcending the mere act of the circumcision. The expressions used at the first specific Jewish law—and a symbolic law at that—could be of the highest importance for the correct appreciation of all similar laws that follow.[62]

R. Hirsch thus explains that the Torah calls circumcision *brit* in Genesis 17:10 to convey that performing circumcision fulfills the covenant—not that the act of circumcision is equivalent to the covenant. It follows, as R. Hirsch states, that the covenant transcends the physical act of circumcision. Furthermore, this interpretation takes every word of the Torah into account. Characterizing circumcision as *brit* in verse 10 expresses the first step for all "symbolic commandments," which is to do the required act. Verse 11, which calls circumcision *ote brit* ("sign of the covenant"), expresses the second step, which is making a symbolic act into a reality by internalizing its covenantal significance.[63] In R. Hirsch's words:

[P]erforming the act only then achieves its full purpose when it does become an "ote" a symbol, if it is taken to heart as such and the idea it expresses becomes a reality for us. . . . What the act is to accomplish is that through it the idea is constantly expressed by us as a declaration of God, and as such is to be firmly held, kept and constantly repeated and revived for ourselves and others.[64]

Doing the act itself and accepting its underlying symbolism are both necessary to fulfill the commandment of circumcision. Said otherwise, the first step of this commandment is milah (verse 10) and the second step is brit (verse 11). According to R. Hirsch, therefore, even Genesis 17:10 demonstrates that circumcision and covenant are distinct and separable, when viewed in juxtaposition with the following verse. This interpretation is consistent in the context of Genesis 17 as a whole. In the first nine verses of chapter 17, God expansively depicts the covenant to include multiplying Abraham's descendants, giving them the Land of Canaan, and "being God to you." Only at this point, in verse 10, does God introduce the commandment of circumcision.

Four centuries before R. Hirsch expounded this interpretation, the Abrabanel addressed the use of *brit* (covenant) and *ote brit* (the sign of the covenant) in a related, if less elaborate, fashion. The Abrabanel explains that *brit* refers to circumcision when it is being performed, and that *ote brit* refers to circumcision after it is performed.[65] In other words, the fact that circumcision is the "sign of the covenant" is the rationale or basis for this commandment.

Some modern feminists have understandably interpreted Genesis 17:10 ("This is My covenant that you will guard between Me and you and between the descendants after you; circumcise for you every male") as creating an assumption that the Jewish religious community consists of men only.[66] The interpretations of R. Hirsch and the Abrabanel, however, demonstrate that circumcision, as important as it is, constitutes but one component of the covenant of Abraham, as we saw in the previous chapter. Thus, while Genesis 17:10 is hardly female-centric, it is also not the only Biblical covenantal expression. Furthermore, circumcision is a symbol or sign of the covenant, not the covenant itself. Understood in this way, even Genesis 17:10 can be construed to demonstrate the separability of covenant and circumcision.

Talmudic Texts

Although the rabbis of the Talmud did not extensively address the theology of covenant, a few selected texts support the key distinction between covenant and circumcision.[67] These texts deal with a variety of subjects.

First is a mishna that describes the repercussions of making certain vows (Nedarim 3:11):

> [Vow #1:] [If one swore,] "May any benefit that I derive from the fore-skinned be as forbidden to me as a sacrificial offering," one is permitted to have benefit from the foreskinned of Israel, but is forbidden to have benefit from the circumcised of the nations.

> [Vow #2:] [If one swore,] "May any benefit that I derive from the circumcised be as forbidden to me as a sacrificial offering," one is forbidden to have benefit from the foreskinned of Israel, but is permitted to have benefit from the circumcised of the nations, since "foreskin" is but another name for "gentiles."

In the first vow, this mishna construes "foreskinned" to mean "gentiles." Although the swearer may not derive benefit from "foreskinned" individuals, he may derive benefit from all of Israel—both foreskinned (despite the oath) and circumcised (who are unaffected by the oath). At the same time, the swearer may not derive benefit from anyone of the nations—whether foreskinned (per the oath) or circumcised (despite the oath's seeming inapplicability to this group). In the second vow, the mishna construes *circumcised* to mean "Jews." Although the swearer may not derive benefit from circumcised individuals, he may not derive benefit from all of Israel—both foreskinned (who are unaffected by the oath) and circumcised (despite the oath). At the same time, the swearer may derive benefit from anyone of the nations—whether foreskinned (despite the oath's seeming inapplicability to this group) or circumcised (per the oath).

In short, this mishna defines *foreskinned* as "gentiles" and *circumcised* as "Jews," regardless of whether an individual is actually circumcised or not. Therefore, a Jew is deemed circumcised, and a covenantal member, even if he lacks the physical mark of circumcision.[68] It follows that women, who also lack circumcision, can be—and, in fact, are—likewise included in the covenant. We see from this mishna that circumcision is not a prerequisite for covenantal membership and that circumcision and the covenant are distinct.

This point can also be inferred from a lengthy Talmudic discourse about the qualifications for bearing witness (BT Bava Kama 88a). The Talmud mentions that women are "eligible to enter the congregation" of Israel and, separately, that they are "subject to commandments," albeit not to all of them. At the same time, the Talmud acknowledges that a woman cannot undergo penile circumcision. It follows that a woman has standing among the Jewish people despite her inability to be circumcised in the manner of men.[69]

A Talmudic inquiry into the qualifications for a circumciser (BT Avodah Zara 27a) results in a similar conclusion:

> It has been stated: What is the scriptural basis for the ruling that circumcision performed by a gentile is invalid? Daru ben Papa said in the name of Rav: "You shall keep My covenant" [Genesis 17:9]. R. Yochanan said: "You shall surely circumcise" [Genesis 17:13]. What [practical difference] is there between these [two positions]? . . . A woman is [a point of disagreement] between them. For the one who says, "You shall keep my covenant"—[the criterion] is [not satisfied], because a woman is not susceptible to circumcision [*lav bat milah hee*] [and therefore a woman may not perform a valid circumcision]. For the one who says "You shall surely circumcise"—[the criterion] is [satisfied], because a woman resembles one who has been circumcised [*k'man d'm'hula d'mai*] [and therefore a woman may perform a valid circumcision].

The rabbis of the Talmud understood "You shall keep My covenant" to refer to those obligated to fulfill the commandment of circumcision. By contrast, the rabbis understood "You shall surely circumcise" to refer to those who are circumcised.[70] It appears that the applicable distinction is between action and result. According to Daru ben Papa (who cites "You shall keep My covenant"), women are not obligated to take action to effect their circumcision since this is physically impossible, and therefore they are deemed not "circumcised." According to R. Yochanan (who cites "You shall surely circumcise"), women "resemble one who has been circumcised," regardless of how that result came about, and therefore are deemed to have the status of "circumcised."

What does it mean for a woman to resemble a circumcised man? Commentators have advanced a number of interesting responses to this question.[71] For our purposes, however, we focus on the response that both women and uncircumcised men are part of the community of Israel (*k'lal yisrael*). At least five prominent rabbis, over the span of many centuries, articulate this approach.[72] R. Tzadok HaKohen Rabinowitz (nineteenth century, Lublin, Poland) even goes so far as to say that women are considered circumcised because their flesh, like that of men, is "holy flesh" (*basar kodesh*).[73] This idea that Jewish women, and likewise uncircumcised Jewish men, are part of the community of Israel despite their lack of physical circumcision demonstrates that, according to R. Yochanan, circumcision is not a prerequisite for membership in the Jewish people or in their national charter, the covenant. It follows that circumcision and covenant are distinct and separable. Later authorities hold that the opinion of R. Yochanan prevails, with the practical result that women may serve as ritual circumcisers.[74] On a deeper level, the acceptance of R. Yochanan's position may further support the broader distinction between circumcision and covenant.

The Philosophy of Maimonides

The perspective of Maimonides (twelfth-century Spain and Egypt) is integral to this discussion because he "decovenantalizes" circumcision,[75] meaning that he conceptualizes circumcision outside the rubric of the Jewish covenant. For example, in his *Book of Commandments (Sefer HaMitzvot)*, Maimonides categorizes circumcision among commandments governing sexual relations.[76] Similarly, in his *Guide for the Perplexed* (3:49), Maimonides discusses circumcision in the context of illicit sexual relations. He maintains, first, that circumcision has the benefit of weakening a man's lust and sexual excitement and decreasing the frequency of his sexual interactions. This reason is similar to an explanation advanced many centuries earlier by Philo, the Greek-influenced Jewish philosopher of the first century CE.[77] Second, Maimonides explains that circumcision creates a covenant, meaning an alliance or league, among circumcised peoples who believe in God's unity. In his words:

> It is also well known what degree of mutual love and mutual help exists between people who all bear the same sign, which forms for them a sort of covenant and alliance. Circumcision is a covenant made by Abraham our father with a view to the belief in the unity of God. Thus, everyone who is circumcised joins Abraham's covenant.[78]

These circumcised peoples include both Jews and Muslims, and Maimonides does not here characterize circumcision in terms of the special, eternal relationship between God and the Jewish people.[79]

In his *Mishneh Torah* (*Repetition of the Torah*), Maimonides emphasizes the covenant of Abraham and devotes the vast majority of his discussion to the technical details of fulfilling the circumcision commandment.[80] Significantly, nowhere in the Mishneh Torah does Maimonides refer to circumcision as *brit milah* (covenant of circumcision); rather, he speaks of *milah* (circumcision) and the *brit Avraham* (covenant of Abraham).

At one point in the Mishneh Torah,[81] Maimonides initially limits circumcision only to those of the same "religion and straight path" of Abraham (Jews), and excludes from this obligation the descendants of Ishmael (Muslims) and those of Esau. Then, Maimonides cites "the sages" for the opinion that the sons of Keturah (Abraham's third wife; Genesis 25:1–4) must perform circumcision. Explaining that the descendants of Ishmael and those of Keturah are today intermingled, Maimonides requires circumcision for both of these peoples (although noting that they are not punishable by death for failure to perform the rite, as Jews are). Maimonides's conclusion that certain non-Jews must perform circumcision (despite his initial position) starkly exemplifies Maimonides's "decovenantalization" of circumcision.

This outlook is apparently a function of Maimonides's lifelong interactions with Muslims who also circumcise.[82] Maimonides may have thought that Muslim circumcision somehow severs the commandment of circumcision from the distinctly Jewish conception of covenant. Indeed, Abraham circumcises Ishmael (albeit not on the eighth day of life) (Genesis 17:23, 25–26) while, at the same time, God excludes Ishmael from the Abrahamic covenant (Genesis 17:19–21). Regardless of his reasoning, Maimonides clearly distinguishes between circumcision and the Jewish covenant.

DIFFERENTIATING BETWEEN COVENANT AND CIRCUMCISION

The covenant and circumcision have been continuously conflated over many centuries for a variety of theological and historical reasons, as we have seen. This conflation, in turn, has popularized the erroneous belief that circumcision is the one and only manifestation of the covenant, or even that the two are practically synonymous. In essence, the physical symbolism of circumcision has subsumed the metaphysical covenant. The substantive effect of this misconception is the widespread belief that only men can be members of the covenant. In other words, if the covenant is the same as circumcision, and if circumcision is only for men, then the covenant also must be only for men.

This conclusion is, however, based on false premises. Traditional Jewish legal texts support the axioms that (1) the covenant and circumcision are distinct and separable (although circumcision is a covenantal symbol) and (2) the metaphysical covenant transcends the specific symbolism of circumcision. Women, therefore, can be—and, in fact, are—members of the divine covenant despite their inability to be circumcised in the manner of men. The only prerequisite for covenantal membership is to be born to a Jewish mother. While it is a given that the symbolic entry of girls into the covenant is not marked by circumcision, covenantal entry for girls is nonetheless as real and significant as that for boys, since all Jews are covenantal members. As R. Eliezer Berkovits inquires rhetorically, "Is it really conceivable that since the sign of the covenant was the circumcision, the covenant was not concluded with all Israel, but only with its male members![?]"[83] It follows that denying women their rightful place in the covenant runs counter to a Torah-based belief system.

The first step toward rectifying this situation is to decouple circumcision and covenant, except to the extent that the former symbolizes the latter. This process reveals that the circumcision ceremony encompasses two important purposes: to commemorate a newborn's symbolic covenantal entry, and to fulfill the Biblical commandment of circumcision. This first purpose is significant for girls, while the second is inapplicable. It follows that a ceremony for newborn girls should commemorate their entry into the covenant (without referencing circumcision). Contrary to the assumption of some,[84] the goal of such a ceremony is not to mimic or reformulate circumcision or the circumcision ceremony. Rather, a covenantal ceremony for newborn girls highlights their inestimable religious value in the eyes of God and the Jewish community and sets the stage for lives devoted to Torah and mitzvot. I call this type of covenantal ceremony for Jewish girls a *Brit Bat*, meaning "Covenant of a Daughter."

COVENANTAL SIGNIFICANCE OF BAT MITZVAH
AND WOMEN'S TORAH STUDY

The theological significance of welcoming ceremonies for newborn girls crystallizes in the context of other modern, ground-breaking trends: the coming-of-age Bat Mitzvah ritual for adolescent girls and women's Torah learning. These two developments emerged as norms and opportunities for women in modern times, and they exploded in the 1970s and 1980s as a result of feminist stirrings. Nevertheless, it is widely believed that both the Bat Mitzvah and women's Torah learning express a sincere devotion to Jewish values and beliefs. We take this conceptualization one step further by recognizing that the Bat Mitzvah and women's Torah learning manifest a commitment not only to the Jewish tradition, but also, more specifically, to the covenant. As a result, these trends frame and reinforce the criticality of covenantal entry for newborn girls.

We begin by sketching the contours of each of these phenomena. We turn first to the Bat Mitzvah, which has rapidly emerged as the newest well-accepted Jewish life-cycle practice. It is easy to forget that R. Mordecai Kaplan (1881–1983, founder of the Reconstructionist movement) relied on scant precedent (including a ritual he witnessed in Italy)[85] to create the first modern Bat Mitzvah as recently as 1922. Judith Kaplan, the eldest of R. Kaplan's four daughters, recited on Shabbat morning the blessings for an aliyah to the Torah and read a part of the Torah portion from her printed Pentateuch (chumash), followed by the English translation.[86] Although this ritual was not replicated initially, the Bat Mitzvah practice—in one form or another—is today widely embraced across the Jewish spectrum, and can be found even in some communities on the extreme right wing.[87]

In all the liberal branches of Judaism that have adopted an egalitarian outlook, there are no ritualistic differences between the Bar Mitzvah for boys and the Bat Mitzvah for girls. To celebrate their coming of age, both boys and girls, typically on Shabbat, chant the Torah portion or Haftarah (reading from the Prophets), lead some portion of the prayers, and/or deliver a speech. Initially, in some communities, *b'not mitzvah* (girls reaching the age of Bat Mitzvah), on Friday night, recited the Haftarah (that was repeated by men at Shabbat morning services) and/or lit the Shabbat candles.[88] Bat Mitzvah rituals could be found as early as the 1950s and 1960s in some Reform synagogues, but the practice became increasingly wide-spread in liberal communities with the advent of "second wave" feminism in the late 1960s and 1970s.

The Bat Mitzvah could not be found in any Orthodox community prior to the 1970s. One of the earliest Bat Mitzvah ceremonies in an Orthodox synagogue occurred on a Friday night in 1973 when twelve-year-old Elana Kagan, today an associate justice of the United States Supreme Court, read from the book of Ruth and analyzed this book in a speech at Lincoln Square Synagogue in New York City.[89] Today, more diversity exists among Ortho-dox communities than among more liberal ones. A few Orthodox b'not mitzvah participate in limited ritualistic settings. For example, they lead services or read the Torah at women's tefillah groups (non-minyan gather-ings for women) or read the Scroll of Esther. At my Bat Mitzvah in 1985, I led services and read from the Torah at a women's gathering in the main sanctuary of an Orthodox synagogue, with all of the men (who had already recited their morning prayers) in attendance—an unusual arrangement even today. Some girls today mark their Bat Mitzvah by undertaking community service, and others participate in popular Torah learning programs. While some girls deliver their own Torah expositions (*divrei Torah*) in the syna-gogue or elsewhere, others listen to their rabbi's d'var Torah and receive a gift from the community. Many girls enjoy a sizable party with many rela-tives and friends. Others have a modest gathering with girlfriends on Shab-bat afternoon or participate in group celebrations organized by schools or synagogues.[90]

This diversity demonstrates how Orthodox communities have crafted inventive Bat Mitzvah practices that commemorate this milestone while upholding a range of ritualistic and social restrictions imposed on girls. This ingenuity, in turn, shows the great extent to which Orthodox communities, in a few short decades, have become inextricably attached to the Bat Mitz-vah practice—despite the strong misgivings of, most prominently, R. Moshe Feinstein (1895–1986), a preeminent American Orthodox rabbi.[91]

Another indicator of the Bat Mitzvah's rapid popularization throughout the Jewish community is that adult women who missed the opportunity to mark this milestone as adolescents are doing so now. For example, my pa-ternal grandmother, Tillie Siegel, celebrated her Bat Mitzvah at age eighty-seven by receiving an aliyah to the Torah and writing a d'var Torah.[92]

Like the Bat Mitzvah, women's Torah study is entrenched today, yet barely a century old. Sara Schenirer (1883–1935), a Polish seamstress, recognized the allure of the secularization and acculturation that young Jewish girls were encountering in eastern Europe in the early twentieth century. As a result, she began teaching Torah to girls in the small school she founded in Cracow in 1915, which she named Beis Yaakov ("House of Jacob"). Schenirer drew on the "neo-Orthodox" ideals of R. Samson Raphael Hirsch to which she was exposed during a brief stay in Vienna.[93] In a few short years, Schenirer's school had swelled into a school system educating thousands of girls. The many prominent Torah leaders who supported this grassroots development did so for practical reasons. They sought to ensure that Jewish women remained religious in the face of encroaching "enlightened" ideals and of rapidly expanding opportunities for secular education. Prominent Torah leaders of the day, including the Chofetz Chaim, easily brushed away much of the well-known halachic precedent discouraging or even preventing women from learning Torah[94] and supported this sea change in the strongest terms.[95] This approval was forthcoming despite the protests of some eminent detractors, such as R. Abraham Isaac Kook (1865–1935, Mandate Palestine).

Since that time, women's Torah learning has been transformed from an accommodation (*b'di'avad*) to a Jewish ideal (*l'chatchila*).[96] As early as 1953, R. Joseph B. Soloveitchik strenuously advocated that girls be taught Talmud at the highest levels in the same classroom as boys and as part of a "uniform program for the entire student body."[97] This was a radical position at the time. In the years following the emergence of "second-wave" feminism in the late 1960s, the revolution of women's Torah learning gained momentum.

The extensive range of opportunities available today for women's Torah learning, particularly in the United States and Israel, is astounding. There is more than a critical mass of schools and synagogues that offer women a complete curriculum of Torah studies, including Talmud, on the most advanced levels. These opportunities, which are multiplying more quickly than they can be counted, are available across—and even beyond—the denominations. Some Torah learning opportunities for women are formal and others less so; some are co-ed, and some are not; some have a traditional orientation, and others a liberal one; some occur in venerable institutions, and others in makeshift accommodations.

The Machon Torani L'Nashim (Women's Torah Institute, known by the acronym Matan) presents one dramatic example of this explosion of

Torah learning opportunities for women, particularly in Israel. When I attended Matan in the mid-1990s, we studied Talmud and Bible in somewhat cramped quarters at the school's only facility, located in Jerusalem. Today, Matan has enough students to sustain a spacious campus in Jerusalem, as well as seven other branches throughout Israel.

The Bat Mitzvah and women's Torah study, despite their different origins, are today well-established throughout the Jewish community. Both have become increasingly accepted as the influence of feminism has become more pronounced. From a theological perspective, however, the Bat Mitzvah and women's Torah study are covenantal expressions. In particular, the Bat Mitzvah expresses girls' embrace of mitzvot, the Jewish people's covenantal obligations, and Torah study expresses women's strong relationship with Torah, the written embodiment of the covenant. As such, the Bat Mitzvah and women's Torah study actually *compel* the prerequisite of covenantal entry, which is symbolically enacted in a Brit Bat. Covenantal entry enables a mature acceptance of the covenant (Bat Mitzvah) and a demonstration of love for the covenant (Torah study). In short, the Bat Mitzvah and women's Torah study are not theologically feasible unless women are recognized as covenantal members in the first place, and both practices fall flat—and even lack meaning—without a covenantal basis.

It follows that the great importance that the Jewish community invests today in Bat Mitzvah celebrations and women's Torah study should likewise be invested in covenantal rituals for newborn girls. A ceremony that welcomes a daughter without explicitly initiating her into the covenant does not suffice in preparing a girl for religious milestones and challenges to come. Unlike a generic welcoming ceremony (or no ceremony at all), a covenantal welcoming ceremony clearly communicates that it is a springboard to the type of Jewish life to which a newborn girl will hopefully aspire, one filled with Torah, mitzvot, and Jewish pride. A Brit Bat thus represents the Jewish community's best effort to instill these specific values at the earliest stage of a Jewish girl's life.

This analysis enhances our understanding of the relationship among circumcision, women, and the covenant. The fact that Jewish women are not circumcised has not precluded them from partaking in the covenantal practices of Bat Mitzvah and Torah study. While these practices have encountered various challenges over the years, a lack of circumcision has not been one of them. The absence of circumcision similarly does not impact the pertinence and significance of ceremonies that symbolically usher newborn girls into the covenant.

The Bat Mitzvah and women's Torah study also expose the fallacy of the contention that parents hold covenantal ceremonies to secure for their daughters the same public attention that their sons receive.[98] No one today would make the analogous argument that the Bat Mitzvah celebration exists only to garner for a girl the same public attention that is showered on a boy becoming a Bar Mitzvah. Nor would one argue today that women are learning Torah to attract attention to themselves. To the contrary, there is a growing consensus that the Bat Mitzvah and women's Torah study enhance the Jewish tradition by enabling women to express their devotion to Torah and mitzvot and, therefore, to the covenant. This is likewise the ultimate goal of a Brit Bat.

ANALOGY TO BAR MITZVAH AND BAT MITZVAH

The relationship between a Bar Mitzvah and a Bat Mitzvah also enables us to better understand the interplay between a circumcision ceremony and a Brit Bat. Circumcision and Brit Bat ceremonies function independently, just as Bar and Bat Mitzvah coming-of-age practices comfortably exist side by side, with neither impinging on the other.[99] Because of this independence, a Brit Bat does not supplant or diminish the Biblical commandment of circumcision, nor does this commandment minimize or otherwise affect the legitimacy and importance of a Brit Bat. A circumcision ceremony and a Brit Bat ceremony incorporate vastly different rituals, yet that difference does not dampen the respective significance of each type of ceremony.

At the same time, the Brit Milah and Brit Bat ceremonies share a common theme, since boys and girls are marking the same occasion of covenantal entry. The Bar and Bat Mitzvah present a similar situation. They both commemorate the milestone of entry into the age of mitzvot, and this thematic parallelism is widely accepted and unquestioned.[100] The notion of a shared covenantal theme for newborn boys and girls is, therefore, well-precedented in modern Jewish life-cycle practices. This thematic commonality is appropriate despite divergent rituals for newborn boys and girls—as demonstrated by the example of Orthodox Bar and Bat Mitzvah celebrations, which express the same coming-of-age theme in different ways.

Separating the circumcision ceremony's strands of covenant and circumcision is also instructive in dissecting the argument that "there is no need to welcome [a girl] into something of which she is already a part," that is, the covenant.[101] This argument misses the point that, when born of a Jewish mother, both boys and girls are inherently and automatically incorporated into the covenant upon birth. This principle is clear from the mishna that deems a Jewish man to be "circumcised," that is, a covenantal member, even if he is actually uncircumcised (M. Nedarim 3:11). Thus, while circumcision is a required act, it also symbolically signifies covenantal entry for baby boys who have been members of the covenant since the moment of birth. It follows that girls likewise can and should symbolically commemorate covenantal entry, even though they have also been included in the covenant since birth. Moreover, it is particularly important to ritualize the covenantal status of girls, since women's covenantal membership is apparently not self-evident, given some people's discomfort with and even rejection of this truism.

The Bat Mitzvah analogy bolsters this explanation. Boys and girls become obligated to perform commandments upon turning thirteen or twelve years old, respectively, regardless of whether or when they formally acknowledge this occasion. This is apparent from the absence of a Bar Mitzvah ritual for most of Jewish history. While classic rabbinic texts identify the age of thirteen as a time of transition,[102] no Bar Mitzvah ceremony developed until many centuries later. The Bar Mitzvah ritual, as we know it today, likely did not coalesce into a common Jewish practice until modern times.[103] Since it is well-accepted to mark ceremonially with a Bat Mitzvah the self-evident fact that girls are obligated to perform commandments upon reaching maturity, it is equally important to commemorate with a Brit Bat the self-evident prerequisite that girls are covenantal members. What we ritualize is often "self-evident" in that it has already happened. This does not make a ritual less important. To the contrary, such a ritual highlights the significance of the milestone that we are emphasizing and formalizing.

IT IS UNLIKELY that covenantal welcoming ceremonies for girls could have emerged before the advent of the "second-wave" feminist movement in the 1960s and 1970s, which sparked a newfound interest in the experiences of girls and women. Regardless, Jewish women have been members of the covenant for as long as it has existed, and this axiom derives from fundamental religious tenets and classic halachic sources—not modern egalitarian impulses. In particular, the distinction between the transcendent covenant and the circumcision symbol reveals how and why covenantal rituals for newborn girls spring from a cornerstone of the Jewish tradition. Indeed, the covenant is the theological foundation for the Bat Mitzvah and women's Torah study, both of which are viable only because of the prerequisite of a newborn girl's covenantal entry.

Those who perform covenantal ceremonies for girls recognize this traditional grounding. For example, Rochelle Millen movingly explains, "It is love of Judaism and deep commitment to the covenant that impels parents to articulate, through ritual, the joy of bringing a girl into their family and the community of Israel."[104] Likewise, R. Sandy Eisenberg Sasso, who performed one of the first covenantal ceremonies for girls, recounts that she and other participants saw themselves "as making holy a moment that has long yearned for sanctification."[105] Thus, while modern feminist sensibilities have precipitated the emergence of covenantal rituals for newborn girls, foundational Jewish principles are the primary basis for performing these rituals.

6

A Central Covenantal Ritual for Girls

We saw in the previous two chapters that covenantal entry is a key life-cycle milestone for girls. As such, it demands a central covenantal ritual that signifies the moment at which a girl is initiated into the covenant of God and Israel. While many meaningful covenantal rituals have been proposed in the past few decades, we focus here on the ritual of swaddling a baby girl in a tallit (a four-cornered prayer shawl).

The tallit has been in use as a garment since at least Mishnaic times (circa first century BCE–second century CE; M. Shabbat 23:1). Today, a standard tallit is made of wool or silk and is white or off-white with black or blue stripes, although some modern styles incorporate a variety of colors and patterns. The most important features of a tallit are the *tzitzit,* eight strands of woolen string topped with five knots, which the Torah mandates for each corner of four-cornered garments. The Torah requires a blue coloring (*techelet*) for one strand on each corner. The tzitzit remind its wearer to observe the commandments and to remember that God redeemed us from Egypt (Numbers 15:37–41).

Swaddling a newborn girl in a tallit as an expression of covenantal entry and communal welcome originated in the 1970s, in some of the earliest Simchat Bat ceremonies. Vanessa Ochs documents such a ceremony performed in the mid-1970s in a New York suburb,[1] and there is at least one more from that era,[2] as well as others in the decades that followed. The tallit swaddling ritual is also suggested as an option in published guidance materials and in a Rabbi's Guide.[3] In short, the tallit swaddling ritual has been quietly percolating since the 1970s.

In our formulation of this ritual, a tallit is spread out on the lap of a grandparent or other close relative. The baby is then placed on this tallit. Alternatively, the grandparent or relative places the baby on a tallit spread out on a table. In either case, the parents take the corners of the tallit and wrap the baby in the tallit, covering her body snugly and completely, as with a swaddling blanket. They then hold up the swaddled baby to those in attendance (whether at home or in the synagogue). As we will explore, this swaddling ritual symbolizes a baby girl's entry into the covenant between God and the Jewish people.

I was recently speaking with Dafna, my seven-year-old daughter, about a Jewish ritual that she was learning about in summer camp. With profundity far beyond her years, Dafna commented that "sometimes a new practice is a continuation of an old practice." But how can a ritual be innovative and, at the same time, perpetuate tradition? Dafna's answer means that sometimes a long-standing practice can be "reborn" as something new. A new ritual can draw so heavily from traditional practices that it fits right into the existing framework. As Vanessa Ochs has pointed out, a new ritual "highlight[s] the presence of the old within the new" to create a continuous "link to the past."[4]

Dafna's explanation is exactly how innovators in the 1970s and 1980s conceptualized new welcoming rituals for newborn girls, including that of swaddling a baby girl in a tallit. We will learn in this chapter about the traditional texts, practices, and imagery that underpin the tallit swaddling ritual and that make it feel natural, fluid, and almost instinctual. We will see how this ritual fits comfortably in the context of contemporary Jewish life-cycle events and how it has the potential to revitalize traditional life-cycle customs that have lapsed. Although the tallit swaddling ritual has not previously been associated with newborn girls, it is not foreign. Rather, this ritual is born out of our tradition.

My husband and I utilized the tallit swaddling ritual at the first ceremony we held, for Dafna. I read about this ritual when I was pregnant with Dafna, and we used it simply because it resonated with both of us at that time. Since then, I have given much thought to this ritual and now understand better why it resonated so deeply. In this chapter, we will articulate these reasons, but with the recognition that they almost need no articulation since they are already found within the Jewish tradition and spirit.

AN ACTIVE RITUAL

The premise underlying the tallit swaddling practice is the idea that an active, religiously evocative ritual most effectively expresses the covenantal entry of a newborn. A vivid ritual creates a focal point, imbuing a ceremony with a clear sense of purpose. In the 1970s, anthropologist Chava Weissler observed in her formative study of birth ceremonies for Jewish girls that "if nothing is done to articulate and symbolize the status transformation of the child, [the ceremonies] are less effective." She notes that "we know from cross-cultural study that most rituals do indeed have such a [symbolic] focus."[5] In 1976, R. Daniel Leifer likewise acknowledged that rituals change one's "status and being[.]" Moreover, "[i]n birth rituals the child passes ritually from a state of non-being and non-membership in the community into a status of being and membership in the community."[6]

Almost two decades later, R. Laura Geller similarly conceptualizes a ceremony for newborn girls as "transformative" in that they "change from baby to Jew; . . . [are] named and given tribe and history; and the community gathered for the ritual must be different because of the ritual."[7] Lori Hope Lefkowitz and R. Rona Shapiro, the first editors of the Ritualwell website, note that a ritual should move from a "before" to an "after," with "something" that falls in the middle. "It is that 'something' that gives participants the feeling that they have witnessed an event."[8]

An active ritual thus marks a distinct point in time when a newborn enters the covenant and the community. It is important to recognize that this "change of status" is symbolic, just as circumcision effects a symbolic covenantal entry for boys. As we have learned, both girls and boys, upon birth from a Jewish mother, are automatically members of the covenant and the Jewish people. This is true regardless of any ceremonial recognition and, for boys, even in the absence of circumcision.

Words cannot match the power of a simple symbolic act in conveying a central covenantal theme. As two rabbis noted in 1993, "Too many of the naming ceremonies for girls that we've read or witnessed are almost painfully wordy, as if only torrents of speech could fill the space that circumcision leaves behind. For a ceremony to be effective, something needs to happen."[9] This is particularly important and appropriate for a birth ceremony. Since babies relate to others on a visceral and primal level, an action involving the baby clearly and powerfully conveys her integration into the Jewish community. Words fall flat when the baby, the central figure in the ceremony, can neither formulate nor understand them.

This disconnect between a baby and the words recited at her ceremony corresponds to R. Leifer's observation that some early ceremonies "are less a ritual happening to the child than a ceremony [expressing the] dedication of the parent[s]" to nurture and educate their newborn child. In these ceremonies, parents recite words to articulate this promise to dedicate themselves to their child. R. Leifer characterizes this phenomenon as "a movement away from the child to the parent."[10] Sharon and Joseph Kaplan, responding to R. Leifer's critique of their 1974 ceremony, have a different perspective. They argue that the prayers and blessings that their family members recited clearly conveyed their daughter's covenantal entry.[11]

Reflecting on this dialogue, I agree that prayers and blessings can be evocative, inspiring, and even essential. The crucial point, however, is that nothing is happening to the baby when adults are reciting words. A ceremony that incorporates a central ritual involving the baby, rather than exclusively readings and speeches by adults, reinstates the all-important focus on the baby.

Furthermore, physicality plays an important role in Jewish life-cycle rituals (not only circumcision). A wedding's poignant turning point is when the groom places a ring on the bride's finger (in traditional communities)[12] or when the couple exchange rings (in liberal communities). At a burial, a heart-wrenching moment is when the mourners shovel dirt on the coffin of their loved one. These physical acts imbue these life-cycle events with power and meaning.

Despite these models, some Simchat Bat practices today continue to suffer from the infirmity of using words rather than action, or using too many words. Some ceremonies include only prayers, readings, blessings, and songs, without any action involving the baby. In addition, introductory comments for Simchat Bat ceremonies are often extensive, due to a belief that whatever is going to happen needs to be explained. In the 1970s, new rituals for girls were commonly explained to Simchat Bat attendees. For example, Chava Weissler observed how one family's use of a kiddush cup in a Simchat Bat ceremony "must be explicitly justified in the course of the ritual. The authors did not assume that its appropriateness would be sensed, that its meaning would be intuitively understood by those present."[13] When a ritual becomes accepted over time, however, this need for explanation dissipates.

SIGNIFICANCE OF TALLIT SWADDLING

We now appreciate why a central active ritual is critical to a welcoming ceremony for girls. But what is it about tallit swaddling, in particular, that enables it to expressively and fluidly represent a baby's entry into the covenant?

Our first observation is that a tallit is strongly associated with wrapping. One who is praying physically wraps the tallit around oneself, first uttering the blessing, "Blessed are You God . . . who commanded us to wrap ourselves in tzitzit—*l'heetatef batzitzit*." The term *wrapping*, rather than *wearing* or *putting on*, is significant in this context.

Swaddling a baby is a primal and natural act that involves the type of physicality that resonates with babies. It follows that this ritual puts the focus on the baby being honored, rather than on peripheral participants, such as parents, other relatives, or friends. Furthermore, a swaddled baby's physical comfort symbolizes the security of divine protection, as well as the embrace of the Jewish people in welcoming a new member. In progressing from the womb to the tallit, a baby goes from one warm, nurturing environment to another.

There are many other facets to the symbolism of tallit wrapping. We explore below how the act of swaddling a baby girl in a tallit signifies holiness, evokes the Torah, and envelops the baby in the covenant.

Tallit Wrapping as a Sign of Holiness

There is a pervasive Jewish impulse to wrap items of extreme holiness in a tallit. For example, Ashkenazim customarily wrap a Torah scroll in a tallit when the scroll is being transported or not being used. In some Sephardic and Mizrachic traditions, brides and/or grooms are traditionally wrapped in a tallit, and, according to some customs, corpses are wrapped in a tallit before burial.

Traditional imagery drives home this point that wrapping in a tallit indicates the presence of extreme holiness. A foremost illustration is that one who dons a tallit during morning prayers recites the following meditation from Psalm 104:

Bless God, O my soul,
God, my Lord, You are very great
You are clothed in glory and majesty
Enveloped in light as a garment
Spreading the heavens as a vast curtain.

R. Kenneth Leitner explains that this psalm's "very strong visual imagery gives meaning to our anticipation of the physical action of wrapping the tallit around the body and head completely." Specifically, "we anticipate becoming surrounded by the Glory and Majesty of God, and being enveloped by God's light. We anticipate the drawing back of the tallit from our eyes as the heavenly curtain is drawn back so that we can see the unfolding of creation."[14] In the ultimate, incomprehensible expression of this idea of "wrapping holiness," the Midrash speaks of God's wrapping Himself in a tallit (were this possible) in a variety of contexts.[15] Wrapping in a tallit is thus an effort to emulate the Divine.

Imagery specific to the tzitzit that hang from the tallit confirms this intimate connection to God's holiness. The Sifrei midrash elaborates that when one fulfills the commandment of tzitzit, it is as if one has welcomed "the face of the Shechina," the Divine Presence. In addition, the Talmud and Midrash compare the blue string of the tzitzit to the sea, which is compared to the sky, which, in turn, is compared to the divine Throne of Honor (*Kisei HaKavod*).[16]

A baby is the ultimate embodiment of holiness and worth, a reflection of the partnership between her parents and God. Due to the awe-inspiring holiness associated with wrapping in a tallit, it is almost instinctual to wrap a baby in a tallit to symbolize her membership in the Jewish people, a "holy nation" (*am kadosh*).

Perhaps for this reason, there is a medieval Ashkenazic custom in which a father would wrap his three-year-old son in a tallit on the boy's first day of Torah education on his way to meeting his teacher. This coming-of-age ritual is part of an elaborate series of customs—including the child's licking honey off a tablet on which the aleph-bet is written—which commemorate this special day. Today, boys are sometimes wrapped in a tallit as part of a ceremony at which they receive a first haircut at age three (*upsherin* in Yiddish). This ceremonial haircut is kabbalistic in origin. Thus, the practice of combining tallit wrapping with a first haircut is a modern-day amalgamation of two wholly unrelated customs. At this juncture, a boy also often receives his first *tallit katan* (four-cornered undershirt with tzitzit on each corner).[17]

Turning to another life-cycle setting, we find traditional circumcision practices in which a tallit is used as a covering. One example is the custom of covering the baby's face with the tallit of the person who is holding the baby (sandek).[18] There is also a custom in some Iraqi and Libyan communities that, both before and during a circumcision, a tallit is draped on the Chair of Elijah, who symbolically presides over the ceremony.[19]

There are other Jewish practices where children are traditionally covered with a tallit. On Simchat Torah, a holiday celebrating the annual completion of the Torah reading cycle, there is a custom to gather all the children under a tallit for a special, collective aliyah (*kol hani'arim,* meaning "all the youngsters"). In addition, fathers (in traditional communities) or parents (in liberal communities) cover both themselves and their children with a tallit during the priests' recitation of the priestly blessing (Birkat Kohanim) in the synagogue. These examples demonstrate how a tallit is used to create a holy space for children. Thus, wrapping a baby in a tallit not only conveys her holiness, but also dovetails with other traditional practices for babies and children.

Wrapped Babies and Torah Scrolls

Another aspect of swaddling baby girls in a tallit involves the strong traditional link between young children and Torah scrolls.[20] Perhaps the most vivid illustration occurs in the synagogue on Simchat Torah when celebrants hold up and dance with Torah scrolls and young children interchangeably.[21] In this energetic and sometimes raucous setting, dancers carry young children in their arms or on their shoulders, and likewise carry Torah scrolls in their arms or above their heads. A related practice is to lift up children to allow them to kiss the Torah as it is paraded around the synagogue when it enters or exits the ark.[22] A historical example is the Ashkenazic wimpel, which is a baby's diaper transformed into a Torah binder. Furthermore, among the Jews of Libya, a man who had no children would purchase Torah scrolls that bear his name. In this way, "[p]erpetuity of seed, and perpetuity of the Torah are closely associated." Libyan Jews also have the custom of giving a *yad,* the pointer that a Torah reader uses to keep his place, to a teething baby as a chewing implement.[23]

This connection between Torah scrolls and young children is amplified in conjunction with the tallit. A baby or small child swaddled in a tallit looks like a Torah scroll wrapped in a tallit, and one holds a wrapped Torah in the same position as one holds a swaddled baby in order to prevent the precious bundle from falling out of one's arms. Professor Ivan Marcus mentions how, upon seeing something wrapped in a tallit, he first assumed it was Torah scroll, but it was, in fact, a boy being taken to his first Torah lesson.[24] Likewise, the custom of covering a baby during his circumcision with a *parochet,* the curtain covering an ark that stores Torah scrolls,[25] conceives of the baby as a Torah that needs to be covered. On a symbolic level, therefore, wrapping a baby in a tallit has the effect of *transforming* a baby into a Torah. A baby wrapped in a tallit embodies the covenant, as does a Torah scroll that records the written contract between God and the Jewish people.

A final example involves the custom of kissing one's tzitzit and then touching them to a Torah scroll as it is paraded around the synagogue after it is removed from the ark and before it is returned. A friend of mine told me how he observed children joining in this parade in a synagogue he was once visiting. My friend then noticed that the rabbi kissed his tzitzit and touched them to the parading Torah and, in precisely the same way, kissed his tzitzit and touched each of the parading children. By virtue of this similar treatment, the rabbi had symbolically transformed the children into Torah scrolls.

This idea of treating a Torah scroll like a person is well established. For example, we dress Torah scrolls with mantles that are considered "clothing," as well as jewelry such as necklaces and crowns on the handles. We also bury Torah scrolls that are no longer usable in the manner of burying a human body. In a modern twist on this anthropomorphism, one synagogue website provides actual "biographies" of its Torah scrolls, which include the Torah's nickname, donors, history, and other pertinent information.[26] These online biographies are styled like those of professionals, thus emphasizing how Torah scrolls are likened to people with personalities and histories of their own. This anthropomorphic conceptualization enables the transformation of babies into Torah scrolls through the act of tallit wrapping.

One brand-new practice for newborns strikingly incorporates both tallit wrapping and Torah scrolls. At a Jewish Renewal synagogue in New York City, a baby's name is announced while the baby is double-wrapped in his or her parents' tallitot. Furthermore, during the naming, the wrapped baby is placed on another tallit that is draped on a Torah scroll, which, in turn, is opened to the portion to be read at the baby's future Bar or Bat Mitzvah. This intricate custom draws a connection among babies, tallitot, and the Torah.[27]

Tallit Wrapping as a Covenantal Embrace
Swaddling a baby in a tallit evokes not only the physicality of Torah, but also the metaphysical embrace of the covenant. When one dons a tallit, one recites:

Through the commandment of [tzitzit], may my life's-breath, spirit, soul and prayer be delivered from external impediments, and may the tallit spread its wings [*k'nafeha*] over them and save them "like an eagle stirs up its nest, hovers over its young[,] [spreads its wings, takes its young, and bears them on its wing]" (Deuteronomy 32:11).[28]

Citing a verse from the poem that Moses recites to the Israelites in his final days (beginning *Ha'azinu*), this prayer beautifully connects the tallit and children by depicting the image of the "wings of the tallit" in combination with a majestic eagle protecting and carrying her offspring. This prayer shows that when a child is wrapped in a tallit, she is nurtured and protected as if by a loving parent. Indeed, Rashi, commenting on this verse, emphasizes the merciful nature of an eagle in that it flutters gently over its eaglets to wake them up, rather than suddenly rushing in upon them.

Moreover, *k'nafeha* means not only "its wings," but also "its corners," in particular, each of the four corners of a tallit to which tzitzit are affixed. This double meaning highlights the link between the eagle and the tallit, each of which has *k'nafeha* (its wings or corners, respectively). It follows that just as the eagle uses its wings to shield its young, so too the tallit can be used to envelop newborn girls.

However, this image runs even deeper: the eagle and its offspring allegorize God and the children of Israel, respectively, in the covenantal framework. The Ha'azinu poem (Deuteronomy 32) opens by characterizing God as just and true and the Israelites as God's portion and inheritance; upon finding the Israelites in the wilderness, God led them about and taught them. At this point, God is compared to an eagle protecting its young, as described in the tallit's prayer; God accompanies the Israelites and gives them from the fat of the land. Over the years, however, when they become satiated, the Israelites abandon God, and God's punishments are harsh and fierce. This poem thus vividly portrays the covenantal dynamic of reward and punishment, and the eagle represents God's overpowering love for the Jewish people in the earliest days of their relationship. Even more powerfully, God commands Moses to write this poem so that it will act as a witness against the Israelites. If they later desecrate the covenant, Moses's poem provides the response to the people's inquiry as to why God has forsaken them (Deuteronomy 31:16–21).

Rashi reinforces the covenantal significance of the eagle allegory by drawing parallels between an eagle's actions toward her young and God's actions toward His fledgling nation at two formative covenantal junctures: the Egyptian Exodus and the Sinaitic Revelation. Rashi explains that an eagle flies with its young on its back, since it would rather take the blow of an arrow from hunters below than expose its young to this risk. In the same way, when the Egyptians advanced on the Israelite encampment at the Red Sea, God moved the angel and the cloud pillar from the front to the back of the Israelite camp in order to shield the people from the Egyptians' arrows (Exodus 14:19–20). Rashi furthermore observes that an eagle carries its eaglets on its back since it fears no predators flying above it. Similarly, when the Israelites reached Mount Sinai and Moses "ascended to God," God's first message to the Israelites is that God "carried [the Israelites out] on the wings of eagles" in redeeming them from Egypt (Exodus 19:4).

In sum, wrapping a baby in a tallit evokes not only the love of parents for their children, like that of an eagle for its young, but also God's love for the Jewish people, especially in the earliest days of the covenant. This emphasis on God's unadulterated love for the nascent Jewish nation is particularly fitting for the covenantal initiation of newborn babies. It follows that the prayer "may the tallit spread its wings over them and save them 'like an eagle stirs up its nest, hover[s] over its young'" can be reinterpreted to apply to newborns. As such, this prayer—which intertwines the imagery of the tallit with that of the covenant—might be appropriately recited by parents while they swaddle their daughter and symbolically enter her into the covenant.

THE TALLIT AS A BROAD COVENANTAL SYMBOL

We have seen how the act of wrapping a newborn in a tallit instinctually evokes the extreme holiness of the Divine, the physicality of the Torah, and the embrace of the covenant. Tallit swaddling is also a meaningful covenantal symbol because of the expansive covenantal associations of the tallit itself. In particular, we will explore how tzitzit prod us to fulfill covenantal responsibilities, and how the tallit alludes to covenantal mutualities and symbolizes a modern covenantalism.

Tzitzit as Perpetual Covenantal Reminders

The tzitzit on each of the four corners of a tallit are a quintessential symbol of the covenant between God and the Jewish nation. The Torah states that upon seeing the tzitzit, "you will remember all the commandments of God and you will perform them" and "you will be holy to your God." God then declares that "I am the Lord your God who brought you out of the land of Egypt to be your God. I am the Lord your God" (Numbers 15:37–41). These passages demonstrate that the tzitzit are ever-present reminders of major components of the covenant: the Exodus from Egypt as a sign of God's love; the Jewish people's responsibility to observe God's commandments; and the relationship between God and the Jewish people.

The Talmud (BT Menachot 44a) relays the story of a Torah student who retained a prostitute. As he climbed into bed with her, the tzitzit hanging from the student's garment swayed freely and hit him in the face. The student, who consequently slipped off the bed and onto the ground, referred to his four sets of tzitzit as four witnesses testifying against him. The tzitzit thus have the ability to—literally—slap someone into remembering his covenantal responsibilities. It follows that the tallit, whose most prominent and significant feature are the tzitzit, evokes the Biblical symbolism of the covenant.

Furthermore, the Talmud states that the mitzvah of tzitzit is equivalent to all the other mitzvot (BT Menachot 43b, Nedarim 25a). According to Rashi, this interpretation is based on the tzitzit's ability to remind their wearer of all the mitzvot (Numbers 15:39). Rashi explains that *tzitzit* has the value of 600 in the gematria system, in which a numerical value is assigned to each Hebrew letter. Adding 600 to the eight strings and five knots of the tzitzit yields 613, the total number of Biblical commandments. This equivalency emphasizes the tzitzit's covenantal significance, since the covenant requires the fulfillment of all the commandments.

Mutuality of a Tallit as a Prayer Shawl

Some traditional uses of a tallit demonstrate how, on the one hand, the Jewish people accept God as their Master and obey the commandments, and how, at the same time, God loves and protects the Jewish people. As a result, the tallit represents the duality and mutuality of the covenantal relationship between God and the Jewish people.

When worn as a shawl during prayer, the tallit symbolizes its wearer's devotion to serving God and recognition of *ole malchut shamayim* (literally, the yoke of the kingdom of Heaven). Some halachic sources state that, to show humility and foster a fear of Heaven, those who are praying should cover their heads with a tallit and keep their heads covered for the entire time they wear the tallit.[29] Likewise, when priests bless a congregation with Birkat Kohanim, both the priests and the recipients of this blessing cover themselves in tallitot to symbolically shield themselves against God's over-powering aura and strength. Indeed, the blessing itself beseeches God to "shine His countenance upon you" (Numbers 6:25). It follows that wrapping oneself in a tallit while praying expresses both humility and a recognition of God's fear-inspiring omnipotence.

The other side of this dynamic is that the tallit also embodies divine be-neficence. The tallit, when wrapped around one who is praying and drawing close to God, represents God's enveloping love and protection during this intimate time. By extension, the tallit symbolizes God's special connection to the Jewish people, a microcosm of which is the minyan, a prayer quo-rum. A midrash on Psalms (90:18) says that "when the children of Israel are wrapped in their tallitot, let them feel as though the glory of the Divine Presence is upon them. For Scripture does not say: 'That you may look upon [the tzitzit],' but rather 'That you may look upon God' (Numbers 15:39)." R. Dov Peretz Elkins comments that "the essence of the feeling one derives from wearing the tallit is the feeling of being covered by the wings of the Divine Presence."[30]

Similarly, a tallit as a wedding canopy envelops a couple in their love and the love of God, while a tallit as a shroud protects the body of someone who has gone on to the next world. Moreover, while using tallitot during Birkat Kohanim can be construed as a sign of God's overwhelming power, it can also be viewed as an act of God's love. Birkat Kohanim is itself an expression of God's love; the priests begin this ritual by reciting a blessing for He who "commanded us to bless His people Israel with love." This idea of the tallit as a shield finds expression in the Talmudic statement (BT Rosh Hashana 33b) that Moses saw God's tallit (were this possible) when God "passed by" Moses after the golden calf episode. Shielding Moses from God's glory and fury in the aftermath of the people's ultimate transgression evokes divine love and forgiveness.

Tallit as a Modern Political Symbol

Another covenantal manifestation of the tallit is that it inspired the flag of the modern State of Israel—a beautiful connection between old and new. The Israeli flag has a blue Shield of David (star with six points) at its center with a blue horizontal stripe on either side, all on a white background. This flag made its debut at the First Zionist Congress in Basel, Switzerland in 1897. David Wolffsohn, an English Jew who succeeded Theodor Herzl in 1905 as president of the World Zionist Organization, explained how he designed this flag:

> [A]n idea struck me. We have a flag—and it is blue and white. The talith [that is, tallit] with which we wrap ourselves when we pray: that is our symbol. Let us take this talith from its bag and unroll it before the eyes of Israel and the eyes of all nations. So I ordered a blue and white flag with the Shield of David painted upon it. That is how our national flag ...came into being. And no one expressed any surprise or asked whence it came or how.[31]

In other words, Wolffsohn modeled the flag's horizontal stripes on those of the tallit and colored the flag blue based on the Biblically mandated techelet coloring for one string of each tzitzit set.

As Wolffsohn observed, the tallit's transition from religious garment to nationalistic symbol went unquestioned. The tallit has become so strongly identified with the State of Israel and the Jewish people that, in at least one instance, Israeli soldiers have used it as an identifying mark. In the Yom Kippur War in 1973, a group of Israeli soldiers were hiding in the Sinai Peninsula after Egyptian forces hit their tank. When Israeli tanks approached, one of the soldiers had the idea of waving his personal tallit at the tanks. As a result, the soldiers in the tanks recognized their own and did not open fire.[32]

Citing the traditional comparison of the tzitzit's blue coloring to the sparkling blues of the sea, the heavens, and the Throne of Glory, R. Dov Peretz Elkins comments that these are "[f]itting colors to choose for the symbolic transposition of a people's ideals and aspirations into a cloth representation!" He observes how the inspiration of the tallit symbolically unites the State of Israel and the covenant: "The modern flag of Israel, the people and the State, ... [combine] in one emblem the religious meaning of the eternal covenant between God and Israel, and the corporate solidarity of God's eternal people."[33] That is, the tallit plays a role in the conceptualization of the modern State of Israel as *reisheet tz'michat g'ulateinu* ("the beginning of the flowering of our redemption"). Embodied in the Israeli flag, the tallit has come to symbolize the modern realization of the covenantal promise of a Jewish nation in the Land of Israel.

The tallit has also been used symbolically in the context of political activism to promote Jewish strength and pride. R. Avraham Weiss has worn a tallit when protesting around the world in defense of the State of Israel, on behalf of oppressed Soviet Jews, and in connection with other Jewish causes. One commentator observes that wearing a tallit in public in this context "is a symbol of religious Jewish presence, perhaps a sign to the world that God is behind the man in the prayer shawl."[34] Relatedly, "at the commemoration marking the fiftieth anniversary of the liberation of Auschwitz, the World Jewish Congress asked all participants to wear prayer shawls as they entered the camp."[35] As with the Israeli flag, these examples demonstrate how the tallit bridges the religious and political spheres, thereby conveying its covenantal significance in a way that is easily recognizable.

THE TALLIT IN LIFE-CYCLE PRACTICE

Tallit swaddling is a meaningful ritual, not only because it evokes the covenant, but also because it fits seamlessly into the full range of Jewish life-cycle practices. As we will see, there is a traditional customary role for the tallit at every major life-cycle event. Incorporating the tallit as part of welcoming ceremonies for newborn girls is thus a natural extension of traditional life-cycle practices.

At a circumcision ceremony, the mohel (circumciser) and sandek both traditionally wear a tallit.[36] One reason offered for this custom is to honor the commandment of circumcision. In some communities, the father of the baby boy also wears a tallit.[37] In addition, there is a custom to cover the baby's face with the sandek's tallit. Perhaps in a modern interpretation of these customs, R. Elyse Goldstein held her tallit high over each of her sons at their circumcisions while the women present recited blessings.[38]

The tallit is also traditionally used as an adornment in connection with circumcision. Among Iraqi Jews, it is customary to bring the Chair of Elijah to a baby boy's home on the night preceding his circumcision, and to place a tallit (as well as other ritual items) on this chair. The adorned chair remains in the room of the newborn boy's mother, and women sit there and sing songs.[39] Libyan Jews practice similar customs.[40]

The tallit likewise played a role in formative Ashkenazic life-cycle rituals. During the Hollekreisch ceremony, a baby boy may have been covered with a tallit or one may have been placed next him.[41] More prevalent was the medieval custom of wrapping a three-year-old boy in a tallit on his first day of Torah education. Today, a boy's upsherin may include wrapping him in a tallit and/or presenting him with his first tallit katan.

Interestingly, at least one synagogue today[42] uses a tallit as a canopy (*chuppat tallit*) as part of its nursery school graduation ceremony. A chuppat tallit consists of a tallit raised high overhead by four bearers, each holding a pole attached to a corner of the tallit or just the tallit corner itself. In this case, the chuppat tallit is held above children during their graduation ceremony, and parents donate funds to have the tallit embroidered with the young graduates' names. This practice echoes the use of a chuppat tallit for a child's aliyah on Simchat Torah.

A bar mitzvah traditionally wears a tallit for the first time when he is called up to the Torah for an aliyah. Today in liberal communities (particularly in the Diaspora), a bat mitzvah does the same. In some communities, a tallit is subsequently always worn during prayer, while in others, the tallit is worn again only after marriage (except when leading prayers or receiving an aliyah). In addition, a bar mitzvah in Israel today may receive his first aliyah under a chuppat tallit, a modern variation on the well-established chuppat tallit wedding custom, described below. This illustrates a broader trend of adapting wedding practices to create new coming-of-age rituals.[43]

The tallit is a long-standing feature of Jewish wedding ceremonies. At Sephardic and Mizrachic weddings since the sixteenth century, brides and/or grooms have been covered or wrapped in a tallit, and there are many versions of this custom. For example, in the Syrian community, during the recitation of the sheva brachot (the seven wedding blessings), the bride's father, the groom's father, and the rabbi spread a tallit over the couple's heads. Moroccan grooms, while standing under the chuppah, recite the blessing on tzitzit and wear the tallit until the *birkat erusin* (the betrothal blessing); at this point, the tallit is spread over the couple's heads as a chuppah until the end of the sheva brachot. In the Judeo-Spanish tradition, a groom wears a newly purchased tallit and recites the Shehechiyanu blessing. The parents of the bride and groom subsequently place this tallit over the couple's heads and thank God for "enabl[ing] them to reach the day of covering their children under the prayer shawl in marriage." Among Sephardim in England and Holland, a groom traditionally wears a new tallit without saying a blessing. In some Yemenite communities, a groom drapes his tallit on the bride. In one contemporary Sephardic practice, a groom puts on a tallit, and then four men remove it and hold it taut over the bride and groom. Another practice today is that a bride purchases a tallit for the groom, and he wraps it around both of them, with a separate chuppah spread out above them.[44]

In Ashkenaz, a tallit was used as a chuppah since at least the High Middle Ages. There is also evidence in Ashkenaz of draping a tallit on the bride and groom and then stretching a separate chuppah above their heads. By contrast, the Dutch custom since the sixteenth century is to cover the bride and groom with a tallit such that no additional chuppah is necessary. After the Holocaust, the chuppat tallit practice remained prevalent in France, particularly in Alsace. Some Ashkenazim today in Israel and North America use a chuppat tallit at weddings.[45] A variation on this custom is to hold a chuppat tallit over a groom receiving an aliyah on the Shabbat preceding his wedding (*Shabbat chatan* in Hebrew; *aufruf* in Yiddish). In this way, the chuppat tallit practice has smoothly expanded from wedding ceremonies to pre-wedding celebrations.

Another feature of Ashkenazic wedding practices today is the adoption of Sephardic and Mizrachic customs related to the tallit. For example, among some Ashkenazim in Israel today, a groom standing under the chuppah wraps himself and the bride with a newly purchased tallit.[46] Similarly, an Ashkenazic friend of mine told me that, at her wedding in the United States, the rabbi wrapped both bride and groom in a tallit and recited Birkat Kohanim. At an Ashkenazic wedding that I attended in London, the groom wore a tallit over his kittel (a white, shroud-like garment) for the length of the ceremony, thus mixing Sephardic and Ashkenazic customs, respectively. Given the contemporary Ashkenazic use of the Sephardic Zeved HaBat liturgy for naming baby girls (as we saw in chapter 3), there may be a tendency today for Ashkenazim to borrow life-cycle customs from Sephardim.

The final chapter of life-cycle practices has also become associated with the tallit, as some Jews customarily wrap a deceased with a tallit. One tradition in the Diaspora is to bury a tallit with its wearer, as an indication that the deceased performed the commandment of tzitzit. In Israel, a tallit typically covers a body being carried to the cemetery, and the tallit can be removed before the burial.[47]

REFORMULATING TRADITIONAL CUSTOMS

Since the tallit plays a role in every major Jewish life-cycle ritual, swaddling newborn girls in a tallit fits fluidly into this life-cycle framework. However, tallit swaddling is special in yet another way, due to its potential to reinterpret and renew one particular Ashkenazic life-cycle custom—the wimpel. A wimpel is a diaper, placed under a baby boy during his circumcision, which was subsequently embroidered and used as a Torah binder. A robust custom for centuries, the wimpel disappeared in the Holocaust era. By alluding to the wimpel custom, a tallit swaddling ritual for newborn girls would connect to tradition while serving as a bridge to the future.

Over time, it became customary to use a boy's wimpel to bind the Torah from which he received his first aliyah as a bar mitzvah, as well as the Torah that was read on the Shabbat preceding his wedding.[48] In this way, the wimpel associated with a boy's birth was reused for life-cycle events that followed. In a variation on these customs, R. Nathan Marcus Adler, chief rabbi of the British Empire in the nineteenth century, was presented with a unique, decorative wimpel on the occasion of his twenty-fifth wedding anniversary to his second wife.[49]

Another significant example of recycling a birth object for subsequent life-cycle events is the Talmudic advice to plant a tree at the birth of a child—a cedar tree for a boy, and a pine tree for a girl—and to use the wood from this tree for the child's eventual wedding *genana* (BT Gittin 57a). The *genana* may have been a wedding chamber, rather than a canopy, which is a later custom. Ritual objects are likewise reused for the *Aqd-el-yas* ("Bond of the Myrtle") ceremony in the Indian Iraqi tradition. In this ceremony, the Chair of Elijah to be used at the next day's circumcision is decorated and the baby boy is blessed. The two large, decorative candles placed next to the chair had been previously used at the wedding of the boy's parents.[50] Along similar lines, the embroidered silk veil placed over the heads of a mother and her newborn daughter at the Turkish Las Fadas welcoming ceremony is re-worn by the daughter on her wedding day.[51] Finally, it is significant that, in one of the earliest instances of welcoming a baby girl into the covenant by swaddling her in a tallit (in 1976), the baby was wrapped in the tallit that had served as her parents' wedding chuppah.[52] This tallit thus linked wedding and birth practices across two generations.

This tradition of keeping a religious object from a birth ritual and reusing it at subsequent life-cycle events leads us to the idea of creating a "modern wimpel." In this formulation, the relevant four-cornered garment is a tallit, rather than a diaper. For baby girls, a tallit would be used at a Brit Bat for swaddling. For baby boys, a tallit would be used in a traditional fashion at a circumcision, either placed under the baby, draped over the Chair of Elijah, or worn by a participant. Parents would embroider or otherwise decorate this tallit, whether used for a boy or a girl, in the manner of a wimpel. These embellishments would include the baby's name, the parents' names, the birth date, and other inscriptions, along with artistic decorations, if desired and feasible. A boy would subsequently wear his special tallit at his Bar Mitzvah and, in liberal communities, a girl would do the same at her Bat Mitzvah. This tallit could then be used as a chuppah at the child's eventual wedding. All told, creating a handmade and personalized modern wimpel meaningfully connects an array of life-cycle events and results in *hiddur mitzvah,* the beautification of Jewish practices.

It is noteworthy that, sometime before 1984, textile artist Ita Aber advanced the idea of creating a Torah covering from the material with which a baby girl was wrapped during her naming ceremony. One side of the covering would have a design related to the girl's Torah portion, and the other side would bear her name and a dedication "on the beginning of her study of Torah." This idea was based on the wimpel model. Aber also presented the related idea of having a baby girl don a dress with the Hebrew inscription that she be blessed with Torah, chuppah, and good deeds.[53] While this innovative Torah covering and dress were offered for sale in the 1980s, it is unclear whether they were ever actually made or used in a ceremony. I recently discovered, however, that there is at least one contemporary fabric artist who creates unique, decorative "modern wimpels" for both boys and girls.[54]

This suggestion of using a tallit as a modern wimpel allows for different variations. One idea is to use, at a welcoming ceremony (i.e., circumcision or Brit Bat), a tallit currently or previously worn by a parent, grandparent, or great-grandparent. At our children's ceremonies, my husband, Dan, and I used the tallit that Dan currently wears and that belonged to his late father. We swaddled our daughters in this special tallit, and Dan wore it at our son's circumcision. In this way, we imbued our newborns' rituals with multigenerational significance and honored the memory of their grandfather.[55]

Another possibility is that children receive a new tallit upon birth and use it throughout their lifetimes, both for life-cycle events and for daily prayer. Such a tallit is a meaningful gift from parents to their children. My children love to see the baby blankets they received as gifts and the baby scrapbooks that I compiled. A tallit used as a modern-day wimpel would channel this sentimentality into commemorating the milestone of covenantal entry.

Alternatively, a single tallit could be used for all the children in one family at their respective birth ceremonies. This "family tallit" would contain all the children's names and birth dates as they are born and ceremonially welcomed. The information recorded on this tallit would be similar to that on a family tree. Each child would then use this same "family tallit" for subsequent life-cycle events. Passed down to the next generation, this tallit would become a cherished family heirloom.

This idea for a family keepsake from a birth ceremony is based on my personal experience. When I was pregnant for the first time and anticipating my firstborn's ceremony (whether boy or girl), I created a handmade covering for a Chair of Elijah. I purchased yards of red velvet material and some mustard-colored felt, colors and fabrics that I thought evoked royalty and rich splendor. Following my freehand sketches, I cut out from the felt the Hebrew letters spelling out *Kisei Eliyahu,* and, with my mother's assistance, sewed them onto the velvet. At all four welcoming ceremonies we held, Dan and I adorned the Chair of Elijah with this covering, and we will hopefully pass it down to our grandchildren. A "family tallit" would likewise function as a personalized ritual object to be passed down to the next generation, and could additionally be used at a range of life-cycle events.

While there are different ways to adopt a "modern wimpel" in contemporary settings, the primary purpose of this tallit is to connect to the covenant, just as an actual wimpel links a circumcision to a Torah scroll, both symbols of the covenant. This special tallit would be used at a circumcision or Brit Bat, which symbolically marks covenantal entry, and at a Bar or Bat Mitzvah when a young person takes on covenantal responsibilities. It likewise would be used at a wedding, which creates a covenant between bride and groom and results in the next generation of covenantal members.

Finally, this new practice would, paradoxically, revitalize traditional customs. The tallit is utilized in the manner of a wimpel—an article containing personal details which enhances birth ceremonies and other life-cycle events and which is lovingly retained for generations. As such, this use memorializes, and even perpetuates, the wimpel custom by reinterpreting it. The "modern wimpel" would also give a new layer of meaning to the Ashkenazic custom of a bride and groom standing under a chuppat tallit.[56] Finally, reusing a tallit from a birth ceremony as a chuppah for a wedding brings us back to the Talmud's advice to plant a tree when a baby is born and then to use the tree's wood for his or her wedding chuppah. Just like this wood, the tallit used at a circumcision or Brit Bat harkens back to a groom or bride's birth and, by using the same ritual object, physically connects birth and marriage in an intensely personal way.

TALLIT SWADDLING AND HALACHA

We next consider tallit swaddling from a perspective that is far-reaching, yet also more technical. Halacha is the Jewish legal system that serves as a backbone of traditional Jewish thought and practices. It is important and interesting to understand whether and how a ritual as new as tallit swaddling for newborn girls fits into a broad traditional context that has been evolving for two thousand years.

There is evidence that in medieval Ashkenaz, some women wore tzitzit or a tallit katan, while others actively participated in the production of tzitzit.[57] Today, many Jewish women wear tallitot, and this practice has been addressed in contemporary halachic literature.[58]

Regardless, swaddling a newborn girl in a tallit is different than an adult woman wearing a tallit during prayer. As a wrapping for a newborn baby, the tallit functions as an object (*chefetz*), and not as a garment (*beged*), a significant technical distinction. The tallit is similarly used as a chefetz, for example, when wrapping a Torah scroll or covering a table where a Torah is placed.

The perspective of R. Raphael Aaron Ben-Shimon (Cairo, Egypt, 1847– 1928) about the use of tallitot in wedding ceremonies is instructive. He inquires why a bride and groom would cover themselves with a tallit under the chuppah rather than with silk embroidered with gold and silver. R. Ben-Shimon responds that the tallit is enhanced with holiness and is "a garment of mitzvah." It is thus appropriate for a bride and groom to "honor and adorn at their time of joy with a garment that has religious holiness."[59] He adds, "And which honor is more elevated than this honor, and what pleasure is more elevated than this spiritual pleasure?" Likewise, R. Binyomin Hamburger of the Institute for German Jewish Heritage concludes that a tallit contains elements of "holiness, honor, and glory."[60] It follows that the tallit is used as a religious article in a wide variety of contexts, as we have seen, because of its holiness and its close association with mitzvot (or perhaps these characteristics derive from the tallit's diverse uses).

Since it is a versatile "garment of mitzvah," the tallit would not become "feminized" due to its role in Brit Bat ceremonies. A newborn girl's once-in-a-lifetime use of a tallit at a Brit Bat is analogous to men's sporadic use of the mikvah (ritual bath) on a customary basis, such as on the eve of Yom Kippur. The mikvah is strongly associated with women because they traditionally use it on a regular basis, for monthly post-menstrual immersions. However, just as a mikvah is not masculinized when men use it sporadically, the tallit is not feminized when girls are wrapped in it once. Put simply, the tallit's symbolism is expansive enough to transcend gender associations.

More generally, wrapping a baby girl in a tallit would be yet another example of the countless Jewish symbols and liturgies that have taken on different meanings or connotations over time. One illustration of this phenomenon is the custom of parents bestowing on their children the priestly blessing (along with an introductory prayer) at the onset of Shabbat. This custom is called Birkat Banim, which means "the Blessing of Children." There is no textual basis or a priori reason for linking the priestly blessing (Numbers 6:24–26) with children or Shabbat. In fact, from a halachic perspective, it is quite radical to encourage non-priests to recite weekly the special blessing that God explicitly reserved in the Torah for the priests. R. Baruch Epstein (Lithuania, 1860–1941) calls this type of custom "foreign" or "strange" (*zar*) and observes that a non-priest who blesses the people in the manner of priests violates a positive Biblical commandment.[61] Despite lacking a halachic basis (or possibly even violating normative halacha), Birkat Banim developed over time, combining the themes of blessings, children, peace, and Shabbat. Today, this custom is widely practiced and appears in the vast majority of siddurim for Shabbat.

It is likely that the Birkat Banim practice spread as people connected the peace of Shabbat with the peaceful nature traditionally associated with priests (M. Avot 1:12). In addition, priests proclaim that they are commanded to bless God's nation "with love," and the priestly blessing is itself an expression of divine love. Birkat Banim therefore may have gained popularity as people linked parents' love for their children with the love of God and His priests for the community of Israel.

Like those of Birkat Banim, the central themes of a tallit swaddling ritual—the covenant, the tallit, and young children—are intertwined and deeply rooted in Jewish tradition. As a result, tallit swaddling has the long-term potential to become identified with welcoming newborn girls into the covenant, just as the priestly blessing evolved into the basis for a Shabbat children's blessing. Birkat Banim illustrates how practices and associations change over time, sometimes drastically, and that halacha is flexible enough to accommodate and even facilitate this process.

OTHER PROPOSED COVENANTAL SYMBOLS

While we have focused here on tallit swaddling, a range of other rituals have been suggested and performed since the 1970s to welcome girls ceremonially into the covenant. Some utilize existing liturgies or rituals, such as candle-lighting, the Shabbat kiddush prayer, the Havdalah ceremony marking the end of Shabbat, and a wedding's sheva brachot. Other covenantal rituals involve physicality or movement, such as having a baby touch a Torah scroll, parading her around the synagogue, placing a religious article in her hand, and carrying her between two lines of people. Some rituals relate to water, including mikvah immersion and hand or feet washing. Others relate to the senses, such as touching with salt water, applying henna or myrtle, and rubbing with olive oil. Still others involve giving gifts to the baby. This is only a partial list; there are certainly many other active covenantal rituals that have been proposed or used in the past four decades.

All these rituals are the product of sincere and thoughtful efforts and are no doubt deeply meaningful to those performing them. Parents should not be discouraged from using rituals that resonate with them. Nonetheless, many of these rituals have drawbacks, particularly in the context of formulating a widely accepted ceremony.

Some may not clearly and instantly convey the concept of covenantal entry. A ritual is most effective when no explanation is required. For example, carrying a baby between two lines of people is a creative suggestion for evoking the brit ben habetarim, Abraham's third covenantal interaction with God, where a fire passed between halves of animals (Genesis 15). However, this connection is not immediately apparent, and the significance of carrying a baby in this manner is likely understood only with the aid of a detailed explanation. Absent an explanation, this type of ritual is more likely to be associated with a burial, where mourners traditionally walk between two lines of people.

Among those rituals with more easily discernible ties to the covenant, one set involves Shabbat symbolism. The Bible explicitly refers to Shabbat as an "eternal covenant" (Exodus 31:16). However, Shabbat rituals, such as the combination of candlelighting and kiddush, are so strongly identified specifically with Shabbat that they may not translate effectively to the different context of a newborn's covenantal entry. The same holds true for the Havdalah ceremony. Since a covenantal ritual should mark an entry into the covenant, Havdalah has the added difficulty of marking an exit (that of Shabbat). A related suggestion is commemorating covenantal entry by holding a ceremony on Shabbat, without any active ritual.[62] Capturing the powerful covenantal symbolism of Shabbat is a beautiful idea. However, this ephemeral symbolism lacks the physicality that is so compelling in connecting ceremonially to an intangible covenant.

Another set of covenantal rituals involves Torah scrolls, which represent the "written contract" between God and the Jewish people. One ritual is touching a baby's hand to a Torah scroll as a means of introducing her to Torah. This ritual also echoes the custom of kissing one's hand after touching a "dressed" Torah and that of touching tzitzit to a Torah's parchment on the line where an aliyah's reading begins. However, touching the baby's hand to a Torah is physically awkward, since newborns lack control of their limbs, naturally tighten their fingers into a fist, and do not yet reach out to touch objects. The same difficulty applies to touching any other ritual object. By contrast, swaddling is naturally comfortable for newborns and engages a baby's entire body.

A second ritual evoking Torah scrolls is to carry a baby around the synagogue, just as Torah scrolls are paraded when they are taken out of the ark and, later, when they are returned. While Torah scrolls and children are closely linked, as we have seen, this minutes-long ritual does not provide a single, focal moment signifying the symbolic status change of covenantal entry.

Two final rituals utilize water. The first is immersing a baby girl in a mikvah. This has been accomplished in either a full-sized mikvah or a miniature tub. Rabbinic sources link mikvah immersion with the covenant, and the mikvah is most commonly construed as a female symbol. Immersing in a mikvah also traditionally bestows a symbolic change of status (for example, menstruating women become ritually pure, and converts become Jewish).

However, the mikvah's connection to the covenant is not widely known. Adopted as a symbol for baby girls, the mikvah would likely conjure up instead its traditional "female" use: the immersion of women resuming sexual relations with their husbands upon the cessation of their monthly menstrual period. In my personal opinion, this overt sexuality of the mikvah symbol is not suitable for newborns who are many years away from developing their sexuality and who should not be viewed in sexual terms. Coming from a different perspective, R. Elyse Goldstein has commented that mikvah symbolism is important for women "[b]ecause we have so little that is ours."[63] To the contrary, I prefer to emphasize that the totality of Judaism "belongs" to all Jews, men and women alike. To confine women to limited aspects of Judaism is to re-assign women to the realm of "other."

Another issue is that complete immersion requires an adult to accompany the baby into the mikvah and then to let go of her underwater for a split second. This release and separation, however, conveys precisely the opposite of what the covenant represents—the continuous, loving embrace of God and the Jewish people. More importantly, this procedure may upset the baby and may pose a safety risk for her. Even a minute risk is, however, unacceptable when there is no religious mandate. While partial immersion in a small, transportable tub alleviates these issues, it does not capture the enveloping water symbolism.[64]

A second water ritual is washing a baby's feet to evoke how Abraham washed the feet of the angels who came to announce Sarah's impending pregnancy (Genesis 18). This symbol alludes to the perpetuation of the Abrahamic line, which is an aspect of the covenant. Foot washing, however, does not fit easily with modern Jewish practices, since it is a social etiquette that has not been practiced for many centuries. By contrast, wrapping with a tallit (as for a Torah scroll or corpse) is a well-known practice today. Moreover, extricating and washing a baby's foot is physically awkward, since babies naturally keep their legs bent and tucked close to their bodies. On the other hand, babies naturally feel comfortable when they are swaddled.

WE HAVE LEARNED in this chapter about the power and simplicity of tallit swaddling as a central ritual for a covenantal ceremony for newborn girls. Tallit swaddling resonates with traditional sensibilities and fits easily into the framework of contemporary Jewish life-cycle practices. It also provides an opportunity for reviving and reinterpreting traditional customs. My hope is that parents and rabbis consider these ideas in thinking about the direction that welcoming ceremonies for newborn girls should take in the years to come.

Conveying the Covenantal Theme

We have seen how a ritual that actively initiates a newborn girl into the covenant can be the focal point of a covenantal welcoming ceremony. However, the symbolism of covenantal entry becomes apparent and seamless, requiring no explanation, only when it suffuses the ceremony and is manifested in multiple ways. Thus, while a central ritual is important, it is not sufficient. A cohesive theme requires more.

In this chapter, we consider ways of expressing a covenantal theme consistently throughout a ceremony for newborn girls (whether it occurs at home, during synagogue services, or otherwise). An array of prayers, symbols, and Scriptural passages have been used creatively in the past few decades to communicate a covenantal theme. However, we turn our attention here to the notion of modeling selected aspects of the circumcision ceremony, the covenantal ceremony for newborn boys, in order to convey the covenantal entry of girls. While the circumcision ceremony has evolved over time and allows for some variation, most Jewish communities today follow certain conventions, and we would draw from this body of traditions.

There are many parents and rabbis who have already utilized the template of the circumcision ceremony in formulating practices for girls. We explore this idea here in detail to understand how and why modeling the circumcision ceremony can compellingly express a girl's entry into the covenant and even add new layers of meaning to this symbolism. We will also discover why this modeling has been controversial and, yet, how this approach comes to feel fluid when we contextualize it in light of other Jewish life-cycle rituals and their historical trajectories.

CONTOURS OF A COVENANTAL CEREMONY FOR GIRLS

The first step in modeling the circumcision ceremony is to identify its most basic elements—a welcoming, a covenantal ritual with blessings, and a naming. In the context of a ceremony for a newborn girl, each of these elements would incorporate excerpts from the circumcision liturgy that emphasize the covenant (rather than the circumcision rite).

For example, a ceremony begins when an honored participant carries the baby girl into the room, and all those in attendance greet her in unison. After the baby is symbolically entered into the covenant (by being swaddled in a tallit), the parents and attendees recite a prayer, such as, "Just as she has entered into the covenant, so shall she enter Torah, chuppah, and good deeds." This powerful prayer, the feminine form of that recited at a circumcision, is particularly appropriate for a newborn because it portrays covenantal fidelity as a lifelong endeavor. The blessing over a cup of wine ("Blessed are You God . . . who creates the fruit of the vine") is likewise fitting since it sanctifies the occasion, as at a circumcision or wedding.[1]

Some might incorporate a more progressive element, namely, a feminized version of a central blessing of the circumcision ceremony: "Blessed are You God, King of the Universe, who has sanctified us with Your commandments and commanded us to enter our daughter into the covenant of Abraham our forefather and Sarah our foremother." Other variations eliminate the concept of commanding us to enter our daughters into the covenant (since, indeed, the Torah does not explicitly command us to do so). One example is: "Blessed are You God, King of the Universe, who has entered our daughter into the covenant of Abraham our forefather and Sarah our foremother."

The issue of whether to include a new blessing in a ceremony for girls has been fraught with controversy. In general, liberal Jews maintain that a covenantal blessing is critically important and stands at the heart of a ceremony, while traditional Jews believe that the creation of new blessings is strictly prohibited today. In the end, whether to recite such a blessing is a personal decision for parents to make.

The Hatov v'Hameitiv blessing ("Blessed are You God, our God, King of the Universe, who is Good and who causes good"), which we learned about in chapter 1, could alternatively function as a Brit Bat's central blessing (in traditional communities) or could meaningfully supplement other blessings (in liberal communities). The Hatov v'Hameitiv blessing, which has existed since at least Mishnaic times (Brachot 9:2), is traditionally recited in connection with the birth of a son.[2] The Talmud explains that Hatov v'Hameitiv is recited for that which is good "for oneself and others"—in other words, for two or more people—and that a father's hearing of the birth of his son falls into this category (BT Brachot 59b). Later authorities explain that the birth of a son merits Hatov v'Hameitiv because both a father and a mother are happy upon learning that they have a new son.[3] Reciting Hatov v'Hameitiv today on the birth of a girl can be understood as an application of halachic principles in light of the contemporary norm that recognizes the birth of a girl as a joyous event for both parents.[4] By extension, the Hatov v'Hameitiv blessing articulates the religious import of newborn girls and, in my opinion, constitutes a key component of an initiation ceremony (to the extent that this blessing was not already recited at the time of the baby's birth).

Another segment of our ceremony is a baby's first and only naming, which we encountered in chapter 2. We now take this idea to the next level by infusing the naming liturgy with covenantal meaning. The purpose of announcing a baby girl's name is to provide her not only with a personal identity, but also with a communal identity as a proud Jew who has a covenantal relationship with God and Torah. In this way, a girl's naming dovetails with her symbolic covenantal entry. The naming becomes an expression of the community's hope that a newborn girl will live a rich Jewish life in the covenantal framework.

This inherent nexus between covenantal entry and a naming harkens back to Abraham and Sarah. "When Avram entered into the 'brit' (covenant), he became known as Avraham; Sarai his wife became Sarah. So the tradition [arose] of giving each new member of the brit a covenant-name[.]"[5] A new name brings with it a new covenantal persona. God gave Abraham and Sarah new names and covenantal identities, and we follow God's example every time we name a baby.

This intrinsic link between the covenant and a Jewish name may be a reason that naming a baby boy developed as part of the circumcision ceremony. While the miracle of birth and the naming of a child are beautiful secondary themes in a welcoming ceremony for newborns, neither captures the essence of Jewish existence as completely as the covenant.

It follows that modeling the overall structure of the elaborate naming liturgy recited after a circumcision is one way to highlight our ceremony's covenantal theme. In the feminine form, this liturgy begins: "Our God, the God of our forefathers and foremothers, preserve this girl for her father and her mother, and her name in Israel will be called . . ." The inclusion of selected Scriptural passages that evoke the eternality of the covenant (modeled on the passages cited at a circumcision) explicitly casts a girl's naming as a means of initiating her into the covenant. The naming liturgy concludes with the prayer that "this small child will become great. Just as she has entered into the covenant, so shall she be entered into Torah, the marriage canopy, and good deeds."

Looking beyond structure and liturgy, we recognize that the circumcision ceremony is held on the eighth day following a baby boy's birth, per God's command (Genesis 17:12, Leviticus 12:3). We consider how and why this timing effectively communicates the entry of a girl into the covenant and, at the same time, enhances the overall experience of participating in a welcoming ceremony. We also note that a symbolic Chair of Elijah (*Kisei Eliyahu*) could serve as a backdrop for the proceedings, as it does at a circumcision ceremony. One approach is to designate this chair with a decorative covering or some other distinguishing ornamentation. Finally, we call the complete ceremony a *Brit Bat,* meaning "Covenant of a Daughter," to succinctly articulate that we are commemorating a girl's entry into the covenant.

Bearing this outline in mind, we examine, in turn, each aspect of this ceremony for newborn girls, which we adapted from the circumcision ceremony —that is, its structure, liturgy, timing, ancillary symbolism, and name.

MODELING THE STRUCTURE AND LITURGY
OF THE CIRCUMCISION CEREMONY

Echoes of the circumcision ceremony can be found, to varying degrees, in the novel ceremonies for newborn girls that emerged in the 1970s and 1980s. For example, some followed the basic structure of the circumcision ceremony. Some included the prayer expressing the hope that a baby will have a life filled with Torah, marriage, and good deeds; the blessing over a cup of wine; or variations of the naming prayer. In some ceremonies, the traditional blessing for entering boys into the covenant was adapted for girls. The most radical attempt at utilizing the circumcision model for girls was Mary

Gendler's hymenectomy proposal. Today, many parents and rabbis continue to use selected aspects of the traditional circumcision liturgy in welcoming newborn girls. These elements may or may not predominate in the overall ceremony.

At the same time, there are both traditionalists and feminists who have rejected this idea of "borrowing" elements from the circumcision ceremony. As a result, this notion has been highly controversial from the start. R. Moshe Meiselman is one traditionalist who disparaged the "[i]mitation of male ceremonies" in his denunciation of new ceremonies for girls.[6] Coming from a different perspective within the Orthodox community, Sharon and Joseph Kaplan, who performed in 1974 what may have been the first Orthodox Simchat Bat, were careful to explain that "[t]he birth ritual should be specifically for a girl." They warned of the "dangers in taking a male ceremony and adapting it for use by females." In particular, "certain inappropriate forms and procedures" might be "foisted upon the ceremony, where none need be."[7]

Some Orthodox adherents today continue to assert staunchly that they are not "mimicking" the circumcision liturgy[8] and thus not detracting from or tampering with this sacred ceremony. One corollary of this position is that some purposefully omit references to the covenant when welcoming their daughters, as we have seen.[9]

To the contrary, however, adapting certain aspects of the circumcision ceremony can be a fitting means of deferring to tradition while, paradoxically, developing a brand-new ritual form. Tradition demands that we make every effort to link a newer custom to well-accepted practices, and especially to those with the same underlying theme. Examining the circumcision ceremony more closely is therefore an appropriate starting point in formulating a welcoming ceremony for girls.

Our investigation reveals a distinction between the act of circumcision, which is as old as Abraham, and the surrounding ceremony, which began to coalesce many centuries later. While the male rite of circumcision is ancient, some central elements of the associated liturgy are recorded much later, in the Tosefta (Brachot 6:12–13) and the Talmud (BT Shabbat 137b). Furthermore, the circumcision ceremony was substantively augmented and reoriented as recently as the early medieval period (circa seventh–eleventh centuries CE). For example, drinking wine and smelling fragrances became part of the circumcision ceremony during this era; in addition, the Chair of Elijah was popularized, and the sandek's role was formalized. More generally, spiritual properties were attributed to the blood of circumcision at this time.[10]

We also learn that there are pre-modern halachic sources that accord the same high standing to both a baby boy's naming at his circumcision and a girl's synagogue naming.[11] This parallelism underscores the idea that the liturgy of a circumcision ceremony, while tied to the circumcision act, can also be considered separately.

It follows that "borrowing" liturgical or structural aspects of the circumcision ceremony does not in any way detract from or emasculate the core circumcision act, which is intensely physical and unquestionably the province of men. The circumcision ceremony is thus no different from any other Jewish liturgy in that it can be adapted to apply in other contexts.

With this understanding, we turn to the circumcision ceremony as a "traditional" model for developing a welcoming ceremony for girls. This approach captures the beauty of the liturgy and practices that have developed over many centuries around the circumcision rite. As a result, we exhibit great respect for Jewish traditions, even while adapting them for a different ritual form. By comparison, a less "traditional" way of creating a ceremony for girls is to divorce it both from the covenant and from the circumcision ceremony, and then to devise it from scratch—precisely the tack followed today in many traditional communities. It is ironic that traditionalists eschew the most traditional model for welcoming a baby into the Jewish people (that is, the circumcision ceremony), in favor of creating something completely new. In short, adapting the circumcision ceremony has nothing to do with "gender equality" and everything to do with keeping a foothold in tradition.

Feminists have advanced different reasons for distancing ceremonies for girls from the circumcision model. As early as 1984, Susan Weidman Schneider mentioned the ongoing debate about whether to use the circumcision ceremony as a basis for developing new ceremonies for girls.[12] Some feminists have been wary of incorporating into new rituals for girls the outline of an androcentric ceremony that elicits a good amount of angst in the first place. Other feminists have maintained that a girl's ritual should look different than that of a boy.[13] One rabbi argues that "imitative rituals ... say nothing of us as women [and] ... express Judaism in ways that still are male ways of envisioning the universe."[14]

To the contrary, a welcoming ceremony for girls that is modeled on the circumcision ceremony says exactly what needs to be said about women: that they are members of the eternal covenant. Communicating this all-important truism should be the paramount concern for feminists in formulating a ceremony for girls. Regardless of one's personal feelings about circumcision, the traditional circumcision ceremony remains so universally recognizable today that any allusion to this ceremony immediately conjures up the covenant. As a result, adapting certain facets of the circumcision ceremony is currently the most effective means of clearly and powerfully conveying the covenantal entry of girls—the central message of a welcoming ceremony.

However, this conclusion may seem troubling to those who have adopted the model of "feminist rituals." This genre is characterized by fluidity, flexibility, and openness and is the de facto template for welcoming practices for girls (especially freestanding ceremonies) across Jewish communities. As such, each practice is different in terms of substance and configuration, and this variability is encouraged and deemed beneficial. The feminist ritual paradigm developed in response to existing rituals that some perceive to be overly rigid, legalistic, and "male."

To my mind, however, these distinctions are overstated. All Jews, whether male or female, can find meaning in a wide range of rituals and can adhere to tradition while considering fresh perspectives. The point of a ceremony for girls is to welcome them into the Jewish community, not into a women's community,[15] and to do so using Jewish means, not "female" means. Furthermore, performing a well-structured ritual repeatedly and consistently yields comfortable expectations. As a result, this mode facilitates the seamless integration of a Brit Bat as a well-accepted Jewish life-cycle ritual. Welcoming ceremonies for girls need not be crafted out of whole cloth because of a supposed call to do so.

Judith Plaskow questions whether openness "is inherent in or necessary to feminism or represents a residue from . . . the 1960s."[16] It seems to be the latter. The openness and other characteristics of "feminist rituals" are due to the zeitgeist in which feminism emerged, rather than from an inherent feminist requirement. Taken to an extreme, drawing these artificial distinctions between male and female rituals portrays women as oppositional and promotes the false stereotype that women are not inclined toward structured approaches. All told, modeling the circumcision ceremony conveys both the Jewish tenets and the feminist ideals embedded in welcoming ceremonies for girls.

MORE BROADLY, modeling new practices for girls on the circumcision ceremony should not evoke dissent or even raise eyebrows, since Jewish rituals of all sorts have long influenced each other as they continuously evolve and amalgamate into our tradition. Some may nonetheless feel that the model of the circumcision ceremony should be cordoned off because it is somehow distinctive among Jewish rituals. It is therefore crucial to recognize that the circumcision ceremony has previously served as the model for a practice that is decidedly female (albeit from a male perspective)—the Tokens of Virginity (*Birkat Betulim*) ceremony. We will examine this parallelism after describing the ceremony itself.

Originating in the early medieval period, the Tokens of Virginity ceremony ritualizes a bride's "blood of virginity," that is, the blood that is discharged if her hymen ruptures during her first intercourse.[17] R. Shimon Kayyarah describes the ceremony as it occurred in ninth-century Babylonia. It took place on a couple's wedding night immediately after the consummation of their marriage. When the groom emerged from the bedroom with a sheet stained with the bride's blood of virginity—the ceremony's central ritual—he recited, "Blessed are You God ... who created the fruits of the vine" over a cup of wine, and "Blessed are You God ... who created the trees of spices" over fragrant spices. The groom then recited the Betulim blessing:

> Blessed are You, Lord our God, King of the Universe, who placed the walnut in the Garden of Eden, the lily of the valley, so that no stranger shall have dominion over the sealed spring; therefore, the loving doe preserved her [holy seed in] purity and did not break the law. Blessed are You, Lord, who chooses the descendants of Abraham.[18]

This ritual was widely practiced in the Middle East into the High Middle Ages, and in Ashkenazic regions as late as the fifteenth century. While it became increasingly common for Ashkenazic grooms to recite the Betulim blessing in private, the complete ceremony continued to be practiced publicly in Arab lands.[19] There is even limited evidence that some version of the Betulim practice survived into early modern times.[20]

A question posed to Maimonides in the twelfth century provides insight into the Betulim ceremony of this time. The questioner depicts how a groom recites the Betulim blessing, along with the blessings over wine and spices, "when the congregation comes to the house of the groom on Shabbat to pray or to bless him" and then again after the seven wedding blessings are recited without a meal. In his response, Maimonides denounces this ceremony in the harshest terms and unequivocally prohibits it.[21] It may be significant that Maimonides forbade the Tokens of Virginity ceremony because it violates standards of modesty and holiness, and not because it models or copies the circumcision ceremony. Other medieval scholars forbade or modified the Betulim blessing because it originated in the post-Talmudic period,[22] but not because of its close relationship to the circumcision liturgy.

The parallels between the circumcision ceremony and the Betulim ceremony are striking. Both begin with the appearance of blood—that of circumcision and of virginity, respectively. Moreover, the Betulim blessing is "similar in literary form and style" to the Talmudic blessing that is recited following the circumcision act:

> Blessed are You, Lord our God, King of the Universe, who made the beloved one [Isaac] holy from the womb, marked the decree of circumcision in his flesh, and gave his descendants the seal and sign of the holy covenant. As a reward for this, the Living God, our Portion, our Rock, did order deliverance from destruction for the beloved of our flesh, for the sake of His covenant that He set in our flesh. Blessed are You, Lord, who establishes the covenant.[23]

Both blessings "use allusive, poetic language beyond the level normally found in prayer books."[24] The conclusion of this circumcision blessing ("Blessed are You, Lord, who establishes the covenant") is particularly similar to that of a Betulim ceremony ("Blessed are You, Lord, who chooses the descendants of Abraham.")[25] Both invoke the covenant, since perpetuation of the Abrahamic line is a vital covenantal element. Both blessings also allude to the womb.

Furthermore, both the Betulim and circumcision ceremonies incorporate drinking wine, smelling fragrances, and reciting blessings for each. At circumcision ceremonies today, wine is a universal element, and, in some Sephardic and Mizrachic communities, fragrances are smelled and the prayer "Blessed are You God . . . who created the trees of spices" is said. The Tokens of Virginity ceremony developed in the early medieval period, which is precisely when wine and fragrances began to be incorporated into the circumcision ceremony. More generally, this is the time that various innovations associated with circumcision emerged; for example, circumcision blood attained sanctity and spiritual significance.[26] It is therefore not surprising that a different type of blood, that of virginity, would also be ritualized and ceremonially blessed.

Despite its ultimate disappearance, the Betulim ceremony exemplifies the thriving use of the circumcision ceremony as a structural and liturgical model, and demonstrates the viability of this model for a Brit Bat ceremony as well. To elaborate on this point, we return to the notion that the circumcision ceremony is composed of the "twin themes" of blood and covenant.[27] During the early medieval period when blood became a prominent symbol, a ceremony about women's blood evolved from the "blood component" of the circumcision ceremony. Today, on the other hand, we are interested in how the "covenant component" of the circumcision ceremony applies to women. Just as the blood theme was ritualized in the early medieval period in the Betulim ceremony, so too, we would ritualize the covenant theme today in a welcoming ceremony for newborn girls.

NEVERTHELESS, SOME MAY continue to feel uncomfortable developing a ceremony for girls based on the model of the circumcision ceremony due simply to the extreme maleness of the circumcision act. However, there are a number of Jewish practices for girls that have, over time, been adapted from those for boys, just as a Brit Bat (for girls) would adapt aspects of the circumcision ceremony (for boys). These examples, which we will discuss in turn, include the Hollekreisch ceremony, Birkat Banim, and the Bat Mitzvah. They demonstrate not only that practices for boys have expanded into related practices for girls, but also that our tradition is continuously evolving to incorporate new rituals that stem directly from existing ones.

Hollekreisch Ceremony

The Ashkenazic Hollekreisch naming ceremony for newborns was performed for many centuries for both boys and girls, but, in later years, became prevalent in some regions for girls (see chapter 1). It may have originated, however, from a ceremony, or set of related ceremonies, conducted for boys only.[28] One such ceremony appears in the Machzor Vitry, a compendium of Jewish practices and rules, published in France in 1107. This ceremony occurred sometime after the circumcision ceremony in the presence of ten men, a prayer quorum (minyan). The baby boy is dressed up, and the father places a Pentateuch next to him and prays, "Let this [child] fulfill what is written in this [Pentateuch]." The gathered men recite Biblical passages and put a quill and ink in the baby's hand "so that he will be a scribe, quick in the Torah of God."[29] R. Yehuda ben Samuel of Regensburg (twelfth–thirteenth century Germany) recounts a related ceremony in which "the book of the Torah of the priests," that is, Leviticus, is put under the head of a baby boy when he is placed in his cradle and given a name.[30] There is another possibly related ceremony, of uncertain origin,[31] that occurred on a boy's eighth day of life, after his circumcision. The baby boy is put on a "bed of sheets with the Pentateuch at his head." A community elder or *rosh yeshiva* (head of a Torah institute) places his hands on the baby and bestows a number of blessings, for example, that the baby will learn what is written in the Pentateuch. The father hosts "a feast of drinking and joy for the circumcision and for the dedication" of a life devoted to God, just as Hannah pledged her son Samuel into the service of God (Samuel I, 1:28).[32]

These obscure cradle ceremonies for baby boys may have been the forerunners of the Hollekreisch ceremony.[33] To the extent that this assumption holds, the placement of a Pentateuch near the baby and the recitation of related blessings, which occurred in these precursor ceremonies, may have persisted on a limited basis in some variations of the Hollekreisch ceremony for boys (or perhaps evolved into the custom of reciting Scriptural verses). These early practices, however, were deemed inappropriate for girls who did not, as a rule, study Torah. Therefore, when the ceremony was gradually adapted for girls, it no longer included the placement of a Pentateuch or the recitation of blessings. This example demonstrates that the transition of life-cycle practices from boys to girls is not foreign to the evolution of Jewish customs, and that this type of transition is marked by flexible changes and adaptations.

Birkat Banim

One contemporary case in point is Birkat Banim, the blessing that parents give their children as Shabbat begins. This blessing incorporates the priestly benediction (Birkat Kohanim, Numbers 6:24–26), but we focus here on

Birkat Banim's introductory prayer—"May God make you like Sarah, Rebecca, Rachel, and Leah" for girls, and "May God make you like Ephraim and Menashe" for boys. The patriarch Jacob blessed his grandsons Ephraim and Menashe with the prophecy that "by you will Israel bless, saying 'May God make you like Ephraim and Menashe'" (Genesis 48:20).[34] This prayer recalls how Jacob breached conventional practices by putting his right hand on the second-born, Ephraim, and his left hand on the firstborn, Menashe (Genesis 48:17–20). However, the prayer for girls, "May God make you like Sarah, Rebecca, Rachel, and Leah," has no parallel basis. Thus, the Biblically significant introductory prayer for boys noticeably contrasts with the generic prayer for girls. This discrepancy suggests that the Birkat Banim custom for girls may have developed from the corresponding, yet more substantively grounded, custom for boys and that the introductory prayer for girls is an adaptation of that for boys.

Intrigued by this observation, I decided to investigate further.[35] I learned that Birkat Banim for boys was apparently well-accepted by the sixteenth century in some locales. R. Elijah Capsali (sixteenth-century Crete) describes the practice of fathers blessing their sons after evening prayers at the onset of Shabbat and holidays. Sons came before their fathers on bent knee and kissed the palms of their fathers' hands, at which point fathers placed their hands on their sons' heads and blessed them. R. Capsali refers to this practice as *minhag vatikin v'atikin*—an ancient custom.[36] Likewise, R. Yosef Yuspa Nordlinger Hahn (sixteenth-century Frankfurt-am-Main, Germany) refers to the custom of blessing sons and relatives upon exiting from the synagogue after evening services at the start of Shabbat and holidays, as well as during Shabbat morning prayers and at the end of Shabbat and holidays. He also notes that this practice is a *minhag vatikin*—a very old custom.[37]

In contrast to these sixteenth-century attestations to the long history of blessing sons, the earliest evidence of blessing daughters comes from the seventeenth century. According to R. Binyomin S. Hamburger of the Institute for German Jewish Heritage,[38] *Chavvot Yair* by R. Yair Chayim Bachrach (1639–1702, Germany) contains the first written statement that girls are blessed with the prayer, "May God make you like Sarah, Rebecca, etc. . ."[39] In the same source, R. Bachrach notes that boys are blessed with the prayer that Jacob said to his grandsons. Thus, the first mention of a blessing for girls includes a reference to an already extant blessing for boys.

As a historical matter, the blessing for sons is almost certainly not "ancient," despite assertions to this effect. In addition, the blessing for daughters may have existed prior to the seventeenth century, the date that it was first recorded. Nonetheless, the sources more broadly characterize the boys' blessing as well-established by the sixteenth century (at least in Frankfurt and Crete) and suggest that the girls' blessing is more recent. Based on this difference—and the fact that the boys' blessing was already in use when the girls' blessing was first recorded—it appears that the blessing for sons predates that for daughters.

Furthermore, based on at least one source, the blessing for sons was deemed to have greater significance than that for daughters. R. Aharon Berachia of Modena (seventeenth-century Italy) describes the custom of blessing a young son on Friday night by placing a hand on his head. R. Aharon Berachia explains the connection to the priestly benediction and the spiritual reasons for blessing sons specifically on Shabbat. He concludes that "it is a great necessity [*tzorech gavoha*] for one to bless his sons on Shabbat." He adds off-handedly that "if one has a daughter, he should also bless her, and particularly on Friday night."[40] This disparity between the vital importance of blessing sons and the option of blessing daughters also supports the theory that the blessing for sons was established prior to that for daughters. Greater significance might have been accorded to the custom of blessing girls if it had a longer tradition and history.

To the extent that this theory holds, the custom of blessing sons may have expanded to daughters as a result of a collective sensibility among parents that they should bless all their children together. Today, it would be unheard-of for a parent to bless only sons and not daughters. If this hypothesis is correct, the development of Birkat Banim is an example where a custom for girls was modeled on an earlier custom for boys. Significantly, the girls' introductory prayer, "May God make you like Sarah, Rebecca, Rachel, and Leah" was apparently adapted directly from the boys' prayer by substituting the matriarchs for Ephraim and Menashe. In a comparable manner, a Brit Bat for girls would model and adapt the structure and liturgy of a circumcision ceremony for boys.

Birkat Banim illustrates an additional point. While circumcision is a Biblical commandment and blessing children on Shabbat evening is predicated on a Biblical episode (a significant distinction), both circumcision and blessing boys on Shabbat evening have a specific Biblical basis. God commands Abraham and his descendents to circumcise (Genesis 17:10–14), and Birkat Banim for boys cites Jacob's prophecy that "by you will Israel bless, saying 'May God make you like Ephraim and Menashe'" (Genesis 48:20). Despite the fact that there is not even an allusion in the Torah to blessing girls, the tradition developed to bless both boys and girls on Shabbat. Just as the custom of blessing girls arose in the absence of an explicit Biblical foundation, so too can girls be ceremoniously welcomed into the covenant despite the absence of a Biblical mandate.

Bat Mitzvah

The Bar Mitzvah ritual for boys probably originated in late medieval or early modern times, although components of it have earlier roots,[41] while the Bat Mitzvah is a twentieth-century invention. Both celebrations recognize the transition of children into adulthood and commemorate an acceptance of religious responsibilities. There is no question that the Bat Mitzvah ritual was devised from and runs parallel to the centuries-older Bar Mitzvah ritual. This obvious derivation of a practice for girls from that for boys has not hampered the rapid spread and community-wide acceptance of the Bat Mitzvah in recent decades. In precisely the same way, the development of ceremonies for newborn girls by modeling the circumcision ceremony is not only legitimate and meaningful, but also has the potential for broad acceptance.

Furthermore, adaptations have been made in translating a coming-of-age commemoration for boys to that for girls. For example, in some early Bat Mitzvah rituals in liberal communities, girls lit candles or read the Haftarah on Friday night because these activities were deemed, at the time, to be an appropriate reformulation of a bar mitzvah's leading prayers and reading from the Torah. In a similar exercise, Orthodox communities have found creative ways (such as school functions and non-minyan prayer groups) to design Bat Mitzvah practices based on, or at least precipitated by, the Bar Mitzvah model. A Brit Bat would adapt the structure and liturgy of the circumcision ceremony in the same way that the Bat Mitzvah resulted from a conscious repurposing of the Bar Mitzvah.

IN THE END, we see that modeling the circumcision ceremony is a compelling means of framing a new ritual in a traditional way and in conformance with past practices.

HOLDING A CEREMONY ON THE EIGHTH DAY OF LIFE

In 1976, R. Daniel Leifer became one of the earliest advocates of performing welcoming ceremonies for baby girls on their eighth day of life. He maintained that a ritual must occur at a specific time and place in order to maintain "its ontological power and effectiveness."[42] The Reform movement in 1977 also proposed eighth-day timing for covenantal ceremonies for girls[43] (similar to an obscure Reform covenantal ritual formulated in the 1840s).[44] However, R. Leifer's advice has been largely disregarded, both then and now, across the range of Jewish communities.

The modern Simchat Bat resources that cite eighth-day timing as an option often dismiss it as too soon or too inconvenient. Citing these reasons, parents and rabbis have overall rejected the notion of holding a ceremony on the eighth day—or on any other specifically designated day.[45] It appears to me that the most prevalent feature of the Simchat Bat practice today is that it generally takes place at a time that is convenient for the parents who are arranging the event and for the family and friends who are attending it. As a result, welcoming ceremonies for girls are often held weeks or even months after a baby's birth. Every freestanding Simchat Bat ceremony that I have personally attended in the United States has taken place on a Sunday, a day when people are not at work and when travel is permitted for those who observe traditional Shabbat restrictions. In Israel, these ceremonies might occur on Fridays (when some do not work), weekday evenings (a standard time for weddings and parties), or holidays. Synagogue Simchat Bat practices almost always occur on Shabbat, the day that attracts the most synagogue goers and, therefore, also a convenient day.

Furthermore, the standard advice for parents holding a ceremony for their daughter is that "the immediate imperatives for the family following the birth of a girl are not as time-pressured" as for that of a boy.[46] Some parents are relieved that they can "take their time" in planning a party or ceremony. They savor this flexibility and characterize the open-ended timing as fitting "the emotional needs and schedules of the celebrants."[47] One parent recounted that after her daughter was born, she "reveled in the luxury of time [she] had to plan a Simchat Bat."[48] Another declared that the "best thing about having a baby girl . . . is that you get to decide when you want to have the party."[49]

It follows that there is often no particular significance, religious or otherwise, to the timing of contemporary welcoming ceremonies for girls. In addition, ceremonies held long after the baby's birth may not fully capture the exhilaration that is at its height in the first days following birth. For these reasons, if given the choice to modify one aspect of the overall Simchat Bat practice today, I would strongly encourage parents and rabbis to hold ceremonies consistently on the eighth day following a baby girl's birth. As compared to the convenient timing that many choose today, eighth-day timing is filled with meaning and consequence.

Significance of the Eighth Day

The eighth day of life is the time that God established for symbolic covenantal entry via male circumcision, and, for millennia, this covenantal rite has been performed accordingly on the eighth day. As a result, this day is universally recognized, almost on an instinctual level, as a time for symbolically entering the covenant. It follows that the eighth day instantly communicates the theme of covenantal entry. No other timing conveys the centrality of the covenant more effectively. We see, therefore, that the purpose of eighth-day timing is not to thoughtlessly mimic circumcision. To the contrary, incorporating the timing of circumcision is, like other elements of our Brit Bat, both thematically expressive and deeply reverent to tradition.

It also appears that this timing falls within traditional bounds, particularly with regard to the naming aspect of a Brit Bat. Jewish law is flexible about when to name a girl, and this timing has varied substantially in different eras and regions, as we learned in chapter 2. At the same time, it seems that girls need not be named any sooner than the eighth day, since boys are named on the eighth day following birth, and boys and girls today utilize names in the same way.

The power of eighth-day timing is that it requires no elaborate explanations or contortions, as other suggested times often do. For example, holding a ceremony at a time that corresponds to the niddah status of the mother (such as the fifteenth day following birth, which marks the end of her ritual impurity) is certain to be missed in the absence of an explanation. More importantly, a ceremony's timing should be tied to the baby, not the mother. Rosh Chodesh (the first day of the lunar month) alludes to femininity, and the thirtieth day from birth alludes to the baby's viability—but neither of these days involves the covenant. Even Shabbat, with its covenantal basis, has no particular connection to a newborn, since Shabbat would have happened whether or not a baby was born that week.

While eighth-day timing needs no explanation, it also has deeper significance beyond its association with circumcision. R. Menachem Leibtag of Yeshivat Har Etzion has eloquently interpreted the eighth day as the time when humanity takes the creation of nature, which occurred in seven days, to a higher level by forming a close relationship with God.[50] This progression is evident from the timing of circumcision, a rite that transforms the natural state of a body to connect with the Divine. As R. Leibtag explains, the transition from *natural* to *spiritual* is also evident from the juxtaposition of the seven-day Sukkot holiday with the Shimini Atzeret holiday that follows on the eighth day. Sukkot is a harvest festival that evokes nature, while Shimini Atzeret, according to rabbinic interpretations, marks God's special love for the Jewish people and thus serves as a means of drawing closer to the Divine.[51]

Another example cited by R. Leibtag is the seven-day priestly consecration of the Tabernacle in the desert, which demanded the intensely physical acts of slaughtering animals for sacrifices, sprinkling the animals' blood, burning their fat, and the like. On the eighth day, however, God revealed His Glory to the Israelites who fell on their faces in awe (Leviticus 8 and 9). Again, seven days of working with the natural elements of life and death are followed by an intimate encounter with the Divine on the eighth day. A final example is that a person with an abnormal bodily ailment that causes ritual impurity (*m'tzora, zav,* or *zava*) returns to the Israelite camp—his or her "natural habitat"—after a seven-day cleansing. On the eighth day, the individual brings a sacrifice that enables re-entry to the Tabernacle (Leviticus 14 and 15). After focusing for seven days on physicality and its challenges, one returns on the eighth day to high levels of spirituality.

R. Leibtag's interpretation demonstrates that, beyond the well-known paradigm of circumcision, there is a broader connection between the eighth day and the special covenantal relationship between God and Israel. While a baby's first seven days of life are embroiled in the physicality of birth and the maintenance of a fragile life, the eighth day should be devoted to aspiring to a higher level of existence in a relationship with God. This conceptualization provides an additional reason that the eighth day following birth is a fitting time to mark covenantal entry.

Immediate Timing

While the eighth day is itself significant, it also results in a compressed time frame that affords ancillary benefits. As with a circumcision ceremony, holding a Brit Bat so soon after birth captures the energy and excitement of inducting a brand-new individual into the Jewish people. Just as a family gears up for the exhilarating physical entrance of a baby into the world, it should do the same for her religious initiation. This juxtaposition conveys that a baby's ceremonial entry into the covenant constitutes the religious dimension of her birth. In addition, performing a Brit Bat so soon after birth requires parents, as with a circumcision, to focus on the baby's religious significance while simultaneously faced with the daunting physical demands of a newborn. In meeting this challenge, parents demonstrate their commitment to the covenant and the Jewish people. By contrast, this feeling of excitement and determination is lost when parents wait some length of time to host a Simchat Bat. Joseph and Sharon Kaplan observed in 1976 that, even by the thirtieth day following a birth, "some of the initial indescribable excitement on the appearance of a brand new human being has worn off."[52]

I recently attended a party celebrating a friend's completion of her doctorate. Her husband commented on the strong congratulatory emotions at the party due to holding it so soon—a week or so—after my friend's defense of her dissertation. I agreed wholeheartedly and felt genuinely happy for my friend and her accomplishment. Later on, it occurred to me how these comments illustrate the importance of promptly welcoming a new member of the Jewish people. As with my friend's celebration, immediate timing captures the sentiments of parents and loved ones when they are fresh and, therefore, most intense. In short, parents and rabbis should seize the moment.

Simchat Bat practices are not only often delayed, but also are frequently held on a convenient day and when the mother's "condition" permits. Some popular sources emphasize that consideration should be given to the convenience of family and friends planning to attend a Simchat Bat. One parent casually suggests that "you can choose to hold your welcoming ceremony on the first convenient Sunday, as we did."[53] Other prevalent advice is that the event should be convenient for the parents, and particularly for the mother. The assumption is that a woman who has recently given birth is not well enough to plan an event and participate in it, and that she has the leisure to wait until she is "fully recovered."[54] Citing these reasons, some sources specifically identify perceived difficulties in holding a ceremony for girls on the eighth day.[55]

However, parents should look forward to marking their children's religious status on a day that is intrinsically significant, rather than doing so at a time that is easy or convenient. To the extent that parents are able to hold ceremonies for their sons at a "less convenient time," they should be able to muster the strength to do the same for their daughters. In fact, many parents of newborn boys host two gatherings within the baby's first week of life—a *Shalom Zachar* (Peace of a Son) on the Friday night following birth, and a circumcision on the eighth day—as well as a *Pidyon HaBen* (Redemption of the Firstborn) three weeks later for firstborn sons. Similarly, grandparents and other relatives and friends manage to attend an eighth-day ritual, as well as these other events, when it is important enough to them. My husband and I have hosted four ceremonies on the eighth day (three for our daughters and one for our son), and we always had a full house.

I am blessed to have a narrative written by my maternal grandmother, Senta Okolica, that describes my second-born daughter's Brit Bat and, in particular, my grandmother's perspective on the ceremony's eighth-day timing. My mother discovered this writing a few years after my grandmother's passing. This account, titled "A Different Party," is close to my heart, and I therefore provide it in full:

> It was in the middle of June when my granddaughter Sharon gave birth to a sweet little baby girl. Mother and baby were doing well so the parents decided to hold the party they had planned. Should the baby be a girl, [her] name would be announced. Since the parents wanted it on the eighth day, everything had to be done in a hurry. Relatives, friends, neighbors all had to be invited, tables and chairs had to be placed in the garden, food had to be ordered. Everything was in order now; only the calls had to be made. We hoped that the guests would be willing to come. Even so, it was in the middle of the week and they all came. Everybody was seated, the baby was brought out, and the parents announced the name. It is Nurit. Nurit's big sister Dafna is looking forward to a new playmate.

This touching account is a tribute to my then-eighty-six-year-old grandmother. She expresses her concern about the eighth-day timing, particularly since the event fell mid-week (on a Wednesday), and her pleasure when all the guests arrived to celebrate her new great-granddaughter. This story demonstrates that concerns about attendance at eighth-day occasions are misplaced and that even my traditionally inclined German grandmother became, I think, a new convert to this timing.

A related point is that planning a ceremony on a day that is convenient for family and friends shifts the focus from the baby, whose centrality should be highlighted, to other participants. While communal endorsement is an important feature of covenantal entry, the essence of a Brit Bat is to ritualize a newborn's religious milestone, and the timing should reinforce this core purpose. Already in 1976, R. Daniel Leifer observed that some early ceremonies for baby girls emphasized the role of parents, rather than that of the child. He clarifies that, to the contrary, the traditional "focus is primarily on the child and only secondarily on the parents, who effect the ritual. It is the child whose ritual status is changed."[56] In this vein, my personal preference is for a ceremony with special timing and fewer guests, rather than a larger party planned for a convenient time.

With respect to the mother's "condition," childbirth has long been dangerous and remains that way in less-developed areas of the world today. However, when modern medical safeguards are utilized, childbirth is the least risky it has ever been. In the absence of complications, childbirth can be an empowering experience—a momentous opportunity to use one's physical and emotional strength to bring forth new life. In addition, while illness or injury can occur in conjunction with childbirth, childbirth itself is a natural process, not a sickness. It is also significant that the timing of a circumcision does not depend on how a mother is feeling. Thus, a concern with a mother's physical or emotional post-partum condition in selecting the time for her daughter's ceremony is, at best, unnecessary and, at worst, patronizing. An eighth-day Brit Bat becomes feasible when childbirth is no longer mischaracterized as a sickness and when the ceremony's focus returns to the baby.

Brit Bat on Any Day of the Year

We turn now to the notion of performing a Brit Bat on the eighth day following birth regardless of when this day falls on the yearly calendar. For example, a Brit Bat does not violate any of the traditional prohibitions assigned to Shabbat or holidays. On these days, friends and family would gather in the home or at the synagogue, just as they would for a circumcision. On Yom Kippur, a ceremony could be conducted without wine or a meal, and a commemorative "break fast" could follow that night.

The standard advice, however, is to tiptoe around days of communal mourning when planning a ceremony for a newborn girl. These include fast days, the three weeks preceding Tisha b'Av (the anniversary of the Temples' destruction), the seven weeks of counting the Omer (the period between Passover and Shavuot, believed to be when 42,000 students of R. Akiva died; BT Yevamot 62b), Israeli Memorial Day, and Holocaust Remembrance Day.[57] I am personally aware of two instances, one in the United States and one in England, where Orthodox rabbis disallowed parents from holding Simchat Bat ceremonies during the counting of the Omer. Rabbis today would also likely bar parents from conducting a Simchat Bat during personal days of mourning following the death of a close relative. These restrictions have been imposed primarily for freestanding Simchat Bat ceremonies, since synagogue practices typically occur on Shabbat, which does not coincide with fast days (except sometimes Yom Kippur) and which supersedes certain mourning practices.

An initial observation is that, unlike a Simchat Bat ceremony at which a name is reiterated, a Brit Bat at which a name is announced for the first time technically functions as a "naming." Generally, there is no difficulty with naming a baby on a day of mourning. Today, girls are named on any day on which the Torah is read and, as we have learned, a naming does not even require a Torah reading. A Brit Bat with a name announcement, therefore, enjoys the enhanced status of a naming, which may result, as a technical matter, in greater leeway with respect to its timing.

Bearing this in mind, we note that there may be a simple way both to ensure a Brit Bat's consistent eighth-day timing and to comply with any mourning restrictions that may arise on that day. On a day of mourning, a Brit Bat ceremony could be performed during or at the conclusion of a daily prayer service—in the synagogue or at home, as appropriate—without reciting a blessing over wine or serving a festive meal. Daily prayers occur on days of mourning, as on every other day, and anyone may attend. In this way, it may be that no issue would arise with respect to attending a gathering solely for social purposes, an act disallowed on some days of mourning. Moreover, the Brit Bat liturgy would have the same status as any other customary prayer recited on days of mourning, such as additional Psalms or dirges (*kinnot*).

A key supposition here is that, absent a festive meal, a Brit Bat is commemorative, not celebratory. The essence of a Brit Bat is to mark a girl's entry into the covenant with substantive rituals and prayers, not to host a party. It seems, therefore, that conducting a Brit Bat during or at the end of a communal prayer service, and without a meal, might not pose a concern with mixing happy and sad occasions. A festive meal and wine could be served when a fast day or mourning period concludes.

It is even arguable that, according to certain sources, a festive meal might be served at a Brit Bat during the seven weeks of the Omer, which is considered to be a period of lesser mourning. Holding weddings and getting haircuts are the only restrictions for the Omer cited in the Shulchan Aruch, the premier Jewish legal code.[58] The Shulchan Aruch explicitly permits *erusin,* the betrothal stage of a wedding, during the Omer, and R. Judah Ashkenazi (eighteenth-century Poland) even allows for a festive meal following erusin. R. Ashkenazi characterizes this meal as "optional," and he bars only "greater festivities," such as those with singing and dancing.[59] Perhaps the meal associated with a Brit Bat, assuming there is no singing or dancing, could be construed according to these opinions as "optional"; if so, it is conceivable that this meal might be permissible during the Omer.

My parents were invited to an ultra-Orthodox Bar Mitzvah held during the nine days preceding Tisha b'Av, the saddest nine days on the Jewish calendar. On these days, a variety of activities—including social gatherings and celebrations—are traditionally prohibited. My understanding is that the Bar Mitzvah was nevertheless held at this time based on the notion that the ostensible significance of celebrating the boy's coming of age on his exact birthday overrode the traditional "nine days" restrictions. Regardless of the extent to which this notion is accepted in other communities, the point is that there may be some room for creative reasoning when a conflict arises between customary life-cycle events and communal days of mourning.

Other sources are pertinent in examining the possibility of conducting a Brit Bat on days of personal mourning for a close relative. The Arba'ah Turim, a fourteenth-century halachic code, rules that one should perform a circumcision prior to tending to a deceased person when both must be done on the same day. Commenting on this ruling, R. Joshua Falk (1555–1614,

Poland) maintains that a girl's synagogue naming is "in place of" a boy's naming at his circumcision and, therefore, enjoys the same high standing as circumcision. R. Falk concludes that, just like circumcision, a girl's naming takes precedence over attending to the needs associated with a death.[60] It may follow that a girl could be named—in conjunction with a broader welcoming ceremony—despite the onset of a personal mourning period.

It is also noteworthy that R. Shmuel Halevi Segal of Mezeritch (seventeenth-century Poland) holds that a new mother may participate in the medieval Ashkenazic customs associated with returning to the synagogue post-partum, although she is mourning for a close relative during the intense first week following death (*shiva*). According to R. Shmuel Halevi, a new mother may be accompanied to the synagogue and back by her female friends, although she may not partake in the meal that would customarily follow her synagogue attendance.[61] The key point is that R. Shmuel Halevi at no time proposes that the mother should postpone her synagogue visit to a later Shabbat.[62] This responsum demonstrates that birth-related customs deemed important enough can be permissible even during the most stringent shiva mourning period (albeit on Shabbat, when mourning practices are scaled down).

Relatedly, R. Yedidah Tia Weil (eighteenth-century Poland) advises a birthing mother, who was mourning for her father during the more lenient twelve-month post-mortem period, that she may host a festive meal in honor of the Hollekreisch.[63] It is arguable that an analogy can be drawn for a Brit Bat. R. Shmuel Halevi, however, disallows the Hollekreisch during the shiva period, but his reasoning is that the Hollekreisch is an unnecessary "unholy" naming and, in any event, was waning at this time. It seems that neither of these reasons applies to a Brit Bat, which includes a "holy" naming and represents an increasingly popular practice.

IN SUM, holding a Brit Bat on the eighth day following a baby girl's birth evokes the covenant and, more particularly, the transition from the physicality of a newborn's demands to the spirituality of her covenantal entry. This immediate timing also conveys the energy and excitement that befits the initiation of a newborn daughter into the covenant. To my mind, the eighth day is so crucial to a girl's covenantal ceremony that every effort should be made to maintain this timing consistently.

THE CHAIR OF ELIJAH

Up to this point, we have examined how and why a Brit Bat's structure, liturgy, and timing express a covenantal theme. We now consider the covenantal symbolism of a specially designated Chair of Elijah, which invites the spirit of Elijah the Prophet (I Kings 17–21; II Kings 1–2) to suffuse the ceremony. This chair would serve as a prominent ritual object at a Brit Bat, as it does at a circumcision. The person holding the baby could sit in the Chair of Elijah while the baby is swaddled. Alternatively, the chair could remain vacant in anticipation of Elijah's visit, just as the Cup of Elijah remains untouched at the Passover seder. (These alternatives correspond to varying customs at circumcision ceremonies.)

In addition, the verses that are traditionally said to recognize the Chair of Elijah at a circumcision (Genesis 49:18; Psalms 119:162, 165, 166; Psalms 65:5) might likewise be recited at a Brit Bat. These verses invoke the expansive themes of messianic deliverance, peace for those who love Torah, and the joy derived from closeness to God. In turn, these themes provide context for the Elijah imagery and translate into communal hopes and prayers for a newborn girl as she joins the covenant.

Pirkei d'Rabbi Eliezer (Chapters of R. Eliezer), a ninth-century midrash, provides the first known mention of the custom of having a Chair of Elijah at a circumcision[64] (a custom that may have pre-dated this written reference). As part of its fanciful lore relating to Abraham's fulfillment of the circumcision commandment, this midrash (chapter 29) recounts an episode in which Elijah flees to the desert and goes to Horeb. When God asks Elijah what he is doing there, Elijah responds that he has been very zealous on God's behalf (I Kings 19:8–10). The midrash then interposes an extra-textual coda to this dialogue. God responds that Elijah has always been zealous and that Elijah was also zealous in the episode where Phineas, Aaron's grandson, slew an Israelite man and Midianite woman who were engaging in licentiousness and idol worship (Numbers 25:6–13). The midrash here assumes that Phineas is Elijah, since the distinctive "zealous" terminology appears in both Numbers (chapter 25) and I Kings (chapter 19), respectively. God continues to speak to Elijah, declaring: "By your life! Israel will not perform a circumcision until you see it with your own eyes." The midrash concludes that "from this, the sages have instituted that there should be a seat of honor for the messenger of the covenant, as it says, 'The messenger of the covenant whom you desire, he is coming' (Malachi 3:1)." Chapter 29 of Pirkei d'Rabbi Eliezer closes with the prayer that God send the Messiah in our lifetimes.

Although the midrash's stated purpose is to provide a basis for a Chair of Elijah at a circumcision, the verses that ground this exegesis deal exclusively with the covenant between God and Israel and say nothing about circumcision. The midrash cites Elijah's statement in I Kings 19:10 only in part. The complete passage (repeated in verse 14) states: "I have been very zealous on behalf of the Lord, God of Hosts, since the children of Israel have forsaken Your covenant and destroyed Your altars; they have killed Your prophets by the sword. I remain alone, and they seek my life to take it away." In other words, Elijah has been zealous on behalf of God's eternal covenant, which Israel has forsaken as a result of its idolatry. Circumcision is not discussed anywhere in this episode. Phineas likewise acts zealously to preserve the covenant and root out idolatry, and, in return, God gives him a "covenant of peace" and an "eternal priestly covenant" (Numbers 25:12–13). Again, circumcision is not mentioned in these passages.

Indeed, Elijah is the quintessential embodiment of the effort to exhort Israel to mend its covenantal relationship with God. In the chapter cited by Pirkei d'Rabbi Eliezer (I Kings 19), Elijah flees to Horeb because Queen Jezebel threatens to take his life on account of a dramatic episode where Elijah challenges hundreds of idolatrous priests to bring fire to their altars on Mount Carmel (I Kings 18). While the priests cannot meet this challenge, God's fire consumes Elijah's sacrifice and altar, and even the water surrounding his altar. As a result, the onlookers fall on their faces and cry out, "The Lord is God; the Lord is God" (I Kings 18:19–40). As epitomized by this episode, Elijah dedicated his life to repairing the covenant and risked his life defending it. It is therefore meaningful to have this defender of the covenant watching over newborns as they assume their place in the covenant. While the midrash connects the Chair of Elijah to a circumcision, the vivid covenantal symbolism of Elijah is likewise compelling at a Brit Bat.

Circumcision also plays no part in Malachi 3:1 ("The messenger of the covenant whom you desire, he is coming"), which the midrash references as a "prooftext" for a Chair of Elijah. Instead, God charges the messenger of the covenant to purify the Levites, who have disregarded the Torah, so that they may again offer sacrifices. The ultimate purpose of this messenger, therefore, is to renew the covenant. A few verses later, the prophet relays God's words, imploring, "Return to Me and I will return to you," a succinct plea for covenantal reconciliation (Malachi 3:7). Thus, in introducing the Chair of Elijah, the midrash cites a verse that has powerful covenantal meaning, rather than any particular relationship to circumcision.

In conclusion, Pirkei d'Rabbi Eliezer's explanation of (and justification for) the Chair of Elijah applies to a covenantal initiation generally and, therefore, pertains as much to a Brit Bat as to a circumcision. Said otherwise, this midrashic exegesis conflates covenant and circumcision by interpreting verses about the covenant to refer to circumcision, when circumcision is nowhere to be found in the text (see chapter 5).

The Chair of Elijah has other associations that are also significant in the context of a Brit Bat, just as they are at a circumcision. First, Elijah is strongly associated with transitions. His spirit is invoked at the Passover seder, which represents the transition from slavery to freedom, and at the Havdalah ceremony at Shabbat's conclusion, which represents the transition from Shabbat to weekdays. At a circumcision, Elijah conjures up the symbolic transition of entering the covenant, and this symbolism likewise animates a Brit Bat ceremony. Second, Elijah is a protector of children, as exemplified by his miraculous resuscitation of a dead child (I Kings 17:17–24). While this imagery is meaningful at a circumcision due to a baby boy's exposure to physical danger, it also applies more broadly as a blessing that all children remain safe and cared for throughout their lifetimes. Finally, Elijah is believed to be the harbinger of the Messiah, as the midrash's conclusion alludes. By acknowledging Elijah, we are effectively praying for the coming of the Messiah, a hope that is pertinent in the context of any Jewish ritual.

Today, a designated Chair of Miriam, rather than a Chair of Elijah, is sometimes incorporated into welcoming ceremonies for girls. This is a means of infusing a female presence and introducing a female role model. A Chair of Miriam can also be interpreted as a symbol of divine nurturing, since Miriam ensures that her mother nurses her brother, Moses, after the Egyptian princess rescues him from the river (Exodus 2:7).[65] Miriam has become a significant Biblical figure in modern Jewish feminist thought and practices, based particularly on her role in leading Israelite women in dancing and singing after the splitting of the Red Sea (Exodus 15:20–21).[66] It follows that some invite the spirit of Miriam to welcoming ceremonies for girls as an expression of thanksgiving to God or to invoke her gift of prophecy.[67]

At a Brit Bat, however, the covenant is paramount, and symbols that most effectively express this theme should be utilized. While Miriam's actions bespeak her strong connection to God and evoke the Exodus from Egypt, Elijah's activities more expansively and recognizably communicate a covenantal theme for all the reasons presented above. In my opinion, imagery should be used because of its well-understood relevance to the subject matter, not because it highlights a particular gender. All told, therefore, the Chair of Elijah is an appropriate covenantal symbol for a Brit Bat.

BRIT BAT NOMENCLATURE

A final covenantal element of a Brit Bat is not part of the actual ceremony. Rather, it is the use of the name *Brit Bat* (Covenant of a Daughter) to describe the ceremony and its accoutrements. This name is used today to some extent in liberal communities. To me, *Brit Bat* is most suitable because it captures the ceremony's focus on the covenant as central to each and every Jewish girl's life.

Following are a few examples of names that have been proposed for modern welcoming ceremonies for newborn girls, although these examples constitute only a fraction of those that have been used to date. *Simchat Bat* (Celebration of a Daughter) is common terminology, particularly in traditional communities. This generic name, however, neither evokes the covenant, nor provides much indication of what the ceremony entails. Other generic names include *Mesibat HaBat* (Party for a Daughter), *Tekes Huledet HaBat* (Ceremony for the Birth of a Daughter), and *Seudat Hodaya* (Thanksgiving Banquet). Ashkenazim have also increasingly adopted the name *Zeved HaBat* (Gift of a Daughter), which refers to traditional Sephardic practices for newborn girls. However, *baby naming* may be the most popular name overall (among English speakers) for all types of ceremonies, whether synagogue or freestanding rituals, and whether covenantal or not. This terminology reflects the perceived primacy of a girl's naming.

By contrast, some parents and rabbis emphasize the covenant. One practice is to reference a specific ritual, for example, *Brit Tallit* (Covenant of a Tallit), *Brit Rechitza* (Covenant of Washing), and *Brit Neirot* (Covenant of Candles). Other names depict particular themes, such as *Brit Eidut* (Covenant of Testimony) and *Brit Sarah* (Covenant of Sarah). Some names feature generalized blessings, such as *Brit Kedusha* (Covenant of Holiness) and *Brit Chayim* (Covenant of Life). Other possibilities include *K'nisa LaBrit*

(Entry into the Covenant), *Brit Bat Tziyon* (Covenant of a Daughter of Zion), and *Brita,* a derived term that is a feminized version of *Brit.*

Some have proposed *Simchat Brit* (Celebration of Covenant) to express joyousness.[68] However, a welcoming ceremony is primarily commemorative, and not celebratory per se. *Brit Banot* (Covenant of Daughters) sounds to me as if there is more than one baby being honored at the ceremony, while *Brit HaBat* (Covenant of the Daughter) may imply that the covenant pertains only to the one daughter being honored. For me, in the end, *Brit Bat* is the simplest way to communicate that this ceremony symbolically initiates a new female member into the covenant of Israel.

WE HAVE SEEN in this chapter how the structure, liturgy, timing, symbols, and nomenclature of our Brit Bat all convey the theme of covenantal entry. These elements, along with the central ritual of tallit swaddling, are mutually reinforcing and provide a rich texture for a ceremony.

We also now understand the significance of, and basis for, modeling a welcoming ceremony for girls on the traditional circumcision ceremony. There is a prevalent sense today that the circumcision ceremony is "off-limits," due to the uniqueness of circumcision itself. However, to the contrary, not only has the circumcision ceremony changed over time, but it has also inspired at least one other practice (the Tokens of Virginity ceremony). Likewise, a number of practices for girls have been adapted from those for boys. This cross-fertilization of customs has been occurring throughout Jewish history and has become intertwined with the evolution of the Jewish legal tradition. In the final Part that follows, we more broadly explore the development of customs and its impact on modern welcoming ceremonies for girls.

Part III

A Tradition of Customs

8

Ceremonies for Newborn Girls
as Developing Customs

The importance of tradition is a central theme of this book. Previous chapters have demonstrated how traditional Ashkenazic customs can inform contemporary naming practices for girls (chapters 1–2), how classic Jewish texts view women as members of the covenant (chapters 4–5), and how contemporary girls' welcoming ceremonies, although novel, integrate traditional themes and imagery (chapters 3, 6–7). In this final part, we broadly examine these ceremonies from the perspective of halacha, the traditional system of Jewish law and practice.

Since welcoming ceremonies are distinctly Jewish practices that emerged as feminism gained momentum, our first step is to survey the wide range of Jewish feminist perspectives on the halachic system. Feminists have observed that halacha has evolved over many centuries, based exclusively on the opinions, experiences, and authority of men, with women often functioning as "enablers." Some feminists nonetheless remain committed to halacha, believing in both its binding authority and its capacity for flexibility and accommodation.[1] Blu Greenberg, for example, advocates for "find[ing] ways within Halakhah to allow for growth and greater equality" and maintains that halacha "cries out for reinterpretation in light of the new awareness for feminine equality [and] feminine potential."[2] Professor Tamar Ross proposes the philosophical approach of "accumulating revelation," which encourages creativity in approaching Torah as a means of "elaborating upon its original meaning." In this framework, feminism is "a new revelation of the divine will" and "a gift from God."[3]

Some view halacha in a relatively positive light, but propose substantial changes. For example, Professor Ellen Umansky sees halacha as a meaningful, authentic expression of Jewish tradition and authority. Her recommendation is to enrich and reshape halacha with women's voices, while retaining the aspects of halacha that address both men and women.[4] Along similar lines, Professor Tikva Frymer-Kensky approaches halacha as "our way of acting in concert to reach God" and views the halachic process as a mandate to "monitor and adjust the path so that it leads to holiness and divine order." She explains that all forms of domination, including patriarchy, cannot "lead to God" and must be dismantled.[5]

Other feminists, such as Judith Plaskow and Rachel Adler, express impatience with halacha and view it as an intractable system that subordinates women and ignores difficult realities. These feminists maintain, to different degrees, that the halachic system puts form over substance and socializes women to accept a peripheral and non-spiritual role.[6] Susan Weidman Schneider (founding editor of *Lilith* magazine) states that halacha excludes women and structures a "restricted legal status" for them, despite the tradition's focus on social justice.[7] A more critical vision, such as that of author Cynthia Ozick, characterizes Torah as "frayed" and innately unjust since it does not outright reject the dehumanization of women.[8] According to this perspective, halacha is "at best, irrelevant and, at worst, insidious."[9]

Despite these diverse opinions about the intersection between halacha and feminism, there is no question that halacha has influenced, and has been influenced by, Jewish life for many centuries. As Rachel Biale put it in 1984 in her landmark book *Women and Jewish Law,* "Whether one lives in harmony with tradition or in tension with [Halakhah], one must contend with that tradition. Comprehending the Halakhah is necessary for a Jewish life, whether one seeks to follow Jewish law or depart from it."[10] In this vein, we consider in this chapter whether and how ceremonies for newborn girls have a place in the halachic system and, if so, what this tells us about how to guide the future development of these rituals.

HALACHIC SENSIBILITIES

We begin with the custom of parents' sponsoring a kiddush (public reception) in the synagogue in honor of their daughter's birth, as well as the halachic sources encouraging parents to hold a festive meal soon after the baby's naming (see chapter 1). Both point to the halachic acceptability—and even encouragement—of celebrating a newborn girl's birth. Indeed, R. Moshe Sternbuch, chief rabbi of the Eidah HaChareidit, asserts that this kiddush is a "*minhag vatikin*"—an ancient custom.[11] In addition, welcoming ceremonies for newborn girls have become increasingly common in halachically observant communities, at times with the sanction of community rabbis.

Nonetheless, some Orthodox rabbis have strongly opposed welcoming ceremonies for newborn girls. When these rituals were beginning to emerge in 1976, R. Moshe Meiselman called ceremonies with a covenantal theme for girls "ridiculous" and, further, that they "mock the very concept of brit" and are "a meaningless form of spiritual autoeroticism." More broadly, R. Meiselman declared that newly created rituals and ceremonies are "certainly" meaningless and futile. However, it is significant that he did not argue that halacha categorically prohibits them. In fact, he stated that the "introduction of new rituals may not be absolutely forbidden," and that producing a "[c]reative divine service may or may not be forbidden."[12]

R. Meiselman's equivocation regarding the halachic acceptability of new practices, coupled with his hyperbolic language, signals a "meta-halachic" argument.[13] This type of argument relies on soft, subjective "traditional values," rather than on hard-nosed legal rulings or precepts. It is thus difficult, if not impossible, to engage this type of argument analytically.

A related argument that shares this difficulty is the principle of not following in the ways of other peoples ("*bechukoteichem lo teileichu*"; Leviticus 18:3). Professor Judith Bleich contended in 1983 that certain types of Simchat Bat rituals violate this principle. This argument, however, could be extended to prohibit all welcoming ceremonies for girls, based on the observation that many other cultures ritualize the birth of girls. The bechukoteichem line of reasoning could even be taken ad absurdum to disallow most Jewish practices, since other cultures celebrate weddings, observe holidays, have dietary restrictions, and so on.

R. Yechiel Yaakov Weinberg (twentieth-century Germany and Switzerland) takes a similar tack when faced with the issue of whether the new Bat Mitzvah practice is halachically acceptable. He rejects the "bechukoteichem" argument, surmising that this argument would likewise prohibit the well-established Bar Mitzvah on the basis that Christians also hold coming-of-age ceremonies. He goes on to speculate that perhaps Jews should not pray since prayer is a staple of other religions as well. Dismissing these specious conclusions, R. Weinberg holds that the "bechukoteichem" argument does not apply to the Bat Mitzvah since other religions "have their practices and we have ours." He also stresses that the motivation of the Bat

Mitzvah is to instill in girls a love for Judaism and pride in being Jewish, not to copy Christian practices.[14] These arguments apply equally to welcoming ceremonies for girls.

The doctrine of not following in the ways of other religions can be stated more broadly as an argument for maintaining tradition for the sake of tradition. R. Weinberg acknowledges that some Jews do not "consider rational arguments when it comes to religious practices, and do not even bother themselves with halachic arguments, but rather judge such matters only on the basis of emotions." He encourages these Jews to accept permissible new practices "in peace," particularly given the pure intentions of innovators.

Despite the conclusion of R. Weinberg, some today continue to espouse the belief that any new practice violates "bechukoteichem" and traditional sensibilities. For some, it is easier to reject new practices indiscriminately than to evaluate them carefully on a case-by-case basis. It is difficult, however, to interface with these "meta-halachic" issues because they are so slippery, subjective, and emotionally fraught.

Instead, we examine welcoming ceremonies for girls by applying an analytic halachic framework pertaining to the function and status of customs (*minhagim;* singular, *minhag*). In this way, we seek to characterize girls' welcoming ceremonies based on halachic principles rather than on meta-halachic sentiments.

CUSTOMS AS HALACHIC CONSTRUCTS

An extensive discussion of the complex role of customs in the halachic system is beyond the scope of this book. Broadly speaking, however, customs constitute grassroots practices, per the famous Talmudic exhortation to "go and see what the people do."[15] Customs "operate anonymously and non-directedly by the agency of the entire people or some particular segment of the people," and "the public as a whole is the direct creative source of normative rules generated by custom."[16] As expressed by R. Abraham Chill (1912–2004, United States), "Minhag was the vehicle by which the Jew demonstrated his devotion to God in a manner wholly spontaneous and embracing something of his own personality."[17]

Customs are an integral part of the halachic system. R. Haym Soloveitchik (b. 1937) explains that "[i]t is no exaggeration to say that the Ashkenazic community saw the law as manifesting itself in two forms: in the canonized written corpus [the Talmud and related codes], and in the regnant practices of the people." R. Soloveitchik characterizes these halachic practices as "a way of life" that is "not learned but rather absorbed. Its transmission is mimetic, imbibed from parents and friends, and patterned on conduct regularly observed in home and street, synagogue and school."[18]

Since customs flow from experience, they are continuously evolving. The "spontaneous and undirected" development of customs involves experimentation, intuition, and outside forces, such as social, cultural, and economic trends.[19] Customs emerge as people come to terms with new realities and, as a result, devise new practices that gain momentum as more people adopt them. It follows that differences among customs arise in both time and space; customs evolve with the passage of time and according to regional or local variations. As such, webs of overlapping and even contradictory customs gradually materialize.[20]

Customs thus proliferate as part of a highly fluid process, guided by what Jacob Katz (1904–1998, Mandate Palestine and Israel), the preeminent social historian of halacha, refers to as "ritual instinct." This is the basis by which the people—entrusted as the guardians of Jewish tradition—generate and sustain a wide range of practices. There is a strong traditional belief in the good will of the people to follow the law: "The people are endowed with this decisive power and authority [to develop customs] because there is a presumption that the people, who base their conduct on the Halakhah, intend their practices to be true to its spirit."[21] Said otherwise, "the classic Ashkenazic position for centuries ... saw the practice of the people as an expression of halakhic truth."[22]

Halachic rules and legal norms evolve when rabbinic authorities recognize changes occurring in the community and apply the law in real-world situations. In the words of Jacob Katz: "Regarding various questions arising in everyday life, there was always a certain tension between basic halachic teachings and the ability and readiness of the public to adapt its behavior."[23] For example, the vast body of responsa literature demonstrates that rabbis have, throughout the ages, taken into account prevailing human circumstances. Generally speaking, however, halachic rules evolve "from the top down" while customs evolve "from the bottom up," and these two processes interact dialectically. Halachic rulings therefore may develop in a somewhat more structured way than customs. These rulings ideally evolve as rabbis examine facts, study the law, and methodically apply the law to the facts, whereas customs develop non-linearly.

The different priorities and approaches of the community and its leaders have resulted in clashes between customs and halachic rules. In one paradigm, a community rejects a permissive ruling by a halachic authority in order to maintain pre-existing customs that are more stringent. In another paradigm, a halachic authority critiques or even denounces a customary practice due to a determination that it conflicts with normative halacha.[24] Historically, this type of controlling "veto" has occurred relatively infrequently. Rabbis have been more likely to offer this type of opinion indirectly or summarily. They have exerted more robust control in the strictly limited cases of customs based on error (*minhag ta'ut*), unreasonable or illogical customs (*minhag sh'tut*), and dreadful or potentially injurious customs (*minhag garu'a*).

Moreover, halachic oversight is applicable primarily in areas of religious prohibitions (*issurim*), whereas areas related to commercial law (*mammon*) are largely free from the oversight of authorities.[25] In fact, the well-known rule that custom overrides the law (*minhag mevattel halacha,* JT Bava Metzia 7:1) or that custom uproots the law (*minhag okare halacha*) is fully effective for areas of commercial law based on a principle of freedom to contract. In issues of religious prohibitions, by contrast, custom may disallow what the halacha permits, but may not permit what halacha disallows.[26]

Perhaps most commonly, clashes between customs and halachic norms can persist without being recognized as such. For example, R. Haym Soloveitchik notes that sorting or separating (*borer*) is traditionally forbidden on Shabbat, yet Jews eat fish on Shabbat and, in doing so, separate the bones from the meat to avoid choking. He concludes that "all Jews who ate fish on Sabbath (and Jews have been eating fish on Sabbath for, at least, some two thousand years) have violated the Sabbath." R. Soloveitchik acknowledges that "[t]his seems absurd, but the truth of the matter is that it is very difficult to provide a cogent justification for separating bones from fish." Despite attempts to offer solutions to this type of dilemma, the end result is that "on frequent occasions, the written word was reread in light of traditional behavior."[27]

It follows that the reality of customs is messy and not easily categorized or conceptualized. A vast majority of customs are uncodified, and many are even undocumented. Since customs develop organically, scholars continuously gather and sort them—a gargantuan and never-ending project.[28] R. Daniel Sperber, for example, has produced the most comprehensive compilation and analysis of Jewish customs to date, and he continues to expand this work.[29]

Notwithstanding the challenge of cataloging this immense and ever-changing universe of Jewish customs, nineteenth-century eastern European halachic sources identify three fundamental categories of customs: *s'yagim* ("fences" around the Torah), *m'orririm* (literally, those that awaken), and *chovivim* (those that exhibit love). The s'yagim safeguard the Torah by establishing extra stringencies to avoid transgressing laws. The m'orririm are subdivided into those that conjure up and revitalize earlier practices and those that promote spirituality. The chovivim are motivated by a sincere love for mitzvot and a desire to beautify them (hiddur mitzvah) by adding special touches and flourishes to ritual objects or practices.[30]

Legal norms have also developed in an attempt to formally frame the vast body of evolving customs. Even these norms, however, largely defer to the "power of the people." First, a small minority of customs serves as a source of law. These customs have the force of law solely because they are practiced, and they do not require any external legal authority.[31] One prototypical example involves Levirate marriage, where an unmarried man is required to marry his widowed and childless sister-in-law (Deuteronomy 25:9–10). The Talmud (BT Yevamot 102a) presents a hypothetical scenario in which Elijah the Prophet declares that *halizah,* the ceremony that cancels the obligation for a Levirate marriage, may not be accomplished by the accepted practice (throwing a sandal). The Talmud explains that even Elijah must not be obeyed under these circumstances, since the people had long ago adopted this practice.

Second, customs may be considered binding if they have been followed for a certain amount of time and "acquire an established place in Jewish law."[32] In the twelfth century, Maimonides viewed customs as akin to legal edicts (*takkanot* and *g'zeirot*), and, in the fourteenth century, R. Nissim of Gerona, Spain (the Ran) deemed the force of customs as comparable to that of takkanot. Furthermore, Ashkenazic halachic scholars devised the notion that the customs of Israel are Torah (*minhagei yisrael Torah hee*), meaning that Jewish customs are authoritative and are binding to the same extent as Torah.[33] Some later halachic authorities took a more stringent approach to customs, even assigning them the strength of a Biblical commandment.[34] Others adopted a more moderate stance. For example, R. Abraham Isaac Kook held that only the customs and decrees of the Sanhedrin, the seventy-one-member supreme court of Israel in the Second Temple era, require strict adherence (Deuteronomy 17:11). All other customs, including those that developed in the past two thousand years, may be observed more leniently.[35]

WELCOMING CEREMONIES AS CUSTOMS

Based on our excursion into the relationship between customs and halacha, we can begin to understand how welcoming ceremonies for newborn girls fit into a halachic framework. We start with the observation that these ceremonies have been developing fluidly in the grassroots since the 1970s. This evolution has been non-linear, as different variations have gained momentum in different communities. Early on, experimentation predominated, and the "people" perpetuated these practices spontaneously and instinctually. Overall, these ceremonies demonstrate an interest in enhancing Jewish life-cycle practices by expressing a love for Judaism and devotion to God. Furthermore, social trends, such as the feminist movement of the late 1960s and 1970s, sparked an interest in this new, yet traditionally grounded, type of ritual.

This description easily fits the definition of customs in the halachic system. Welcoming ceremonies for girls evince the key hallmarks of customs— they are spontaneous practices of the people, products of people's good intentions, and the result of instinct and experience, rather than a written dictate. In addition, social trends were an impetus for the emergence of these ceremonies, just as diverse social, cultural, and economic circumstances have spurred many other customs. Furthermore, welcoming ceremonies easily fit into two identified categories for customs. These rituals are both m'oririm since they promote spirituality and a strong connection to Judaism, and chovivim since they are motivated by a love of Torah and an interest in beautifying it.

Customs play an essential halachic role by encompassing a wide range of religious and quasi-religious practices. Customs function within the system, not outside it—although they are not consistently recorded in the written rabbinic corpus. As part of the halachic system, customs remain subject to halachic standards (although these standards have, historically, sometimes been overlooked). It follows that welcoming ceremonies for girls appear to be legitimate customs in the eyes of halacha, to the extent that they comply internally with halachic requirements. This compliance is critical, since customs, except sometimes for those relating to commercial law, may not permit what halacha disallows.

The distinction of being a legitimate custom brings with it halacha's remarkable assumption that those performing these ceremonies intend to abide by the spirit of halacha. Furthermore, while there are varying stances regarding the binding nature of customs, some authorities maintain that halacha demands strict adherence to accepted customs. This may be difficult to implement in light of the reality of overlapping or conflicting customs. Nonetheless, the mere articulation of such opinions demonstrates the extent to which customs are valued within the halachic system. While initiation ceremonies for girls are brand-new on the evolutionary scale of customs, these practices have become well-accepted and even commonplace in many different communities. Welcoming ceremonies for newborn girls are thus customs that, viewed from a halachic perspective, are worthy of respect.

THE MAGIC OF CUSTOMS

In the course of thinking about customs as a crucial component of the halachic system, I came across an article from the *Arizona Jewish Post*. Titled "Baby Naming Becomes Part of Tradition," the article focuses on the development of modern welcoming ceremonies for newborn girls.[36] This title is paradoxical: How can these emergent, evolving customs become part of "tradition," a set of sustained religious practices?

The answer is a matter of perception. Customs are continuously adopted and formulated by the "people" as expressions of their devotion to God. Customs become more firmly woven into the fabric of Jewish life, however, when they become indistinguishable from pre-existing, or even longstanding, practices. This hazy transition from an undirected, variable custom to a well-accepted "tradition" is a sleight of hand that I conceptualize as "the magic of customs." Unlike a rabbit coming out of a hat, this transformation happens relatively slowly. But it is a magical transformation nonetheless; a custom becomes traditional while everyone is closely watching, yet no one can pinpoint exactly when or how it happened. This process can occur regardless of whether a custom's origin is known or unidentifiable.

I encountered this notion for the first time in *Inventing Jewish Ritual* by Vanessa Ochs. She vividly describes this process:

> Our personal or cultural memory of a time when the new custom did not exist or when it was first introduced grows fuzzy and is eventually erased. A new memory is constructed, and we say to ourselves, this custom has existed for as long as we can remember. It feels rooted in the most ancient practices and affirms and honors our connections to our ancestors and their most sacred commitments. It defines one's Jewish identity.... We know only this: a given ritual is one we perform now, and we probably have been doing so since the beginning of time.[37]

This notion is best illustrated with a story. R. Moses Sofer (the Chatam Sofer, nineteenth-century Hungary) was once visiting a synagogue. There, he observed that when the congregation recited the prayer Aleinu, they stood and turned around to face the synagogue's back wall. The Chatam Sofer investigated and discovered that, many years earlier, a large sign with the words for Aleinu had been affixed to the synagogue's back wall because there were not enough individual prayer books to accommodate everyone. However, even when the sign was later taken down, the congregants continued to turn to the back wall when reciting Aleinu and, ironically, even held their prayer books while doing so.[38] While this story may or may not have happened, the point is that a custom can become "traditional" so "magically" that its original purpose fades away.

There are many actual examples of this type of "magical" transformation in Judaism. Some customs take center stage in Jewish life, even though they had earlier been vociferously denounced. One prominent example is the Kol Nidrei (literally, "All Vows") prayer that opens the service on Yom Kippur, the most solemn day on the Jewish calendar. Kol Nidrei's melodies and content set the tone for the holiday today. However, Gaonim (leading scholars) in ninth- and tenth-century Babylonia vigorously opposed the recitation of this prayer, and European rabbis in the centuries that followed revised Kol Nidrei in an attempt to make it consistent with halachic norms.[39] Over the years, these substantial concerns have been forgotten, and, in the minds of Jews today, Kol Nidrei is considered timeless.

Vanessa Ochs also provides case studies. The first involves *matzah* (plural, *matzot*), the unleavened bread eaten on Passover, which had been made by hand since ancient times. When machine-made matzot were introduced in the mid-nineteenth century in France, a strenuous controversy ensued.[40] "[S]ome rabbis proclaimed that [machine-made matzot] were 'a dangerous instrument of modernity leading inevitably to assimilation, reform, and apostasy,' and would uproot the Torah." Today, however, "[g]iven the iconic nature not just of the store-bought matzah, but the matzah box itself, it is hard to imagine how threateningly novel this practice was in the recent past."[41] Again, intense controversy gave way to unquestioning acceptance, but it is difficult to pinpoint exactly when or how machine-made matzah became "traditional." Ochs also cites the example of women using wigs as head coverings in some Orthodox communities:

> [W]hen married women wanted to wear wigs as a sign of modesty, rabbis of the late nineteenth century argued against it, preferring the less attractive hat, kerchief, or shawl. For the rabbis, the wigs were lewd and provocative borrowings from secular culture. But the wig-wearing women prevailed, especially as more of them could afford wigs. Now wearing wigs is *the* sign of the highest standards of modesty and piety in certain communities, and the rabbis would be the first to pronounce the practice de rigueur.[42]

Here, as with Kol Nidrei and machine-made matzot, opposition to a custom "magically" transformed into an embrace of that very same custom.

Customs can become "magically" accepted despite apparent inconsistencies with basic tenets. Some prime examples include variants on the practice of ingesting the blood of circumcision. In certain North African Jewish communities, the mother of a recently circumcised son would customarily eat her son's foreskin. Likewise, women seeking to become pregnant in certain Egyptian, Libyan, Greek, Turkish, Bucharian, and Tadjik communities would eat a foreskin to facilitate pregnancy, with the goal of giving birth to a boy. Barren Libyan women would eat two eggs placed on the sand in which a ritual circumciser had spat out the blood of circumcision and buried the foreskin. Yemenite brides and barren Sephardic women in Israel would drink water mixed with the residual blood from a circumcision.[43] In 1931, R. Yaakov Moses Toledano (1880–1960, Israel) analyzed the complex question of whether these superstitious folk practices violate a Biblical injunction against eating human flesh (Leviticus 11:2).[44] It is likewise questionable whether these practices are permissible in light of Biblical prohibitions against drinking blood (Leviticus 7:26–27, 17:10–14). It is not known when and how customs involving the ingestion of foreskins and circumcision blood became accepted in these communities and whether halachic issues played any part in the process. But these customs "magically" became "traditional" in the face of halachic pitfalls.

Other Jewish customs have developed as a result of practices in the prevailing external culture. For example, in a wide swath of Jewish communities, particularly in North Africa and central and south Asia, brides decorate themselves, as part of their wedding preparation rituals, with red or orange dye extracted from the henna plant. Some variations include creating intricate patterns on a bride's hands or feet or smudging henna on a bride's hand. Sometimes henna is applied as part of an elaborate pre-wedding "henna ceremony." Jews apparently adopted these customs from the non-Jewish communities in these regions where henna use had been long established. However, it is not known precisely how or when dyeing a bride's skin with henna became deeply entrenched and "traditional" in many Mizrachic communities.

Finally, in some Ashkenazic communities today, there is a practice of kissing one's pinky finger and then holding it up toward an open Torah scroll while the scroll is lifted overhead, either before or after it is read aloud. It seems that the idea is to exhibit a love for the Torah when it is in a paradoxical state that is both intimate (since the scroll is open) and yet inaccessible (since it is raised high above the congregation). While pointing to a lifted Torah scroll with an index finger is perhaps a precursor practice, there is a dearth of documentation tracing the trajectory of this pinky gesture, which may well be fairly recent.[45] Nonetheless, there are some who fervently greet a raised Torah scroll with an outstretched pinky, based on the belief that this is an enduring tradition. Somehow, this custom "magically" became traditional.

MAKING THE MAGIC WORK

We have now seen that functioning customs can gradually transition into "traditions" across the wide spectrum of Jewish practice. Although we cannot identify exactly when or how this happens, we can broadly characterize some of the factors that precipitate or foster this transition. One important factor is longevity, since the passage of time obscures the machinations involved in gaining acceptance. For well-liked customs, sometimes even a relatively short period can have this effect. A functionality or technical advantage is another means by which a practice can become more readily accepted. For example, people were ultimately inclined to use machine-made matzah because it is more cost-effective than handmade matzah. Superstitions or beliefs in supernatural powers can also pave the way for a practice to become traditional. The Mizrachic customs of ingesting foreskins or circumcision blood demonstrate this dynamic. External social or cultural forces, including aesthetic conventions, may also create traditions, as with the examples of women's wigs in Orthodox communities and henna decorations in Mizrachic communities. Finally, some "traditions" enrich religious or cultural experiences. Pointing a pinky finger toward a raised Torah scroll, for example, can be construed as an enhancement in the context of communal prayer.

For customs that involve a liturgy, however, one powerful factor that facilitates the transformation from recognizable practice to "tradition" is the gradual adoption of a uniform text. This standardization signals that the text is significant to the larger community and has gained the community's imprimatur. As R. Daniel Sperber has pointed out, "The printed book has become the canon"—for better or worse. While contemporary liturgy is by no means completely standardized, there is a tendency today to resist change with regard to liturgy.[46] This holds true, to varying extents, in all denominations, since attachment to the liturgies in prayer books has grown and radical innovations in synagogue prayer are relatively atypical today. It follows that uniform liturgies—and particularly those found in prayer books—are taken seriously and viewed today as legitimate in their respective communities. These perceptions are precisely what "magically" convert a liturgy into a "tradition."

At the same time, it is important to remember that, as R. Daniel Sperber explains, "our liturgy has always been evolving" and that there was "never a fixed text or a tefillat keva [a set liturgy] in which everything was fully formed so that no further changes could be introduced." One well-known mishna (Avot 2:13) instructs, "When you pray, do not make your prayer fixed, but rather, [invoke] mercy and supplications before God, Blessed is He." Furthermore, one can pray anytime without any set liturgy.[47] Thus, Jewish prayer is not limited to a recorded body of liturgy, despite the Talmudic opinion of R. Jose that "one who changes the liturgy fixed by the sages does not fulfill his obligation" (BT Brachot 40b). While acknowledging that ultra-traditionalists are likely to keep rejecting the liturgical changes that continue to arise, R. Sperber observes that "the conflict will go on well into the future, but so too will changes continue to appear throughout the pages of our prayer books."[48]

Once a liturgy is recited in one community, it may gain acceptance in other communities. Beyond a certain point in time, the liturgy is perceived as more "traditional" each time it is recited. The emphasis on a minyan (prayer quorum), in which all participants recite the same prayers at the pace set by a prayer leader, exemplifies the robust Jewish belief in the potency of uniform public practices. As a liturgy becomes more "traditional," it both reflects and influences the communal outlook and culture. Thus, with respect to liturgy, tradition can promote standardization, just as standardization can promote tradition. A "traditional" liturgy also instills a sense of confidence that derives from reciting venerated, established prayers. As Professor Tova Hartman has stated, "Fixed liturgy enables us to partake in something larger, older, greater than our immediate reality."[49]

A UNIFORM CORE PRACTICE FOR NEWBORN GIRLS

My ultimate hope for the modern practice of initiating newborn girls is that it becomes widely accepted to the point that it "magically" becomes "traditional." This means that holding welcoming ceremonies for girls would become such a natural part of the Jewish life-cycle that no one could precisely pinpoint when this practice began to feel irrevocable, entrenched, and maybe even timeless. We would remain cognizant of the actual historical origin of initiating girls, while, at the same time, somewhat obscuring this history, as our perception would become more attuned to this ritual's pervasiveness and its compatibility with older practices.

As with other liturgy-based customs, a trend toward standardizing a liturgy for newborn girls would be an effective first step toward integrating the initiation of girls into the body of "traditional" life-cycle practices. My hope is that one core practice emerges gradually from the multitude of options and is thrust into the cauldron of popular opinions, preferences, and observances. Over a span of time, the "people" would use their "ritual instincts" to assess whether a single basic practice—with some potential for modifications—is meaningful to them in welcoming a daughter into the covenant of Israel. If such a practice slowly gains popularity, it could evolve in the same way that the body of Jewish liturgy has been evolving for centuries. This approach would necessarily shift away from the widespread belief today that the content of ceremonies for newborn girls can or should vary according to personal predilections.

Performed throughout the Jewish community, a single core practice would gain the legitimacy required for a ritual to become significant and, over the course of time, "traditional." Relative uniformity would free parents from the need to rely on the ad hoc advice of friends or the interpretation of individual rabbis. While it might be fun or personally fulfilling for a parent or rabbi to formulate a ceremony for a newborn girl, the lack of a standard, accepted text inhibits the Jewish community from taking its practices for newborn girls to the next level. Some measure of uniformity is thus a crucial step toward continuing to build on the modern instinct to celebrate newborn daughters.

The key is sustainability. The grassroots can maintain a new liturgy for a short or long time, but formalizing a liturgy provides a better chance for its long-term acceptance and integration. For example, it is likely that *"L'cha Dodi,"* the sixteenth-century kabbalistic poem sung to usher in Shabbat, might have become forgotten over time, like so many other beautiful Jewish poems, had it not become an established central feature of the prayer services that welcome Shabbat. In addition, there are countless *techinot* (Yiddish prayers written by and for women), which have been composed since the sixteenth century. However, this body of uncodified prayers was not easily accessible and, for the most part, lay temporarily dormant until the advent of a modern feminist surge of interest in collecting and reciting them.[50] Gary Rosenblatt, who held a Simchat Bat for his daughter in the 1970s, reflected on the status of ceremonies for girls today:

> There is still no ritualized ceremony to mark the occasion [of the birth of a baby girl] as, of course, the Brit Milah does for a boy. This is both good and bad. Good because it allows for creativity and flexibility in allowing parents to design a ceremony to their liking. . . . Not so good, though, is that in more than three decades, the ceremony is still far from the norm in many communities.[51]

It appears that the fact that girls' welcoming rituals are, in Rosenblatt's opinion, "still far from the norm" is the direct result of the "creativity and flexibility" encouraged for these rituals.

This suggestion of reorienting ourselves toward uniformity is not impractical, since the wide variety of Simchat Bat welcoming rituals for girls has already begun to contract slowly. These rituals are developing today based less on experimentation and more on modeling earlier ceremonies. Synagogue Simchat Bat practices tend to conform to templates that are well-known and accepted in individual communities. Popular resources also have narrowed the field of readings and rituals by cataloging them and presenting them as a cohesive set of options. Furthermore, traditional parents who hold Simchat Bat ceremonies utilize a relatively narrow scope of prayers and readings, limiting themselves to those that satisfy halachic constraints and conform with communally accepted sensibilities.

The combined result of all these trends is that common ritualistic and liturgical elements have emerged for the Simchat Bat, and they have become increasingly acceptable, and even expected, in some communities. Although the Simchat Bat remains innovative, in that parents and rabbis continue to formulate new rituals freely (or at least retain the license to do so), Simchat Bat practices are nonetheless experiencing a degree of homogenization. While parents and rabbis might balk initially at the idea of a uniform practice, they are in fact already heading—ever so slowly—in that direction. As R. Debra Orenstein has recognized, "It is not difficult to imagine, in the not too distant future, when the format of girls' naming ceremonies will be more nearly standardized."[52]

This slow, yet perceptible, move toward homogenization answers the question of why now is the time to begin to gravitate toward a uniform practice for newborn girls. We stand at a crossroads at the second stage in the development of welcoming ceremonies for girls. The first stage of experimenting and brainstorming has, for the most part, drawn to a close. While practices remain splintered among different communities, individual rabbis and parents are beginning to follow broad patterns of practice, with liberal rabbis leading their communities and traditional parents using well-defined resources and models. Now, before these patterns become fixed, is the time to take a step back and assess what we have. We can strengthen current practices substantially by coming together to accept central features of a ceremony, and now is the right time to do so. Moreover, consolidating our practices with respect to newborn girls could be one avenue, albeit a small one, to strengthen ties today among different factions in the Jewish community at large.

Striving for a measure of uniformity need not require the loss of personal expression. A Brit Bat ceremony could welcome embellishments to the same extent as any other Jewish prayer or ritual. At its core, a Brit Bat consists of one central ritual, a basic liturgical text, and set timing. Above and beyond these components, parents and rabbis might add personalized prayers, readings, or other touches—but, importantly, not to the extent of diluting the ceremony's central covenantal theme and ritual. If they choose to make additions (or deletions), parents and rabbis should endeavor to enhance (or at least preserve) the covenantal message, and some of these variations might even become more broadly accepted in the future. However, excessive readings or rituals, particularly those that are disparate or unfamiliar, may feel awkward or run the risk of clouding the covenantal theme. "Less is more," as the concise, yet evocative, traditional circumcision and Jewish wedding ceremonies demonstrate.

A Brit Bat's general composition should be no different than that of any other Jewish life-cycle event as practiced today. Circumcisions, Bar and Bat Mitzvah celebrations, weddings, and funerals all consist today of certain uniform elements—despite notable differences among the purpose, status, and history of each event. At the same time, each occasion also allows for highly personalized contributions. These range from substantive content to the array of participants, type of speeches, or style of meal. Furthermore, particularly at weddings, the ceremony is often sprinkled with supplemental customs, from using a quilt made by friends as a chuppah to escorting a newly married couple from the chuppah with song and dance—and everything in between. This common ritualistic model for life-cycle ceremonies, which combines a central practice with the potential for some embellishment, provides the benefits of uniformity with the opportunity to make it feel like one's own. This is likewise an effective model for welcoming rituals for girls.

Some feminists have identified and, to some extent, promoted the model of an "open, flexible, and creative" ritual for new practices for girls and women, including welcoming ceremonies for newborns. This translates to a belief that individual families or communities should craft their own rituals for newborn girls and that these practices should be continuously modified, based on personal preferences, interests, and creative output. Most significant, however, is that the resulting fluidity is a positive, encouraged value.

However, no other Jewish life-cycle commemoration is deemed "enhanced" by its indeterminate structure and inconsistent practice. It is difficult for a community to embrace practices that are free-form, without set rituals and timing. As a result, if rituals for newborn girls continue to utilize the "open and flexible" model, these rituals will continue to be deemed secondary in some communities. By contrast, a ceremony that fits seamlessly with the model of other Jewish life-cycle practices may have the potential, in the long term, to become "traditional"—meaning fully integrated and accepted, not old-fashioned or ossified.

Furthermore, ceremonies for newborn girls remain needlessly separate and "other" when they use a different structure than that of well-established life-cycle rituals. Ironically, therefore, the result of encouraging fluid and creative rituals is to portray women as "other," a characterization feminists have long criticized. A new structure should not be sought in order to distinguish "female" rituals from existing "male" rituals. This is analogous to a hypothetical scenario in which female scientists would create a new scientific method in order to differentiate their work from the previous advances of a male-dominated field. Even more troubling is the suggestion that a fluid and open ritualistic structure is "appropriate to female anatomy."[53] The idea that rituals for Jewish women should somehow correspond to their anatomy is objectifying in a way that would ordinarily be denounced. In short, women will cease being "other" only when their rituals and other practices are no longer separated out from mainstream Judaism.

LITURGICAL TEXTS

As I slowly began to recognize the importance of a core uniform practice for newborn girls, my first step was to inquire if there were welcoming liturgies published in Ashkenazic prayer books (siddurim; singular, siddur) or rabbi's guides (madrichim; singular, madrich). (Traditional Sephardic and Mizrachic prayer books record longstanding liturgies in those communities.) As I began to investigate, I noted with interest that Blu Greenberg wrote in the late 1980s about the possibility of adopting a standard welcoming ceremony for newborn girls by publishing it in a prayer book:

> As has happened many times before, it will take a few decades before [a ceremony] will become standardized and formalized. Or it could happen next year: the publisher of a traditional siddur might select one ceremony and include it in his siddur—and it would henceforth become fixed for all time.[54]

When I first began to compile welcoming liturgies for girls found in prayer books and rabbi's guides, I shared Blu Greenberg's belief in the "power of the siddur" and, therefore, took for granted that I was gathering "codified" texts. My assumption was that recording a ritual in a prayer book or a rabbi's guide reflects the fact that this ritual is widely performed and accepted. However, I slowly became disabused of this notion. What I discovered is that publication in a prayer book or rabbi's guide does not guarantee, and may not even signify, standardization. It turns out that, while a handful of modern Ashkenazic prayer books and rabbis' manuals contain liturgies for the birth of a girl, these liturgies are little known, seldom followed, and sometimes even difficult to understand.

The Reform liturgy is the most complicated, since it encompasses four different ceremonies for newborn girls (two in a "home prayer book" and two in a rabbi's manual), but without an explanation about when or why each should be used. Published in 1994, *On the Doorposts of Your House: Prayers and Ceremonies for the Jewish Home,* which is a "ritual guide for home use" rather than a "prayer book" per se, has a naming ceremony for both boys and girls and a separate covenantal naming ceremony specifically for girls.[55] The "Naming of a Child" ceremony for both boys and girls does not mention the covenant and features a naming liturgy that blesses a newborn with good judgment, wisdom, and kindness, as well as other blessings and prayers. The text specifies that this ceremony may be conducted either in the synagogue or at home. By contrast, the "Covenant of Life" ceremony for girls, which parallels the "Covenant of Milah" ceremony for boys, is performed on the eighth day of life. Each of the parents kindles a light and welcomes their daughter into the covenant with prayers and blessings. The mother recites a blessing praising God for "command[ing] us to bring our daughters in the Covenant of Life." The father's blessing praises God for "command[ing] us to sanctify our life."

The Reform *Rabbi's Manual,* published in 1988, likewise presents both a naming ceremony for boys and girls and a separate covenantal naming ceremony for girls.[56] In the non-covenantal "Naming a Child in the Synagogue" ceremony, conducted for both boys and girls, the rabbi recites a Mi Shebairach, along with a prayer that gives thanks for the joys of parenthood, seeks guidance for the new parents, and names the baby. This liturgy, however, is different than the one in the home ritual guide. The "Hachnasat Bat l'Brit" (Entry of a Daughter into the Covenant) in the *Rabbi's Manual,* which is held either at home or in the synagogue, conforms to the broad outline of a traditional circumcision ceremony. However, the covenantal blessing recited here—praising God "who commands us to bring our daughter into the covenant of our people, Israel"—is also different from that in the home ritual guide. Another difference is that the *Rabbi's Manual* includes the blessing that "just as she has entered the covenant, so shall she enter Torah, the marriage canopy, and good deeds," which is absent in the home ritual guide.

The Conservative *Siddur Sim Shalom* provides only a naming Mi Shebairach in the Torah service.[57] On the other hand, the Conservative *Rabbi's Manual* contains a total of five possible ways to welcome a newborn girl—two alternatives for a synagogue naming ritual,[58] and three options for a freestanding Simchat Bat ceremony.[59] In particular, the *Manual* presents a "conventional" synagogue naming with the same Mi Shebairach that is in the siddur, as well as an "innovative" alternative in which a more extensive Mi Shebairach is recited in English while the baby touches the handle of a Torah scroll. The *Manual* asks rabbis to encourage parents to attend synagogue with their daughter, receive an aliyah, and name the baby "according to the traditional ritual."

Nevertheless, the *Manual* also has a separate freestanding Simchat Bat ceremony "that deliberately affirms [a girl's] inclusion in the covenant." This ceremony "offers three options within a single structure"[60] and invites rabbis to select one ritual from the following choices: (1) lighting candles, (2) placing the baby's hand on the handle of a Torah scroll, and (3) enfolding the baby in the four corners of a tallit. The candle ritual allows for the additional alternatives of carrying the baby between rows of guests, each of whom holds a candle, or lighting six candles to represent the six days of creation. The *Manual* sets out three full-length ceremonies, each of which centers on one of the ritualistic options and includes various readings and blessings that correlate with that particular ritual, respectively. The naming liturgy that closes each of these ceremonies incorporates the prayer that a girl's parents will be "privileged to raise her to Torah, the marriage canopy, and good deeds." This prayer does not recognize that a girl has entered the covenant.

The Reconstructionist siddur *Kol Haneshama* has a "Mi Sheberah for Newborn Children and Their Parents" and an additional English blessing regarding Torah study.[61] However, the Reconstructionist *Rabbi's Man-*

ual[62] offers both a naming liturgy and a covenantal ceremony, and suggests that the naming liturgy be recited in the synagogue or *chavurah* (informal prayer group) after holding a covenantal ceremony in the home. The non-covenantal naming liturgy for a "Public Welcoming of Parents and a New-Born Child," consists of a Mi Shebairach substantially similar to that in the prayer book, as well as other blessings. By contrast, the more expansive *Brit Rechitza* (Covenant of Washing) ceremony follows the basic outline of the circumcision ceremony. After reciting the blessing for "command[ing] us to bring her into the covenant of the people of Israel," the parents wash their daughter's feet to symbolize her covenantal entry, and they bless God "who remembers the covenant through washing feet." The baby is named with a Mi Shebairach that shares some elements of the traditional Sephardic Zeved HaBat naming prayer, and she is blessed with verses from the Zeved HaBat liturgy.

To my knowledge, the only Orthodox Ashkenazic siddur in use today that has a ceremony for newborn girls is the *Koren Siddur, Nusah Ashkenaz,* published in 2009. Chief Rabbi Lord Sacks of the United Kingdom wrote this prayer book's introduction, translation, and commentary, and the prayer book is co-sponsored by the Orthodox Union in the United States.[63] The siddur contains a naming Mi Shebairach for girls as part of the Torah service. Separately, alongside other life-cycle rituals, the siddur provides a modified Zeved HaBat ceremony. This ceremony begins with the introductory Zeved HaBat verses, followed by an Ashkenazic Mi Shebairach that is slightly different from that in the Torah service. Significantly, this Mi Shebairach explicitly permits the option of announcing a baby girl's name for the first time at this freestanding ceremony. The ceremony also incorporates a parental prayer and Biblical verses.

The RCA *Lifecycle Madrikh* (*Rabbi's Manual*) published in 1995 by the Rabbinical Council of America, an organization of Orthodox American rabbis, has both a "Baby Naming" and a "Baby Naming Celebration."[64] The "Baby Naming," which occurs during a synagogue Torah service, consists of a Mi Shebairach that blesses the mother and daughter, prays for the mother's recovery, and names the daughter. The *Madrikh* recommends that "a festive meal or some repast" is appropriate "[f]ollowing the conclusion of the services." The *Madrikh* introduces the separate "Baby Naming Celebration" by explaining that "one may also call a special gathering of family and friends for the express purpose of celebrating the special joy of the birth." This may occur "after due time has been given for the mother to recover, gain some strength, and thus participate in the event." The ceremony includes the recitation of selected Psalms and the Shema prayer, as well as a "reaffirmation" of the baby's name that was previously announced in the synagogue. "The mother, wearing a new dress, may then recite" the Shehechiyanu blessing.

In reviewing all of these ceremonies, I was first struck by how the Conservative *Rabbi's Manual* offers a choice among three options for a ceremony's central ritual. I had never before seen such a blatant presentation of multiple options in a single published liturgy. When I mentioned this observation to a friend of mine who is a rabbi and a professor, she was likewise astounded by this panoply of choices. She commented that so many alternatives result in the perception that the ceremony is not an important life-cycle ritual. Were this ritual perceived as significant, it would be presented as a standard practice, rather than as a menu of options.

Soon after this conversation, I noticed that many of these published texts explicitly acknowledge that they are works in progress. The Conservative *Rabbi's Manual* states that the "final form" of its ceremony for girls "has not yet been canonized" and that "[a]ll those who use these rituals are partners in their creation."[65] The Reconstructionist *Rabbi's Manual* conveys the same fundamental message. This *Manual* explains that its ceremony "was conceived, and is designed, as a laboratory project for immediate use and ongoing revision. Proposed sections will be added, and additional changes made, as the project continues."[66] Despite its vastly different outlook, the Orthodox RCA *Madrikh* notes in a similar vein that its ceremony "is one of many possible formats for this gathering."[67]

In studying these ceremonies and attempting to understand how different practices in corresponding prayer books and rabbi's manuals fit together, I found the interplay among the texts confusing. I had a particularly difficult time trying to follow the connections among the four different ceremonies in the Reform home ritual guide and *Rabbi's Manual*. It is also unclear why the Conservative and Reconstructionist prayer books record only a Mi Shebairach, while the corresponding rabbi's manuals include detailed ceremonies. Furthermore, why does the Conservative rabbi's manual strongly encourage the synagogue Mi Shebairach, yet also provide a freestanding ceremony? Similarly, neither the *Koren Siddur* nor the RCA *Madrikh* explain why they have both a synagogue naming and a more elaborate ceremony. The *Koren Siddur* leaves unanswered some additional questions: Why has this Ashkenazic prayer book adopted a Sephardic liturgy? And should a baby girl be named for the first time in the synagogue or at a freestanding ceremony?

After years of struggling with these published texts, it finally occurred to me that each of the different rituals in these prayer books and rabbi's manuals conform to either the "synagogue naming" model (which has a Mi Shebairach and does not mention the covenant) or the "freestanding Simchat Bat" model (which is a covenantal ceremony, except in Orthodox variants). Yet, nowhere is it explained why one model or the other should be used, since contemporary rabbis themselves, across the denominations, have not selected one model or the other. As a result, none of these prayer books and rabbis' manuals offer clear direction and instructions to parents and rabbis seeking to welcome a newborn girl into the Jewish community. Said otherwise, it is difficult to think of any of these published rituals as codified when so many questions are left hanging.

My conversations with a handful of liberal rabbis confirmed some of my observations. I began these discussions by inquiring about "codified ceremonies" for newborn girls. The rabbis, however, were perplexed about what I meant. When I explained that I was referring to ceremonies for baby girls that are found in prayer books and rabbi's manuals, most of these rabbis clarified that these ceremonies are not "codified" simply because they appear in prayer books or rabbi's manuals. The rabbis explained that, to the contrary, these published ceremonies are, in essence, suggestions.

At the same time, when my Orthodox-affiliated friends and acquaintances have planned welcoming ceremonies for newborn daughters in the past few years, it did not occur to most of them to consult the *Koren Siddur,* although they were well-acquainted with it for weekday and Shabbat services. The vast majority did not even realize that the siddur contained a welcoming ceremony for girls. I subsequently began to realize that laypeople in more liberal denominations were likewise often unaware that there were "officially published" texts for rituals for newborn girls.

In sum, the ceremonies for newborn girls appearing in prayer books and rabbis' manuals across the denominations are not considered to be codified, although this is a common assumption for most other liturgies appearing in these publications. Furthermore, these prayer books and rabbis' manuals explicitly encourage a multiplicity of practices for newborn girls, although the ostensible purpose of these books is to standardize practices. Thus, welcoming ceremonies published in a range of "liturgical texts" have not promoted a uniformity of practice, nor are they intended to do so.

WE HAVE LEARNED that ceremonies for newborn Jewish girls are "customs" that constitute an integral and vibrant component of the halachic legal system. Thus, contrary to the sentiments of some, these ceremonies—like all other customs—play a significant role within the halachic framework and have the potential to "magically" evolve into "tradition." While a variety of factors have facilitated this transition, reorienting practices for newborn girls on a path toward standardization can be an effective first step in this "magical" process. In keeping with the model of all other Jewish life-cycle rituals today, we can develop a "tradition" for newborn girls while still making each individual ceremony feel special.

Although practices for newborn girls are slowly beginning to converge, there is today no single accepted form. Even the texts published in prayer books or rabbi's manuals are neither widely used, nor even well known. Thus, the only chance for a measure of standardization lies in the power of the people, with the support of their leadership. While this notion of striving for homogenization may be novel or controversial in the context of rituals for newborn girls, it presents the best chance for continuing to strengthen this genre and for integrating it fully into Jewish life-cycle practices.

A Jewish Ceremony for Newborn Girls

I have set out below my thoughts for a Brit Bat ("Covenant of a Daughter") ceremony. This ceremony ties together all of the themes in this book, from a first and only naming to a central covenantal theme animated by tallit swaddling, aspects of the circumcision liturgy, and eighth-day timing.

My hope is that this basic text could serve as a starting point for a wide-ranging discussion and that it might be debated, evaluated, fine-tuned, and performed over time. I am hopeful that, in the long term, a version of this ceremony—or another practice that coalesces over time—could become an accepted custom with the potential to begin to evolve slowly and "magically" into "tradition." Only the people have the ability and authority to make this collective determination.

The Jewish community encompasses widely divergent, deeply held world-views, which are both our greatest strength and greatest challenge. In considering this ceremony, many will use their pre-existing opinions regarding the rituals with which they may be familiar. Some will contemplate whether the ceremony expresses liberal ideals; others will evaluate its connection to tradition; yet others will assess whether it conforms to halachic principles. As a result, care has been taken to respect halachic tenets and sensitivities, while, at the same time, providing an opportunity to utilize more progressive modes of expression. Simplicity is key in finding common ground.

In the end, there is a sustained interest in commemorating the birth of daughters as a religiously significant event. My hope is that the ideas offered below can play a part in shaping this future. Moreover, engaging in a community-wide conversation about the future of Jewish practices for newborn girls presents a distinct opportunity for the entire Jewish community to work together toward a shared goal.

This ceremony is performed on the eighth day following the birth of a girl.

WELCOMING THE BABY

When the baby is carried in by a grandparent or other honored participant, those attending the ceremony say:

Blessed is she who comes.   בְּרוּכָה הַבָּאָה.

CHAIR OF ELIJAH

A second honored participant is sitting in the Chair of Elijah the prophet or, alternatively, standing next to it. This chair is symbolically designated using a decorative covering or other ornamentation.

The person carrying the baby passes her to the second participant, and the rabbi or a parent recites:

זֶה הַכִּסֵא שֶׁל אֵלִיָּהוּ הַנָּבִיא, זָכוּר לַטּוֹב.
לִישׁוּעָתְךָ קִוִּיתִי יהוה (בְּרֵאשִׁית מט:יח). שִׂבַּרְתִּי לִישׁוּעָתְךָ יהוה, וּמִצְוֹתֶיךָ עָשִׂיתִי
(תְּהִלִּים קיט:קסו). שָׂשׂ אָנֹכִי עַל אִמְרָתֶךָ, כְּמוֹצֵא שָׁלָל רָב (תְּהִלִּים קיט:קסב). שָׁלוֹם
רָב לְאוֹהֲבֵי תוֹרָתֶךָ, וְאֵין לָמוֹ מִכְשׁוֹל (תְּהִלִּים קיט:קסה). אַשְׁרֵי תִּבְחַר וּתְקָרֵב, יִשְׁכּוֹן
חֲצֵרֶיךָ (תְּהִלִּים סה:ה).

This is the Chair of Elijah the prophet, may he be remembered for good. For Your salvation I hope, God (Genesis 49:18). I wait for Your deliverance, God, and Your commandments I have performed (Psalms 119:166). I rejoice in Your sayings, like one who finds great spoils (Psalms 119:162). Great peace for lovers of Your Torah, and there is no stumbling block for them (Psalms 119:165). Happy are those You choose and bring close; let them dwell in Your courtyards (Psalms 65:5).

The attendees respond:

נִשְׂבְּעָה בְּטוּב בֵּיתֶךָ, קְדֹשׁ הֵיכָלֶךָ (תְּהִלִּים סה:ה).

May we be satisfied with the goodness of Your House, the holiness of Your Tabernacle (Psalms 65:5).

A tallit (prayer shawl) is spread out on the lap of the second participant, who is sitting in the Chair of Elijah. This participant gently positions the baby at the center of the tallit. Alternatively, this participant, if standing, places the baby on a tallit that is spread out on a table.

The parents take the corners of the tallit and lovingly swaddle their daughter, thus symbolizing her entry into the covenant between God and the Jewish people.

While performing this ritual, the parents say:

הַטַּלִּית תִּפְרוֹשׂ כְּנָפֶיהָ עָלֶיהָ וְתַצִּילֶהָ, כְּנֶשֶׁר יָעִיר קִנּוֹ עַל גּוֹזָלָיו יְרַחֵף (דְּבָרִים לב:יא).

May the tallit spread its wings over her and protect her "like an eagle stirring up its nest, hovering over its young" (Deuteronomy 32:11).

The parents then hold up their swaddled daughter.

Optional blessing. The parents recite:

בָּרוּךְ אַתָּה יהוה, אֱלֹהֵנוּ מֶלֶךְ הָעוֹלָם, אֲשֶׁר קִדְּשָׁנוּ בְּמִצְוֹתָיו וְצִוָּנוּ לְהַכְנִיסָהּ בִּבְרִית שֶׁל אַבְרָהָם אָבִינוּ וְשָׂרָה אִמֵּנוּ.

Blessed are You God, our God, King of the Universe, who has sanctified us with His commandments and commanded us to enter our daughter into the covenant of Abraham our forefather and Sarah our foremother.

or, alternatively,

בָּרוּךְ אַתָּה יהוה, אֱלֹהֵנוּ מֶלֶךְ הָעוֹלָם, שֶׁהִכְנִיסָהּ בִּבְרִית שֶׁל אַבְרָהָם אָבִינוּ וְשָׂרָה אִמֵּנוּ.

Blessed are You God, our God, King of the Universe, who has entered our daughter into the covenant of Abraham our forefather and Sarah our foremother.

COVENANTAL AFFIRMATION

The parents proclaim:

כְּשֵׁם שֶׁנִּכְנְסָה לַבְּרִית, כֵּן תִּכָּנֵס לְתוֹרָה וּלְחוּפָּה וּלְמַעֲשִׂים טוֹבִים.

Just as she has entered into the covenant, so shall she be entered into Torah, the marriage canopy, and good deeds.

The attendees respond in agreement:

כְּשֵׁם שֶׁנִּכְנְסָה לַבְּרִית, כֵּן תִּכָּנֵס לְתוֹרָה וּלְחוּפָּה וּלְמַעֲשִׂים טוֹבִים.

Just as she has entered into the covenant, so shall she be entered into Torah, the marriage canopy, and good deeds.

PARENTAL BLESSING

The parents recite together:

בָּרוּךְ אַתָּה יהוה, אֱלוֹהֵנוּ מֶלֶךְ הָעוֹלָם, הַטוֹב וְהַמֵּטִיב.

Blessed are You God, our God, King of the universe, who is Good and who causes good.

BLESSING OVER THE WINE

The rabbi or a parent recites and afterwards drinks from a cup of wine:

בָּרוּךְ אַתָּה יהוה, אֱלוֹהֵנוּ מֶלֶךְ הָעוֹלָם, בּוֹרֵא פְּרִי הַגָּפֶן.

Blessed are You God, our God, King of the universe, who creates the fruit of the vine.

The rabbi or a parent names the baby for the first and only time:

אֱלֹהֵינוּ וֵאלֹהֵי אֲבוֹתֵינוּ וְאִימוֹתֵינוּ, קַיֵּם אֶת הַיַּלְדָּה הַזֹּאת לְאָבִיהָ וּלְאִמָּהּ, וְיִקָּרֵא
שְׁמָהּ בְּיִשְׂרָאֵל, _____ בַּת _____ וְ _____. יִשְׂמַח הָאָב בְּיוֹצֵא חֲלָצָיו,
וְתָגֵל אִמָּה בִּפְרִי בִטְנָהּ, כַּכָּתוּב: יִשְׂמַח אָבִיךָ וְאִמֶּךָ, וְתָגֵל יוֹלַדְתֶּךָ (מִשְׁלֵי כג:כה).
וְנֶאֱמַר: וַהֲקִימוֹתִי אֶת בְּרִיתִי בֵּינִי וּבֵינֶךָ וּבֵין זַרְעֲךָ אַחֲרֶיךָ לְדוֹרוֹתָם לִבְרִית עוֹלָם
לִהְיוֹת לְךָ לֵאלֹהִים וּלְזַרְעֲךָ אַחֲרֶיךָ (בְּרֵאשִׁית יז:ז). וְנֶאֱמַר: זָכַר לְעוֹלָם בְּרִיתוֹ, דָּבָר
צִוָּה לְאֶלֶף דּוֹר. אֲשֶׁר כָּרַת אֶת אַבְרָהָם, וּשְׁבוּעָתוֹ לְיִשְׂחָק. וַיַּעֲמִידֶהָ לְיַעֲקֹב לְחֹק,
לְיִשְׂרָאֵל בְּרִית עוֹלָם (תְּהִלִּים קה:ח-י). וְנֶאֱמַר: וְזָכַרְתִּי אֲנִי אֶת בְּרִיתָךְ בִּימֵי
נְעוּרָיִךְ וַהֲקִימוֹתִי לָךְ בְּרִית עוֹלָם (יְחֶזְקֵאל טז:ס). הוֹדוּ לַיהוה כִּי טוֹב, כִּי לְעוֹלָם
חַסְדּוֹ (תְּהִלִּים קיח:כט). זֹאת הַקְּטַנָּה _____ גְּדוֹלָה תִּהְיֶה. כְּשֵׁם שֶׁנִּכְנְסָה
לַבְּרִית, כֵּן תִּכָּנֵס לְתוֹרָה וּלְחוּפָּה וּלְמַעֲשִׂים טוֹבִים.

Our God, the God of our forefathers and foremothers, preserve this
girl for her father and her mother, and her name will be called in Israel
_____, the daughter of _____ and _____. May the father be
happy in the issue of his body, and may the mother rejoice in the fruit
of her womb, as it is said: "May your father and mother be happy, and
may she who gave birth to you rejoice" (Proverbs 23:25). And it is said:
"I will establish My covenant between Me and you and between your
descendants who follow you for all generations, for an eternal covenant, to be a God for you and for your descendants who follow you"
(Genesis 17:7). And it is said: "Remember forever His covenant, that
which He commanded to a thousand generations, which He made
with Abraham, and swore to Isaac; and it was established for Jacob as a
law, for Israel as an eternal covenant" (Psalms 105:8–10). And it is said:
"I will remember My covenant with you in the days of your youth,
and I will establish with you an everlasting covenant" (Ezekiel 16:60).
"Praise God because He is Good, because His kindness lasts forever"
(Psalms 118:29). [We pray that] this small child _____ will become
great. Just as she has entered into the covenant, so shall she be entered
into Torah, the marriage canopy, and good deeds.

SPEECHES AND FESTIVE MEAL

A parent discusses the significance of the baby's name.
The rabbi or a parent delivers a d'var Torah (Torah exposition).
The parents serve a seudat mitzvah (festive meal with religious significance).

Epilogue

It is the eighth day following the birth of my youngest child. I sit upstairs in my home nursing my baby in anticipation of her Brit Bat. A few minutes later, I gently hand the baby to my father and join my mother and my husband, Dan, at the back of the living room downstairs. The baby emerges in my father's arms to the sound of our guests greeting the child with the traditional Hebrew welcome. My father sits in the specially designated Chair of Elijah, as our guests welcome Elijah with a prayer. The baby is then passed to my mother who has the honor of placing the child on Dan's tallit, which is spread out on the table in front of us.

As the ceremony begins, I think about how the covenant encapsulates the essence of Jewish existence and the eternal relationship between God and the Jewish people. I reflect on how the covenant embodies the Jewish people's acceptance of God's commandments and God's promise to love the Jewish people in perpetuity, grant them a homeland, and multiply their numbers to match those of the stars.

The ceremony also evokes for me the covenant's chain of generations and reminds me how much I miss my grandparents and my husband's grandfather. Dan's father is also in my heart as we use the tallit that belonged to him before his untimely passing thirty years ago.

The baby is remarkably silent as the ceremony proceeds. Our daughter symbolically enters the covenant when Dan and I lovingly swaddle her in Dan's tallit. With her frilly pink dress obscured, our daughter lies there for a second, still wrapped up, until we pick her up to embrace her. She is swaddled in the warm embrace not only of her family, but also of the entire community of Israel. We recite traditional blessings, one of which expresses our hope that, just as she has entered the covenant, so will she be entered into a life that includes Torah, the marriage canopy, and good deeds. Our guests respond, echoing these wishes. I remember when we shared the same beautiful moment with our baby's older brother and sisters.

In the final segment of the ceremony, Dan and I reveal our daughter's name for the first time to the eager anticipation of our family and friends. In the years to come, when Tamar Sarit asks us how we welcomed her into the Jewish community, we will be proud to tell her what happened on her special eighth day, her first step toward what we pray will be a lifetime of Torah.

AS I WRITE THIS EPILOGUE, I think back to Tamar's Brit Bat, which occurred a year ago. It is unbelievable to me that writing this book has been my professional vocation for all of Tamar's life, as well as the culmination of my work from the previous eight years. I have spent countless hours in the library and in front of my computer, studied wide-ranging Jewish texts, and read numerous books and articles (both popular and scholarly). I have also spoken with many Jews across the spectrum of outlooks and beliefs. I never could have imagined the extent to which I have devoted myself to this project and how much of a passion it has become. My family has likewise become engrossed in this project; my parents read every word I write, and my three older children draw pictures to illustrate the book that they promise to read when they grow up.

I also think back to the ceremonies Dan and I held for our daughters Dafna and Nurit and our son Yakir. I realize that the parallel texts that I typed up while pregnant for the first time (the "pink program" and the "blue program") have not changed much over the years. Each of the four ceremonies we held was indescribably joyous and, each time, our family and friends participated with us. I hope that the model Brit Bat ceremony, provided above, might enrich the experiences of others, as it has enriched mine.

The covenant that stands at the heart of this ceremony is as traditional as the Torah itself, and classical sources demonstrate women's covenantal membership. By distinguishing between the covenant and male circumcision, we enable newborn girls to claim their full and rightful place in the covenant, and we commemorate this status with a substantive life-cycle event.

Other ideas in this book incorporate, yet reframe, tradition. For example, historical Ashkenazic practices for new mothers and their offspring have inspired our conception of a first and only naming for girls. Furthermore, the central tallit swaddling ritual, while novel at first glance, emanates from a tapestry of traditional imagery, symbolism, and practices. In addition, the notion of adapting aspects of the circumcision liturgy is based on the observation that this liturgy's dual themes of circumcision and covenant, while tightly related, are separable.

This book thus springs from a sincere desire to enhance and beautify Jewish practices from within our tradition. The same can be said for the full expanse of welcoming ceremonies for girls, as well as Bat Mitzvah rituals, women's Torah learning, and the countless Jewish customs that have evolved over time.

Furthermore, this book has afforded me a distinct opportunity to study a range of Jewish texts. Learning Torah is a mainstay of Jewish life, and I hope that readers will enjoy delving into these sources as much as I have enjoyed doing so.

A family friend asked me some time ago about my current occupation, and I responded that I am writing a book about Jewish practices for newborn girls. She replied, "But everyone knows what to do; there's nothing to write about!" I beg to differ, as this book demonstrates. As with any other area of Jewish law or practice (or any intellectual pursuit), there is always more to learn, and each exciting discovery leads to more interesting questions.

Despite these good intentions, roadblocks are inevitable with any suggestions that threaten the status quo. I have no doubt that efforts to guide the development of practices for newborn Jewish girls will face challenges and controversy. Nonetheless, I believe that now is the right time to initiate a serious discussion about the future of these practices. Welcoming ceremonies for girls are here to stay and, on the whole, are today the result of expectations and existing models, not experimentation. Glimmers of commonality are even beginning to emerge. Correspondingly, there is a growing realization that the current Ashkenazic synagogue naming is, at best, insufficient or, at worst, demoralizing to families seeking to mark a substantive event.

This is the time to affirm the Torah's covenant, as this book is subtitled, by clearly and consistently conveying girls' admission into the covenant, a status that has until recently been marked only with silence.

I have offered some ideas in this book; the rest is up to us.

Notes

Introduction

1. Defendant's Motion in Limine, *United States v. Lacey, et al.,* No. 1:09-cr-00507-KMW (S.D.N.Y. November 18, 2010). Chaim Saiman was the first of many friends to e-mail me this motion. Thank you to all.

2. *United States v. Lacey, et al.,* No. 1:09-cr-00507-KMW (order conditionally granting Motion in Limine).

3. Ashby Jones, "If It's a Girl, Judge Kimba Woods Will Celebrate!" *Wall Street Journal* Law Blog, November 19, 2010, http://blogs.wsj.com/law/2010/11/19/if-its-a-girl-judge-kimba-wood-will-celebrate/ (accessed December 1, 2010).

4. Debra Cassens Weiss, "It's a Boy! Manhattan Lawyer Gets Trial Reprieve for Grandson's Bris," *ABA Journal* (November 30, 2010), http://www.abajournal.com /news/article/its_a_boy_manhattan_lawyer_gets_trial_reprieve_for_grandsons_bris/ (accessed December 2, 2010).

5. Daniel Sperber, "Congregational Dignity and Human Dignity: Women and Public Torah Reading," in *Women and Men in Communal Prayer: Halakhic Perspectives,* ed. Chaim Trachtman (New York: Jewish Orthodox Feminist Alliance, 2010), 90 and Appendix 3.

6. Rachel Adler, "I've Had Nothing Yet So I Can't Take More," *Moment* 8 (September 1983): 22, 24.

7. Rachel Biale, *Women and Jewish Law: An Exploration of Women's Issues in Halakhic Sources* (New York: Schocken Books, 1984), 8. See also Leonard D. Gordon, "Toward a Gender-Inclusive Account of Halakhah," in *Gender and Judaism: The Transformation of Tradition,* ed. T. M. Rudavsky (New York: New York University Press, 1995), 10.

8. Haym Soloveitchik, "Rupture and Reconstruction: The Transformation of Contemporary Orthodoxy," *Tradition* 28 (Summer 1994): 69. My thanks to Sid Vidaver for recommending this article to me.

9. Gail Collins, *When Everything Changed: The Amazing Journey of American Women from 1960 to the Present* (New York: Little, Brown and Company, 2009), 22–23, 250–51.

Chapter 1. Traditional Ashkenazic Naming Practices for Girls

1. Yitzchak Yaakov Weiss, *Minchat Yitzchak,* vol. 4, siman 107, paragraph 2.

2. E.g., Jules Harlow, ed., *Siddur Sim Shalom: A Prayerbook for Shabbat, Festivals, and Weekdays* (New York: The Rabbinical Assembly, 1985), 406–7; *Kol Haneshama: Shabbat Vehagim,* 3rd ed. (Wyncote, PA: Reconstructionist Press, 1996), 691, 785. See also *Siddur Sim Shalom for Weekdays* (New York: The Rabbinical Assembly, 2002), 244–45 (additions for Grace After Meals). This also holds true for many prayer books used in Orthodox synagogues.

3. *Siddur Rinat Yisrael, Nusach Ashkenaz* (for Israel) (Jerusalem: Moreshet Ltd. Publishing House, 1976), 273; *Siddur Rinat Yisrael, Nusach Ashkenaz* (for outside of Israel) (Jerusalem: Moreshet Ltd. Publishing House, 1972), 257; *The Koren Siddur, Nusah Ashkenaz*, with introduction, translation, and commentary by Jonathan Sacks (Jerusalem: Koren Publishers Jerusalem Ltd., 2009), 510–11; *The Artscroll Siddur, Weekday/Sabbath/Festival*, 2nd ed., translated and with commentary by Nosson Scherman (Brooklyn: Mesorah Publications, Ltd., 1990), 442–43; Aharon Cohen, *Zeved HaBat* (Jerusalem: Kaneh, 1990), 14.

4. Reuven P. Bulka, *The RCA Lifecycle Madrikh* (New York: Rabbinical Council of America, 1995), 2; Binyomin S. Hamburger, *Shorshei Minhag Ashkenaz*, vol. 3 (Bnei Brak, Israel: Machon Moreshes Ashkenaz, 2001), 397 (citing *Siddur Ateret Yerushalayim* [Jerusalem: Ateret Publications, 1989], 211, and *Siddur Shaar Harachamim with Commentary of the Magid Tzedek*, vol. 1 [Jerusalem: n.p., 1992], 328). See also Yosef David Weisberg, *Otzar HaBrit: Encyclopedia on Topics of Circumcision*, vol. 1 (Jerusalem: The Torat Habrit Institute, 1993), 333; Shlomo Zalman Auerbach, *Halichot Beita*, 13:13 and note 31.

5. See, e.g., Scherman, ed., *Artscroll Siddur*, 442–43; Philip Birnbaum, *Daily Prayer Book (Siddur Ha-Shalem)* (New York: Hebrew Publishing Company, 1977), 372.

6. Blu Greenberg, *How to Run a Traditional Jewish Household* (Northvale, NJ: Jason Aronson Inc., 1989), 248. See also Harvey E. Goldberg, *Jewish Passages: Cycles of Jewish Life* (Berkeley: University of California Press, 2003), 68.

7. BT Brachot 54a; Shulchan Aruch, Orach Chaim 219:1.

8. I use masculine God language throughout this book, with the recognition that God is, of course, neither masculine nor feminine.

9. David de Sola Pool, *Book of Prayer According to the Custom of the Spanish and Portuguese Jews*, 2nd ed. (New York: Union of Sephardic Congregations, 1947), 417.

10. Ibid. (my translation). See also, e.g., A. Cohen, *Zeved HaBat*, 15–19; David Levi, ed., *Siddur Tefilat HeChodesh* (Jerusalem: Erez, 2004), 657; *Siddur Ahava V'Achva* (Jerusalem: Yichva Da'at Institute, 1997/1998), 542–43; Eliezer Toledano, ed., *Siddur Kol Sasson: The Orot Sephardic Shabbat Siddur* (Lakewood, NJ: Orot, Inc., 1995), 779. See also Leopold Low, *Die Lebensalter in der Judischen Literatur* (Szegedin, Hungary: Druck von Sigmund Burger's Wwe., 1875), 104; cf. Rochelle L. Millen, *Women, Birth, and Death in Jewish Law and Practice* (Hanover, NH: Brandeis University Press, 2004), 96.

11. See, e.g., Millen, *Women, Birth, and Death in Jewish Law and Practice*.

12. A. Cohen, *Zeved HaBat*, 18; *Siddur Tefilat HeChodesh*, 657.

13. *Book of Prayer According to the Custom of the Spanish and Portuguese Jews*, 417; A. Cohen, *Zeved HaBat*, 20–25; *Siddur Tefilat HeChodesh*, 657.

14. *Sheer Ushbahah Hallel Ve-Zimrah*, 9th ed. (New York: The Sephardic Heritage Foundation, Inc., 2002), 144, 146, 240, 351. See also Sandy Eisenberg Sasso, *Call Them Builders* (New York: Reconstructionist Federation of Congregations and Havurot, 1977), 34.

15. Deborah Nussbaum Cohen, *Celebrating Your New Jewish Daughter: Creating Jewish Ways to Welcome Baby Girls into the Covenant* (Woodstock, VT: Jewish Lights Pub-

lishing, 2001), 8–9; A. Cohen, *Zeved HaBat*, 8–9, 24; Aharon Cohen, "Bat Mitzvah: A Challenge for Religious Education," *Ten Da'at* 3 (Spring 1989): 32, note 2.

16. Avraham Yaari, "Misheberach Prayers: Their Development, Customs, and Nusach," *Kiryat Sefer* 33 (1958): 118–30, 233–50. See also Avraham Yaari, "Continuations to My Article 'Misheberach Prayers: Their Development, Customs, and Nusach'," *Kiryat Sefer* 36 (1961): 103–18; Daniel Y. Cohen, "Remarks and Completions to the Study of A. Yaari on the Misheberach Prayers," *Kiryat Sefer* 40 (1965): 542–59. My gratitude to R. Daniel Sperber for recommending these extraordinary articles to me.

17. *Seder Rav Amram Gaon*, ed. Daniel Shlomo Goldschmidt (Jerusalem: Mossad Harav Kook, 2004), 59, lines 12–14.

18. *Machzor Vitry*, paragraph 166.

19. Yaari, "Misheberach Prayers," 124.

20. Ismar Elbogen, *Jewish Liturgy: A Comprehensive History* (Philadelphia: The Jewish Publication Society, 1993), 160–61, § 30(3).

21. *Ohr Zarua*, Hilchot Shabbat, paragraph 50.

22. Yaari, "Misheberach Prayers," 125.

23. Elisheva Baumgarten, *Mothers and Children: Jewish Family Life in Medieval Europe* (Princeton, NJ: Princeton University Press, 2004), 1, 93.

24. Seligman Baer, ed., *Tikkun Hasofer V'Hakoreh*, 2nd ed. (Frankfurt: Druck und Verlag von M. Lehrberger & Co., 1886), 18 (cited in Hamburger, *Shorshei Minhag Ashkenaz*, vol. 3, 396).

25. Yaari, "Misheberach Prayers," 125.

26. Ibid., 246, note 154.

27. Professor Elisheva Baumgarten of Bar-Ilan University offered this insightful suggestion to me.

28. Samuel Krauss, *Talmudische Archaologie*, vol. 2 (Hilesheim, Germany: Georg Olms Verlagsbuchhandlung, 1966), 12 (§ 114); see also David Golinkin, "When Should Baby Girls Be Named?" *Insight Israel* 6 (November 2005), http://www.schechter.edu/insightIsrael.aspx?ID=65, § II (citing, e.g., Genesis 30:21) (accessed March 7, 2013). My gratitude to Professor Wilhelm (Bill) and Louise Braun, and their daughter Alisa Braun, for graciously translating a number of German sources for me.

29. Golinkin, "When Should Baby Girls Be Named?" § II.

30. Dov Herman, *Ma'gal Hachaim B'bayit Hayehudi* (Life Cycle in the Jewish Home) (Rosh Ha'ayin, Israel: Prolog Publishers, 2005), 214.

31. *Seder Rav Amram Gaon*, vol. 1 (New York: Saphrograph Company, 1955), 52; *Siddur R. Saadia Gaon*, eds. I. Davidson, S. Assaf, and B. I. Joel (Jerusalem: Mekize Nirdamim, 1941), 99.

32. Krauss, *Talmudische Archaologie*, 12 (§ 114).

33. M. Semachot (Evel Rabbati), "Breitot from Evel Rabbati Not in S'machot Before Us," 2:3, ed. Michael Higger (New York: Bloch Publishing Company, 1931), 231.

34. Isaac ibn Giat, *Meah Sh'arim*, in *Shaarei Simcha* Hilchot Avel, paragraph 152.

35. Nachmonides, *Torat HaAdam*, "Inyan HaHotza'ah," paragraph beginning, "In the chapter of the widowed woman."

36. Seligman Baer Bamberger, *Yitzchak Yiranen,* in *Shaarei Simcha,* Hilchot Avel, note 153 (citing Derisha on Arba'ah Turim, Yoreh Dei'a, Hilchot K'vurah, 360:2). Based on his citation to the Derisha, R. Bamberger seems to be referencing the synagogue naming for girls. It appears, however, that this practice emerged after the redaction of Evel Rabbati.

37. Reuven Margoliot, *Margoliot HaYam al Mesechet Sanhedrin,* Sanhedrin 32b, paragraph 15; Saul Lieberman, *Tosefta Kifshuta,* vol. 5, Seder Moed, Megillah 3:357 (citing as a hypothesis); Lawrence A. Hoffman, *Covenant of Blood: Circumcision and Gender in Rabbinic Judaism* (Chicago: University of Chicago Press, 1996), 178–79; Golinkin, "When Should Baby Girls Be Named?" § III (suggesting as an unconfirmed hypothesis); see also Ivan G. Marcus, *The Jewish Life Cycle* (Seattle: University of Washington Press, 2004), 36.

38. Golinkin, "When Should Baby Girls Be Named?" § III.

39. Margoliot, *Margoliot HaYam al Mesechet Sanhedrin,* Sanhedrin 32b, paragraph 15.

40. Rashi, BT Bava Batra 60b, "L'Shavuah Haben."

41. Nissan Rubin, *The Beginning of Life: Rites of Birth, Circumcision and Redemption of the Firstborn in the Talmud and Midrash* (Tel Aviv: HaKibbutz HaMeuchad Publishing House Ltd., 1995), 117–19 and 188, note 226; see also Baumgarten, *Mothers and Children,* 99 and 217, note 33 (citing N. Rubin, *The Beginning of Life*).

42. Shaye J. D. Cohen, *Why Aren't Jewish Women Circumcised? Gender and Covenant in Judaism* (Berkeley: University of California Press, 2005), 215 and 269, note 23; see also N. Rubin, *The Beginning of Life,* 7.

43. Hamburger, *Shorshei Minhag Ashkenaz,* vol. 1, 407–8.

44. Baumgarten, *Mothers and Children,* 101.

45. Ibid., 101–2, 117–18.

46. Ibid., 105, 112; Marcus, *Jewish Life Cycle,* 63. A woman would undergo these rituals even if her baby died immediately after birth. Baumgarten, *Mothers and Children,* 102.

47. Joseph Steinhardt, *Responsa of Zichron Yaakov,* Orach Chaim, responsum 5 (cited in Hamburger, *Shorshei Minhag Ashkenaz,* vol. 1, 436); Weiss, *Minchat Yitzchak,* vol. 4, siman 107; see also Hamburger, *Shorshei Minhag Ashkenaz,* vol. 1, 392–93.

48. Marcus, *Jewish Life Cycle,* 64.

49. Jacob Emden, *Birat* Migdal Oz, 2:9; Steinhardt, *Responsa of Zichron Yaakov,* Orach Chaim, responsum 5; Auerbach, *Halichot Beita,* 13:11 and note 25; *Responsa of Yedidya Tia Weil,* Yoreh Dei'ah, responsum 108; Hamburger, *Shorshei Minhag Ashkenaz,* vol. 1, 389–92.

50. Aliza Lavie, ed., *A Jewish Woman's Prayer Book* (New York: Spiegel & Grau, 2008), 106–7.

51. Hamburger, *Shorshei Minhag Ashkenaz,* vol. 3, 393–96.

52. Hamburger, *Shorshei Minhag Ashkenaz,* vol. 1, 389–92; see discussion in Emden, *Birat Migdal Oz,* 2:11 and 2:13.

53. Hamburger, *Shorshei Minhag Ashkenaz,* vol. 1, 393–96, 409–10.

54. Emden, *Birat Migdal Oz,* 2:12 and 2:15; see also Weiss, *Minchat Yitzchak,* vol. 4, siman 107, paragraph 1.

55. Hamburger, *Shorshei Minhag Ashkenaz,* vol. 1, 439 (citing *Beit HaKeneset HaKadum* Manuscript, vol. 18 [Berlin: Sinai, 1946], 235).

56. Emden, *Birat Migdal Oz,* 2:10.

57. Hamburger, *Shorshei Minhag Ashkenaz,* vol. 1, 398–405.

58. *Responsa of Yedidya Tia Weil,* Yoreh Dei'ah, responsum 108; Baumgarten, *Mothers and Children,* 102–5; compare Marcus, *Jewish Life Cycle,* 63.

59. Hamburger, *Shorshei Minhag Ashkenaz,* vol. 1, 383–89; Auerbach, *Halichot Beita,* 13:11 and note 25.

60. Hamburger, *Shorshei Minhag Ashkenaz,* vol. 3, 398.

61. Hamburger, *Shorshei Minhag Ashkenaz,* vol. 2, 322, 356–57, 366–69; Baumgarten, *Mothers and Children,* 102, 117, and 221, note 106; Michele Klein, *A Time to Be Born: Customs and Folklore of Jewish Birth* (Philadelphia: The Jewish Publication Society, 2000), 245–46.

62. Marcus, *Jewish Life Cycle,* 65; Klein, *A Time to Be Born,* 246; Hamburger, *Shorshei Minhag Ashkenaz,* vol. 2, 414–17, 421–24, 580–83.

63. Ivan G. Marcus, *Rituals of Childhood: Jewish Acculturation in Medieval Europe* (New Haven: Yale University Press, 1998), 77; Hamburger, *Shorshei Minhag Ashkenaz,* vol. 2, 390–98, 408; Klein, *A Time to Be Born,* 245.

64. Hamburger, *Shorshei Minhag Ashkenaz,* vol. 2, 351, 575–80; Klein, *A Time to Be Born,* 246; see also Baumgarten, *Mothers and Children,* 117.

65. Baumgarten, *Mothers and Children,* 102; Hamburger, *Shorshei Minhag Ashkenaz,* vol. 2, 514–15. Christian mothers, upon their reinstatement into the community, customarily returned baptism cloths to the church. Baumgarten, *Mothers and Children,* 110; Marcus, *Jewish Life Cycle,* 65.

66. Hamburger, *Shorshei Minhag Ashkenaz,* vol. 2, 322, 502–27; Klein, *A Time to Be Born,* 246; Daniel Sperber, *The Jewish Life Cycle: Custom, Lore and Iconography: Jewish Customs from the Cradle to the Grave,* trans. Ed Levin (Ramat Gan, Israel: Bar-Ilan University Press, 2008), 146, 147–49.

67. Hamburger, *Shorshei Minhag Ashkenaz,* vol. 2, 347, 352–53.

68. Ibid., 353–55, 527–28; Sperber, *Jewish Life Cycle,* 143; Marcus, *Jewish Life Cycle,* 65; Klein, *A Time to Be Born,* 246.

69. Hamburger, *Shorshei Minhag Ashkenaz,* vol. 2, 347, 350–51; Klein, *A Time to Be Born,* 245–46; Sperber, *Jewish Life Cycle,* 144.

70. Marcus, *Rituals of Childhood,* 77; Hamburger, *Shorshei Minhag Ashkenaz,* vol. 2, 533.

71. Hamburger, *Shorshei Minhag Ashkenaz,* vol. 1, 415, 417; Golinkin, "When Should Baby Girls Be Named?" § IV.

72. There are a number of variant English spellings, such as *Hol Graasch* and *Holekrash.*

73. Hamburger, *Shorshei Minhag Ashkenaz,* vol. 1, 416; see also Baumgarten, *Mothers and Children,* 215, note 8; H. J. Zimmels, *Ashkenazim and Sephardim* (London: Oxford University Press, 1958), 165.

74. Hamburger, *Shorshei Minhag Ashkenaz,* vol. 1, 433–35.

75. Marcus, *Jewish Life Cycle,* 64; Baumgarten, *Mothers and Children,* 96; Hamburger, *Shorshei Minhag Ashkenaz,* vol. 1, 419.

76. Ibid., 420.

77. But see Leo Trepp, "The Naming of the Child—The Secular Name," *CCAR Journal* 20 (Winter 1975): 95.

78. Klein, *A Time to Be Born,* 229; Baumgarten, *Mothers and Children,* 93; Hamburger, *Shorshei Minhag Ashkenaz,* vol. 1, 417, 429–33; Noa Hochstein Gorlin, "And Her Name Will Be Called in Israel," in *To Be a Jewish Woman: Papers of the First International Conference: Woman and Her Judaism,* ed. Margalit Shilo (Jerusalem: Urim Publications / Kolech, 2001), 218; Goldberg, *Jewish Passages,* 67; Trepp, "The Naming of the Child," 94. See Emden, *Birat Migdal Oz,* 2:9, 2:16, 2:17, and 2:19. I also note my January 23, 2013 conversation on this topic with R. Binyomin Hamburger.

79. Seligman Baer, ed., *Seder Avodat Yisrael* (Rodelheim [Frankfurt]: Druck Verlag von Schrberger & Co., 1901), 494 (citing Genesis 1:1, 2:1, 48:16; Exodus 1:1; Leviticus 1:1; Numbers 1:1; and Deuteronomy 1:1, 33:1, 34:12).

80. Hamburger, *Shorshei Minhag Ashkenaz,* vol. 1, 424.

81. Emden, *Birat Migdal Oz,* 2:19.

82. Baumgarten, *Mothers and Children,* 93; Klein, *A Time to Be Born,* 229; Hamburger, *Shorshei Minhag Ashkenaz,* vol. 1, 427–28, 435; Baer, ed., *Seder Avodat Yisrael,* 494.

83. Hamburger, *Shorshei Minhag Ashkenaz,* vol. 1, 417, 424–27; Klein, *A Time to Be Born,* 229; Gorlin, "And Her Name Will Be Called in Israel," 218.

84. Hamburger, *Shorshei Minhag Ashkenaz,* vol. 1, 423 (citing Joseph Yuzpa Shamash, *Customs of the Worms Community*).

85. See, e.g., Hamburger, *Shorshei Minhag Ashkenaz,* vol. 1, 416–17, 423; Golinkin, "When Should Baby Girls Be Named?" § IV; Gorlin, "And Her Name Will Be Called in Israel," 218–19.

86. R. Binyomin Hamburger relayed this opinion to me in our conversation on January 23, 2013.

87. See e.g., Baumgarten, *Mothers and Children,* 96; Low, *Die Lebensalter in der Judischen Literatur,* 104.

88. Trepp, "The Naming of the Child," 95.

89. Goldberg, *Jewish Passages,* 67.

90. Baumgarten, *Mothers and Children,* 96; Marcus, *Jewish Life Cycle,* 64; Golinkin, "When Should Baby Girls Be Named?" § IV.

91. Baumgarten, *Mothers and Children,* 97–98; Golinkin, "When Should Baby Girls Be Named?" § IV. See also Jill Hammer, "Holle's Cry: Unearthing a Birth Goddess in a German Jewish Naming Ceremony," *Nashim: A Journal of Jewish Women's Studies and & Gender Issues* 9 (Spring 2005): 62–87.

92. Hamburger, *Shorshei Minhag Ashkenaz,* vol. 1, 415.

93. Trepp, "The Naming of the Child," 95–96.

94. Golinkin, "When Should Baby Girls Be Named?" § IV; see also Goldberg, *Jewish Passages,* 67–68.

95. *Old Responsa of the Bach,* section 95, paragraph starting *V'ein.*
96. Shmuel Halevi Segal, *Nachalat Shiva,* vol. 3, responsum 17.
97. Derisha on Arba'ah Turim, Yoreh Dei'a, Hilchot K'vurah, 360:2; Hamburger, *Shorshei Minhag Ashkenaz,* vol. 1, 435.
98. Klein, *A Time to Be Born,* 229 and 320, note 81.
99. Hamburger, *Shorshei Minhag Ashkenaz,* vol. 1, 415, 422.
100. I found both of these ceremonies in Blu Greenberg's private collection. One is "Simchat Bat of Yonah Eliana Bruder Pretsfelder" by Nina Bruder and Gary Pretsfelder, November 17, 2002. The other is "Simchat Bat of Baby Berman" by Sara and David Berman, June 2, 2005.
101. Baumgarten, *Mothers and Children,* 93. But see Low, *Die Lebensalter in der Judischen Literatur,* 104 (dating to the fifteenth century the synagogue naming for girls, the circumcision naming for boys, and the Hollekreish).
102. Marcus, *Jewish Life Cycle,* 64–65.
103. Hamburger, *Shorshei Minhag Ashkenaz,* vol. 1, 435.
104. Shmuel Halevi Segal, *Nachalat Shiva,* vol. 3, responsum 17.
105. Steinhardt, *Responsa of Zichron Yaakov,* Orach Chaim, responsum 5.
106. Emden, *Birat Migdal Oz,* 2:9, 2:16, 2:17, and 2:19.
107. Salomon Carlebach, *Pelah Yoetz* (Berlin: n.p.,1918), 79–80.
108. Menachem Gottlieb, *Darchei Noam,* vol. 1 (Hanover, Germany, n.p., 1896), 99 (chapter 67, paragraph 12).
109. Hamburger, *Shorshei Minhag Ashkenaz,* vol. 1, 438 (citing R. Y. Tvisig, *Beit Yisrael HaShalem,* vol. 8 [Jerusalem: Tanina, 1982], 303).
110. Markus Horovitz, *Mateh Levi,* vol. 1 (Frankfurt: A. Slobottski, 1891), 66 (siman 15) (relevant statement is in parentheses).
111. Derisha on Arba'ah Turim, Yoreh Dei'a, Hilchot K'vurah, 360:2.
112. Goldberg, *Jewish Passages,* 51
113. In our January 23, 2013, conversation, R. Binyomin Hamburger stated that, as a general rule, fathers attended Hollekreisch ceremonies throughout the ages.
114. Hamburger, *Shorshei Minhag Ashkenaz,* vol. 3, 397–99.
115. Hamburger, *Shorshei Minhag Ashkenaz,* vol. 1, 403–4; see also Sacks, ed., *Koren Siddur,* 1030–33.
116. Susan Weidman Schneider, *Jewish and Female: Choices and Changes in Our Lives Today* (New York: Simon and Schuster, 1984), 121–22.
117. Millen, *Women, Birth, and Death,* 70.
118. Bulka, *RCA Lifecycle Madrikh,* 1.
119. Weiss, *Minchat Yitzchak,* vol. 4, siman 107, paragraph 2; Auerbach, *Halichot Beita,* 13:14 and note 32; Weisberg, *Otzar HaBrit,* vol. 1, 333.
120. Moshe Meiselman, *Jewish Woman in Jewish Law* (New York: Ktav Publishing House, 1978), 61.
121. Moshe Sternbuch, *Teshuvot V'Hanhagot,* Orach Chaim, vol. 2, siman 132.
122. See, e.g., Mordechai Kamenetzky, Drasha for Parshat Vayera 5758, "Blessings in Disguise," 4:4, www.torah.org.il/learning/drasha/5758/vayera.hyml?print=1# (accessed

July 3, 2010); Josh Waxman, parshablog, Shofetim—Ki Seitzei, http://parsha.blogspot
.com/2007/07/making-kiddush-for-grown-daughters.html (accessed July 3, 2010). My
thanks to Chaim Saiman for telling me about this story.

123. Netziv, *Meromei Sadeh,* BT Brachot 44a.

124. Chofetz Chaim, *Mishna Berura,* Orach Chaim 223:1; see also Chofetz Chaim,
Sha'ar HaTziyun, note 5, on *Mishna Berura,* Orach Chaim 225:2.

125. Chaim Elazar Spira, *Darchei Chaim V'Shalom,* (Brooklyn, NY: Jacob Gold, 1986),
95 (Laws of Shehechiyanu, paragraph 256, note 1); Eliezer Waldenberg, *Tzitz Eliezer,* vol.
13, siman 20. See also ibid., vol. 14, simanim 21–22.

126. See also, e.g., Shulchan Aruch, Orach Chaim, Hilchot Brachot 223:1.

127. Sharon R. Siegel, "Reciting the *Hatov V'Hameitiv* Blessing on the Birth of a
Daughter: A Survey of Halakhic Sources," *Tradition: A Journal of Orthodox Jewish
Thought* 44 (Winter 2012): 23–39.

Chapter 2. A First and Only Naming

1. Vanessa Ochs makes a similar point. See Vanessa L. Ochs, *Inventing Jewish Ritual,*
(Philadelphia: The Jewish Publication Society, 2007), 161.

2. Steinhardt, *Responsa of Zichron Yaakov,* Orach Chaim, responsum 5.

3. Sternbuch, *Teshuvot V'Hanhagot,* Orach Chaim, vol. 2, siman 132.

4. Sacks, ed., *Koren Siddur,* 1034–37; Shlomo Riskin, *Around the Family Table: A
Comprehensive "Bencher" and Companion for Shabbat and Festival Meals and Other Fam-
ily Occasions* (Efrat and Jerusalem, Israel: Ohr Torah Stone / Urim Publications, 2005),
196–201; Bulka, RCA *Lifecycle Madrikh,* 1–3; Jennifer Breger, "Crafting a Welcoming
Ceremony for Girls Today," in *The Orthodox Jewish Woman and Ritual: Options and
Opportunities: Birth,* Jewish Orthodox Feminist Alliance, http://www.jofa.org/uploaded
Files/site/Education/Ritual_Opportunities/Birth%20Ritual%20Guide.pdf (accessed
March 7, 2013), 6.

5. For these reasons, I suggest that a boy's circumcision should likewise be conducted
at home, if feasible.

6. See, e.g., Shlomit Kislev, "Zeved Ha'Eim," in *To Be a Jewish Woman,* 222–29 (also
reprinted in Lavie, ed., *A Jewish Woman's Prayer Book,* 112–23); Naomi Bromberg Bar-
Yam, "Simchat Yoledet," Ritualwell, http://www.ritualwell.org/ritual/simchat-yoledet
(accessed March 14, 2013).

7. Lavie, *A Jewish Woman's Prayer Book,* 98–99.

8. Bar-on Dasberg, "Restart," Zomet Institute, *Insights for the Shabbat Table* news-
letter 1420: T'azria-Metzora (April 21, 2012), http://www.zomet.org.il/Eng/?Category
ID=160&SectionID=-1&ChapterID=-1&Archive=&ArchVolID=&AuthorID=60&
searchMode=0&Search=1&SString=&Page=2 (accessed June 25, 2012). My thanks to
David Jacobowitz who relayed these thoughts at the Simchat Bat of his granddaughter
Emanuela Nitza Perelis on June 17, 2012, and was kind enough to e-mail me the text.

9. BT Brachot 54a; Shulchan Aruch, Orach Chaim 219:1. According to the Shulchan
Aruch, Birkat HaGomel is also recited for surviving a number of specific situations, but
these are not applicable in the context of childbirth.

10. Hamburger, *Shorshei Minhag Ashkenaz,* vol. 3, 398.

11. See, e.g., Moshe B. Pirutinsky, *Sefer HaBrit on the Shulchan Aruch, Yoreh Dei'ah: Halachot of Circumcision* (New York: Gross Bros. Printing Co., Inc., 1972), 282 (Likutei Halachot 265:1, paragraph 53); Weisberg, *Otzar Habris: Encyclopedia of the Laws and Customs of Bris and Pidyon Haben* (English edition) (Jerusalem: n.p., 2002), 74–75; David Weinberger, *The Simchah Handbook* (Brooklyn, NY: Mesorah Publications, Ltd., 2008), 121–22; Abraham Chill, *The Minhagim: The Customs and Ceremonies of Judaism: Their Origins and Rationale* (New York: Sepher-Hermon Press, Inc., 1979), 306.

12. Weiss, *Minchat Yitzchak,* vol. 4, siman 107, paragraph 1.

13. Waldenberg, *Tzitz Eliezer,* vol. 13, siman 20; see also Pirutinsky, *Sefer HaBrit,* 282 (Likutei Halachot 265:1, paragraph 53).

14. Waldenberg, *Tzitz Eliezer,* vol. 13, siman 20; Weiss, *Minchat Yitzchak,* vol. 4, siman 107, paragraph 5; Auerbach, *Halichot Beita,* 13:11 and note 26; see also Pirutinsky, *Sefer HaBrit,* 282 (Likutei Halachot 265:1, paragraph 53); Weisberg, *Otzar HaBrit,* vol. 1, 331.

15. Hamburger, *Shorshei Minhag Ashkenaz,* vol. 1, 437. See generally Machon Itim, "Simchat Bat: Where and When," http://itim.org.il/eng/?CategoryID=203&ArticleID=385 (accessed March 14, 2013).

16. Weiss, *Minchat Yitzchak,* vol. 4, siman 107, paragraph 1; see also Josef Lewy, *Minhag Yisrael Torah* (North Bergen, NJ: Edison Lithographing Corp. 1990) 331 (283:4); Gorlin, "And Her Name Will Be Called in Israel," 218.

17. Sacks, ed., *Koren Siddur,* 1034–35.

18. My thanks to Gila Ahdoot for making this important point and for investigating Persian practices in her local community.

19. A. Cohen, *Zeved HaBat,* 9; Herbert C. Dobrinsky, *A Treasury of Sephardic Laws and Customs* (Hoboken, NJ: Ktav Publishing House, Inc., 1988), 11, 20; see also Marcus, *Jewish Life Cycle,* 39.

20. Dobrinsky, *A Treasury of Sephardic Laws and Customs,* 11, 20, 25; see also Marcus, *Jewish Life Cycle,* 39.

21. Klein, *A Time to Be Borm,* 230. See also Goldberg, *Jewish Passages,* 67; Baruch Moshavi "Customs and Folklore of Nineteenth Century Bukharian Jews in Central Asia," (PhD diss., Yeshiva University, 1974), 84–88, 94–96.

22. Millen, *Women, Birth, and Death,* 94.

23. A. Cohen, *Zeved HaBat,* 9.

24. Dobrinsky, *A Treasury of Sephardic Laws and Customs,* 11.

25. Ari L. Goldman, *Being Jewish: The Spiritual and Cultural Practice of Judaism Today* (New York: Simon & Schuster, 2000), 46; Dobrinsky, *A Treasury of Sephardic Laws and Customs,* 3, 11, 20, 25; A. Cohen, *Zeved HaBat,* 9.

26. Dobrinsky, *A Treasury of Sephardic Laws and Customs,* 20; D. Cohen, *Celebrating Your New Jewish Daughter,* 13–14; Anita Diamant, *The New Jewish Baby Book: Names, Ceremonies & Customs: A Guide for Today's Families,* 2nd ed. (Woodstock, VT: Jewish Lights Publishing, 2008), 131; Roselyn Bell, "Thank Heaven for Little Girls," in *The Hadassah Magazine Jewish Parenting Book,* ed. Roselyn Bell (New York: Avon Books,

1989), 20; Breger, "Historical Precedents of Welcoming Ceremonies for Girls," 3; Millen, *Women, Birth, and Death,* 96.

27. Compare D. Cohen, *Celebrating Your New Jewish Daughter,* 14, with Klein, *A Time to Be Born,* 231.

28. Millen, *Women, Birth, and Death,* 96; see also Klein, *A Time to Be Born,* 228.

29. Ibid., 206, 230; Golinkin, "When Should Baby Girls Be Named?" § III.

30. Goldberg, *Jewish Passages,* 67; Orpa Salpak, ed., *The Jews of India: A Story of Three Communities,* (Jerusalem: The Israel Museum, 1995), 146–47. My thanks to Daniel Wolf for referring me to *The Jews of India,* to which his parents contributed their first-hand knowledge.

31. Salpak, ed., *Jews of India,* 159.

32. Klein, *A Time to Be Born,* 230.

33. Salpak, ed., *Jews of India,* 159.

34. Flora Samuel, "The Bene Israel Cradle Ceremony: An Indian Jewish Ritual for the Birth of a Girl," *Bridges* 7 (Winter 1997/1998): 43.

35. Ibid., 43–44; Salpak, ed., *Jews of India,* 146–47.

Chapter 3. New Modern Practices for Baby Girls

1. My thanks to R. Tamar Malino for astutely pointing out this reality to me.

2. Weinberger, *The Simchah Handbook.*

3. D. Cohen, *Celebrating Your New Jewish Daughter,* 4.

4. Michael A. Meyer, "The First Identical Ceremony for Giving a Hebrew Name to Girls and Boys," *Journal of Reform Judaism* 32 (Winter 1985): 84-87.

5. Saul J. Berman, "The Status of Women in Halakhic Judaism," *Tradition* 14 (1973): 5–28.

6. Naamah Kelman, "A Thirty-Year Perspective on Women and Israeli Feminism," in *New Jewish Feminism,* ed. Elyse Goldstein (Woodstock, VT: Jewish Lights Publishing, 2008), 198.

7. Elizabeth Koltun, introduction to *The Jewish Woman: New Perspectives,* (New York: Schocken Books, 1976), xi.

8. Kelman, "A Thirty-Year Perspective on Women and Israeli Feminism," 199.

9. Alice Shalvi, "The Geopolitics of Jewish Feminism," in *Gender and Judaism: The Transformation of Tradition,* ed. T. M. Rudavsky (New York: New York University Press, 1995), 236–39; Alice Shalvi, "Israel Women's Network," in Jewish Women's Archive, jwa .org/encyclopedia/article/Israel-womens-network (accessed January 10, 2012).

10. Shalvi, "The Geopolitics of Jewish Feminism," 231.

11. My mother, Judith Okolica, who helped to organize this conference, provided me with the program and related documents.

12. Arlene Agus, "This Month Is for You: Observing Rosh Hodesh As a Woman's Holiday," in *The Jewish Woman,* 84–93. See also Schneider, *Jewish and Female,* 94–97.

13. See Lori Hope Lefkovitz, "Sacred Screaming," in *Lifecycles: Jewish Women on Life Passages & Personal Milestones,* ed. Debra Orenstein, vol. 1 (Woodstock, VT: Jewish Lights Publishing, 1994), 5–15.

14. Schneider, *Jewish and Female*, 117–121, 130–133, 142–143; Orenstein, ed., *Lifecycles*, vol. 1, especially chs. 1, 2, 4, 12, and 13.

15. Judith Plaskow, *Standing Again at Sinai: Judaism from a Feminist Perspective* (San Francisco: Harper San Francisco, 1991), 67–68; Ochs, *Inventing Jewish Ritual*, 48–52; see also Leonard D. Gordon, "Toward a Gender-Inclusive Account of Halakhah" in *Gender and Judaism*, ed. Rudavsky, 4–5.

16. Orenstein, introduction to *Lifecycles*, vol. 1, xxi.

17. See Richard Siegel, Michael Strassfeld, and Sharon Strassfeld, *The Jewish Catalog* (Philadelphia: The Jewish Publication Society, 1973), 8; Sharon Strassfeld and Michael Strassfeld, introduction to *The Second Jewish Catalog* (Philadelphia: The Jewish Publication Society, 1973); Ochs, *Inventing Jewish Ritual*, 40.

18. Chava Weissler, "New Jewish Birth Rituals for Baby Girls," Simchat Bat Collection of the Jewish Women's Resource Center, JWRC #260 (undated; after 1977), 4; see also Susanna Heschel, introduction to *On Being a Jewish Feminist*, (New York: Schocken Books, 1983), xvi.

19. Ochs, *Inventing Jewish Ritual*, 39–40.

20. Siegel, Strassfeld, and Strassfeld, *The Jewish Catalog*, 9.

21. Sandy Eisenberg Sasso, foreword to D. Cohen, *Celebrating Your New Jewish Daughter*, xi.

22. Sandy Eisenberg Sasso, "B'rit B'not Israel: Observations on Women and Reconstructionism," *Response* 7 (Summer 1973): 101–5; Sandy Sasso, "Brit B'not Yisrael: Covenant for the Daughters of Israel," *Moment* 1 (May/June 1975): 50–51; see also Sasso, *Call Them Builders,* 18–21; Toby Fishbein Reifman with Ezrat Nashim, eds., *Blessing the Birth of a Daughter: Jewish Naming Ceremonies for Girls* (Englewood, NJ: Ezrat Nashim, 1978), 9–12.

23. Sharon and Michael Strassfeld, "Ceremonial Welcoming for a Newborn Jewish Daughter," *Lilith* 1 (Winter 1976/1977): 22.

24. Daniel I. and Myra Leifer, "On the Birth of a Daughter," in *Blessing the Birth of a Daughter*, ed. Reifman, 28; Strassfeld and Strassfeld, eds., *Second Jewish Catalog*, 33–34.

25. Ellen and Dana Charry, "Brit Kedusha," in *Blessing the Birth of a Daughter,* ed. Reifman, 5; see also Strassfeld and Strassfeld, eds., *Second Jewish Catalog*, 32–33.

26. Weissler, "New Jewish Birth Rituals for Baby Girls," 10–11.

27. Shoshana and Mel Silberman, "A Brit Ceremony for a Baby Girl," in *Blessing the Birth of a Daughter*, ed. Reifman, 13.

28. Linda Holtzman, "Welcoming Daughters," Ritualwell, http://www.ritualwell.org/blog/welcoming-daughters-rabbi-linda-holtzman (accessed March 10, 2013); Schneider, *Jewish and Female*, 124–27.

29. Schneider, *Jewish and Female*, 127–28.

30. Strassfeld and Strassfeld, eds., *Second Jewish Catalog*, 31.

31. Ochs, *Inventing Jewish Ritual*, 21–22.

32. Mary Gendler, "Sarah's Seed: A New Ritual for Women," *Response* 8 (Winter 1974–75): 74.

33. Strassfeld and Strassfeld, eds., *Second Jewish Catalog*, 36.

34. Judith Plaskow, "Bringing a Daughter into the Covenant," in *WomanSpirit Rising: A Feminist Reader in Religion,* eds. Carol P. Christ and Judith Plaskow, 2nd ed. (New York: HarperCollins Publishers, 1992), 180–84.

35. Schneider, *Jewish and Female,* 123.

36. Ibid.

37. Sharon and Joseph Kaplan, "Innovation within Halachah for Daughters," *Sh'ma: A Journal of Jewish Responsibility* 6 (April 30, 1976): 103.

38. Joseph C. Kaplan, "An Orthodox Simchat Bat," *Sh'ma: A Journal of Jewish Responsibility* 5 (March 21, 1975): 237–238; see also D. Cohen, *Celebrating Your New Jewish Daughter,* 7 and 225, note 4.

39. Gary Rosenblatt, "A Welcome Ceremony for Baby Girls," *New York Jewish Week,* September 14, 2007, 7.

40. Nadine Brozan, "A Share for Girls in Jewish Birthright," *New York Times,* March 14, 1977, 34.

41. Yechiel Eckstein, e-mail message to author, December 25, 2011.

42. Gary and Sheila Rubin, "Preserving Tradition by Expanding It: The Creation of Our Simchat Bat," *Response* 13 (Fall/Winter 1982): 60–68.

43. Meiselman, *Jewish Woman in Jewish Law,* 60–61.

44. Judith Bleich, "The Symbolism in Innovative Rituals," *Sh'ma: A Journal of Jewish Responsibility* 14 (December 23, 1983): 1–2.

45. Sharon and Michael Strassfeld, "An Appropriate Ceremony for Daughters," *Sh'ma: A Journal of Jewish Responsibility* 14 (December 23, 1983): 2–3.

46. Ibid.

47. See, e.g., Laura Geller, "Brit Milah and Brit Banot," in *Lifecycles,* ed. Orenstein, vol. 1, 64.

48. *Shaarei Habayit, Gates of the House: The New Union Home Prayer Book* (New York: Central Conference of American Rabbis, 1977), 114–117.

49. Brozan, "A Share for Girls in Jewish Birthright"; Weissler, "New Jewish Birth Rituals for Baby Girls"; Simchat Bat Collection of the Jewish Women's Resource Center, JWRC #3308 (handwritten text titled "Lincoln Square Synagogue, New York City").

50. Strassfeld and Strassfeld, eds., *Second Jewish Catalog,* 30–37.

51. Daniel I. Leifer, "Birth Rituals and Jewish Daughters," *Sh'ma: A Journal of Jewish Responsibility* 6 (April 2, 1976): 85, 88.

52. Sharon and Joseph Kaplan, "Innovation within Halachah for Daughters," 103–4.

53. My sincere thanks to R. Sandy Eisenberg Sasso for graciously providing me with this booklet and taking the time to speak with me.

54. Reifman, ed., *Blessing the Birth of a Daughter,* 1, 3.

55. Barbara Penzer, "Women and the Reconstructionst Movement," in *New Jewish Feminism,* ed. Goldstein, 337–38.

56. Schneider, *Jewish and Female,* 122.

57. Ibid., 128–130. See also Joel Lurie Grishaver, *The Life Cycle Workbook* (Denver: Alternatives in Religious Education, Inc., 1983), especially p. 16. This workbook, identi-

fied in *Jewish and Female* (p. 129), is an educational tool for middle school students and includes brief references to Brit Banot ("Covenant of Daughters") ceremonies.

58. *A Guide toward Celebrating the Birth of a Daughter,* Simchat Bat Collection of the Jewish Women's Resource Center, JWRC #94, 1, 4, Appendix p. 1. I have a copy of this guide in my personal file.

59. Blu Greenberg, *On Women and Judaism* (Philadelphia: The Jewish Publication Society of America, 1981), 20, note 3.

60. Brozan, "A Share for Girls in Jewish Birthright."

61. I originally found this booklet in the Simchat Bat collection of the Jewish Theological Seminary in New York. It is also in my personal file.

62. Sacks, ed., *Koren Siddur,* 1034–37. See also Jonathan Sacks, "Simchat Bat, Weinberg Family: Ceremony for the Naming of a Daughter" (November 30, 2003), which interestingly includes both Ashkenazic and Sephardic naming formulas. My thanks to Anna Mass London for providing me with this ceremony.

63. See, e.g., Shlomo Riskin, *Around the Family Table,* 196–201; Adena K. Berkowitz and Rivka Haut, eds., *Shaarei Simcha / Gates of Joy* (Jersey City, NJ: Ktav Publishing House, 2007), 132–39; Gorlin, "And Her Name Will Be Called in Israel," 217–21.

64. *Jewish Encyclopedia,* "Acrostics," http://www.jewishencyclopedia.com/articles/750 -acrostics (accessed March 14, 2013).

65. See, e.g., Shelley List and Yael Penkower, "Prayer upon the Birth of a Child [Boy/Girl]," http://www.jofa.org/pdf/uploaded/1533-XLFV6111.pdf (accessed March 7, 2013).

66. E.g., Jonathan Sacks, "Simchat Bat, Weinberg Family: Ceremony for the Naming of a Daughter."

67. Devora Steinmetz and David Silber, ceremony in the Simchat Bat Collection of the Jewish Women's Resource Center, #VF 10609 (June 16, 1991). I also found this ceremony, in Blu Greenberg's private collection.

68. I found this ceremony in Blu Greenberg's private collection. It is also available online. Larry and Diane Cohler-Esses, "The Brit of Ayelet Kalila Vivianne Cohler-Esses," Ritualwell, http://www.ritualwellorg/ritual/brit-ayelet-kalila-vivianne-cohler-esses (accessed March 14, 2013).

69. "Awakening the Senses," from the Brit Bat of Rebecca Yael Morrow-Spitzer, Ritualwell, http://www.ritualwell.org/ritual/awakening-senses (accessed March 14, 2013); originally found in the files of the Reconstructionist Rabbinical College.

70. Avi S. Olitzky, "A New Simchat Bat Ritual—Pidyon HaIsha." R. Olitzky kindly emailed this text to me on June 23, 2011.

71. "The Covenant of Sarah Our Foremother," for Alice Bean Tecotzky, Simchat Bat Collection of the Jewish Women's Resource Center, #14393.

72. I found this "Simchat Bat Ceremony in Celebration of the Birth of a Daughter" in Blu Greenberg's private collection. The text explains that this is "an expanded version of the Seder *Zeved Habat*" and that "[t]his ceremony was developed by Rabbi Saul J. Berman for use at Lincoln Square Synagogue."

73. Alexandra Volin Avelin, "Annointing with Breast Milk," http://www.ritualwell.

org/ritual/anointing-breast-milk (accessed March 14, 2013); Debra Ruth Kolodny, "Mystery of the Covenant: A New Ceremony of Simchat Brit," *Kerem*, vol. 11 (2007–2008): 9–13.

74. Shira Shazeer, "Brit Otiyot," http://www.ritualwell.org/ritual/brit-otiyot-covenant -letters (accessed March 14, 2013).

75. Geller, "Brit Milah and Brit Banot," 63 (citing Richard and Carol Levy, "Covenant and Redemption Ceremony for Sarah Levy" [unpublished]). See, e.g., Gabrielle Birkner, "Parsing the 'Menstrual Slap,'" Sisterhood Blog (February 23, 2010), http://blogs .forward.com/sisterhood-blog/126293/parsing-the-menstrual-slap/ (accessed March 14, 2013).

76. See, e.g., Haviva Ner-David, *Life on the Fringes: A Feminist Journey Towards Traditional Rabbinic Ordination* (Needham, MA: JFL Books, 2000), 26–27; Kolodny, "Mystery of the Covenant," 8–9; Devora Steinmetz and David Silber, ceremony in the Simchat Bat Collection of the Jewish Women's Resource Center, #VF 10609.

77. Sharon and Joseph Kaplan, "Innovation within Halachah for Daughters," 103.

78. D. Cohen, *Celebrating Your Jewish Daughter*, 46.

79. Ner-David, *Life on the Fringes*, 26.

80. *A Guide toward Celebrating the Birth of a Jewish Daughter*, Simchat Bat Collection of the Jewish Women's Resource Center, JWRC #94, 2; Bell, "Thank Heaven for Little Girls," 21.

81. This is the collection of Blu Greenberg, which she very kindly sent to me.

82. D. Cohen, *Celebrating Your New Jewish Daughter*; Diamant, *New Jewish Baby Book*, 2nd ed., 128–69.

83. Women's League of Conservative Judaism "Simhat Bat: Ceremonies to Welcome a Baby Girl." This folder is available from the League, www.wlcj.org.

84. Available from Machon Itim, http://itim.org.il/eng/?CategoryID=203 (accessed March 14, 2013).

85. Laura Janner-Klausner, ed., *Neshama Hadasha (A New Life): An Anthology of New Birth Celebrations from Kehilat Kol Haneshama* (Jerusalem: Kihalat Kol Haneshama, 1999).

86. *The Orthodox Jewish Woman and Ritual: Options and Opportunities: Birth*, Jewish Orthodox Feminist Alliance. In addition, R. Debra Orenstein has edited an anthology focused on life-cycle rituals for women, with an afterword that provides step-by-step instructions for creating rituals (although not specifically those for newborn girls). Orenstein, ed., *Lifecycles*, vol. 1, especially chapter 3 and the Afterword.

87. D. Cohen, introduction to *Celebrating Your New Jewish Daughter*, xviii; Orenstein, ed., *Lifecycles*, vol. 1, 4.

88. "Welcoming and Raising Children," Ritualwell, http://www.ritualwell.org /categories/8 (accessed March 14, 2013).

89. "Simchat Bat Ceremony," Machon Itim, http://itim.org.il/eng/?CategoryID=307 (accessed March 14, 2013).

90. Janner-Klausner, ed., *Neshama Hadasha*, 10 (emphasis in original).

91. Haym Soloveitchik, "Rupture and Reconstruction," 68, 72.

92. Seth Farber, e-mail message to author, August 22, 2007.

93. Weissler, "New Jewish Birth Rituals for Baby Girls," 9.

94. Rachel Adler, *Engendering Judaism: An Inclusive Theology and Ethics* (Philadelphia: The Jewish Publication Society, 1998) 84.

95. Ochs, *Inventing Jewish Ritual*, 115–17.

Chapter 4. Women and Covenant

1. Joseph B. Soloveitchik, *Kol Dodi Dofek* (*Listen–My Beloved Knocks*), translated and annotated by David Z. Gordon, ed. Jeffrey R. Woolf (New York: Yeshiva University Press, 2006), 51–68, 73.

2. Jonathan Sacks, *Crisis and Covenant: Jewish Thought after the Holocaust* (Manchester: Manchester University Press, 1992), 1, 5, 27, 48, 227, 241.

3. Jonathan Sacks, "Ki Tavo 5771—Covenant & Conversation—Thoughts on the Weekly Parsha from the Chief Rabbi," http://www.youtube.com/watch?feature=endscreen& NR=1&v=RLQUK6SX81k (accessed December 1, 2011).

4. Sacks, *Crisis and Covenant*, 1–2.

5. Jonathan Sacks, *Covenant and Conversation: A Weekly Reading of the Jewish Bible: Exodus: The Book of Redemption* (New Milford, CT: Maggid Books, 2010), 151–52.

6. Eugene B. Borowitz, *Renewing the Covenant: A Theology for the Postmodern Jew* (Philadelphia: The Jewish Publication Society, 1991), 221, 224, 226–227. See also Peter Ochs with Eugene B. Borowitz, ed., *Reviewing the Covenant: Eugene B. Borowitz and the Postmodern Renewal of Jewish Theology* (Albany: State University of New York Press, 2000).

7. See, e.g., Rashi on Genesis 17:10.

8. See, e.g., Sacks, ed., *Koren Siddur,* 37; Scherman, ed., *Artscroll Siddur,* 26.

9. See, e.g., Sacks, ed., *Koren Siddur,* 175; Scherman, ed., *Artscroll Siddur,* 154.

10. Millen, *Women, Birth, and Death*, 100.

11. See, e.g., Rachel Adler, "I've Had Nothing Yet So I Can't Take More," *Moment,* 22–23; Plaskow, *Standing Again at Sinai,* 27–28, 63–64, 82–85.

12. Menachem Leibtag, Tanach Study Center, Shiurim on Chumash and Navi, http://www.tanachapterorg/breishit/lech/lechapterhtm (accessed August 20, 2008).

13. For contrary opinions, see, e.g., Ner-David, *Life on the Fringes,* 21; Millen, *Women, Birth, and Death,* 74; Idana Goldberg, "Orthodoxy and Feminism," in *New Jewish Feminism,* ed. Goldstein, 288.

14. Isaac Abrabanel, *Commentary on the Torah*, Genesis 17:15.

15. Some contemporary rabbis emphasize Sarah's distinct role in the establishment of the covenant. See, e.g., Elyse Goldstein, *ReVisions: Seeing Torah Through a Feminist Lens* (Woodstock, VT: Jewish Lights Publishing, 1998), 117–18; Ann Moline, "Baby Naming Becomes Part of Tradition," *Arizona Jewish Post,* September 29, 1995, 14 (quoting R. Hayyim Kassorla of Sephardic Temple Magen David in Rockville, MD).

16. Kolodny, "Mystery of the Covenant," 3.

17. *Tosafot HaShalem: Otzar Peirushei Baalei Tosfot al Torah, N'vi'im, K'tuvim,* vol. 3, Yaakov Galis, ed. (Jerusalem: Tosfot HaShalem Productions, 1984), 249 (Genesis 34:14, paragraph 3).

18. Sacks, *Covenant and Conversation: Exodus,* 153.

19. According to exegesis on Deuteronomy 31:10–12, "men come to learn [and] women come to listen" or, alternatively, "men come to listen, and women [come] in order to receive a reward for bringing the children." BT Chagiga 3a; M. Sofrim 18:6. It was natural for Talmudic and post-Talmudic rabbis to understand these passages in terms of the gender-based division of labor that was commonplace in these eras. Viewed more broadly, however, this gloss confirms women's inclusion in hakhel and, thus, in the covenant.

20. See, e.g., Plaskow *Standing Again at Sinai,* 26; Cynthia Ozick, "Notes toward Finding the Right Question," in *On Being a Jewish Feminist,* ed. Heschel, 149–50.

21. Judith Plaskow, "The Right Question Is Theological," in *On Being a Jewish Feminist,* ed. Heschel, 231; Plaskow, *Standing Again at Sinai,* 25–28.

22. Adler, "I've Had Nothing Yet So I Can't Take More," 23.

23. Plaskow, *Standing Again at Sinai,* 82.

24. Eliezer Berkovits, *Jewish Women in Time and Torah* (Hoboken, NJ: Ktav Publishing House, Inc., 1990), 59. But see Ozick, "Notes toward Finding the Right Question," 148, for a substantially different viewpoint.

25. Greenberg, *On Women and Judaism,* 41.

26. Isaiah 42:6, 55:3.

27. Isaiah 49:8; Ezekiel 16:62–63; Psalms 105:1–13.

28. Isaiah 55:3; Jeremiah 50:5; Ezekiel 37:26, 16:60; Psalms 105:10.

29. Isaiah 59:21; Jeremiah 31:31–33, 32:37–40; Ezekiel 20:33–39, 37:23–28; Malachi 3:1.

30. II Kings 17:35–38; Jeremiah 11:2–10, 32:40.

31. I found this ceremony in Blu Greenberg's private collection. It is also available online. Larry and Diane Cohler-Esses, "The Brit of Ayelet Kalila Vivianne Cohler-Esses," Ritualwell, http://www.ritualwellorg/ritual/brit-ayelet-kalila-vivianne-cohler-esses (accessed March 14, 2013).

32. II Chronicles 34:14–33 also describes this episode.

33. S. Cohen, *Why Aren't Jewish Women Circumcised?,* 133. I have drawn many of the sources discussed here from *Why Aren't Jewish Women Circumcised?* (pp. 133–34), and from Shaye J. D. Cohen, "Are Women in the Covenant?" in *A Feminist Commentary on the Babylonian Talmud,* ed. Tal Ilan, et al. (Tübingen, Germany: Mohr Siebeck, 2007), 33–35. I am grateful for access to Professor Cohen's scholarship.

34. Since Rachel and Leah are considered one, the three mentions of *et* encompass all four foremothers. Vilna Gaon, *Hagahot HaG'ra* on Sifra, Parshat B'chukotai, chapter 8, halacha 9.

35. Mechilta, Mesechta Dibachodesh, Yitro, parsha 7 (*Avdecha V'Amatecha*).

36. Geza Vermes, *The Dead Sea Scrolls in English* (London: Sheffield Academic Press Ltd., 1962), 95; Lawrence H. Schiffman and James C. VanderKam, eds., *Encyclopedia of the Dead Sea Scrolls,* vol. 1 (London: Oxford University Press, 2000), 169–70.

37. Vermes, *The Dead Sea Scrolls in English*, 95–96.

38. Florentino Garvia Martinez and Eibert J.C. Tigchelaar, eds., *The Dead Sea Scrolls Study Edition*, vol. 1 (Leiden, The Netherlands: Koninklijke Brill NV, 1997), 570–71 (Damascus Document, CD-A, col. 12, lines 10–11 [my translation]; cited in S. Cohen, *Why Aren't Jewish Women Circumcised?*, 254–55, note 83).

39. See, e.g., Shmuel Safrai, "The Obligations of Women in Mitzvot in the Mishnayot of the Tanaim," in *The Annual of Bar-Ilan University*, ed. Tzvi Aryeh Sheinfeld (Ramat Gan: Bar-Ilan University, 1985), 227–36; S. Cohen, "Are Women in the Covenant?" 33–35.

40. Mechilta Dibachodesh, Yitro, parsha 3 (Exodus 19:15).

41. Meiri on M. Shabbat 9:3 in *Beit HaB'chira*, commentary on fourth mishna, following discussion of BT Shabbat 85.

42. Tanchuma, Metzorah, chapter 9; Tanchuma (Buber), Metzorah, 27:18.

43. Mechilta Dibachodesh, Yitro, parsha 2 (Exodus 19:3, 19:7).

44. Yair Chaim Bachrach, *Mekor Chaim*, Hilchot Tzitzit 17:2 (cited in Daniel Sperber, *On Changes in Jewish Liturgy: Options and Limitations* [Jerusalem: Urim Publications, 2010], 202–3, note 8).

45. Tanchuma, Metzorah, chapter 9; Tanchuma (Buber), Metzorah 27:18.

46. See S. Cohen, *Why Aren't Jewish Women Circumcised?*, 28–32. By contrast, R. Lawrence Hoffman dates the trend associating circumcision blood with salvation to the Tannaitic period. *Covenant of Blood*, 90–95, 107, 191.

47. Goldstein, *ReVisions*, 113; see also S. Cohen, *Why Aren't Jewish Women Circumcised?*, 203–4; Gary Shapiro, "Sealed in Our Flesh—Women as Members of the Brit," in *The Pardes Reader: Celebrating 25 Years of Learning* (Jerusalem: The Pardes Institute, 1997), 94; cf. Ruth Langer, *To Worship God Properly: Tensions Between Liturgical Custom and Halakhah in Judaism* (Cincinnati: Hebrew Union College Press, 1998), 60–73.

48. Abrabanel, *Commentary on the Torah*, Genesis 17:9.

49. B. Netanyahu, *Don Isaac Abravanel: Statesman & Philosopher*, 5th ed. (Ithaca, NY: Cornell University Press, 1998), 86.

50. Yehuda Brandes, *Mada Toratecha: Masekhet Ketubot* (Jerusalem: Machon Ha-Yisraeli Le-Pirsumim Talmudi'im, 2008), 40–42. My thanks to Chaim Saiman for providing me with this source.

51. Maimonides, *Sefer HaMitzvot*, discussion at the conclusion of positive mitzvot; see also ibid., first nine positive mitzvot.

52. Bachrach, *Mekor Chaim*, Hilchot Tzitzit, 17:2 (cited in Sperber, *On Changes in Jewish Liturgy*, 202–3, note 8).

53. Nachmonides on Deuteronomy 4:9–10; Nachmonides, "Mitzvot that Maimonides Excluded from the Negative Commandments," Addendum to Maimonides's *Sefer Hamitzvot*, mitzvah 2.

54. See, e.g., Maimonides, *Mishneh Torah*, Sefer Madah, Hilchot Talmud Torah, 1:1, 1:13. See also BT Kiddushin 31a; Sifrei Deuteronomy 46.

55. See, e.g., M. Sotah 3:4; JT Sotah 3:4.

56. See, e.g., BT Shabbat 127a.

57. See Berkovits, *Jewish Women in Time and Torah,* 86. For a different opinion, see S. Cohen, "Are Women in the Covenant?" 30–33.

58. Introduction to *Sefer Mitzvot Gadol.*

59. See, e.g., Be'er Hatov on Shulchan Aruch, Orach Chaim 47:14; Beit Yosef on Arba'ah Turim, Orach Chaim, 47; *New Responsa of the Maharil* 45:2; *Levush HaTechelet,* Orach Chaim, Hilchot Brachot, 47:14.

60. Beit Yosef on Arba'ah Turim, Orach Chaim, 47; *Sefer HaAgur HaShalem,* Hilchot Tefilah, siman 2; *Levush HaTechelet,* Orach Chaim, Hilchot Brachot 47:14, 106:2; *Shulchan Aruch of Schneur Zalman,* Orach Chaim, Hilchot Brachot 47:10; ibid., Hilchot Tefillah, 106:2.

61. M. Brachot 3:3; BT Brachot 20b.

62. Orach Chaim 70:1.

63. *Levush HaTechelet,* Orach Chaim, Hilchot Keriyat Shema, 70:1.

64. *Bayit Chadash,* Orach Chaim 70:1.

65. Perisha on Arba'ah Turim, Orach Chaim, Hilchot Keriyat Shema, 70:1.

66. Shulchan Aruch, Orach Chaim 47:14; see also Beit Yosef on Arba'ah Turim, Orach Chaim 47. For alternate versions of this blessing, see BT Brachot 11b and Arba'ah Turim, Orach Chaim 47.

67. Shulchan Aruch, Orach Chaim 47:1, based on Arba'ah Turim, Orach Chaim 47.

68. Beit Yosef on Arba'ah Turim, Orach Chaim 47.

69. *Levush HaTechelet,* Orach Chaim, Hilchot Brachot, 47:14.

70. Rashi on BT Rosh Hashana 29a; see also Rashi on Leviticus 26:37. My thanks to R. Dov Linzer for pointing out this topic to me. See Dov Linzer, e-mail message to author, January 6, 2009.

71. Rosh on BT Brachot 20b; see also Rosh on BT Rosh Hashana 33a (citing Baal HaItur); Moshe Feinstein, *Iggrot Moshe,* Orach Chaim, 1:190). See also Rahel Berkovits, "Kol Yisrael Areivim Zeh LaZeh? Women and the Principle of Areivut," *Bikurim* 2 (1993): 43. *Bikurim* is a publication of Midreshet Lindenbaum in Jerusalem with a limited circulation.

72. Akiva Eger, *Tosafot on the Mishna,* Megillah 2:4:19; Yechiel Michal Epstein, *Aruch HaShulchan,* Orach Chaim, Hilchot Shabbat, 271:6.

73. See, e.g., Sifra, 2 parshata, paragraph 2.

74. Sperber, *On Changes in Jewish Liturgy,* 202.

75. Berkovits, *Jewish Women in Time and Torah,* 87; see also ibid., 5, 81, 86.

76. Sacks, *Covenant and Conversation: Exodus,* 153–54.

77. Meiselman, *Jewish Woman in Jewish Law,* 61–62.

78. Adler, "I've Had Nothing Yet So I Can't Take More," 22–23.

79. Plaskow, *Standing Again at Sinai,* 27–28, 59, 83–85; S. Cohen, "Are Women in the Covenant?" 25–42; S. Cohen, *Why Aren't Jewish Women Circumcised?,* 133–38; Hoffman, *Covenant of Blood,* 26, 47, 135. See also Orenstein, introduction to chapter 3, *Lifecycles,* vol. 1, 55–56 (noting "lingering disparities with respect to Brit").

80. Millen, *Women, Birth, and Death,* 190, note 18.

81. Berkovits, *Jewish Women in Time and Torah,* 131.

Chapter 5. The Conflation of Covenant and Circumcision

1. Joseph B. Soloveitchik, *Halakhic Man,* trans. Lawrence Kaplan (Philadelphia: The Jewish Publication Society of America, 1983), 90.

2. See Robin Judd, "Circumcision and Modern Life: A German Case Study, 1843–1914," in *The Covenant of Circumcision,* ed. Elizabeth Wyner Mark (Hanover, NH: Brandeis University Press, 2003), 146–47, 151–53; Goldberg, *Jewish Passages,* 57–58.

3. Soloveitchik, *Halakhic Man,* 90.

4. I refer here to traditional sources providing for matrilineal descent. See, e.g., M. Kiddushin 3:12; BT Kiddushin 68b; BT Yevamot 23a; Shulchan Aruch, Even HaEzer 8:5; see also Shaye J. D. Cohen, "The Origins of the Matrilineal Principle in Rabbinic Law," *AJS Review* 10 (Spring 1985): 19–53. The Reform movement has adopted the position that Jewish status requires one Jewish parent, whether father or mother. According to this viewpoint, one becomes a covenantal member upon birth as long as one parent is Jewish. See Central Conference of American Rabbis, Resolution, "The Status of Children of Mixed Marriages" (March 15, 1983), ccarnet.org/rabbis-speak/resolutions/all/status-of-children-of-mixed-marriages-1983 (accessed March 14, 2013); Central Conference of American Rabbis, Contemporary American Reform Responsa No. 38, "Patrilineal and Matrilineal Descent" (October 1983), ccarnet.org/responsa/carr-61-68 (accessed March 14, 2013).

5. Academy of the Hebrew Language, e-mail messages to author, March 26–27, 2008 (search of the Historical Dictionary database); see Mechilta D'Bachodesh, Yitro, parsha 2, *U'Shemartem et briti.*

6. Avraham Even-Shoshan, *HaMilon HeChadash* (The New Dictionary), vol. 1 (Jerusalem: Kiryat Sefer, 1966), 280 (footnotes on entry for "Brit").

7. By contrast, R. Lawrence Hoffman claims, "*Milah* is really a metonymic shorthand of the larger nominal phrase, *brit milah.*" *Covenant of Blood,* 25–26.

8. See, e.g., Weisberg, *Otzar HaBrit;* Pirutinsky, *Sefer HaBrit.*

9. Defendant's Motion in Limine, *United States v. Lacey, et al.,* No. 1:09-cr-00507-KMW, note 6.

10. Klein, *A Time to Be Born,* 215; Goldberg, *Jewish Passages,* 60–61; Ephraim Tabory and Sharon Erez, "Circumscribed Circumcision," in *Covenant of Circumcision,* ed. Mark, 163.

11. Hoffman, *Covenant of Blood,* 212. See also "Bris, Britah: Parents' First Lessons in Balancing Gender, Culture, Tradition, and Religion" in *Patterns in a Feminist Sampler,* eds. Rachel Josefowitz Siegel and Ellen Cole (New York: The Haworth Press, 1997), 9–14.

12. See, e.g., Geller, "Brit Milah and Brit Banot," 58.

13. Hoffman, *Covenant of Blood,* 211.

14. Ibid.

15. Eva Kovacs and Julia Vajda, "Circumcision in Hungary after the Shoah," in *Covenant of Circumcision,* ed. Mark, 187; see also Hoffman, *Covenant of Blood,* 220.

16. Ibid.

17. Elizabeth Wyner Mark, "Crossing the Gender Divide: Public Ceremonies, Private Parts, Mixed Feelings," introduction to *Covenant of Circumcision,* xxv.

18. See Hoffman, *Covenant of Blood,* 37.

19. Mechilta D'Bachodesh, Yitro, parsha 2, *U'Shemartem et briti.*

20. S. Cohen, *Why Aren't Jewish Women Circumcised?,* 128–33; cf. Sperber, *On Changes in Jewish Liturgy,* 199–201.

21. *Siddur R. Saadia Gaon,* 102 (cited in S. Cohen, *Why Aren't Jewish Women Circumcised?,* 254, note 80).

22. Avi Shmidman, "Developments with the Statutory Text of the *Birkat ha-Mazon* in the Light of its Poetic Counterparts," in *Jewish and Christian Liturgy and Worship: New Insights into its History and Interactions,* eds. Albert Gerhards and Clemens Leonhard (Leiden, The Netherlands: Koninklijke Brill NV, 2007), 109–26 and note 1 (cited in Sperber, *On Changes in Jewish Liturgy,* 201–2).

23. An alternate interpretation is that the verse's repetition of "in your bloods live" evokes both two types of blood and two types of salvation. Hoffman, *Covenant of Blood,* 101–2.

24. See ibid., 92, for a proposed reason for this custom.

25. See, e.g., Weisberg, *Otzar HaBrit,* vol. 1, 493–511; Goldberg, *Jewish Passages,* 51.

26. See, e.g., M. Nedarim 3:11; BT Brachot 48b-49a, Shabbat 132a and 133a, Pesachim 69b, Yevamot 5b.

27. See BT Menachot 43b; David Kimchi (Radak), *Commentary on the Torah,* Genesis 17:11; Abrabanel, *Commentary on the Torah,* Genesis 17:9; Joseph ben Isaac Bechor Shor, *Commentaries on the Torah,* Genesis 17:2; Gottlieb, *Darchei Noam,* chapter 67, paragraph 1; see also Pirutinsky, *Sefer HaBrit,* 11 (Likutei Halachot 260:1, paragraph 62).

28. Some conceptualize circumcision as a "birthing experience" for fathers. Geller, "Brit Milah and Brit Banot," 59. This anthropological perspective, however, leaves me with more questions than answers. Other explanations for circumcision are posited in Michael V. Fox, "The Sign of the Covenant: Circumcision in Light of the Priestly 'Ot' Etiologies," *Revue Biblique* 81 (1974): 591–94.

29. Ra'anan Abusch, "Circumcision and Castration under Roman Law in the Early Empire," in *Covenant of Circumcision,* ed. Mark, 75–76; Goldberg, *Jewish Passages,* 39; Robert G. Hall, "Epispasm: Circumcision in Reverse," *Bible Review* 8 (August 1992): 52–53; Nissan Rubin, "Brit Milah: A Study of Change in Custom," in *Covenant of Circumcision,* 90.

30. "The Life of Hadrian," in *Historia Augusta,* vol. 1 (Loeb Classical Library, 1921), 14.2, http://penelope.uchicago.edu/Thayer/E/Roman/Texts/Historia_Augusta/Hadrian/1*.html#ref118 (accessed March 24, 2013).

31. Abusch, "Circumcision and Castration," 85.

32. S. P. Scott, ed., *The Visigothic Code: (Forum judicum),* Library of Iberian Resources Online (LIBRO), Book XII, Title II, Laws III and VII, http://libro.uca.edu/vcode/vg12-2.pdf (accessed March 24, 2013); see also Jacob R. Marcus, *The Jew in the Medieval World: A Source Book* (Cincinnati: Sinai Press, 1938), 20; Klein, *A Time to Be Born,* 212.

33. Rubin, "Brit Milah," 92–96 and note 43; Goldberg, *Jewish Passages,* 40.

34. See, e.g., S. Cohen, *Why Aren't Jewish Women Circumcised?,* 27–28.

35. See Weisberg, *Otzar HaBrit,* vol. 1, 369–383; BT Nedarim 31b–32a; Yalkut Shimoni, Lech L'cha, remez 81 (Genesis 17:1–4).

36. Midrash Tanchuma (Buber), Lech L'cha, 20; Genesis Rabba 46:4; see also Yalkut Shimoni, Lech L'cha, remez 80 (Genesis 17:1–4).

37. Ibid., remez 81; Tanya Rabbati, Hilchot Milah, 96.

38. Midrash Tanchuma (Buber), Vayera, paragraph 4; Midrash Tanchuma, Vayera, paragraph 2 (parallel source).

39. Sperber, *Jewish Life Cycle,* 79–83; see also Shaye J.D. Cohen, "A Brief History of Jewish Circumcision Blood," in *Covenant of Circumcision,* ed. Mark, 39.

40. See also BT Nedarim 32a.

41. Yoreh Dai'ah, 260:1.

42. Pirutinsky, *Sefer HaBrit,* 13 (Likutei Halachot 260:1, paragraph 62).

43. Pirkei d'Rabbi Eliezer, chapter 29.

44. Yalkut Michiri, Psalms 136:19; Yalkut Shimoni, B'Shalach (Exodus), chapter 14, remez 236.

45. Genesis Rabba 46:9; Yalkut Shimoni, Lech L'cha, remez 82 (Genesis 17:8–14).

46. Pirkei d'Rabbi Eliezer, chapter 29.

47. Genesis Rabba, Vayerah, 48:8; see also Midrash Tanchuma (Tanchuma C), Lech L'cha, 20.

48. Exodus Rabba 1:8.

49. Genesis Rabba, Vayerah, 48:8.

50. Midrash Tanchuma (Tanchuma C), Lech L'cha, 20.

51. Weissler, "New Jewish Birth Rituals for Baby Girls," 7–8. By contrast, Lawrence Hoffman claims that "[b]lood is the dominant symbol of circumcision." *Covenant of Blood,* 171.

52. Ibid., 27, 31. Hoffman also asserts that "the covenant is a covenant of blood," ibid., 103. Shaye J. D. Cohen observes, however, that "Biblical and rabbinic texts . . . seldom mention the blood of circumcision." S. Cohen, *Why Aren't Jewish Women Circumcised?,* 28.

53. Leviticus 26:15, 42, 44–45; Deuteronomy 8:18.

54. Exodus 24:7–8, 34:27; Deuteronomy 5:2.

55. Exodus 34:28, Deuteronomy 4:13.

56. Deuteronomy 9:9–15.

57. Numbers 10:33, Deuteronomy 10:8.

58. Deuteronomy 4:31.

59. See, e.g., Deuteronomy 7:8–9.

60. See, e.g., Isaiah 1:10–17, Jeremiah 11:6–8.

61. See, e.g., Jeremiah 4:4, 9:24–25.

62. Samson Raphael Hirsch, *The Pentateuch,* vol. 1, trans. Isaac Levy (London: L. Honig & Sons Ltd., 1959), 299–300 (Genesis 17:10).

63. For a perspective on "ote" that could not be more different than that of R. Hirsch, see Fox, "The Sign of the Covenant."

64. Hirsch, *The Pentateuch,* vol. 1, 299–300 (Genesis 17:10).

65. Abrabanel, *Commentary on the Torah*, Genesis 17:9.

66. See, e.g., Plaskow, *Standing Again at Sinai,* 82. On the other hand, Rochelle Millen notes a distinction between the circumcision commandment and the underlying covenant in Genesis 17. Millen, *Women, Birth, and Death,* 74–75.

67. I have drawn these sources from *Why Aren't Jewish Women Circumcised?* by Shaye J. D. Cohen (pp. 94–99) and *Women, Birth, and Death in Jewish Law and Practice* by Rochelle Millen (pp. 74–75). I am indebted to Professors Cohen and Millen for access to their scholarship.

68. See S. Cohen, *Why Aren't Jewish Women Circumcised?,* 95. A Jewish boy might remain uncircumcised due to, for example, his poor health or the circumcision-related deaths of his older brothers.

69. Throughout this book, a woman's "inability to be circumcised" means her inability to undergo penile circumcision. Female circumcision (also known as female genital mutilation or FGM), while common in some cultures, is not known to have ever existed among Jews, even in ancient times. S. Cohen, *Why Aren't Jewish Women Circumcised?,* chapter 2.

70. Ibid., 97; Shapiro, "Sealed in Our Flesh," 92.

71. See Yael Levin, "A Woman Resembles One Who Is Circumcised," *Mesechet* 2 (2004): 27–45 (collecting sources).

72. *Sh'iltot d'Rav Achai Gaon,* Vayerah (Genesis), 10; Shimon Kayyara, *Sefer Halachot Gedolot,* Hilchot Milah, 46; Isaac ben Jacob Alfasi (Rif), BT Shabbat, end of chapter 19; Asher ben Yechiel (Rosh), BT Shabbat, end of chapter 19; Tzadok HaCohen Rabinowitz, *Poked Akarim,* section 5, *V'ha'milah.*

73. Ibid.

74. Rif and Rosh, BT Shabbat, end of chapter 19.

75. S. Cohen, *Why Aren't Jewish Women Circumcised?,* 150–54.

76. Maimonides, *Sefer HaMitzvot,* positive mitzvah no. 215.

77. Philo, *Questions and Answers on Genesis,* trans. Ralph Marcus (Cambridge, MA: Harvard University Press, 1953), Supp. I, 3:47 and 3:48, 241–42. See also S. Cohen, *Why Aren't Jewish Women Circumcised?,* 148; Ra'anan Abusch, "Circumcision and Castration," 81–82.

78. Maimonides, *Guide for the Perplexed,* 3:49, trans. Shlomo Pines (Chicago: University of Chicago Press, 1962), 610.

79. S. Cohen, *Why Aren't Jewish Women Circumcised?,* 146–54; Elizabeth Wyner Mark, "Crossing the Gender Divide: Public Ceremonies, Private Parts, Mixed Feelings," introduction to *Covenant of Circumcision,* 207, note 48.

80. Maimonides, Mishneh Torah, Sefer Ahava, Hilchot Milah, chapters 1–3. In one instance, however, Maimonides may allude to the generalized covenant. Ibid., 3:9.

81. Maimonides, Mishneh Torah, Sefer Shoftim, Hilchot Melachim, 10:7–8. My thanks to R. Michael Broyde for pointing out this source to me.

82. S. Cohen, *Why Aren't Jewish Women Circumcised?,* 151–52; Mark, "Crossing the Gender Divide," 207, note 48.

83. Berkovits, *Jewish Women in Time and Torah,* 5.

84. Meiselman, *Jewish Woman in Jewish Law,* 61; Joel B. Wolowelsky, *Women, Jewish Law, and Modernity: New Opportunities in a Post-Feminist Age* (Hoboken, NJ: Ktav Publishing House, Inc., 1997), 46.

85. See Selma Kaplan Goldman, personal account, in *Today I Am a Woman: Stories of Bat Mitzvah around the World,* eds. Barbara Vinick and Shulamit Reinharz (Bloomington: Indiana University Press, 2012), 258 (citing Mel Scult, ed., *Communings of the Spirit: The Journals of Mordecai M. Kaplan,* vol. 1: 1913–1914 [Detroit: Wayne State University Press, 2001], 159, 163). For coming-of-age practices for girls in the late nineteenth century, see, e.g., Marcus, *Jewish Life Cycle,* 105–7; Goldberg, *Jewish Passages,* 106; Vinick, introduction to *Today I Am a Woman,* 3.

86. Marcus, *Jewish Life Cycle,* 107; Judith Kaplan Eisenstein, Hadassah Kaplan Musher, and Selma Kaplan Goldman, personal accounts, in *Today I Am a Woman,* 255–59.

87. Moshe Sternbuch, *Teshuvot V'Hanhagot,* Orach Chaim, vol. 1, siman 156.

88. Goldberg, *Jewish Passages,* 105; Schneider, *Jewish and Female,* 134–35.

89. Lisa W. Foderaro, "Growing Up, Kagan Tested Boundaries of Her Faith," *New York Times* (May 12, 2010), http://www.nytimes.com/2010/05/13/nyregion/13synagogue .html?_r=0 (accessed March 24, 2013).

90. See generally, Marcus, *Jewish Life Cycle,* 105–116; Ora Wiskind Elper, ed., *Traditions and Celebrations for the Bat Mitzvah* (Jerusalem: Urim Publications / MaTaN: The Sadie Rennert Women's Institute for Torah Studies, 2003); *The Orthodox Jewish Woman and Ritual: Options and Opportunities: Bat Mitzvah,* Jewish Orthodox Feminist Alliance, http://www.jofa.org/uploadedFiles/site/Education/Ritual_Opportunities/Bat% 20Mitzvah%20Guide.pdf (accessed March 7, 2013); Goldberg, *Jewish Passages,* 107; Bea Rosenfield and Jerry Rosenfield, "In Our Bookbag," *Ten Da'at* 3 (Spring 1989): 37; A. Cohen, "Bat Mitzvah: A Challenge for Religious Education," 32.

91. Feinstein, *Iggrot Moshe,* Orach Chaim, 1:104, 2:30, 2:97, and 4:36. See also Norma Baumel Joseph, "Ritual, Law, and Praxis: An American Response to Bat Mitzvah Celebrations," *Modern Judaism* 22 (2002): 234–60.

92. Steve Chambers, "Coming of Age—At 87, Older Voices Fill Bat Mitzvahs," *New Jersey Star-Ledger,* July 14, 1998, 1, 20.

93. Asaf Kaniel, "Sarah Schenirer," in *The YIVO Encyclopedia of the Jews of Eastern Europe,* trans. Carrie Friedman-Cohen, http://www.yivoencyclopedia.org/article.aspx /Schenirer_Sarah (accessed March 24, 2013).

94. M. Sotah 3:4; JT Sotah 3:4, Chagigah 1:1; BT Sotah 21a, Kiddushin 34a, Chagigah 3a; Mesechet Sofrim 18:6. Tosfot on BT Chagigah 3a, "Nashim"; Maimonides, Mishneh Torah, Sefer Madah, Hilchot Talmud Torah 1:1; Shulchan Aruch, Yoreh Dei'ah, Hilchot Talmud Torah, 246:6. The following sources allow for certain leniencies: Maimonides, Mishneh Torah, Sefer Madah, Hilchot Talmud Torah 1:13; Moses Isserles (Rama) on Shulchan Aruch, Yoreh Deah, Hilchot Talmud Torah, 246:6; Taz on Shulchan Aruch, Yoreh Deah, Hilchot Talmud Torah, 246:4; Perisha on Arba'ah Turim, Yoreh De'ah, Hilchot Talmud Torah, 246:6, note 15. On the other hand, the following sources apply certain stringencies: Yechiel Michal Epstein, Aruch Hashulchan, Yoreh Deah, Hilchot

Talmud Torah, 246:19; Baruch Epstein, *Torah Temima* on Deuteronomy 11:19, notes 44 and 45.

95. Chofetz Chaim, *Likkutei Halachot* on Sotah 21a, note 3; Chofetz Chaim, letter in *Beit Yaakov: A Monthly Journal for Issues of Education, Literature, and Philosophy* (1960): 3; Avraham Mordechai Alter, letter in *Beit Yaakov* (1960): 3; Zalman Sorotzkin, *Maoznaim LaMishpat*, siman 42. See also letter in *Beit Yaakov* (1960): 3 for the opinions of Avraham Yeshaya Karelitz, Yosef Tzvi Dushinsky, and Issachar Baer Rokeach. Cf. Meiselman, *Jewish Woman in Jewish Law*, 40.

96. Joel B. Wolowelsky, introduction to *Women and the Study of Torah: Essays from the Pages of Tradition* (Hoboken, NJ: Ktav / Rabbinical Council of America, 1992), xi; see generally Moshe Kaveh, "The Status of the Woman in Judaism with Respect to Bold Halachic Determinations," in ed. Shilo, *To Be a Jewish Woman*, 31.

97. Joseph B. Soloveitchik, *Community, Covenant, and Commitment*, ed. Nathaniel Helfgot (Jersey City, NJ: Ktav Publishing House, Inc., 2005), 83 (the Rav's letter is dated May 27, 1953); see also Mayer Twersky, "A Glimpse of the Rav: Talmud Torah for Women and the Mehitsa Controversy," in *Women and the Study of Torah*, ed. Wolowelsky, 49.

98. Wolowelsky, *Women, Jewish Law, and Modernity*, 46; Meiselman, *Jewish Woman in Jewish Law*, 61.

99. See, e.g., Weinberger, *Simchah Handbook*, 193–201. Cf. Yechiel Yaakov Weinberg, *Seridei Aish*, vol. 3, responsum 93; Berkovits, *Jewish Women in Time and Torah*, 80–81.

100. Yardena Cope-Yossef, "Celebrating *Bat Mitzvah* with a *Seudat Mitzvah*—Should a Girl Give a *Derashah* or Make a *Siyyum*?" in *Traditions and Celebrations for the Bat Mitzvah*, ed. Wiskind, 69, note 20.

101. Recounted in D. Cohen, *Celebrating Your New Jewish Daughter*, 73.

102. See, e.g., M. Avot 5:21; BT Yoma 82a; Genesis Rabba, Toldot, 63:10 (on Genesis 25:27), *Vayigadlu hani'arim*.

103. Marcus, *Jewish Life Cycle*, 85, 100; Goldberg, *Jewish Passages*, 90. By contrast, Leon Katz claims that the Bar Mitzvah "was practiced long before the Middle Ages." "Halakhic Aspects of Bar-Mitzvah and Bat-Mitzvah," *Journal of Jewish Music and Liturgy* 9 (1986): 24.

104. Millen, *Women, Birth, and Death*, 83. See also Plaskow, *Standing Again at Sinai*, 58.

105. Sandy Eisenberg Sasso, forward to *Celebrating Your New Jewish Daughter*, by D. Cohen, xi.

Chapter 6. A Central Covenantal Ritual for Girls

1. Ochs, *Inventing Jewish Ritual*, 21–22.

2. "Circumcision of the Heart," Simchat Bat Collection of the Jewish Women's Resource Center, JWRC #83.

3. Perry Raphael Rank and Gordon M. Freeman, eds., *Moreh Derekh: The Rabbinical Assembly Rabbi's Manual* (New York: The Rabbinical Assembly, 1998), A-42–A-45. Relatedly, in a 1976 ceremony, parents presented their baby daughter with a tallit, Weissler, "New Jewish Birth Rituals for Baby Girls," 10–11, and, more recently, parents placed

bracelets of tzitzit on their daughter's wrists and ankles. James Greene, "Simkhat Bat—A Welcoming Ceremony For a New Daughter," Ritualwell, http://www.ritualwell.org/rituals/ simkhat-bat-welcoming-ceremony-new-daughter (accessed March 24, 2013).

4. Ochs, *Inventing Jewish Ritual,* 141, 159.

5. Weissler, "New Jewish Birth Rituals for Baby Girls," 7–8.

6. Leifer, "Birth Rituals and Jewish Daughters," 86.

7. Geller, "Brit Milah and Brit Banot," 62. Similarly, R. Debra Ruth Kolodny maintains that a welcoming ceremony should "leave those in attendance transformed." Kolodny, "Mystery of the Covenant," 2.

8. Lori Hope Lefkowitz and Rona Shapiro, "The Politics and Aesthetics of Jewish Women's Spirituality," in *New Jewish Feminism,* ed. Goldstein, 78. See also Geller, "Brit Milah and Brit Banot," 59 (describing the liminality of the circumcision ritual).

9. Debra Cantor and Rebecca Jacobs, "Brit Banot Covenant Ceremonies for Daughters," *Kerem* 1 (Winter 1992–93): 47.

10. Leifer, "Birth Rituals and Jewish Daughters," 87.

11. Sharon and Joseph Kaplan, "Innovation within Halachah for Daughters," 104.

12. Traditionally, this act signifies a couple's engagement.

13. Chava Weissler, "New Jewish Birth Rituals for Baby Girls," 9.

14. Kenneth R. Leitner, "Lehitatef Batzitzit: Recovering the Meaning of the Tallit," in *Enveloped in Light: A Tallit Sourcebook,* eds. Dov Peretz Elkins and Steven Schwarzman (Princeton, NJ: Pomegranate Books, 2004), 99 (citing Abraham Isaac Kook, *Siddur Olat Re'iyah*). My warm thanks to my uncle, Abraham Kinstlinger, for providing me with this wonderful book, which also contains his poetry.

15. BT Rosh Hashana 17b, 33b; Genesis Rabba 3:4; Yalkut Shimoni 191.

16. BT Menachot 43b; Sifrei, Parshat Sh'lach, 115, *V'asu Lahem Tzitzit;* Numbers Rabba, Parshat Sh'lach, 5.

17. Marcus, *Jewish Life Cycle,* 76, 79. Today, there are at least a handful of Chabad-Lubavitch families who also commemorate the third birthday of their daughters. On Friday night, the girl lights candles for the first time with her mother. On Shabbat day, the girl's father receives an aliyah on Shabbat, she gives out candy to the women, words of Torah are spoken, and a kiddush follows services.

18. Weisberg, *Otzar HaBrit,* vol. 1, 206 and note 37.

19. Goldberg, *Jewish Passages,* 30; Eliyahu Bitton, *Sefer Nachalat Avot* (Birya, Israel: n.p., 2007), 181; Eliyahu Bitton, *Ohr Yahadut Luv* (Birya, Israel: Yeshivat Beit Yosef, 1994), 24. See also Harvey E. Goldberg, "Torah and Children: Some Symbolic Aspects of the Reproduction of Jews and Judaism" in *Judaism Viewed from Within and from Without* (Albany: State University of New York Press, 1987), 114, note 15.

20. Marcus, *Rituals of Childhood,* 77 and 150, notes 14–16 (collecting sources).

21. See Goldberg, "Torah and Children," 111 and note 2.

22. Marcus, *Rituals of Childhood,* 150, note 16.

23. Goldberg, "Torah and Children," 112, 115; Bitton, *Sefer Nachalat Avot,* 188.

24. Marcus, *Rituals of Childhood,* 150, note 14.

25. Weisberg, *Otzar HaBrit,* vol. 1, 206 and note 37.

26. Congregation Agudas Achim in Austin, Texas, "Our Sifrei Torah," http://www
.caa-austin.org/congregation/index.php?page=sefrei (accessed fall 2010).

27. David Ingbar, "Ritual at Romemu," *Contact: The Journal of the Steinhardt Foundation for Jewish Life* 12 (Winter 2010): 12, http://www.jewishlife.org/pdf/winter_2010
.pdf (accessed November 7, 2010). See also Lehman Weichselbaum, "Renewal for Babies," *New York Jewish Week* (November 3, 2010), www.thejewishweek.com/news/new
_york/renewal_newbies (accessed January 19, 2011). My thanks to R. Ingbar for speaking with me. My independent research has not confirmed R. Ingbar's claim that the
Romemu ritual revives a traditional Libyan custom.

28. Translation taken, in large part, from Sacks, ed., *Koren Siddur*, 12.

29. Henoch Morris, "Yarmulkas and Hats: Societal Custom or Halachic Imperative?"
The Journal of Halacha and Contemporary Society 52 (Fall 2006), 26–28.

30. Elkins, "The Tallit and Its Messages," 25.

31. Ibid., 15–16.

32. Ibid., 18.

33. Ibid., 16.

34. Rebecca Shulman Herz, "The Transformation of Tallitot: How Jewish Prayer
Shawls Have Changed Since Women Began Wearing Them," *Women and Judaism: Contemporary Writings,* http://www.utoronto.ca/wjudaism/contemporary/articles/Tallitot
/a_shulman_herz_3.html (accessed October 29, 2011); see also Avraham Weiss, *Spiritual
Activism: A Jewish Guide to Leadership and Repairing the World* (Woodstock, VT: Jewish Lights Publishing, 2008), 83.

35. Ibid.

36. See, e.g., Pirutinsky, *Sefer HaBrit,* 14 (Likutei Halachot 260:1, paragraph 68).

37. Shmuel Pinchas Gelbard, *Rite and Reason: 1050 Jewish Customs and Their Sources*
(Petach Tikva, Israel: Mifal Rashi Publications, 1998), 585.

38. Goldstein, *ReVisions,* 121.

39. Weisberg, *Otzar Habris* (English edition), 191.

40. Bitton, *Sefer Nachalat Avot,* 181; Bitton, *Ohr Yahadut Luv,* 24.

41. See, e.g., Hamburger, *Shorshei Minhag Ashkenaz,* vol. 1, 416–17, 423.

42. This synagogue is the Fair Lawn Jewish Center / Congregation Bnai Israel of Fair
Lawn, New Jersey. My thanks to R. Ronald Roth for taking the time to speak with me
about this custom.

43. Marcus, *Jewish Life Cycle,* 116–18.

44. Dobrinsky, *A Treasury of Sephardic Laws and Customs,* 45, 53, 58; Hamburger,
Shorshei Minhag Ashkenaz, vol. 3, 452–59, 468–72.

45. Hamburger, *Shorshei Minhag Ashkenaz,* vol. 3, 432–42, 460–67, 473–83; Marcus,
Jewish Life Cycle, 163–66.

46. Shlomo Riskin, "Marriage and the Wings of Desire," *New York Jewish Week,* September 6, 2011, www.thejewishweek.com/jewish_life/sabbath_week/marriage_and_wings
_desire (accessed March 8, 2013).

47. Menachem Raab, "The Tallit: A Halakhic Summary," in *Enveloped in Light,* eds.
Elkins and Schwarzman 227 and 238, notes 76–78.

48. Marcus, *Jewish Life Cycle*, 65; Hamburger, *Shorshei Minhag Ashkenaz*, vol. 2, 527–28; see also Klein, *A Time to Be Born*, 246.

49. Hamburger, *Shorshei Minhag Ashkenaz*, vol. 2, 420, 528.

50. Salpak, ed., *Jews of India*, 159–60.

51. D. Cohen, *Celebrating Your New Jewish Daughter?*, 14.

52. Ochs, *Inventing Jewish Ritual*, 22.

53. Schneider, *Jewish and Female*, 129–30. I discovered these proposals long after independently formulating my own.

54. Diana Drew with Robert Grayson, *Jewish Threads: A Hands-On Guide to Stitching Spiritual Intention into Jewish Fabric Crafts* (Woodstock, VT: Jewish Lights Publishing, 2011), 181–87 (project designer is Vicki Pieser). My thanks to Diana Drew for sending me a signed copy of her book. This book likewise came to my attention long after I set out my own ideas.

55. Along similar lines, one modern artist made a wimpel from a duvet in her mother's trousseau which was sent to the United States from Prague in 1939 "ahead of her parents' daring escape from the Nazis." Ibid., 182.

56. Hamburger, *Shorshei Minhag Ashkenaz*, vol. 2, 481–82.

57. Avraham Grossman, *Pious and Rebellious: Jewish Women in Medieval Europe*, trans. Jonathan Chipman (Waltham, MA: Brandeis University Press, 2004), 194.

58. See, e.g., Feinstein, *Iggrot Moshe*, Orach Chaim, 4:49; Yehuda Henkin, *Responsa on Contemporary Jewish Women's Issues* (Hoboken, NJ: Ktav Publishing House, 2003), 32–33; see also Aviva Cayam, "Fringe Benefits: Women and Tzitzit," in *Jewish Legal Writings by Women*, eds. Micah D. Halpern and Chana Safrai (Jerusalem: Urim Publications, 1998), 119–42; BT Menachot 43a; Shulchan Aruch, Orach Chaim, 17:2. But see Meiselman, *Jewish Woman in Jewish Law*, 152–54.

59. Raphael Aaron Ben-Shimon, *Sha'ar HaMefaked*, vol. 1, Orach Chaim, Hilchot Tzitzit, Nahar Pakod commentary, paragraph 1.

60. Hamburger, *Shorshei Minhag Ashkenaz*, vol. 2, 440.

61. Baruch Epstein, *Torah Temima*, Numbers 6:25, paragraph 131. For a different perspective, see Ovadiah Yosef, *Yechaveh Da'at*, part 5, siman 14; see also Yosef Tzvi Rimon, "Halakha: A Weekly Shiur in Halakhic Topics: Blessing Children on Shabbat Evening," Yeshivat Har Etzion and Israel Koschitzky Virtual Beit Midrash, trans. Eliezer Kwass, ed. David Silverberg, adapted from "Daf Kesher" #579, vol. 6 (Tevet 5757): 384–88, www .vbm-torah.org/archive/halak59/23bless.doc (accessed December 31, 2008).

62. Sasso, "Brit B'not Israel: Observations on Women and Reconstructionism," 104.

63. Goldstein, *ReVisions*, 131.

64. For opposing viewpoints, see Sharon and Michael Strassfeld, "Brit Mikvah," in *Blessing the Birth of a Daughter*, 21–22, and Ner-David, *Life on the Fringes*, 27.

Chapter 7. Conveying the Covenantal Theme

1. S. Cohen, *Why Aren't Jewish Women Circumcised?*, 35.

2. BT Brachot 59b; Shulchan Aruch, Orach Chaim, Hilchot Brachot 223:1.

3. See, e.g., Responsa of the Rashba, part 4, siman 77.

4. See, e.g., Nachum Rabinovich, *Yad Peshuta on Mishneh Torah*, Berachot 10:7 (cited in Jonathan Sacks, "Creativity and Innovation in Halakhah," in *Rabbinic Authority and Personal Autonomy,* ed. Moses Z. Sokol [Northvale, NJ: Jason Aronson, Inc., 1992], 150–51); Benny Lau, "Birchat 'Hatov V'Hameitiv' for the Birth of a Daughter," Kolech, http://www.kolechaptercom/print.asp?id=18644 (accessed December 16, 2010); Ephraim Betzalel Halivni, "A Daughter Is Born—What Do You Bless?" *Hadarom* 65 (1996): 20–22, http://www.itim.org.il/?CategoryID=342&ArticleID=426 (accessed December 16, 2010); Riskin, *Around the Family Table,* 198. Others reject the recitation of Hatov v'Hameitiv for a girl. See, e.g., Weisberg, *Otzar HaBrit,* vol. 1, 85 and note 7; cf. Sternbuch, *Teshuvot V'Hanhagot,* Orach Chaim, vol. 2, siman 132; Yekutiel Yehuda Halberstam, *Yetziv Pitgam,* ed. Yitzchak Shlomo Wertheimer (Netanya, Israel: Machon Shefa Chaim, 1986), 65. All of these sources are cited in Siegel, "Reciting the 'Ha-Tov ve-haMeitiv' Blessing on the Birth of a Daughter," 38, notes 48 and 49.

5. Sally Friedman and David Gmach, "Simchat Banot," Ritualwell, http://www.ritual well.org/rituals/simchat-banot (accessed March 24, 2013).

6. Meiselman, *Jewish Woman in Jewish Law,* 61.

7. Sharon and Joseph Kaplan, "Innovation within Halachah for Daughters," 103.

8. See, e.g., Wolowelsky, *Women, Jewish Law, and Modernity,* 46; Introduction to *The Orthodox Jewish Woman and Ritual: Options and Opportunities: Birth,* Jewish Orthodox Feminist Alliance, 1.

9. See, e.g., Gary and Sheila Rubin, "Preserving Tradition by Expanding It," 60–68.

10. S. Cohen, *Why Aren't Jewish Women Circumcised?,* chapter 1.

11. Derisha on Arba'ah Turim, Yoreh Dei'a, Hilchot K'vurah, 360:2; Waldenberg, *Tzitz Eliezer,* vol. 14, siman 21.

12. Schneider, *Jewish and Female,* 123.

13. See, e.g., Plaskow, *Standing Again at Sinai,* 67.

14. Goldstein, "The Pink Tallit," 85.

15. For a contrary position, see Kolodny, "Mystery of the Covenant," 8.

16. Plaskow, *Standing Again at Sinai,* 68.

17. Notwithstanding this expectation, some women do not bleed when having intercourse for the first time. Furthermore, whether a woman's hymen is intact is not indicative of her sexual history.

18. Langer, *To Worship God Properly,* 60–64.

19. Israel M. Ta-Shma, *The Early Ashkenazic Prayer: Literary and Historical Aspects* (Jerusalem: The Hebrew University Magnes Press, 2004), 182–84; Langer, *To Worship God Properly,* 62–65. My thanks to Ethan Rotenberg for providing me with Professor Ta-Shma's book.

20. Shulchan Aruch, Even Ha'ezer, Hilchot Kedushin 63:2, and corresponding Be'er Heitev, notes 3 and 4; Langer, *To Worship God Properly,* 71–72. Even today, the traditional Jewish marriage contract (*ketubah*)—which is read aloud at traditional weddings and often hangs prominently in a couple's home—doubles the amount of money held in escrow for the bride on account of her virginity.

21. Responsa of Maimonides, vol. 2, no. 207. This responsum was accessed on the Bar-Ilan University Global Jewish Database (the Responsa Project CDs).

22. Shulchan Aruch, Even Ha'ezer, Hilchot Kedushin 63:2, and corresponding Be'er Heitev, notes 3 and 4.

23. Translation in Sacks, ed., *Koren Siddur,* 1018.

24. Langer, *To Worship God Properly,* 61 and note 77.

25. Brandes, *Mada Toratecha: Masekhet Ketubot,* 41.

26. S. Cohen, *Why Aren't Jewish Women Circumcised?,* 28–43; S. Cohen, "A Brief History of Jewish Circumcision Blood," 39.

27. Weissler, "New Jewish Birth Rituals for Baby Girls," 7–8.

28. Hamburger, *Shorshei Minhag Ashkenaz,* vol. 1, 417.

29. *Machzor Vitry,* paragraph 507 (Hilchot Milah); see also Baumgarten, *Mothers and Children,* 93; Klein, *A Time to Be Born,* 228–29.

30. Yehuda ben Samuel of Regensburg, *Sefer Hasidim,* paragraph 1140.

31. Baumgarten, *Mothers and Children,* 215, note 7.

32. Simcha Assaf, ed., *Mekorot L'Toldot HaChinuch B'Yisrael* [Sources for the History of Education in Israel] (from the Early Middle Ages until the Enlightenment), vol. 1 (Tel Aviv: D'vir Co. Ltd., 1925), 13 (2:5).

33. Hamburger, *Shorshei Minhag Ashkenaz,* vol. 1, 417–18. Baumgarten notes some similarities between these early ceremonies and the Hollekreisch. *Mothers and Children,* 93, 96.

34. See, e.g., Rashbam on Genesis 48:20.

35. I am indebted to R. Binyomin Hamburger of the Institute for German Jewish Heritage (Machon Moreshes Ashkenaz) for graciously providing me with the sources cited in this subsection and for taking the time to speak with me about this topic on January 20, 2010.

36. Elijah Kafshaeli, *Me'ah Sh'arim* (Jerusalem: Ofeq Institute, Inc., 2000), part 2, 283–84.

37. Joseph Yuspa Nördlinger Hahn, *Yosef Ometz,* paragraph 70.

38. Binyomin S. Hamburger, e-mail message to author, January 28, 2010.

39. Yair Chaim Bachrach, *Mekor Chaim,* vol. 2, Hilchot Shabbat, siman 270.

40. Aharon Berachia of Modina, *Ma'avar Yabok,* Siftei R'nanot, chapter 43.

41. Marcus, *Jewish Life Cycle,* 84–105.

42. Leifer, "Birth Rituals and Jewish Daughters," 86.

43. *Shaarei Habayit, Gates of the House,* 114; see also *On the Doorposts of Your House: Prayers and Ceremonies for the Jewish Home* (New York: Central Conference of American Rabbis, 1994), 116.

44. Meyer, "The First Identical Ceremony for Giving a Hebrew Name to Girls and Boys," 86.

45. See, e.g., Ochs, *Inventing Jewish Ritual,* 51; Geller, "Brit Milah and Brit Banot," 411, note 18. R. Elyse Goldstein notes her experience that eighth-day timing is today "fairly common." "The Pink Tallit," 83. Nonetheless, I believe that this timing is not normative in the Jewish community as a whole.

46. Bulka, *RCA Lifecycle Madrikh,* introduction to "Baby Naming," 1.

47. Ochs, *Inventing Jewish Ritual,* 51.

48. Adena K. Berkowitz, "All Jewish Children Are Our Guarantors: A Mother Looks Back at Her Children's Welcoming Rituals," in *The Orthodox Jewish Woman and Ritual: Options and Opportunities: Birth,* Jewish Orthodox Feminist Alliance, 10.

49. Bell, "Thank Heaven for Little Girls," 21; see also, e.g., D. Cohen, *Celebrating Your New Jewish Daughter,* 45.

50. Menachem Leibtag, "Parshat Tazria—From Seven to Eight," Tanach Study Center, http://www.tanachapterorg/vayikra/taz/tazs1.htm (accessed August 20, 2008).

51. BT Sukkah 55b; Rashi on Numbers 29:36; Chezekiah ben Manoah, Chizkuni on Leviticus 23:36.

52. Sharon and Joseph Kaplan, "Innovation within Halachah for Daughters," 103.

53. D. Cohen, *Celebrating Your New Jewish Daughter,* 47. See also, e.g., Diamant, *New Jewish Baby Book,* 2nd ed., 132; Women's League for Conservative Judaism, "Simhat Bat: Ceremonies to Welcome a Baby Girl."

54. See, e.g., Breger, "Creating a Welcoming Ceremony for Girls Today," 6; Sharon and Joseph Kaplan, "Innovation within Halachah for Daughters," 103. See also Bulka, *RCA Lifecycle Madrikh,* 2; Douglas Weber and Jessica Brodsky Weber, *The Jewish Baby Handbook: A Guide for Expectant Parents* (West Orange, NJ: Behrman House, 1990), 46–47; Machon Itim, "Simchat Bat: Where and When," http://eng.itim.org.il/?CategoryID=203&ArticleID=385 (accessed March 14, 2013).

55. Diamant, *New Jewish Baby Book,* 2nd ed., 133; Women's League for Conservative Judaism, "Simhat Bat: Ceremonies to Welcome a Baby Girl"; Goldman, *Being Jewish,* 48; Berkowitz, "All Jewish Children Are Our Guarantors," 10.

56. Leifer, "Birth Rituals and Jewish Daughters," 86–87.

57. See, e.g., Machon Itim, "Simchat Bat: Where and When," http://eng.itim.org.il/?CategoryID=203&ArticleID=385 (accessed March 14, 2013); D. Cohen, *Celebrating Your New Jewish Daughter,* 48–49.

58. Shulchan Aruch, Orach Chaim, Hilchot Pesach, 493:1.

59. B'er Heiteiv on Shulchan Aruch, Orach Chaim, Hilchot Pesach 493:1, note 2.

60. Derisha on Arba'ah Turim, Yoreh Dei'a, Hilchot K'vurah, 360:2.

61. Shmuel Halevi Segal, *Nachalat Shiva,* vol. 3, responsum 17.

62. Hamburger, *Shorshei Minhag Ashkenaz,* vol. 3, 406.

63. *Responsa of Yedidya Tia Weil,* Yoreh Dei'ah, responsum 108.

64. S. Cohen, *Why Aren't Jewish Women Circumcised?,* 38–39.

65. D. Cohen, *Celebrating Your New Jewish Daughter,* 60–61.

66. One interesting example of this phenomenon is the use of a "Miriam's tambourine" by Chabad-Lubavitch women. Ochs, *Inventing Jewish Ritual,* chapter 6.

67. See, e.g., Carol and Neal Rose, "Gift of a Daughter: *Zeved Habat,*" Ritualwell, http://www.ritualwell.org/ritual/gift-daughter-zeved-habat (accessed March 28, 2013).

68. See, e.g., Kolodny, "Mystery of the Covenant," 2.

Chapter 8. Ceremonies for Newborn Girls As Developing Customs

1. See, e.g., Greenberg, *On Women and Judaism*, 6; Tova Hartman, *Feminism Encounters Traditional Judaism* (Waltham, MA: Brandeis University Press, 2007), 73; Tamar Ross, *Expanding the Palace of Torah: Orthodoxy and Feminism* (Waltham, MA: Brandeis University Press, 2004), xxi, 182–83, 197–200.

2. Greenberg, *On Women and Judaism*, 40–41, 42, 46.

3. Ross, *Expanding the Palace of Torah*, 198–200, 210; see also Ochs, *Inventing Jewish Ritual*, 52. R. Debra Orenstein states that "I am utterly convinced that, despite any quarrels or differences, the marriage between [feminism and Judaism] is one made in heaven." Introduction to *Lifecycles*, vol. 1, xiii.

4. Ellen M. Umansky, "Roundtable Discussion: What Are the Sources of My Theology?" *Journal of Feminist Studies in Religion* 1 (Spring 1985): 124–26.

5. Tikva Frymer-Kensky, "Toward a Liberal Theory of Halakha," *Tikkun* 10 (July/Aug. 1995): 46–47.

6. Plaskow, *Standing Again at Sinai*, 61–64, 69–70; Adler, "I've Had Nothing Yet So I Can't Take More," 28; Rachel Adler, "The Jew Who Wasn't There," in *On Being a Jewish Feminist*, ed. Heschel, 14, 15; Heschel, introduction to *On Being a Jewish Feminist*, xxi–xxvi. See also Thena Kendall, "Memories of an Orthodox Youth," in *On Being a Jewish Feminist*, 100.

7. Schneider, *Jewish and Female*, 33.

8. Ozick, "Notes toward Finding the Right Question," 148–51; see also Plaskow, "The Right Question Is Theological," 224, 227.

9. Gordon, "Toward a Gender-Inclusive Account of Halakhah," 3.

10. Biale, *Women and Jewish Law*, 8; see also Gordon, "Toward a Gender-Inclusive Account of Halakhah," 10.

11. Sternbuch, *Teshuvot V' Hanhagot*, Orach Chaim, vol. 2, siman 132.

12. Meiselman, *Jewish Woman in Jewish Law*, 60–62.

13. See Hartman, *Feminism Encounters Traditional Judaism*, 100–101.

14. Weinberg, *Seridei Aish*, vol. 3, responsum 93.

15. BT Brachot 45a, Eruvin 14b; see also e.g., JT Pe'ah 7:5, Bava Metziah 7:1.

16. Menachem Elon, *Jewish Law: History, Sources, Principles / HaMishpat HaIvri*, vol. 2, trans. Bernard Auerbach and Melvin J. Sykes (Philadelphia: The Jewish Publication Society, 1994), 881–82.

17. Chill, introduction to *The Minhagim*, xix.

18. Soloveitchik, "Rupture and Reconstruction," 66.

19. Elon, *Jewish Law*, vol. 2, 937.

20. See, e.g., Jacob Katz, *The "Shabbes Goy": A Study in Halakhic Flexibility*, trans. Yoel Lerner (Philadelphia: The Jewish Publication Society, 1989), 236–37, and chapters 6–8 and 10–11; Soloveitchik, "Rupture and Reconstruction," 66; Isadore Twersky, *Introduction to the Code of Maimonides (Mishneh Torah)* (New Haven, CT: Yale University Press, 1980), 125; Elon, *Jewish Law*, vol. 2, 932–36; Langer, *To Worship God Properly*, 107–9.

21. Elon, *Jewish Law,* vol. 2, 882 (citing BT Pesachim 66a).

22. Soloveitchik, "Rupture and Reconstruction," 67.

23. J. Katz, *"Shabbes Goy,"* 4, 231–36; see also Sperber, "Women and Men in Communal Prayer," 117.

24. See, e.g., Twersky, *Introduction to the Code of Maimonides,* 124–34.

25. Elon, *Jewish Law,* vol. 2, 882, 896, 937–38, 941–42; Daniel Sperber, *Minhagei Yisrael: Origins and History,* vol. 1 (Jerusalem: Mossad Harav Kook, 1990), 31–38; Katz, *"Shabbes Goy,"* 231–32.

26. Elon, *Jewish Law,* vol. 2, 896, 903–4; Sperber, *Minhagei Yisrael,* vol. 1, 24.

27. Soloveitchik, "Rupture and Reconstruction," 67.

28. Sperber, *Minhagei Yisrael,* vol. 1, 9–13.

29. This is R. Sperber's *Minhagei Yisrael,* which currently encompasses eight volumes.

30. Yaakov David Pieskin, *Tumat Yesharim,* chapter 5, "Derech Chochma" (cited in Yitzhak Lipietz, introduction to *Sefer Matamim,* and in Chill, introduction to *The Minhagim,* xx and note 6).

31. Elon, *Jewish Law,* 881.

32. Ibid., 894; see also Daniel Sperber, *Minhagei Yisrael: Origins and History,* vol. 2 (Jerusalem: Mossad Harav Kook, 1991), 4–5.

33. Tosafot, BT Menachot 20b, "Nifsal"; see Sperber, *Minhagei Yisrael,* vol. 2, 4–8.

34. Ibid., 17–19.

35. Ibid., 19–20 (citing Abraham Isaac Kook, *Daat Kohen,* 18:49, 84:189).

36. Ann Moline, "Baby Naming Becomes Part of Tradition," *Arizona Jewish Post,* September 29, 1995, 13. This article is in Blu Greenberg's collection of Simchat Bat materials.

37. Ochs, *Inventing Jewish Ritual,* 155–56, 157; see also Adler, *Engendering Judaism,* 84–85.

38. Azi, comment on "Raising the Pinky," YWN Coffeehouse, Yeshiva World News, http://www.theyeshivaworld.com/coffeeroom/topic/raising-the-pinky (accessed March 28, 2013).

39. Daniel Goldschmidt, *Machzor for the Days of Awe,* vol. 2 (Jerusalem: Koren Publishers, 1970), 26–28. My gratitude to Professor Avraham Holtz for speaking with me and providing me with this source.

40. Shmuel Singer, "The Great Matzah Controversy: Should Matzah Be Made by Hand or Machine?" Orthodox Union (March 28, 2006), http://www.ou.org/news/article/the_great_matzah_controversy_should_matzah_be_made_by_hand_or_machine (accessed November 22, 2012).

41. Ochs, *Inventing Jewish Ritual,* 32–33 (citing Jonathan D. Sarna, "How Matzah Became Square," sixth annual lecture of the Victor J. Selmanowitz Chair of Jewish History, Touro College, New York, 2005). R. Daniel Sperber also cited the example of machine-made matzah in his lecture at Congregation Netivot Shalom, Teaneck, New Jersey, on June 26, 2010.

42. Ochs, *Inventing Jewish Ritual,* 148–49 (emphasis in original).

43. Sperber, *Jewish Life Cycle,* 14–17; Moshavi, "Customs and Folklore of Nineteenth Century Bukharian Jews," 85; Bitton, *Ohr Yahadut Luv,* 24.

44. Yaakov Moses Toledano, *Yam HaGadol*, responsum 53.

45. "Raising the Pinky," YWN Coffeehouse, Yeshiva World News, http://www.the yeshivaworld.com/coffeeroom/topic/raising-the-pinky (accessed March 28, 2013).

46. Sperber, *On Changes in Jewish Liturgy*, 112, 122–24.

47. BT Brachot 20b; see also *L'vush HaTechelet*, Orach Chaim, Hilchot Tefillah, 106:2; ibid., Hilchot Brachot 47:14; *Shulchan Aruch of Schneur Zalman*, Orach Chaim, Hilchot Tefillah, 106:2.

48. Sperber, *On Changes in Jewish Liturgy*, 24–25, 123.

49. Hartman, *Feminism Encounters Traditional Judaism*, 69.

50. See, e.g., Chava Weissler, *Voices of the Matriarchs: Listening to the Prayers of Early Modern Jewish Women* (Boston: Beacon Press, 1998); Dinah Berland, *Hours of Devotion: Fanny Neuda's Book of Prayers for Jewish Women* (New York: Schocken Books, 2007); Lavie, *A Jewish Woman's Prayer Book*.

51. Rosenblatt, "A Welcome Ceremony for Baby Girls," 7.

52. Orenstein, introduction to *Lifecycles,* vol. 1, xix.

53. Lori Hope Lefkovitz, "Eavesdropping on Angels," in *Gender and Judaism,* ed. Rudavsky, 158.

54. Greenberg, *How to Run a Traditional Jewish Household,* 250.

55. *On the Doorposts of Your House: Prayers and Ceremonies for the Jewish Home* (New York: Central Conference of American Rabbis, 1994), 116–22. See *Shaarei Habayit, Gates of the House,* 114–17.

56. David Polish and W. Gunther Plaut, eds., *Rabbi's Manual (Ma'aglei Tzedek)* (New York: Central Conference of American Rabbis, 1988), 16–23, 39–42.

57. *Siddur Sim Shalom for Weekdays,* 244–45.

58. *Moreh Derekh,* A-10.

59. Ibid., A-29–A-45.

60. Ibid., A-29; see also Cantor and Jacobs, "Brit Banot Covenant Ceremonies for Daughters," 45.

61. *Kol Haneshamah: Shabbat Vehagim,* 691, 785.

62. Seth Daniel Riemer, ed., *Reconstructionist Rabbinical Association: Rabbi's Manual,* (Wyncote, PA: The Reconstructionist Rabbinical Association, 1997), B-16–B-31.

63. Sacks, ed., *Koren Siddur,* 510–11, 1034–37.

64. Bulka, RCA *Lifecycle Madrikh,* 2–7.

65. *Moreh Derekh,* A-30; see also Cantor and Jacobs, "Brit Banot Covenant Ceremonies for Daughters," 46.

66. Riemer, ed., *Reconstructionist Rabbinical Association: Rabbi's Manual,* i–viii.

67. Bulka, RCA *Lifecycle Madrikh,* 2.

Index